Putin's Revenge

Woodrow Wilson Center Series

Woodrow Wilson Center Series

The Woodrow Wilson International Center for Scholars was chartered by the U.S. Congress in 1968 as the living memorial to the nation's twenty-eighth president. It serves as the country's key nonpartisan policy forum, tackling global challenges through independent research and open dialogue. Bridging the worlds of academia and public policy, the Center's diverse programmatic activity informs actionable ideas for Congress, the administration, and the broader policy community.

The Woodrow Wilson Center Series shares in the Center's mission by publishing outstanding scholarly and public policy-related books for a global readership. Written by the Center's expert staff and international network of scholars, our books shed light on a wide range of topics, including U.S. foreign and domestic policy, security, the environment, energy, and area studies.

Conclusions or opinions expressed in Center publications and programs are those of the authors and speakers and do not necessarily reflect the views of the Center staff, fellows, trustees, advisory groups, or any individuals or organizations that provide financial support for the Center.

Please visit us online at www.wilsoncenter.org.

Kevin J. Middlebrook, *The International Defense of Workers: Labor Rights, U.S. Trade Agreements, and State Sovereignty*

Margarita M. Balmaceda, *Russian Energy Chains: The Remaking of Technopolitics from Siberia to Ukraine to the European Union*

Abraham M. Denmark, *U.S. Strategy in the Asian Century: Empowering Allies and Partners*

Samuel F. Wells Jr., *Fearing the Worst: How Korea Transformed the Cold War*

Donald R. Wolfensberger, *Changing Cultures in Congress: From Fair Play to Power Plays*

William H. Hill, *No Place for Russia: European Security Institutions Since 1989*

Putin's Revenge

Why Russia Invaded Ukraine

LUCIAN KIM

Columbia

University

Press

New York

Columbia University Press
Publishers Since 1893
New York   Chichester, West Sussex
cup.columbia.edu

Library of Congress Cataloging-in-Publication Data
Names: Kim, Lucian, author.
Title: Putin's revenge : why Russia invaded Ukraine / Lucian Kim.
Other titles: Why Russia invaded Ukraine
Description: New York : Columbia University Press, [2024] |
    Includes bibliographical references and index.
Identifiers: LCCN 2024020928 | ISBN 9780231214025 (hardback) |
    ISBN 9780231560153 (ebook)
Subjects: LCSH: Russo-Ukrainian War, 2014—Causes. | Russian Invasion
    of Ukraine, 2022—Causes. | Russia (Federation)—Foreign relations—
    21st century. | Ukraine—Foreign relations—21st century. | United States—
    Foreign relations—21st century.
Classification: LCC DK5417 .K56 2024 | DDC 947.7086—dc23/eng/20240805
LC record available at https://lccn.loc.gov/2024020928

Printed in the United States of America

Cover design: Julia Kushnirsky
Cover image: Reuters/Pavel Klimov

To Sveta and Leo

Contents

Acknowledgments

Writing a book is an intensely lonely activity, but pulling it off requires many small acts of kindness from friends and strangers alike. I am most indebted to my family for supporting me throughout the process and tolerating my long absences on evenings, weekends, and vacations. One of my son's first complete sentences was "Daddy is writing a book," soon followed up by the question "Why are you writing a book?"

This book would not have come about without the backing of Robert Litwak of the Wilson Center in Washington, where I was a residential fellow from 2021 to 2022. Stephen Wesley, my editor at Columbia University Press, helped shepherd the book through the review and production process. Matthew Bloch created the maps.

Many people encouraged me to write this book following the full-scale invasion of Ukraine in February 2022. Matthew Rojansky and William Pomeranz at the Wilson Center's Kennan Institute gave me their full support, and Larry Weissman helped turn my initial idea into a proposal. I received useful words of advice on how to write a book from Fiona Hill, David Hoffman, and Edward Wong.

Good friends helped by discussing ideas, reading drafts, and giving me moral support. Tetiana Chub and Mykhailo Maslovskyi were always available for questions large and small. I also relied on Melissa Eddy, Todd

Prince, Terry Martin, Greg Walters, William Flemming, Oleksandr Holubov, and Brendan Goodman.

Sergey Radchenko made invaluably useful comments on my manuscript. Fellow journalists Herwig Höller, Ilya Zhegulev, Pavel Kanygin, Konstantin Skorkin, and Steven Lee Myers compared their notes with mine. I received additional support from Stephan Kieninger, Natalie Jaresko, Diana Dumitru, James Goldgeier, and Alex Little. Many people helped by sharing their recollections with me off the record.

Writing this book would have been infinitely more difficult had it not been for Kathleen Smith and Lisa Gordinier, who welcomed me to the Center for Eurasian, Russian, and East European Studies at Georgetown University. Mark Winek and Jeffrey Popovich made it possible for me to find a writing nook in the Georgetown University Library and benefit from its vast resources.

Special thanks go to my parents-in-law, Tatiana and Alexander; my parents, Dorothee and Ha Poong; my brother, Alan; and my sister, Natalie.

To all these people I am deeply grateful for their generosity and support.

Note on Spellings

The transliteration of Ukrainian and Russian into English is complicated. Both are East Slavic languages that use the Cyrillic alphabet, and each one is transliterated in more than one way. In the transliteration of names in this book, I aim for consistency and simplicity.

For Ukrainian names, I use the 2010 Ukrainian government system of romanization as a guide. For Russian names, I follow a modification of the U.S. Library of Congress style developed by the *Moscow Times*, Russia's oldest English-language newspaper. There are plenty of exceptions to these guidelines because alternate spellings have come into common usage, for example Zelensky (Zelenskyi), Gorbachev (Gorbachyov), or Vitali Klitschko (Vitaliy Klychko).

For Ukrainian actors in this book I use their Ukrainian names, except for those who identified as Russian and willingly went over to the Russian side. Place names are spelled according to the language of the country in which they are located: Kyiv (as opposed to Kiev, the common transliteration of the Russian spelling), Odesa (Russian: Odessa), Donbas (Russian: Donbass), or Kharkiv (Russian: Kharkov). The one exception is Chernobyl (Ukrainian: Chornobyl), as the site of the 1986 nuclear disaster is universally known.

Belarusian names pose a separate problem as most Belarusians speak Russian as their first language and often transliterate their names from the Russian. I use Alexander Lukashenko (Belarusian: Alyaksandr Lukashenka) for the dictator of Belarus as he uses the Russian spelling of his name. The Belarusian prodemocracy leader Sviatlana Tsikhanouskaya (Russian: Svetlana Tikhanovskaya) prefers the transliteration of her name from Belarusian.

Cast of Characters

Rinat Akhmetov: A Ukrainian oligarch from Donetsk and former backer of Viktor Yanukovych.

Sergei Aksyonov: The Kremlin's puppet leader of Crimea and former leader of a small, pro-Russian political party.

Sergei Beseda: The FSB general in charge of operations in the former Soviet Union.

Hunter Biden: Joe Biden's son, who sat on the board of a Ukrainian oil company while his father was vice president.

Joe Biden: The forty-sixth U.S. president, vice president to Barack Obama, and a longtime member of the U.S. Senate Committee on Foreign Relations.

Antony Blinken: Joe Biden's secretary of state.

Alexander Borodai: The Moscow PR consultant who became "prime minister" of the Russian proxy statelet in Donetsk.

William Burns: Joe Biden's CIA director and a former U.S. ambassador to Russia.

George W. Bush: The forty-third U.S. president.

Refat Chubarov: The head of the Crimean Tatar community during the Russian occupation of Crimea.

Bill Clinton: The forty-second U.S. president and husband of Hillary.

Hillary Clinton: Barack Obama's first secretary of state, Donald Trump's main challenger in 2016, and wife of Bill.

Mykhailo Dobkin: The governor of the Kharkiv region and an ally of Viktor Yanukovych.

Valery Gerasimov: The chief of the Russian general staff.

Igor Girkin, aka Igor Strelkov: The former FSB colonel who advised Sergei Aksyonov in Crimea and became "defense minister" of the Russian proxy statelet in Donetsk.

Rudy Giuliani: The former New York mayor who served as Donald Trump's personal lawyer.

Sergei Glazyev: A nationalist Russian politician and economic adviser to Vladimir Putin.

Mikhail Gorbachev: The last leader of the Soviet Union.

Leonid Grach: A Communist politician and former speaker of the Crimean parliament who supported the Russian takeover.

Pavel Gubarev: A leader of the pro-Russian uprising in Donetsk.

François Hollande: The twenty-fourth president of France.

Mikhail Khodorkovsky: An exiled Russian opposition leader and former oil tycoon who was imprisoned by the Kremlin for ten years.

Vitali Klitschko: A Ukrainian politician, Kyiv mayor, and former boxing champion.

Ihor Kolomoiskyi: A Ukrainian oligarch and the governor of the Dnipropetrovsk region during the 2014 Russian invasion.

Vladimir Konstantinov: The pro-Russian head of Crimea's parliament and a real estate developer.

Yury Kovalchuk: A Russian billionaire and friend of Vladimir Putin.

Dmitry Kozak: The Kremlin official in charge of Ukraine from 2020 to 2022.

Leonid Kuchma: The second president of independent Ukraine.

Dmytro Kuleba: Volodymyr Zelensky's second foreign minister.

Sergei Lavrov: Russia's foreign minister.

Alexander Lukashenko: The dictator of Belarus and a former collective farm boss.

Emmanuel Macron: The twenty-fifth president of France.

Konstantin Malofeyev: A Russian businessman and monarchist nicknamed "the Orthodox oligarch" for his connections to the Russian Orthodox Church.

Viktor Medvedchuk: A Ukrainian businessman and politician closely connected to Vladimir Putin.

Dmitry Medvedev: The third president of post-Communist Russia, later prime minister and deputy head of Russia's Security Council.

Angela Merkel: Germany's eighth chancellor since World War II.

Anatoliy Mohylov: The prime minister of Crimea when the Russian occupation began.

Sergei Naryshkin: The head of the SVR, Russia's military intelligence service, and a former speaker of the Russian Duma.

Alexei Navalny: A Russian opposition leader and anticorruption activist.

Boris Nemtsov: A Russian opposition leader and former Russian deputy prime minister.

Victoria Nuland: The assistant secretary of state for European and Eurasian affairs during Barack Obama's second term in office.

Barack Obama: The forty-fourth U.S. president.

Andriy Parubiy: A Ukrainian politician who was a leader of the Euromaidan protest and headed the National Security and Defense Council during the 2014 Russian invasion.

Nikolai Patrushev: The head of Russia's Security Council, a former FSB director, and a confidant of Vladimir Putin.

Mike Pompeo: Donald Trump's second secretary of state and first CIA director.

Petro Poroshenko: The fifth president of independent Ukraine.

Vladimir Putin: Russia's supreme leader, post-Communist Russia's second and fourth president.

Condoleezza Rice: George W. Bush's national security adviser and second secretary of state.

Mikheil Saakashvili: The third president of independent Georgia.

Nicolas Sarkozy: The twenty-third president of France.

Olaf Scholz: Germany's ninth chancellor since World War II.

Gerhard Schröder: Germany's seventh chancellor since World War II and a friend of Vladimir Putin.

Sergei Shoigu: Russia's defense minister.

Frank-Walter Steinmeier: The president of Germany and a foreign minister under Angela Merkel.

Vladislav Surkov: The Kremlin aide in charge of Ukraine from 2013 to 2020.

Serhiy Taruta: The governor of the Donetsk region at the time of the pro-Russian uprising.

Rustam Temirgaliyev: The first deputy prime minister of Crimea and a supporter of the Russian takeover.

Rex Tillerson: Donald Trump's first secretary of state and the former CEO of ExxonMobil.

Donald Trump: The forty-fifth U.S. president.

Oleg Tsaryov: A Ukrainian lawmaker who went over to the Russian side.

Sviatlana Tsikhanouskaya: A Belarusian prodemocracy leader who went into exile after challenging Alexander Lukashenko in the 2020 presidential election.

Oleksandr Turchynov: A Ukrainian lawmaker who served as Ukraine's acting president after Viktor Yanukovych's flight from Kyiv.

Yulia Tymoshenko: A Ukrainian lawmaker who served as prime minister and ran for president against Viktor Yanukovych in 2010 and against Volodymyr Zelensky in 2019.

Viktor Yanukovych: The fourth president of independent Ukraine, a former prime minister and governor of the Donetsk region.

Arseniy Yatsenyuk: Ukraine's prime minister during the 2014 Russian invasion.

Boris Yeltsin: The first president of post-Communist Russia.

Viktor Yushchenko: The third president of independent Ukraine, a former prime minister and central bank chairman.

Konstantin Zatulin: A Russian nationalist lawmaker.

Volodymyr Zelensky: The sixth president of independent Ukraine and a former comedian.

Vladimir Zhirinovsky: A Russian politician, head of the ultranationalist Liberal Democratic Party of Russia.

Maps

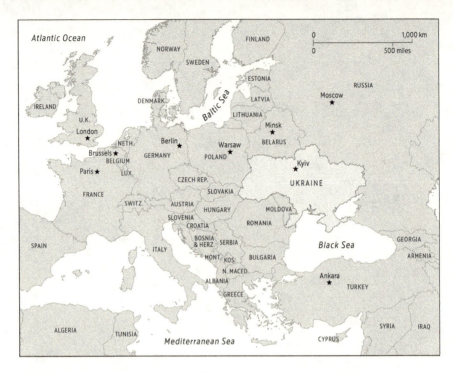

Ukraine and its neighbors

Map created by Matthew Bloch.

Ukraine

Map created by Matthew Bloch.

Ukraine after Russia's 2014 invasion

Map created by Matthew Bloch.

Russia and its neighbors

Map created by Matthew Bloch.

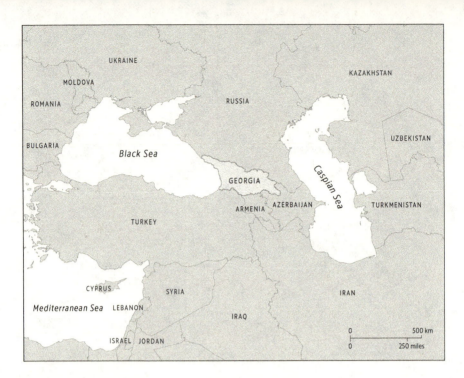

Georgia and its neighbors

Map created by Matthew Bloch.

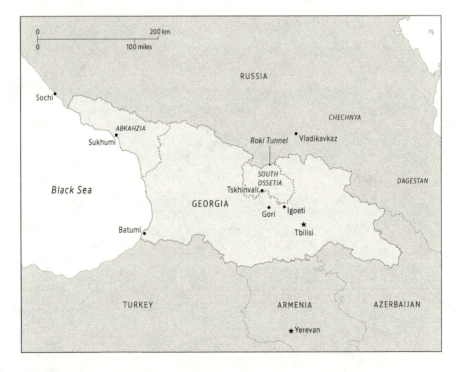

Georgia

Map created by Matthew Bloch.

Putin's Revenge

Introduction

It was still evening in America when Vladimir Putin launched a full-scale invasion of Ukraine in the early hours of February 24, 2022. Seven time zones and five thousand miles away, I was sitting in my kitchen in Washington, DC, watching Putin declare the start of a "special military operation." I immediately messaged my two best Ukrainian friends, Tanya and Misha, who both lived in Kyiv. Tanya is an investment banker who had a toddler the same age as mine. Misha is a photographer originally from the industrial Donetsk region.

In the age of instant messaging, I could reach out to them across continents and missile barrages. They shared their fear and rage and disbelief at what was happening. I felt absolutely powerless to help them. "In bomb shelter" were the first words I received from Tanya. On the second day of the attack she managed to get out of Kyiv with her little boy, husband, and a couple of friends. Her mother was trapped in a cellar in Chernihiv, a city north of Kyiv directly in the path of the Russian invaders. Tanya wanted to make a dash to Ukraine's western border, but her husband and friends were against it. From the house where they were staying they could hear explosions and warplanes. Bandits were robbing people on the highways. "Would you leave?" Tanya asked me. It was the most difficult question anyone had ever asked me.

Misha also got out of Kyiv. As he lived down the street from the Ukrainian General Staff, Misha decided not to trust the precision of Russian missiles and went to stay with friends on the outskirts of the city. Their house did not have a basement where they could take shelter overnight, so Misha faced the dilemma of sleeping above ground or walking to the nearest metro station, which required crossing a wooded area where he risked running into Russian scouts. "We can hear the front, sometimes it's very loud," he messaged me. I had met Misha while reporting on Russia's first attack on Ukraine in 2014, and he had become like a younger brother to me. I told him that I was sorry I had been unable to stop the awful turn of events. Misha laughed and said the only thing I could have done was to assassinate Putin during a press conference in my days as a Moscow correspondent.

Misha disagreed with my prognosis that the Ukrainian military would not withstand the Russian juggernaut. He headed east to be with his parents, fifty miles from the front line. His father was too ill to move, and his mother still went to work in the management of a local coal mine.

Tanya and her little family eventually fled west, first to Romania and then to the United States. Amazingly, they ended up just an hour's drive from my parents' home in Oregon. Like millions of other Ukrainians, they had suddenly become refugees in Europe's largest land war since World War II.

Why did Putin invade Ukraine? Before the attack, the idea of a full-scale invasion seemed insane, even to Kremlin propagandists who mocked persistent U.S. warnings that Russia was about to go to war. The invasion appeared all the crazier after the initial Russian assault on Kyiv faltered, stalled, and was finally repelled. Putin's special military operation foundered on the resistance of the Ukrainian people and the unexpected leadership of their president, Volodymyr Zelensky. What was supposed to be a blitzkrieg to restore Russian domination over Ukraine turned into a grinding, multifront war that has cost countless lives and reduced cities to ruins.

All wars are senseless in the lives that they destroy, but they differ in their origins. The war between Ukraine and Russia was not motivated by a long-standing hatred between Ukrainians and Russians. To a large extent, it was driven by a small coterie of men who had usurped power in Russia. To be sure, millions of Russians supported the Kremlin and followed its orders, but the war against Ukraine was ultimately a product of Putin's mind and his unchecked dictatorial powers. That is why the title of this book is *Putin's Revenge*.

The root cause of the war is the legacy of Russian imperialism, the idea of Russia as the center of a Eurasian empire, whether it was ruled by the czars or by the Communist Party. In that empire, Ukraine played a crucial supporting role as bread basket, industrial powerhouse, and strategic buffer zone, straddling the Black Sea and stretching into central Europe. When the Soviet Union collapsed in 1991, many Russians viewed the loss of their empire as a humiliating defeat. The West's triumphalism further inflamed their sense of injury. As the world's sole superpower, the United States was free to pursue a unilateralist foreign policy that Russia was in no position to stop or even modulate.

For Putin, the defeat was personal. In 1989, as a KGB officer stationed in East Germany, Putin witnessed peaceful prodemocracy protests sweep away Soviet puppet regimes in East Berlin and Prague. The once mighty Soviet Union, on the verge of economic collapse, was powerless to prevent its European vassals from going their own way. Two years later the Soviet Union itself fell apart into fifteen independent states, including Russia and Ukraine.

Once free of Soviet domination, the countries of central Europe embraced the Western model of free-market democracy and rushed to join NATO and the European Union. While many Russians watched grudgingly as former Soviet satellites left Moscow's orbit, there was nothing they could do about it. But the newly independent states that emerged from the Soviet Union—many of which had been Russian possessions for centuries—were a different matter. Russians referred to those countries as the "near abroad," foreign countries only on paper. Those who mourned the Soviet collapse never regarded their new neighbors as fully independent, sovereign states. At the end of Putin's first term in 2004, the three Baltic nations became the first former Soviet republics to join NATO. Putin was determined to make sure they would be the last.

I begin this book with Ukraine's 2004 Orange Revolution, a popular uprising reminiscent of the peaceful street revolutions of 1989. The protests prevented the Kremlin's favored Ukrainian presidential candidate, Viktor Yanukovych, from taking power following a rigged election. The Orange Revolution also convinced Putin that the West was pulling

Ukraine away from Russia. That view seemed to be confirmed three years later when U.S. President George W. Bush pushed for Ukraine, alongside Georgia, to be given a clear path into NATO. Four months after the alliance pledged to admit the two former Soviet republics in the future, Russia invaded Georgia. The Kremlin punished Ukraine's pro-Western government with energy cutoffs until Yanukovych clinched victory in the 2010 presidential election. Yet even Yanukovych wanted to tie Ukraine closer to the West. When Putin pressured him to back out of an association agreement with the EU, street protests erupted that ended in bloodshed and Yanukovych's flight from Kyiv.

Putin responded by seizing Crimea and fomenting a separatist uprising in eastern Ukraine, wrecking the country's prospects for Western integration. But the war that Putin started in 2014 was about much more than just keeping Ukraine under Russia's control. It was a belated, bloody counterrevolution against the wave of prodemocracy protests that had helped bring down the Soviet empire twenty-five years earlier.

In that sense, Putin's war represented a generational clash between those who had freed themselves from the Soviet mindset and those who were still captive to it, wherever they lived. In Russia, that clash was starkest because the Soviet past was completely intertwined with Russia's past. For Russians like Putin, renouncing the Soviet past was tantamount to renouncing their own history. But Putin's nostalgia was devoid of any ideological dimension. It was opportunistic and propagandistic, a chance to appropriate the glory of the Soviet victory over Nazi Germany. The end of World War II had been the moment of the Soviet Union's greatest triumph, when the country stood side by side with the Western allies, shaped the postwar world order, and became the nuclear superpower that held the United States in check for decades.

A product of the KGB, Putin gradually reverted post-Communist Russia to the police state the Soviet Union had once been. Although he enjoyed broad popular support at the beginning of his rule, Putin increasingly derived his legitimacy from the imitation of democratic procedures. He silenced his critics and resurrected the state propaganda machine. The Kremlin discouraged individual initiative and sought to co-opt any grassroots movements.

A new generation of Russians rejected the Soviet legacy and wanted to turn Russia into a modern democracy. They were represented by the oligarch Mikhail Khodorkovsky, Putin's first serious challenger, and later by the anticorruption activist Alexei Navalny. Young Russians with no memory of the Soviet collapse demanded that their voices be heard. The clash of generations inside Russia set the scene for Putin's war against Ukraine.

In Ukraine, Soviet nostalgia also survived, although to a far lesser degree than in Russia. Older Ukrainians were often ambivalent about the Soviet legacy as Ukraine had made many important contributions to the Soviet Union. But younger Ukrainians took independence from Moscow as a given and preferred Western democracy to Russian autocracy as a model of development. By the time of Russia's 2014 invasion, an entire generation had grown up knowing only Ukraine as their homeland. Ukrainians were becoming citizens of their own country, while Russians remained subjects of their ruler.

As a fundamentally Soviet man, Putin could not comprehend Ukraine as an independent country. His view of Ukraine was based on outdated ideas of shared empire, and he could not accept that a new generation of Ukrainians—so close to Russians in language, culture, and religion—was choosing a future in Europe. Before Putin seized Crimea, Ukrainians did not deny their country's deep ties to Russia, and few saw a turn to the West as a repudiation of their neighbor. For the Kremlin, however, maintaining influence over Ukraine was a zero-sum game. Ironically, Russia's 2014 attack only galvanized Ukrainians' sense of national identity, and Ukraine irrevocably disowned its Soviet past.

The 2014 invasion was also inspired by Russia's desire to strike back at U.S. hegemony. Putin and his entourage were afflicted with an inferiority complex that made them envy and loathe the West at the same time. By unilaterally redrawing the map of Europe, the Kremlin presented the biggest challenge to Pax Americana since the Cold War. Even if Western countries did not fully realize it at the time, Russia was now at war with them too.

Putin blamed the West for sowing conflict between Russia and Ukraine. The Kremlin narrative held that the United States and its allies were dragging Ukraine westward as they crept ever closer to their ultimate target, Russia. Although the West did bear responsibility for events in Ukraine, I will show that the Kremlin, for the most part, imagined its struggle for Ukraine. The EU and NATO were not interested in accepting Ukraine as a full-fledged member because of its large size, widespread poverty, and endemic corruption. Furthermore, many Europeans were understanding of Russia's objections. Tragically, by symbolically holding open the doors to the EU and NATO with no intention of letting Ukraine in, the West increased the country's vulnerability to a revanchist Russia.

Among Western leaders, George W. Bush bore special responsibility for raising expectations among Western-oriented Ukrainians that their country had a chance to achieve NATO membership. Pompous empty promises not only deceived Ukrainians but also needlessly irritated the Kremlin. None of Bush's successors were even remotely interested in bringing Ukraine into NATO, and all of them wanted to refocus U.S. foreign policy on Asia. When Russia first invaded Ukraine in 2014, the United States was withdrawing forces from Europe, and U.S. troop levels on the continent were at their lowest since the beginning of World War II.

Without a doubt, talk of NATO enlargement and U.S.-led naval exercises in the Black Sea grated on the Kremlin and fed its sense of grievance. But Putin's obsession with controlling Ukraine was the driving force behind the Russian invasion, and his increasingly autocratic rule made it possible. A democratic Russia would not have seen a threat in an alliance of democracies on its borders, and it would not have attacked a democratic Ukraine.

This book presents an accessible but detailed history of Russia's path to war. In eleven chapters, I chronicle Putin's evolution from a leader who was cheered as a reformer, even by many Ukrainians, to an angry and isolated dictator who understood the reconquest of Ukraine as his historical mission.

The book is based on almost twenty years of reporting from Ukraine and Russia. I first traveled to the Soviet Union in 1991, the last year of its existence, and I began covering Putin's Russia as a journalist in 2003. I made my first visit to Ukraine shortly after the Orange Revolution and spent much of 2014 covering Russia's invasion, from the start of the occupation of Crimea to the bloody insurgency in eastern Ukraine. The book contains material that I reported at that time and draws on hundreds of interviews, conversations, and encounters. I also rely heavily on the reporting of many outstanding colleagues.

The first chapter of the book opens with Putin's visit to Kyiv in 2004, when he openly interfered in a Ukrainian election that ended in mass protests and saw Ukraine's first explicitly pro-Western president, Viktor

Yushchenko, come to power. Putin took the Orange Revolution as a warning that Ukraine was in danger of slipping out of Russian control.

Chapter 2 covers George W. Bush's effort to usher Ukraine and Georgia into NATO. Russia responded by invading Georgia in August 2008. More than any other U.S. president, Bush shaped Ukraine's coming confrontation with Russia. At the same time, Bush's unfettered use of U.S. military power provided Putin with an example he sought to emulate in Georgia, Syria, and eventually Ukraine.

In chapter 3, I go to Russia, where a young, charismatic activist named Alexei Navalny emerged at the head of mass protests against Putin's plan to rule Russia for an unprecedented third presidential term. The Kremlin blamed the United States for trying to export Ukraine's Orange Revolution to Russia.

In the next three chapters I deal with 2014, the year Ukraine experienced a bloody street revolution followed by Russia's lightning seizure of Crimea and the beginning of a pro-Russian uprising in eastern Ukraine. The events of that fateful year are key to understanding why Putin went on to launch a full-scale invasion eight years later. The Kremlin maintained that the CIA instigated a coup to overthrow the Russian-backed president, Viktor Yanukovych, and that Russia had no choice but to intervene militarily to prevent reprisals, even a genocide, against ethnic Russians. I demonstrate that it was actually Putin who spirited Yanukovych out of Ukraine, and I show how Russia laid the groundwork for the occupation of Crimea and fomented an uprising in eastern Ukraine.

In chapter 7, I examine the role the United States played in European security before and after 2014. Bush's successor, Barack Obama, was decidedly uninterested in Europe, which appeared to be prosperous, peaceful, and perfectly capable of defending itself. For Obama, Russia was a nuisance, not a threat, and Ukraine did not even appear on his radar.

In chapter 8, I return to Russia, where Putin's opponents were split over the military intervention in Ukraine. Navalny, who had been shaped by Russian nationalism early in his political career, began a quixotic presidential campaign that showed the growing rift between young Russians and older generations traumatized by the Soviet collapse.

In chapter 9, I track the unlikely rise of the comedian Volodymyr Zelensky to Ukraine's presidency and into the heart of America's polarized political fight before the 2020 U.S. presidential election.

In chapter 10, I show how Putin became increasingly isolated during the COVID-19 pandemic, which led to a hardening of his views on Ukraine. And in the concluding chapter, I focus on the confluence of factors that led Putin to order the full-scale, unprovoked invasion of Ukraine.

Of course the origins of the conflict between Ukraine and Russia go back much further than 2004, and Vladimir Putin was not its sole instigator. But I start my story here, with the Russian leader, because his radicalization began with the prospect of Russia's most coveted former territory going its own way. The Orange Revolution was a turning point for Putin and the beginning of his path to all-out war.

1

Putin in Kyiv

V ladimir Putin gazed down from the reviewing stand on the victory parade in the heart of Kyiv. To the energetic accompaniment of a military band, a vintage T-34 tank flying a Soviet battle flag rolled past Maidan Nezalezhnosti, Independence Square, followed by goose-stepping Ukrainian soldiers in the uniforms of World War II infantrymen, pilots, and sailors. Next came war veterans in open cars, then thousands of troops representing all the branches of Ukraine's armed forces. From on high, the Russian president presided over the extravaganza with other dignitaries in dark coats and generals in enormous peaked caps. Leonid Kuchma, the Ukrainian president, and his prime minister, Viktor Yanukovych, flanked their guest of honor from Moscow.

It was October 28, 2004. Officially, Putin was in the Ukrainian capital to celebrate the sixtieth anniversary of the liberation of Ukraine from Nazi occupation by the Red Army. Unofficially, he was on a three-day visit to stump for Yanukovych, whom Kuchma had chosen as his successor in a hotly contested presidential election to be held three days later.

Yanukovych's main opponent, Viktor Yushchenko, called Putin's visit "untimely" and said it was evidence that Yanukovych lacked the authority to win the election on his own.[1] Putin, who had just begun his second term as Russia's can-do president, was popular among Ukrainians. Russia was experiencing an unprecedented oil boom and had become an attractive destination for millions of Ukrainian migrant workers. A dense web of rail, road, and air connections tied Ukraine to Russia; Ukrainian citizens could travel to Russia without visas; and most Ukrainians spoke Russian fluently, either as their first or second language. Russia and Ukraine, the two most populous countries to emerge from the Soviet Union in 1991, were partners, not rivals.

Ukrainian opposition politicians were careful to direct their ire over Putin's visit at the Yanukovych campaign, not at the Kremlin. Oleksandr Turchynov, the head of the Batkivshchyna (Fatherland) party in the Ukrainian parliament, blamed Yanukovych and his patron, Kuchma, for inviting Putin to bolster a failing campaign that relied on dirty tricks and brute force.[2] Turchynov said that by endorsing Yanukovych, an oafish former governor with a criminal record, Putin risked damaging his own reputation. Petro Poroshenko, the deputy head of the Yushchenko campaign and a member of parliament, regretted that Putin was not meeting any presidential candidates other than Yanukovych—and he expressed the hope that as "an experienced, farsighted politician and outstanding diplomat," Putin would stick to his promise to respect the will of the Ukrainian people.[3]

The Ukrainian opposition's deference to Putin was understandable because, even if Yushchenko won, Russia would remain Ukraine's most important trade partner and a vital source of energy supplies. But the suggestion that Putin was unwittingly being manipulated to serve Yanukovych's political ambitions was disingenuous. In fact, the Kremlin was pulling out all the stops to influence the outcome of the Ukrainian election. Putin's visit to Kyiv was his sixth trip to Ukraine that year, as the Kremlin threw its weight behind the Kuchma-Yanukovych succession as the key to Ukraine's economic integration with Russia. As the election campaign heated up, the Kremlin dispatched a team of Moscow spin doctors to advise the Yanukovych campaign and set up a "Russian Club" in Kyiv as a platform for Russian politicians to reach a Ukrainian audience.[4] The grand finale of the Kremlin's efforts to sway the election was Putin's appearance on a live call-in show on Ukrainian television.

During his first term in office, Putin had started the tradition of taking calls from Russian citizens in marathon sessions on national TV. Carefully staged and lasting for hours, the "Direct Line" programs were designed to project the image of a leader who cared about fixing the problems of ordinary folk.

With a majority of Ukrainians consistently approving of Putin in opinion polls, the Russian president took his call-in show to Ukraine to plug Yanukovych's candidacy—and tighter cooperation with Russia.

Ukraine's three major TV channels broadcast the one-hour show live during prime time. Sitting between the Ukrainian and Russian flags, Putin took questions from three Ukrainian journalists and callers from around the country. He presented a vision of Ukraine and Russia as two young democracies that would prosper together on the foundation of a common past.

Putin acknowledged that Russians had needed time to realize that the other former Soviet republics were "not quasi-Soviet formations but full-fledged, independent countries."[5] In the case of Ukraine, he said, the acceptance of this new relationship was creating economic opportunities. "We have settled all our border issues. What this amounts to is full and absolute recognition of and respect for Ukraine's sovereignty, not only as concerns its land borders, but also its sea borders," he said. All outstanding issues that had burdened bilateral relations—such as Ukrainian debt repayments or the Russian Black Sea Fleet's base on the Crimean Peninsula—were now resolved, Putin boasted.

"No one is going to try to re-create the Soviet Union, no one is in a position to do so, and no one makes it their aim. Any such attempt would be counterproductive and, unfortunately, would not bring any benefits," Putin said. He explained that the closer cooperation he was seeking with Ukraine was economic and not political or military. Anything resembling the common political structures of the European Union was not on the agenda and would be for politicians of the future to decide, Putin said.

As for the politicians of the present, Putin did not hide his endorsement of the Kuchma-Yanukovych tandem. He praised Ukraine's double-digit economic growth and attributed it to the government's efforts to diversify the economy. Asked if it was true that he had recently celebrated his fifty-second birthday together with Yanukovych, Putin revealed that he had invited both the Ukrainian prime minister and the president to his party. Putin even deflected anger with the Yanukovych government over a new rule that required Ukrainians traveling to Russia to have passports. Putin took all the blame for the unpopular rule and summarily retracted it, promising Ukrainians that they would once again be able to visit Russia with only their internal IDs.

Well-planted critical questions were a part of Putin's call-in repertoire, and he happily took a query about the aim of his visit to Ukraine. Looking directly into the camera, Putin said the sixtieth anniversary of Ukraine's liberation from Nazi invaders was a "sufficiently serious occasion" to commemorate with "our friends." Asked if Russia would create or support political forces within Ukraine to bring the two countries together, Putin admitted that he would be happy if such forces gained in strength. "But it is very dangerous to initiate and support political forces inside Ukraine from abroad, especially on the part of Russia," he added. "It is counterproductive and may lead to the opposite result."

Another element of Putin's call-in format was juxtaposing weighty issues of state with a personal touch. The show was conducted in Russian, which Ukrainians understand, even if they do not speak it. When an elderly woman called in from a village outside Kyiv speaking Ukrainian, Putin brushed off a presenter's offer to interpret, saying he had understood the question. In response to another caller, Putin said he regretted not speaking Ukrainian but that he liked the language "very much." The Russian president recounted that in his student days he had tried to read *Kobzar*, a book of poems by Ukraine's national poet, Taras Shevchenko. Putin then recited a few verses in the original Ukrainian. Putin's flattery of his Ukrainian audience went on and on. He said that he and his wife, Lyudmila, had spent their honeymoon in western Ukraine. Asked if he had Ukrainian roots, Putin replied that his ancestors were all Russian, but if he found out that he also had Ukrainian blood, "I would be proud. I like Ukraine."

The flattery was mutual. In the middle of the show, one of the Ukrainian presenters mentioned that viewer calls were coming in at a rate of 520 per minute. One man asked Putin if he had considered running for president of Ukraine once his second term as Russian president expired. One of the last questions came from a first-grader in Kyiv who requested a photo with the Russian president. The next day Putin met the boy in Kuchma's office, posed for a picture, and gave him a laptop computer.[6]

Putin's smooth performance created the impression that there were no problems, only solutions, in Ukrainian-Russian relations. The sincerity of his words was debatable. But Putin's efforts to win over Ukrainians to the cause of closer economic integration with Russia were genuine, and he was playing to an audience that was at least receptive. A significant number of Ukrainians, especially in the Russian-speaking east, missed the security and prestige of living in a superpower called the Soviet Union. Other Ukrainians had wholly pragmatic reasons for aligning with their resource-rich neighbor, which appeared to be under the guidance of a modern, dynamic leader. From Putin's point of view, Russia still held many levers of control over Ukraine; a Yanukovych presidency was the best guarantee that the Kremlin's domination would not just continue but also grow.

Putin's designs were no secret. He was accelerating efforts to create an economic union with the core republics that had made up the Soviet Union—Russia, Ukraine, Belarus, and Kazakhstan. In spring 2004, Estonia, Latvia, and Lithuania became the first former Soviet republics to join the EU and NATO. Putin viewed the Baltic states' membership in the West's two premier clubs as an affront, if not a direct threat, to what he considered Russia's traditional sphere of influence. Viktor Yushchenko, Yanukovych's main rival, was running on a platform of closer integration with the EU and NATO with the eventual goal of full membership.

Yushchenko was the leader of the Our Ukraine political bloc, which styled itself as a European center-right party espousing free-market economics, moderate nationalism, and Christianity.[7] As chairman of the central bank in the 1990s, Yushchenko had overseen the introduction of Ukraine's currency, the hryvnia, and brought runaway inflation under control. With his promise to turn Ukraine westward, Yushchenko threatened to disrupt the cozy relationship with the Kremlin that Kuchma had started and Yanukovych promised to continue.

There were different ways to view Ukrainian society. Geographically there were linguistic, cultural, and religious fault lines that could be traced back to Ukraine's history as a shifting borderland between Russia, Poland, and Turkey. The western part of the country was Ukrainian-speaking and the heartland of Ukrainian national identity; the eastern part was Russian-speaking and more sympathetic to Russia; and central Ukraine, including Kyiv, was somewhere in between.

Generationally, there were also emerging divisions. The popularity of the Communists, Ukraine's single largest political party in parliament during the 1990s, was rapidly fading as more and more young Ukrainians saw their country's future in a democratic Europe. Lingering nostalgia for the Soviet Union was being exploited by Yanukovych's Party of Regions.

For the Ukrainian opposition, the 2004 presidential election was do or die. Kuchma, who had been in power for a decade, was about to pass on an increasingly autocratic government to Yanukovych. That summer, Yushchenko formed an alliance with the charismatic opposition leader Yulia Tymoshenko. Yushchenko campaigned for economic liberalization, good governance, and European integration.[8] Universal Western values, as opposed to a narrow Ukrainian nationalism, were the emphasis of the Yushchenko campaign. Yet the Kremlin rebuffed Yushchenko's outreach before the election to discuss the future of bilateral relations.[9]

Putin would not even entertain the possibility of a Yushchenko victory as he had placed all his bets on Yanukovych. This zero-sum approach made the Kremlin reliant on Kuchma, a wily political operator playing his own game. Kuchma was deeply unpopular after the publication in 2000 of secret tapes that implicated him in the gruesome murder of a critical journalist, Heorhiy Gongadze.[10] The "Kuchmagate" scandal set off huge protests demanding his resignation, and Kuchma's approval ratings slumped into the single digits.[11] Even though he found a legal loophole to run for a third term, Kuchma finally designated Yanukovych as his successor. Yet Kuchma's support for Yanukovych was hardly enthusiastic, fueling speculation that Kuchma was hoping that he might be able to hang on to power if the election somehow failed.[12]

It is unlikely that the inarticulate, lumbering Yanukovych impressed Putin, but that was beside the point. Putin's goal was the continuation of a friendly regime in Kyiv that was unacceptable to the West.[13] The Kremlin's strategy for the Yanukovych campaign was to frame the election as a struggle between eastern and western Ukraine, a choice between good and evil.[14] A series of political and economic concessions demonstrated the benefits of good relations with Russia. As a result of a bilateral agreement on the collection of value-added tax on oil and gas, the Kremlin transferred $800 million to the Ukrainian treasury, allowing Yanukovych to double pensions before the election.[15]

Yanukovych, a native of the eastern Donetsk region, appealed to the Russophone part of the Ukrainian electorate by promising to grant Russian the status of an "official language" (although Ukrainian would continue to be the only state language), permitting dual citizenship for Ukrainians and Russians, and ending closer cooperation with NATO.[16] To tip the balance and prevail in the election, Yanukovych relied on so-called administrative resources, namely the government's influence over media, civil servants, and key institutions such as the Central Election Commission. On top of that came tens of millions of dollars, if not more, from Russia.[17]

Yushchenko was constantly under attack. His plane was denied permission to land in six cities, and campaign events were often disrupted.[18] Yushchenko's opponents accused him of being an American agent because his wife Kateryna had grown up in the Ukrainian diaspora in Chicago and worked for the U.S. State Department during the Cold War. Media in the Donbas, the rust belt coal basin of eastern Ukraine, portrayed Yushchenko as a neo-Nazi and a Ukrainian nationalist who hated Russian speakers.[19] The worst blow came less than two months before the election, when Yushchenko fell violently ill after having dinner with the head of the SBU, Ukraine's main intelligence service. Yushchenko suffered excruciating pain and his face became covered with cysts. He was treated in Austria, where doctors later concluded Yushchenko had been poisoned with a high dose of dioxin.[20] His face disfigured with pockmarks, Yushchenko returned to Kyiv, accusing unnamed forces of trying to stop him from running.[21] The poisoning galvanized his supporters. On October 23, 2004, he held his last big rally in Kyiv, attracting tens of thousands of people. Three days later, Putin flew in to make his last-minute pitch for Yanukovych on Ukrainian television.

Antigovernment protests were nothing unusual in Kyiv after "Kuchmagate" brought thousands of angry citizens out into the street. In the summer before the presidential election, there was a widespread expectation in Kyiv that Yanukovych would try to steal the vote. The question was whether the opposition could mobilize enough people to stop him.[22] A citizens' revolt in the former Soviet republic of Georgia had set a precedent a year earlier, when protesters swept out a corrupt government after a rigged election.

On October 31, in the first round of voting, Yushchenko unexpectedly took 39.9 percent of the vote, just squeaking past Yanukovych's 39.3 percent. With neither man winning an outright majority in a crowded field of two dozen candidates, a runoff was scheduled to take place three weeks later. The official results, however, were not released until ten days after the vote, and evidence later emerged that Yanukovych's allies had hacked into the Central Election Commission's server to manipulate results.[23]

Putin again visited Ukraine, meeting Kuchma and Yanukovych to inaugurate a new ferry service between the Crimean Peninsula and Russia across the Kerch Strait. Although the Kremlin's public message was that Russia was opening yet a new transportation link to its common economic zone, Putin reportedly urged Yanukovych to step up the use of "administrative resources" if he hoped to defeat Yushchenko in the second round.[24]

Yanukovych appeared to heed Putin's advice. After voting ended in the November 21 runoff, EU observers noticed a discrepancy between exit polls, which favored Yushchenko, and vote counting at the Central Election Commission.[25] Voter turnout in the Donetsk region, Yanukovych's home base, jumped by almost twenty percentage points from the first round, to an improbable 96.7 percent.[26] In its final report on the election, the Organization for Security and Cooperation in Europe (OSCE) said its observers had found a raft of violations in the second round, including instances of voters being bussed from polling station to polling station; ballot stuffing; "serious irregularities" in absentee balloting; and examples of "implausibly high voter turnout figures."[27] Putin, on an official visit to Brazil, called Yanukovych to congratulate him.

That night Yushchenko supporters, wearing his campaign color orange, spilled into the streets of Kyiv and assembled on Independence Square, or the Maidan. The next day, tens of thousands of people packed the square after the Central Election Commission announced preliminary results giving Yanukovych 49.5 percent of the vote against Yushchenko's 46.9 percent. Independent exit polling showed a completely different picture, with Yushchenko winning 53 percent over Yanukovych's 44 percent.[28] The Kremlin pushed Kuchma to deal with the protesters decisively.[29] But the White House, which had largely stood by during the election campaign, now urged Kuchma to exercise restraint. Richard Lugar, the chairman of the U.S. Senate Foreign Relations Committee, was in Ukraine to observe the runoff as the personal representative of President George W. Bush. "A tarnished election will lead us to review our relations with Ukraine," Bush wrote in a letter that Lugar delivered to Kuchma.[30]

Activists from the student organization Pora, which means "it is time," pitched tents on the Maidan, and a protest camp rose in the same place where Putin had reviewed a military parade a month earlier. The spiraling protest would have been impossible without Ukraine's burgeoning civic groups. Ordinary Ukrainians descended on Kyiv from across the country, and hundreds of thousands of people peacefully demonstrated at the biggest rallies. Yulia Tymoshenko, Yushchenko's ally and prime minister designate, became the photogenic face of the protest with a blond braid crowning her head. The Kyiv uprising became a global news story, putting independent Ukraine on the map for people around the world.

For Russian politicians, Ukraine was more than a neighbor; it was a place on which to project their greatest hopes—and worst fears. Russian opposition leader Boris Nemtsov, whose liberal party had failed to get reelected to parliament a year earlier, joined Yushchenko's team. Inspired by the democratic wave in Kyiv, Nemtsov showed up on the Maidan in an orange scarf and called Putin's support for Yanukovych a "perverse" union between a secret policeman and a repeat offender.[31] "We need a democratic Ukraine the same way as we need a democratic Russia," Nemtsov said.

Putin, on the other hand, was furious. As he returned from Latin America, he stopped in Portugal for an official visit on November 23. At a press conference in Lisbon, he bristled when a Portuguese journalist brought up his premature congratulatory call to Yanukovych. Putin then assailed the OSCE for criticizing the Ukrainian vote but recognizing recent elections in Afghanistan and Kosovo.[32] The next day, the Duma, Russia's lower house, passed a resolution expressing "deep concern over the extremist actions by the radical opposition forces in Ukraine, which could lead to tragic consequences."[33] Meanwhile, Ukraine's Central Election Commission declared Yanukovych the winner of the second round. On November 25, Putin promptly congratulated Yanukovych a second time, in writing, and traveled to The Hague for a meeting with EU leaders. He blamed them for inciting unrest in Kyiv and accused U.S. Senator Lugar of having taken up residence in Yushchenko's campaign headquarters.[34]

The outsized role that Ukraine played in Putin's mind was the inverse of the country's importance for the U.S. administration, which had been focused on Bush's reelection and stabilizing Iraq and Afghanistan. If Ukraine appeared on Bush's radar at all, it was as the contributor of a peacekeeping contingent to Iraq. Both Yushchenko and Yanukovych had campaigned to bring the Ukrainian troops home. When the Orange Revolution broke out, it came as a "total surprise," according to a former senior Bush administration official.[35] "We were scrambling," he remembered. Some senior U.S. diplomats argued that the United States should not wade into the political crisis in Kyiv. But after the official vote count was released, Secretary of State Colin Powell said: "We cannot accept this result as legitimate because it does not meet international standards and because there has not been an investigation of the numerous and credible reports of fraud and abuse."[36] He called for a "full review" of how the election had been conducted and the votes tallied.

In Kyiv the protesters did not go home, and Yushchenko took a symbolic oath of office on the Maidan. Amid the stalemate, prominent members of the diplomatic service, the SBU, and the military defected from the regime.[37] Unwilling to risk violence, Kuchma invited the Polish president, Aleksander Kwasniewski, and the Lithuanian president, Valdas Adamkus, to help mediate negotiations between the two sides. Yanukovych continued hemorrhaging supporters. On November 27 Ukraine's parliament, the Rada, voted to declare the elections invalid, and four days later dismissed Yanukovych as prime minister.[38] Kuchma flew to Moscow and caught Putin at the airport before the Russian president departed on a trip to India. Kuchma was now promoting the idea of a new election with fresh candidates, which would give him the option of running for a third term.[39] Although wary of his Ukrainian counterpart, Putin supported Kuchma's plan and ridiculed Yushchenko's insistence that the second round be repeated. "Will there have to be a third, a fourth, a twenty-fifth round until one of the sides obtains the necessary result?" Putin asked.[40]

Kuchma's control over the levers of power was slipping. The day after he met Putin in Moscow, the Ukrainian Supreme Court ruled that the authorities had committed mass fraud, invalidated Yanukovych's win, and ordered a repeat of the runoff. Yanukovych conceded. Yet the compromise, brokered by the European leaders, came at a price for Yushchenko: a constitutional reform that would curb the powers of the presidency.[41] The Rada put the compromise into law, and on December 26 the runoff was held again, with 77 percent turnout. Yushchenko convincingly beat Yanukovych 52 percent to 44 percent. OSCE observers compared the vote "much more favorably" to the previous two rounds and reported "few serious violations."[42] The Maidan and Yushchenko had prevailed. Yanukovych, or rather Putin, had suffered a crushing defeat.

I arrived on the Maidan one week after the December 26 vote. At the time I was living in Moscow, where I worked at the local English-language newspaper, the *Moscow Times*. I had been closely following events in Kyiv, but as an editor I could not get away from my desk until the holidays, which in Russia were celebrated in the first ten days of the new year. On January 1, 2005, I boarded an overnight train to Kyiv. As we entered the city's dreary suburbs in the pale morning light, I caught my first glimpses of orange: a little ribbon fluttering from a car's antenna, a young woman's orange hair, an orange ski jacket. As the train trundled across the wide gray Dnipro River, I spotted the fabled golden domes of Kyiv in the distance. Behind them loomed the *Batkivshchyna-Maty*, the giant World War II monument depicting the motherland as a fearless woman holding aloft a sword and shield.

When I exited the metro, I found myself in front of a McDonald's on the Khreshchatyk, the city's main thoroughfare. Before me, the famous tent city stretched up the middle of the street to the Maidan. The day before, the young president of Georgia, Mikheil Saakashvili, had visited to congratulate Ukrainians on their peaceful revolution. He had led Georgians in a popular uprising known as the Rose Revolution a year earlier. The street was packed with people wearing orange, and even with my small bag I found it difficult to navigate the throngs. Music blared from everywhere, and suddenly two mules, ridden by children, came weaving through the crowd. It was a carnival. I checked into the Kozatskiy (Cossack) Hotel, an aging hotel with cheap, clean rooms at one end of the Maidan. Little did I know that time and again it would become my base in the years to come.

Ukraine was a mysterious country for people in the West, in part because a cumbersome, Soviet-era visa policy made it difficult for foreigners to visit. In Moscow, I found it easier to apply for a Ukrainian journalist visa than a tourist visa.[43] For someone coming from Russia, Ukraine seemed instantly familiar but subtly different. In Kyiv, as in many cities of central and eastern Ukraine, Russian was the dominant language on the street and in homes. In the Russian Empire and later the Soviet Union, Russian had been the language of government, trade, and social mobility. Many Ukrainians used both languages in daily life, and it was not uncommon for a person to switch from one to the other in the same conversation. Some Ukrainians spoke a hybrid of Ukrainian and Russian, known as Surzhyk. As East Slavic languages, Ukrainian and Russian are closely related, roughly in the same way that Spanish and Italian are. While Ukrainians were for the most part bilingual, Russians not exposed to Ukrainian had difficulty understanding it. My Russian was far from perfect, but I communicated with most people with ease.

Visually, Ukraine also did not appear to be so different from Russia; its cities were filled with grand czarist buildings, Orthodox churches, and structures representing all the phases of Soviet architecture, from edgy Constructivism and Stalinist pomp to the shabby monotony of the late Communist era. On closer examination, however, there were plenty of differences, from the signage in Ukrainian to the symbols of an independent state: the Ukrainian trident and the ubiquitous use of blue and yellow, the colors of the national flag. In Kyiv I saw billboards with simple patriotic messages: the imperative "Love Ukraine" over a field of sunflowers with a blue sky, or two little girls holding hands under the words "My Ukraine!" In pursuit of a Soviet patriotism, the Communists had persecuted expressions of national pride. Most Ukrainians I met were happy to live in their own country, even if they were still getting used to it. The same people who told me they resented Putin openly campaigning for Yanukovych went on to say how warm their feelings were for Russia.

One difference with Russia that I noticed immediately was the absence of fear. Russia had just experienced a horrifying terrorist attack on a school that killed more than 330 people, the majority of them children, and suicide bombings in Moscow were a constant threat, blowback from the pitiless war Putin was prosecuting against an Islamist insurgency in the North Caucasus region. In Moscow, announcements constantly warned passengers descending into the metro to report suspicious people and packages. In the Kyiv metro, music played in the escalator shafts. Kyivans were in a holiday mood, and not only because Orthodox Christmas was around the corner. The contagious jubilance of the Maidan filled the city. I realized then that the absence of fear is freedom.

The revolution might have been over, but the protesters who remained on the Maidan vowed not to move until Yushchenko was inaugurated. Muscular young men in black wool caps and orange armbands manned the perimeter to keep out provocateurs and to maintain order. The camp consisted of army tents, some heated by wood stoves. There was a "staff" tent, a press center, and a couple of field kitchens. I saw the flags of Georgia, Canada, and Belarus. One tent flew the red and black flag of the Ukrainian Insurgent Army, the nationalist guerilla army responsible for atrocities against Jews and Poles during World War II. An old man with a handlebar moustache stumbled out of the tent wearing red pantaloons, a long sheepskin coat, a shaggy Cossack hat, and a sword. The Maidan had sparked the hopes not only of democrats but also of ultranationalists and other marginal groups disillusioned with the status quo.

During the Soviet era, the Maidan had been known as October Revolution Square. Five days after the Chernobyl nuclear accident on April 26, 1986, the Communist authorities decided to hold the traditional May Day parade despite an alarming rise of radiation levels blowing in from Chernobyl, sixty miles away. Photos of that day show people in traditional costumes, schoolgirls with giant bows in their hair, and students holding pictures of Soviet leaders marching over the square, oblivious to the danger in the air. Four years later, as people around the Soviet Union began demanding freedom from the Communist dictatorship, October Revolution Square became the site of an antigovernment protest. Students set up a tent city and went on a hunger strike, making a series of political demands, including the resignation of the head of Ukraine's Communist government, Vitaliy Masol. The so-called Revolution on Granite forced Masol to stand down and gave Ukraine's independence movement a powerful boost. The Revolution on Granite set an important precedent for the Orange Revolution. After the Soviet Union fell apart and Ukraine became an independent country a year later, the square was renamed Independence Square.

Taras Loginov came to the Maidan on the day after the disputed runoff in November 2004 and ended up staying a month. When protesters began pitching tents on the Maidan, Loginov's experience organizing youth camps was suddenly in high demand. "Nobody expected there would be such a large number of people," he told me. On the third day of the protest, it was impossible to buy a tent in Kyiv. Material support came from managers at big companies, local entrepreneurs, and even civil servants. "If we needed a power generator, the problem was solved within twenty minutes," Loginov said.

Protest organizers feared that mobile phone providers would switch off service, but instead they boosted capacity in the city center. Digital technology played an important role in building momentum for the protest. Social media and smartphones were still in their infancy, but text messaging and the internet became the Maidan's vital link to the outside world. Media attention and the large number of protesters made a violent crackdown all but impossible, Loginov said.

"People went on the square not because they were strongly in favor of Yushchenko but to show that they are people who have an opinion,"

Loginov said. "The people have felt their power." Not only did the outside world get a new image of Ukrainians, he said, but also Ukrainians started to see themselves differently.

I was curious about what was outside Kyiv, the epicenter of the Orange Revolution. I wanted to learn what people thought in the east and west of Ukraine, which typically were portrayed as polar opposites of each other. Fortunately, Ukraine's rail network put every large city within reach of an overnight train ride from Kyiv. I first set out for Lviv near the Polish border. Ukrainians with the strongest sense of national identity were concentrated in the far west of the country, an area that had never been part of the Russian Empire and was seized by the Soviet Union during World War II. After the war, the Soviet authorities were suspicious of any display of Ukrainian national feeling and were quick to brand Ukrainians opposed to the Communist regime as "fascists" or "Banderites," a reference to the followers of the nationalist leader Stepan Bandera. Those old insults reemerged during the 2004 presidential race, when Yanukovych supporters hurled them at the Yushchenko campaign.

My companions in the four-bunk compartment were surprised to have an American join them. A middle-aged woman who lived in Russia was going home to visit her mother. She said her brother had sneaked into the United States on a fake passport, went back after he was deported, and now was living legally in Florida. "That was dangerous," I said. "Yes, but to live here is simply impossible," she replied. Her mother's monthly pension was the equivalent of $17—"one trip to the store." The young man in my compartment, a student, had spent two nights in a tent on the Maidan. Even though he was doubtful that Yushchenko and Tymoshenko could deliver change, he saw his future in Ukraine.

With its cobbled Market Square and ancient churches, Lviv felt distinctly central European, a reflection of its earlier incarnations as the Polish city of Lwów and the Austrian city of Lemberg. Lviv's poverty was plain to see, with people peddling shoelaces and used books on the street. The city felt so quaint, I realized, because there were hardly any modern signs or outdoor advertisements. Its architectural monuments slowly crumbling, Lviv seemed frozen in time.

"Our little Paris" was how Liliya Kovalyk affectionately referred to her hometown. She and her husband, Ihor, invited me into their apartment so

I could interview them for a story I was writing for an American children's magazine. She worked as an editor for a website for the Ukrainian Greek Catholic Church; he ran a small trucking company. When the protests broke out on the Maidan, Liliya and Ihor drove to Kyiv with their twelve-year-old son, Nazar, to take part. It was his first trip to the capital. Nazar was born in 1992, the year after independence, and when I asked him what he knew about the Soviet Union, he only had the vaguest of notions. Nazar already had five years of English and three years of German language instruction, but no Russian. "I'm a big patriot," Liliya said. "I don't like Russians that much, but I think it's wrong that children can't learn Russian." Good neighborly relations with Moscow were important, she said, but Ukraine's future was in Europe—and their son's future was in Ukraine.

Yushchenko swept Lviv and other regions of western Ukraine. But in the Donetsk region, where Yanukovych had started his political career as governor, Yushchenko won a mere 4 percent in the repeat runoff. On my visit to Donetsk, the only orange I saw were the smocks of the street sweepers. My guide was a young man named Volodya, who headed a nongovernmental educational organization funded by the billionaire philanthropist George Soros.[44] Volodya picked me up when my overnight train pulled into Donetsk. The McDonald's on Lenin Square, the city's central plaza, was the only place to grab a coffee that early in the morning. Out on the square, below a black statue of Vladimir Lenin, the founder of the Soviet Union, there was a little camp of about fifteen tents, the answer from Yanukovych's Party of Regions to the mass uprising in Kyiv. Volodya said he had at first been sympathetic to Yushchenko but changed his mind as the campaign rhetoric got uglier. All the Donetsk bashing by Yushchenko's campaign made Volodya vote for Yanukovych in the second round.

Compared to Kyiv or Lviv, Donetsk was a young city. Founded in 1869 by the Welsh industrialist John Hughes, it was first called Yuzovka and later Stalino. The Donets River coal basin, Donbas for short, became one of the most important industrial centers of the Soviet Union. As the dawn glowed pink, Volodya drove me around his hometown, a monument to Soviet industrial planning with its sprawling factories, prefab housing blocks, and hillocks of slag. The new landmarks were shopping centers, an Orthodox cathedral, and the pompous Donbas Palace, a five-star hotel owned by Rinat Akhmetov, the local oligarch and Yanukovych's main backer. Things were looking up in Donetsk, Volodya said. A miner could make up to $500 a month, and real estate prices were similar to those in Kyiv. Because people had started to feel a certain level of stability, Volodya said, they did not support a change in the country's government.

I heard exactly the same view from a local entrepreneur named Roman Medvedev, whom I met with his twelve-year-old daughter, Masha, in the plush lobby of the Donbas Palace. Roman said he thought that what had happened in Kyiv was more of a putsch than a revolution. He was deeply skeptical that Yushchenko would be able to live up to his promises to democratize Ukraine and bring it closer to the EU. "We didn't choose between Europe and Russia," he said. "We voted for our families." Roman identified as Ukrainian and could speak the language, even if most people in the Donetsk region spoke Russian in their daily lives. "We can speak Ukrainian, but it's just easier to communicate in Russian because we're used to it," said Masha, a vivacious sixth-grader. The language of instruction in her school was Russian, with Ukrainian taught as a separate subject. Masha said only one boy in her entire school had voiced support for Yushchenko. "Our people don't want to join Russia," Roman said. He paused, adding that there were many in Donetsk who did. Roman was not against European integration, although he feared the competitive risks of open borders to the Ukrainian economy. Masha said she saw her future in Ukraine, perhaps as a computer programmer. "I was born here, and I'll live here," she said. "I'm an optimist."

The supposed friendship between Ukraine and Russia that Putin touted during his visits belied underlying tensions in bilateral relations. Just a year before the Kremlin's extraordinary interference in Ukraine's elections, the two countries appeared to be on the brink of war—or at least a skirmish—over the Crimean Peninsula. When I moved to Moscow in November 2003 to join the *Moscow Times*, the top news story was a dispute over a causeway Russia was building across the Kerch Strait, the bottleneck separating the Crimean Peninsula from Russia. The new Russian dam was approaching Tuzla Island, which Russia claimed as its own even though Tuzla had been a part of Crimea since 1941—and Soviet authorities had transferred Crimea from Russia to Ukraine in 1954. At the time, the redrawing of internal Soviet borders had been a bureaucratic technicality. But after Ukrainian independence, Russians first became aware of the "loss" of Crimea, which for more than two centuries had served as a strategic, sun-dappled Russian outpost in the Black Sea. Construction on the causeway began in September 2003, and by late October the Ukrainian border guards deployed to Tuzla Island were in a state of "maximum readiness" in case Russian workers violated Ukraine's border.[45] A Kyiv newspaper cited Alexander Voloshin, head of Putin's administration, as telling Ukrainian journalists that it was bad enough that Crimea was Ukrainian, and that Russia was ready to drop "the bomb" to keep control of the Kerch Strait.[46] (A Kremlin official later told the *Kommersant* newspaper that the Ukrainian journalists clearly lacked a sense of humor.) Only a phone call between Kuchma and Putin helped defuse the standoff and stopped the dam from being completed.[47]

In Kyiv there was speculation that Kuchma had manufactured the Tuzla crisis to make him look like the savior of Ukrainian sovereignty and boost his single-digit popularity as he considered a third run for office.[48] A more likely explanation is that Putin was pressuring the weakened Ukrainian president to abandon a foreign policy that sought a middle way between the West and Russia. Half a year later the Ukrainian and Russian parliaments ratified a border agreement that left open the exact delimitation of the Kerch Strait but fixed Crimea as Ukrainian territory. At the same time, the Ukrainian and Russian parliaments ratified an agreement on Putin's pet project, the creation of a single economic space together with Belarus and Kazakhstan.[49] Kuchma had been walking a fine line, seeking closer relations with the EU and NATO even as Ukraine benefited from old economic ties with Russia. After he was implicated in the murder of the journalist Heorhiy Gongadze, Kuchma was at pains to patch up relations with the West and sent Ukrainian troops to Iraq to support the U.S.-led occupation. With the 2004 presidential election on the horizon, Kuchma became more reliant on the Kremlin as he sought ways to preserve his influence over the next administration, if not to stage a political comeback of his own. In July 2004, Kuchma met Putin in the Crimean resort of Yalta. Reversing his own government's policy, Kuchma said that Ukraine was giving up its aspiration to join the EU and NATO and would merely seek to "deepen relations" with the two blocs.[50] Putin warned that "agents" of the West were doing everything possible to thwart the integration of Russia and Ukraine.

The Kremlin left it up to Kuchma to choose his own successor.[51] Viktor Medvedchuk, the suave head of the Ukrainian presidential administration, was interested in running.[52] As one of the central players in Kuchma's

administration, Medvedchuk worked closely with his Russian counter-
parts, first with Alexander Voloshin (who threatened to drop "the bomb"
during the Tuzla crisis) and later with Dmitry Medvedev, Putin's protégé.
In 2004, Medvedchuk traveled to St. Petersburg to christen his daughter
Daria in one of the city's main cathedrals. Putin became her godfather and
Medvedev's wife, Svetlana, her godmother.[53]

Still, Kuchma considered Medvedchuk "unelectable" and chose Yanukovych, his malleable prime minister, as his successor.[54] Putin accepted the
decision and promptly signaled his endorsement of Yanukovych to Washington. Condoleezza Rice, at the time Bush's national security adviser, later
recalled that on a visit to Putin's residence outside Moscow in May 2004,
Yanukovych suddenly emerged from a side room. "Oh, please meet Viktor,"
Putin told Rice. "He is a candidate for president of Ukraine."[55] The main
thing for the Kremlin was not who its candidate was but that it had one.
Putin was never particularly interested in Ukraine's presidents, according
to Sergei Pugachyov, a former Putin confidant. "They are like governors
for him—it's just by accident that he isn't called a governor but a president," Pugachyov remembered.[56] And if Russian governors were any indication, competence or intelligence were far less important to the Kremlin
than loyalty and the ability to carry out orders.

Putin's imperious attitude toward his Ukrainian counterparts was
rooted in centuries of Russian domination over Ukraine. For Russians who
were nostalgic for empire after the collapse of the Soviet Union, Russia was
unimaginable without Ukraine—if not as an integral part than at least as a
vassal state. Because of a common religious and historical heritage, many
Russians claimed medieval Kyiv as the origin of their statehood. In the
Russian Empire and the Soviet Union, Ukraine had served as an agricultural and industrial powerhouse. It had been a gateway for European influence and trade as well as to invaders. Some of the most decisive battles
in Russian history were fought on the territory of Ukraine. Traces of Russia's imperial past were everywhere: from Peter the Great's house in Kyiv
and the Catherine the Great monument in Odesa to Lenin statues in towns
large and small. But if Ukraine had seeped into Russia's understanding of
itself, the reverse was also true. For many Ukrainians, the border with Russia was a blurred line.

Fired up by the divisive rhetoric of the 2004 election campaign, politicians in eastern Ukraine reacted furiously when protests broke out in

Kyiv after the second round of voting. On November 28, 3,500 lawmakers from southeastern Ukraine gathered in the ice hockey stadium in the eastern town of Sievierodonetsk.[57] Borys Kolesnikov, the head of the Donetsk regional legislature, proposed establishing a southeastern Ukrainian state as a federative republic with its capital in Kharkiv. Yevheniy Kushnarov, the governor of the Kharkiv region, said: "I'd like to remind the hotheads under orange banners: from Kharkiv to Kyiv it's 480 kilometers—and to the border with Russia, forty!"[58] The most prominent Russian guest was Moscow Mayor Yury Luzhkov, who compared the protesters on the Maidan to a "Sabbath of witches who have been fattened up with oranges and pretend they represent the whole nation."[59] Yanukovych, who also attended the convention, appealed for calm and the preservation of Ukraine's territorial integrity. But after he left, the delegates unanimously passed an ultimatum warning that if an "illegitimate president" came to power in Kyiv they would pursue a referendum on reorganizing Ukraine's "administrative-territorial system."

The separatist fury in Sievierodonetsk appeared to be a flash in the pan. The next day Kuchma denounced the calls for autonomy by Ukraine's eastern regions, and the angry threats of a split came to nothing.[60]

Putin was as unprepared for the secession of southeastern Ukraine as he was for the Orange Revolution. The Kremlin's spin doctors had no Plan B, because with the administrative juggernaut of the Ukrainian state behind Yanukovych, his victory was supposed to have been guaranteed. By turning the election into a geopolitical contest with the West, Putin set the stakes so high that Yanukovych's defeat became an unmitigated foreign policy disaster.[61] The Maidan was Putin's first big defeat in Ukraine based on faulty intelligence. If the Kremlin's base assumption was that Ukraine was merely a western extension of Russia, then Ukrainian elections should have been as easy for the local authorities to manipulate as Russian elections were. What Putin could not grasp was how far many Ukrainians had come from the days of the Ukrainian Soviet Socialist Republic. Western Ukraine, which had been the center of Ukrainian resistance to Soviet power, contributed to an emerging national identity that rejected centuries of Russian dominion. Free to select a model for their country's development, Ukrainians were increasingly drawn to Europe. Furthermore, Ukraine's regions were divided among rival oligarchs who competed among each other and weakened the power of the central government in

Kyiv. In this more pluralistic, if chaotic, political climate, Ukrainian civil society was thriving and Ukrainians were unafraid to take their demands to the street. As much as Kuchma tried to consolidate power, he lacked the control the Kremlin wielded domestically, making it possible for the Ukrainian Supreme Court to reach an independent decision on the conduct of the presidential election.

The Kremlin ended up getting entangled in Kuchma's machinations to hang on to power. Ironically, Kuchma had cautioned Russians from mistaking Ukraine for Russia when he presented his memoirs, *Ukraine Is Not Russia*, at a Moscow book fair in September 2003. The Ukrainian president embodied the ambivalent relationship between Ukraine and Russia. As Russian was his first language, Kuchma admitted that he was not comfortable writing in Ukrainian and had therefore written the book in Russian. It was published in Moscow and translated into Ukrainian.[62] Kuchma explained that while Russians were not in danger of losing their Russian identity, millions of Ukrainians were still in search of their "Ukrainian-ness."[63] He criticized Russians who begrudged Ukraine its independence and said he "sympathized" with Putin, who was under pressure to find "Russia's man" in the upcoming presidential election. Any Ukrainian president would be for Russia, Kuchma explained, in the sense that Ukraine's genuine independence was in Russia's interests.

Kuchma's words fell on deaf ears. Putin received Yushchenko in the Kremlin in January 2005, pledging to work with the new Ukrainian administration. "As you know, Russia never works behind the scenes in the post-Soviet area," Putin said with a straight face. The Kremlin then did its best to hobble Yushchenko, who proved to be a weak and ineffective president. Russia slashed subsidies that had been used to keep Ukraine hooked on Siberian natural gas. Twice, in 2006 and 2009, Gazprom, Russia's state-run energy giant, switched off natural gas deliveries to Ukraine in the depth of winter. The Kremlin's so-called gas wars also served to demonstrate that Ukraine—which carried 80 percent of Russian natural gas exports to Europe—was an unreliable transit country. Together with European partners, Putin came up with alternative pipeline projects that would circumvent and "discipline" Ukraine. The most notable bypass project was called Nord Stream, connecting Germany directly to Russia via a pipeline under the Baltic Sea.

For Putin, the materialization of a people power revolution on the Maidan smelled like a Western conspiracy. After the adulation he had received during his Kyiv visit in October, such a turn of events was totally unexpected. Putin drew his own conclusions. To stop the "orange plague" from infecting Russia, Putin continued a crackdown on the democratic opposition and on internationally funded nongovernmental organizations, which the Kremlin viewed as a Trojan horse for foreign influence. In response to the Ukrainian student group Pora, which had played a crucial role in organizing the Maidan, the Kremlin preemptively created the progovernment Nashi ("Ours") youth movement.[64] The Orange Revolution fueled paranoia in the Kremlin that the United States and its allies were creeping ever closer under the guise of democracy promotion. Everything had to be done to ensure that Russia would not be next.

2

Warning Shots

George W. Bush bowed his head before Kyiv's new memorial to the Holodomor, the 1932–33 famine that Ukrainians consider a genocide by the Soviet regime. With less than a year left in office, the American president was paying his first visit to Ukraine in April 2008 to reassure Ukrainians that he was doing everything in his power to bring their country into NATO. As part of his "freedom agenda" to promote democracy around the world, Bush was advocating for Ukraine and Georgia to be given a clear road map to membership in the U.S.-led alliance. On the way to Bucharest, Romania, for his last NATO summit, Bush stopped in Kyiv to meet with Viktor Yushchenko, the hero of the Orange Revolution. Three years into Yushchenko's presidency, the hopes raised by the Maidan protest were foundering on dysfunction and infighting within the ruling coalition. And Bush, following his disastrous invasion of Iraq and pursuit of a unilateralist foreign policy, was struggling to convince key European allies of the wisdom of bringing the two former Soviet republics into NATO.

Appropriately enough, Bush and Yushchenko met in the House with Chimeras, an Art Nouveau landmark used for official receptions by Ukrainian presidents. "Your nation has made a bold decision, and the United States strongly supports your request," Bush said about Yushchenko's wish for a Membership Action Plan, or MAP, from NATO.[1] "In Bucharest this week, I will continue to make America's position clear. We support MAP for Ukraine and Georgia. Helping Ukraine move towards NATO membership is in the interest of every member in the alliance and will help advance security and freedom in this region and around the world." The Kremlin, already furious over Bush's plans to deploy components of a U.S. missile shield in Poland and the Czech Republic, had made its opposition to any further NATO enlargement well-known. Vladimir Putin was so intent on thwarting Bush's push to offer MAPs to Ukraine and Georgia that the Russian leader planned to take his case personally to the Bucharest summit. "You will forgive me, but I would not like to see the key, fundamental principle of the alliance's activity, open doors, to be replaced by a veto for a country which is not even a member," Yushchenko said.[2] Bush reassured him that Russia had no veto over NATO membership. But Bush did not dwell on the fact that NATO members Germany and France did hold vetoes—and that both countries were opposed to extending MAPs to Ukraine and Georgia.

Bush's insistence on granting Ukraine a MAP also ignored the country's political reality. In early 2008, 21 percent of Ukrainians supported NATO membership while more than 50 percent opposed it, according to polling by the Kyiv-based Razumkov Centre.[3] At the end of his joint press conference with Bush, Yushchenko acknowledged that "profound work" remained to bring along most Ukrainians before a referendum on the issue. Flying red flags and chanting anti-American slogans, Communists and Socialists protested on the Maidan against a Ukrainian MAP during Bush's visit.[4] A similar rally took place in Simferopol, the capital of Crimea.

Bush's words of support for Ukraine sounded tough and contrasted with a speech his father, George H. W. Bush, had made as president in Kyiv in 1991, the last year of the Soviet Union's existence. At the time, Ukraine and the Baltic states were leading the drive for independence from Moscow. Bush Sr., who had just met the Soviet leader Mikhail Gorbachev in the Kremlin, arrived in Kyiv to warn Ukrainians against "suicidal nationalism based on ethnic hatred."[5] Bush Sr.'s address became known as the "Chicken Kiev speech" for its caution and deference to the crumbling status quo. Now, with his stubborn determination to bring Ukraine and Georgia into NATO against the Kremlin's wishes, Bush Jr. was once again outdoing his father—just as in Iraq, where Bush Sr. had stopped before the gates of Baghdad while Bush Jr. overran them, the consequences be damned.

In the spring of 2008, George W. Bush's second term was nearing its end amid the rubble of the Iraq War. Bequeathing a path to NATO membership was one way to reward Ukraine and Georgia for contributing troops to his "coalition of the willing," the group of countries that had provided a flimsy alibi for an American war of aggression. Ukraine and Georgia fit the narrative of Bush's freedom agenda, having both experienced peaceful, popular uprisings that swept pro-American presidents into office. Although Bush appeared insensitive to the Kremlin's protestations, he continued to maintain a curiously warm relationship with Putin. No affront by Bush was too big for Putin not to forgive. Following the Bucharest summit, Bush was due to visit Russia on the Russian president's invitation. Putin's contradictory relationship with Bush reflected his overall attitude toward the United States: open-eyed admiration mixed with burning envy. That attitude went a long way toward explaining Putin's increasingly aggressive foreign policy.

For Putin, Bush was a model worthy of emulation: "a strong leader, forever breaking the rules" in the words of Gleb Pavlovsky, a political consultant who advised the Kremlin during Putin's first two terms.[6] According to the journalist Mikhail Zygar, Bush was referred to as a "military emperor" in the Kremlin. The term would have sounded like an insult in a democracy, but in the Russian context it encapsulated Putin's grudging respect for the American president.

The relationship began fortuitously enough at the presidents' first meeting, less than six months after Bush took office in 2001. Bush's idea was to establish a personal rapport with his Russian counterpart, who was still stepping out gingerly on the international stage.[7] In his memoirs, Bush recalled how Putin began their meeting in Slovenia reading from a stack of note cards. Bush interrupted him and asked about a cross Putin had received from his mother. Bush had learned about the cross during an intelligence briefing, and Putin launched into the dramatic story of how it had miraculously survived a fire in his dacha. The ice was broken, and after the meeting Bush delivered his famous line that he had looked Putin in the eye and been able "to get a sense of his soul."

Putin also received intelligence briefings, and Bush's religiosity was no secret. Putin was eager to impress the new U.S. president. The Kremlin had been criticized for its pitiless war against separatists in the Muslim province of Chechnya, and Putin wanted to demonstrate that Russia was facing the same threats from Islamic extremists there as the United States was globally. Condoleezza Rice, Bush's national security adviser, was surprised when Putin began to rail against Pakistan for its links to the Taliban rulers of Afghanistan and the shadowy Al Qaeda terrorist network.[8] Putin warned that it was only a matter of time before a major catastrophe struck. Less than three months after the Slovenian summit, a few days before September 11, 2001, Putin phoned Bush to warn him that Russian intelligence had picked up an imminent terrorist threat from Afghanistan.[9]

Putin was the first foreign leader to call the White House after the 9/11 terrorist attacks. When he finally got through to Bush, Putin said: "Good will triumph over evil. I want you to know that in this struggle, we will stand together."[10] The outpouring of Russian goodwill was unprecedented. As the United States planned a military strike against the Taliban for harboring the 9/11 mastermind, Osama bin Laden, Putin pledged intelligence sharing with the United States, opened Russian airspace to flights carrying humanitarian aid, and helped secure the transit of U.S. troops through former Soviet republics in Central Asia.[11] Putin even ordered Russian generals to share with their American counterparts their experience fighting in Afghanistan in the 1980s.[12] The following month Russia announced the closing of its sprawling spy base in Cuba, a source of irritation with the United States since the Cold War.[13]

Bush rewarded Putin's show of support with a meeting in the White House, followed by a visit to the family ranch in Crawford, Texas, the first by a foreign leader.[14] When Putin arrived in Houston, he was received by enthusiastic Texans waving American and Russian flags. Smiling broadly, Putin shook the hands jutting from the crowd, then raised both arms in greeting. Later a Marine helicopter flew Putin and his wife, Lyudmila, to Crawford, where George W. and Laura Bush met them in the rain holding umbrellas. After being treated to a barbecue and country music, the Putins spent the night in Crawford. The next day the two presidents spoke at the local high school. Putin appeared awestruck by the warm welcome, waving and smiling awkwardly. He flew on to New York to pay his respects at Ground Zero. Afterward, Putin gave an interview to National Public Radio and took calls from listeners. Despite disagreement over NATO enlargement and Bush's intention to leave the Anti-Ballistic Missile (ABM) Treaty, Putin struck a conciliatory note, even accepting an invitation from a caller to visit Moscow, Idaho.[15]

The terrorist attacks against the United States opened a unique opportunity for Putin. "After 9/11, he became our best partner in the war on terror—in Afghanistan, in intelligence cooperation, across the board," Condoleezza Rice remembered later.[16] "He thought he'd found the strategic concept that worked with the United States: 'We can both be warriors against terror.'" It was not the last time that Putin would try to insinuate Russia into the ranks of Western nations by equating his war against an Islamic insurgency in southern Russia with the West's fight against militant Islamists. But Putin's honeymoon with the United States was short-lived, even if his special relationship with Bush survived. The United States withdrew from the ABM Treaty in June 2002, freeing Bush to pursue his dream of building a missile defense shield, ostensibly against "rogue states" such as Iran or North Korea. Within a year of Putin's visit to Texas, the United States was preparing to pivot from Afghanistan and invade Iraq. Russia, together with U.S. allies Germany and France, was among the most vocal opponents of the coming war.

Because of the friction with Germany and France, Bush may have been more accommodating toward Putin, according to a former senior Bush administration official.[17] During Putin's visit to Camp David in September 2003, Bush addressed the Russian president as "my friend" and described Putin's vision of Russia as a democracy at peace with itself, its neighbors, and the world.[18] Their "trustworthy relationship," Bush told reporters, allowed the two men to hold "very frank discussions about Iraq" and move beyond disagreements over a single issue. "I like him, he's a good fellow to spend quality time with," Bush said.

Less than a month later, developments inside Russia shattered any wishful thinking in the Bush administration that Putin was a democrat simply administering strong medicine to a reluctant, backward nation. The jailing of Mikhail Khodorkovsky, Russia's richest man and the owner of the country's largest oil company, sent a signal that the Kremlin was seeking to sideline any rivals and take back control of the energy industry. "That was a turning point," the former senior Bush administration official said.[19] "It was clear that Bush started to get Putin."

The reality of Putin's Russia was clashing with the lofty ideals of Bush's freedom agenda. After his reelection in 2004, Bush declared in his inaugural address that "the survival of liberty in our land increasingly depends on the success of liberty in other lands." In the wake of the Orange Revolution in Ukraine, the Kremlin interpreted those words to mean that Russia would soon be next on Bush's democratization checklist.[20]

The two presidents had their first meeting following the U.S. election in Bratislava, the capital of Slovakia. Putin was combative. He turned the conversation into a tiresome exercise of whataboutism, countering every point made by Bush about Russia with a relativizing and irrelevant counterpoint about the United States. "You talk about Khodorkovsky, and I talk about Enron," Putin said, referring to the U.S. energy giant brought down by fraudulent accounting practices. "You appoint the Electoral College, and I appoint governors. What's the difference?"[21] Putin even suggested that Bush had personally fired the TV anchor Dan Rather, who resigned after publishing a story based on forged documents claiming that Bush had shirked military service. In a videoconference with the British prime minister Tony Blair, Bush later recalled his "fairly unpleasant" encounter with Putin.[22] "Seriously, it was a whole series of these juvenile arguments. There was no breakthrough with this guy," Bush said. "At one point, the interpreter made me so mad that I nearly reached over the table and slapped the hell out of the guy. He had a mocking tone, making accusations about America. He was just sarcastic."

Competition and envy marked Bush's relationship with Putin. According to Bush, he introduced Putin to his Scottish terrier, Barney, during their Camp David meeting.[23] A few years later, on a visit to Russia, Putin showed off his black Labrador, Connie, saying: "Bigger, stronger, and faster than Barney." When the Canadian prime minister Stephen Harper heard the story, he told Bush: "You're lucky he only showed you his dog."

The Kremlin soured on the United States. From Putin's point of view, the Bush administration had taken his acts of friendship for granted and refused to treat Russia as an equal. The laundry list of Russian grievances was long: the U.S. withdrawal from the ABM Treaty and Bush's unbending commitment to a missile defense shield; the 2004 wave of NATO enlargement that included the former Soviet republics of Estonia, Latvia, and Lithuania; open American support for street revolutionaries in Georgia and Ukraine; and a lack of movement in the repeal of U.S. sanctions on Russia dating back to the Cold War. The invasion of Iraq was the breaking point.

Although he had first kept the Bush administration guessing about which side Russia would take on Iraq, Putin finally joined France and Germany in the so-called *non-nein-nyet* alliance.[24] Bush suspected that the Kremlin's opposition to the war was based in part on "Russia's lucrative oil contracts" in Iraq.[25] But while Russian oil companies did have billions of dollars at stake there, Bush seemed oblivious to the rage building in the Kremlin over recent U.S.-led combat operations, from the 1999 bombing campaign against the Serbian dictator Slobodan Milošević to the invasion of Afghanistan, which placed the U.S. military in a country the Soviet Union had spent a futile decade fighting to control. When the United States talked about democracy and liberty, Russia saw American hegemony and hypocrisy.

Bush's first term set a bad example for Putin, the former Kremlin adviser Gleb Pavlovsky said in a 2021 radio interview. "At the time, Bush was behaving like the president of the world, and a war president at that. He decided who was right and who was wrong," Pavlovsky said.[26] "Unfortunately Putin internalized all of this, and when he saw that Bush had weakened, he dealt him a coup de grâce in Munich."

Putin's verbal attack on the United States simply became known as "the Munich speech." His 2007 address to an annual international security conference in Germany marked a turning point in the Kremlin's foreign policy: overtly anti-American and unapologetically confrontational. As the German chancellor Angela Merkel, the U.S. defense secretary Robert Gates, and a high-level delegation of U.S. congresspeople sat in the audience, Putin launched into a full-frontal assault on the "unipolar" world order the United States had inherited after the Cold War and that Bush had put on steroids after 9/11. "It is a world in which there is one master, one sovereign. And at the end of the day this is pernicious not only for all those within this system, but also for the sovereign itself because it destroys itself from within," Putin said.[27] He lamented America's "almost uncontained hyper-use of force" and professed concern for the "hundreds of thousands of civilians" who had died in U.S.-led military operations. The unipolar world order was unacceptable and left nobody feeling safe anymore, Putin said. "Russia is constantly being taught about democracy. But for some reason those who teach us do not want to learn themselves." Practically every sentence in his half-hour speech was a poison arrow, as Putin unloaded years of bitterness over Russia's inability to stop, or even slow, the American juggernaut. The only response to U.S. hegemony was a "multipolar" world order, he said, where the United Nations would make all decisions on the use of military force.

Despite his bluster toward the United States, Putin defended Bush personally, as if the U.S. president had nothing to do with the policies he had just excoriated. In the question-and-answer session after the speech, Putin described Bush as a "friend" and a "decent person" who was unfairly blamed for what was happening globally by his domestic opponents. In other words, there was nothing wrong with what Bush was doing—the problem was that it was the United States, and not Russia, that was doing it.

A year after Putin's Munich speech, the idea of granting Membership Action Plans to Ukraine and Georgia seemed like a long shot, even within the Bush administration. The alliance was divided on whether the two countries were ready to receive a road map to membership, and to many European allies it seemed like an unnecessary provocation of the Kremlin. In January 2008, Condoleezza Rice, now Bush's secretary of state, met with Viktor Yushchenko during the World Economic Forum in Switzerland. When she told him that there was very little chance Ukraine would get a MAP on Bush's watch, "the Ukrainian president almost cried," Rice recalled.[28] Ukraine had just submitted its application for a MAP and was soon followed by Georgia in a coordinated move by Yushchenko and the Georgian president Mikheil Saakashvili.[29]

The chief opponents to offering MAPs were the Bush administration's old naysayers, Germany and France, although both countries were now under leaders ready to turn a new page in transatlantic relations. Their arguments were clear: Georgia had open territorial disputes with two separatist regions; only a minority of Ukrainians supported joining NATO; and both countries were struggling to build democratic institutions. The Munich speech was still vivid in Merkel's mind, and she believed Putin would view MAPs for Georgia and Ukraine as a direct threat, according to Christoph Heusgen, the chancellor's top foreign policy adviser at the time.[30] Furthermore, he said, Merkel could not see what benefits the two countries would contribute to the alliance. It did not help that Merkel and Saakashvili had talked past each other in their first encounter, which the chancellor's aides described as one of her worst meetings ever.[31] France's new president, Nicolas Sarkozy, was more sympathetic toward Georgia but was reluctant to clash with Merkel because he also had a difficult relationship with her.[32]

In the White House, Rice laid out the pros and cons of the situation with no recommendation of her own.[33] Bush did not waver from his position that the United States should support the two countries' NATO aspirations as a matter of principle. "I thought the threat from Russia strengthened the case for extending MAPs to Georgia and Ukraine," Bush recalled later.[34] "Russia would be less likely to engage in aggression if these countries were on a path into NATO. As for the governance issues, a step toward membership would encourage them to clean up corruption." Even though Bush was not interested in Russia's objections, he was ready, as always, to let Putin say his piece. Technically, the Russian president was more of a lame duck than Bush, as Putin was stepping down due to a constitutional term limit. Putin invited Bush to Sochi, his balmy getaway on the Black Sea, to say goodbye and to introduce his handpicked successor, Dmitry Medvedev. As the Bucharest summit approached, Bush called Putin to say that he could only accept the invitation if Putin did not cause a "dustup" over Georgia and Ukraine.[35] Putin promised there would be no scandal in Bucharest. Merkel, however, could not make the same assurances. In a videoconference before the summit, Bush said: "Looks like a shootout at the OK Corral," a Wild West reference that neither the chancellor nor her interpreter understood.[36] Having just hosted Saakashvili in the White House, Bush set off for eastern Europe, first stopping in Kyiv before flying on to Bucharest. The stage was set for the most contentious summit in NATO's history.

The gathering was held in the Palace of the Parliament, the gargantuan neoclassical wedding cake commissioned by Romania's Communist dictator, Nicolae Ceaușescu. On the first evening, the dinner of the twenty-six NATO leaders went two hours over schedule as Bush failed in a last-ditch effort to build consensus over welcoming Ukraine and Georgia into the alliance.[37] Meanwhile, he charged Rice to win over the NATO foreign ministers at a separate dinner, which she later described as "the most heated" debate among allies she witnessed in her time as secretary of state.[38] Foreign ministers from former Soviet vassal states piled onto their German colleague, Frank-Walter Steinmeier, when he said Georgia could not be given a MAP because of the "frozen conflicts" it had with two Russian-backed breakaway regions. One foreign minister argued that under that criterion, West Germany would never have been admitted to NATO because East Germany had been under Soviet occupation. Radek Sikorski, Poland's foreign minister, then accused Steinmeier of being more sensitive to Moscow than to Germany's own allies. "Steinmeier was devastated," Rice recalled. "He would later say it was the most brutal experience of his time as foreign minister."

The next morning advisers from key NATO countries, including Poland and Romania, came up with a compromise formulation. But at the general session, the central and eastern Europeans once again rebelled. Merkel, who had grown up in East Germany, and Rice, a trained Soviet specialist, huddled with the presidents of Poland, Romania, and Lithuania, speaking the only language they all had in common: Russian.[39] "We cannot let Russia have a veto. This is not fair to Georgia and Ukraine," the Polish president Lech Kaczyński said.[40] "This is not about Russia and whether it has a veto," Merkel countered. "This is about whether these countries are ready and if we think this is the right time to take this step." After some discussion, it became clear that the sticking point was not *whether* Georgia and Ukraine should become NATO members but *when*. The leaders hammered out a statement that said: "We agreed today that these countries will become members of NATO." Discussions about MAPs were put off for later in the year. NATO's unity was restored, and Rice said she was happy with the outcome. The British prime minister Gordon Brown told Bush: "We didn't give them MAPs, but we may have just made them members!"[41] It was exactly that ambiguity that would bring far-reaching consequences to Georgia, Ukraine—and NATO.

Putin arrived in Bucharest later that day to attend a meeting of the NATO-Russia Council, a body that had been set up in 2002 to elevate the growing partnership between Moscow and the alliance at the time. Both sides were interested in avoiding an open confrontation: NATO was keen on securing an agreement with Russia on the transit of supplies to Afghanistan, and Putin was preparing to host Bush after the summit. As a result, Putin's address to a closed session of the NATO-Russia Council turned into a passive-aggressive screed, with thinly veiled threats combined with appeals to sit down and work through disagreements. Putin's main message was that NATO was disregarding Russian interests and that the Kremlin would be forced to take countermeasures against the alliance's enlargement. Russia had withdrawn troops from European countries where NATO was now moving in, reduced its nuclear arsenal, and closed Soviet-era bases in Vietnam and Cuba. "Of course we expected reciprocal steps from NATO, but we haven't seen that," he said.[42]

Putin said he was "satisfied overall" with NATO's decision not to grant Georgia and Ukraine MAPs. But then he warned that Georgia was trying to drag NATO into deep-rooted ethnic conflicts in the breakaway regions of Abkhazia and South Ossetia. Following Western countries' support for the independence of Kosovo from Serbia in February 2008, Putin reminded his NATO colleagues that Russia could very well recognize Abkhazia and South Ossetia as independent states. As for Ukraine, Putin claimed that one-third of its population, or seventeen million people, were "ethnic Russians." The issue of NATO membership could threaten the country's very statehood, he said. In passing, Putin added that the Soviet leadership had given the Crimean Peninsula to Ukraine without following the proper procedures. At dinner the previous evening, Putin had been even more frank. Unaware that a microphone was still on, he told Bush: "You don't understand, George, that Ukraine is not even a state. What is Ukraine? Part of its territory is eastern Europe, but the greater part is a gift from us."[43]

Russia's opposition to NATO enlargement was not new, so Putin's remarks behind closed doors may have sounded like bluster and hyperbole. The only public statements he made in Bucharest were during an almost hour-long press conference, where Putin stressed Russia's desire to cooperate with NATO and moderated his criticism of the alliance's future plans to include Ukraine and Georgia. The leaders of the two countries were elated. "I'm happy that we reached a compromise," Yushchenko said. "Ukraine has deserved it. There's not a country that has paid so dearly for its independence."[44] Saakashvili said Bush had "fought like a lion," calling the NATO statement on eventual membership nothing less than a "political guarantee."[45]

In Bucharest, Putin left a top Russian diplomat, Sergei Ryabkov, to fulminate. In a briefing to the Russian press, Ryabkov lambasted the alliance's decision and declared that "business as usual with NATO is over."[46] Ryabkov was particularly incensed that NATO, in its final statement, delegated the alliance's foreign ministers to decide on the MAP applications of Ukraine and Georgia, with the first progress report due in December 2008. Where NATO had been intentionally vague on dates, the Russians saw a hard deadline. In Moscow, the Bucharest compromise was taken as little more than a delaying tactic until NATO no longer needed Russian assistance in Afghanistan.[47]

Whatever Putin thought of the true intentions of the United States, he did not let it reflect on his relationship with Bush. Their personal rapport was real, and the U.S. president flattered Putin with his attention. During his eight years in office, Bush met with Putin more than forty times and traveled to Russia more often than to any other foreign country.[48] In his memoirs, Bush fondly recalled visiting Putin's private chapel at his residence outside Moscow, driving the Russian leader's vintage 1956 Volga sedan, and taking a "beautiful boat ride" in St. Petersburg during White Nights.

When Bush landed in Sochi after the Bucharest summit, it was his seventh and final trip to Russia as president. For Putin, who was leaving office the next month, it was also a farewell visit. Putin received Bush and his wife, Laura, at Bocharov Ruchei, the presidential residence on the Black Sea coast. The Sochi Winter Olympics were still six years off, and work had hardly begun on turning the sleepy Soviet-era town into a world-class winter resort. Putin showed Bush a model of the Olympic-facilities-to-be before taking him on a seaside stroll. A photograph published by the Kremlin showed the two presidents silhouetted against the setting sun as they looked out across the Black Sea. At dinner that night, Bush was introduced to Medvedev, the boyish president-elect, over a feast of Russian specialties. Footage released by the Kremlin showed Putin and Bush dancing with performers in traditional costumes. Condoleezza Rice later remembered Bush "unwisely" trying to do the Cossack splits, "almost failing to get up despite his legendary fitness."[49]

Their two terms in office having largely overlapped, the presidents issued a "strategic framework declaration" the next day. Missile defense, the most contentious issue in bilateral relations, was mentioned first, with a pledge by both sides to "intensify" dialogue on it.[50] In the press conference before Bush's departure, the two men complimented each other's honesty and truthfulness, despite any disagreements they may have had. While nobody expected Putin to vanish from the scene, the fact that he was relinquishing the presidency left open the possibility that his successor might take a less abrasive approach to foreign policy. Bush called the still bashful Medvedev a "smart fellow" and said he looked forward to working with him for the remainder of his time in office. Their next conversation would take place under very different circumstances.

Mikheil Saakashvili rose to power during the 2003 Rose Revolution, a peaceful demonstration of people power that presaged Ukraine's Orange Revolution a year later. The charismatic, Columbia-educated lawyer promised to turn Georgia from a failing state run by gangsters into a free-market democracy based on the rule of law. Reestablishing control over the separatist regions of Abkhazia and South Ossetia was a top priority.

The South Ossetians, Orthodox Christians, are separated from their ethnic kin in Russia's North Ossetia province by the towering Caucasus mountains. Abkhazia, with a mixed Christian and Muslim population, is located on the Black Sea, right down the coast from Sochi. Both regions became administrative parts of Georgia during the Soviet era.

The Caucasus region, the craggy land bridge between the Caspian and Black seas, is home to dozens of ethnic groups speaking as many languages and dialects. Russia became a dominant player in the Caucasus in the nineteenth century, when the czars absorbed the ancient Christian nations of Georgia and Armenia and pushed out Turkish and Persian influence. At the same time, Muslim mountain tribes led by the Chechens fought a twenty-five-year-long guerilla war before finally surrendering to the Russians. In the twentieth century, the Soviet Union sought to stamp control over the region with mass deportations and the redrawing of administrative boundaries. The checkerboard of ethnicity and religion continues to bedevil efforts of any state trying to establish its authority.

After the Soviet Union fell apart, South Ossetia and Abkhazia refused to accept the authority of newly independent Georgia and fought brief but bloody wars of secession that cost thousands of lives and created two hundred thousand internally displaced people. The two separatist regions enjoyed de facto independence since the early 1990s thanks to Russia, which first provided military support and later deployed "peacekeeping" troops to oversee the ceasefire lines. South Ossetians and Abkhaz viewed Russia as a protector against Georgian domination.

For the Kremlin, a military presence in the separatist regions meant keeping control over Georgia, a nation of less than four million, despite its formal independence from Moscow. After Saakashvili had four Russian soldiers arrested on espionage charges in 2006, Russia reacted by banning imports of Georgian wine and mineral water on phony food safety concerns. Flights between Georgia and Russia were suspended, and hundreds of Georgian migrant laborers working in Moscow were deported. Meanwhile the situation on the southern borders of South Ossetia and Abkhazia remained tense, with occasional exchanges of gunfire and mortar rounds.

I made my first trip to Georgia in May 2008, when direct flights between Russia and Georgia were briefly reinstated. I was now working as a reporter in the Bloomberg bureau in Moscow and joined some friends on a vacation to a country renowned for its natural beauty, hospitality, and hearty cuisine. When I phoned to book a room in a family-run hotel in Tbilisi, the Georgian capital, the receptionist told me that my $95-per-night room included breakfast, dinner and "all the wine you can drink." Sure enough, after we flew into Tbilisi on the Aeroflot redeye and reached the hotel at 5 A.M., the receptionist first forced me and my companions to have a glass of wine before going to bed.

What I found remarkable about Georgia was that it bore few physical traces of seven decades of Soviet rule. While statues of Vladimir Lenin still dotted town squares across Russia and Ukraine, virtually all symbols of the Soviet past had disappeared in Georgia. The notable exception was Joseph Stalin's hometown of Gori, fifty miles west of Tbilisi. At the town's palatial Stalin Museum, the halls were filled with photographs, documents, and maps depicting Stalin's life. One glass display case showed works of the great dictator translated into English, Arabic, Korean, and a dozen other languages. There were marble statues and busts of the man who had ruled the Soviet Union with an iron fist for more than twenty-five years. Our guide explained that the exhibit would soon be overhauled to shed light on Stalin's repressions that killed untold millions. Outside, Stalin's humble two-room birth house was enclosed by a structure resembling a temple. His personal railway carriage was also on display, featuring a full-size bathtub. As Gori was an otherwise forgettable place, we headed back to Tbilisi. Never would I have imagined that in three months I would be returning to Gori in the back of a Russian army truck.

Georgia's frozen conflicts quickly thawed in the summer of 2008. Claims of intrusions by drones and other ceasefire violations followed my visit. Russian military engineers refurbished a cross-border rail line into Abkhazia, and the Russian army staged its Kavkaz (Caucasus) 2008 maneuvers in July, simulating a mission to assist peacekeepers in the Georgian rebel regions. Ominously, the Russian troops did not return to their home bases but remained mobilized just on the other side of the border. At the same time, Saakashvili's army held its Immediate Response 2008 exercises together with one thousand U.S. troops. August began with a series of shooting incidents along South Ossetia's border with Georgia proper. Then, on August 8, the world woke up to the news that Georgian troops had shelled the South Ossetian capital Tskhinvali overnight and fought their way into the city.

Saakashvili had blundered into a Russian trap. Grossly overestimating his support from Washington and the capabilities of his U.S.-trained troops, the brash Georgian president gave in to repeated provocations and ordered the storming of Tskhinvali. He believed a quick victory would make the reintegration of South Ossetia into Georgia a fait accompli. Instead, the Georgians failed to seal the Roki Tunnel connecting South Ossetia to Russia, and the Russian armor waiting on the other side came streaming through.

Saakashvili claimed that his army was repelling a Russian invasion designed to break Georgian independence. But as an international fact-finding mission led by the Swiss diplomat Heidi Tagliavini concluded in 2009, Georgian troops launched a "large-scale military operation" against Tskhinvali on the night of August 7.[51] The report also discarded the version propagated by Russian state media that Saakashvili's army had sprung a cowardly attack on a city of sleeping civilians and unsuspecting Russian peacekeepers. The arrival of volunteers and Russian reporters before the fighting, as well as the earlier evacuation of civilians, indicated that the Kremlin had been preparing for a fight.

The battle for Tskhinvali took place just as the world was focusing on the start of the 2008 Summer Olympics in Beijing. Following protocol, Bush first phoned Medvedev, his new Russian counterpart, to tell the Kremlin to de-escalate.[52] Medvedev compared Saakashvili to Saddam Hussein and claimed—falsely—that 1,500 civilians had been killed.[53] Bush next confronted Putin at the opening ceremony. Bush said he had been warning Putin that Saakashvili was "hot-blooded," to which Putin replied: "I'm hot-blooded, too." Bush said: "No, Vladimir, you're cold-blooded."

I did not reach Tbilisi until August 10, flying from Moscow to Yerevan, the capital of Armenia, and traveling the rest of the way by car. Children played soccer on a brightly lit field on the outskirts of town. As I approached the city center, the only thing out of the ordinary were honking cars, filled with young men waving Georgian flags as if their country had won a sports competition. At that very moment, Saakashvili's crack troops were being routed in Tskhinvali, less than sixty miles away.

The next day Saakashvili hastily called a press conference as Russian aircraft bombed targets around the country and the last Georgian outposts in Abkhazia were overrun. He spoke in the sunbaked courtyard of his unfinished residence, which with its glass cupola looked like a copy of the Reichstag building in Berlin. Saakashvili said the Russians were pushing closer to Tbilisi and committing atrocities "reminiscent of the Balkans." But out on the streets of the city, life continued as usual. After filing my dispatches that night, I hailed a cab to see how the Georgian capital was preparing its defenses. Earlier in the day the Russians had taken control of Gori, Stalin's hometown, perched strategically on Georgia's main east-west highway. The road to Gori led right past the U.S. embassy, so if Russian tanks entered Tbilisi, the Americans would be among the first to know.[54] Besides a few armored personnel carriers and trucks filled with Georgian troops, there were no signs of serious preparations to defend the city. The flag-waving patriots from the night before were nowhere to be seen. When I returned to my hotel, I wrote in my diary: "Tbilisi sleeps without a care while the Russian bear prowls at the gates."

Behind the scenes, Nicolas Sarkozy was furiously mediating a ceasefire. France, which was holding the rotating presidency of the European Union at the time, had close relations with Russia and a very capable ambassador in Georgia. Traveling first to Moscow and then to Tbilisi, the French president came up with a six-point plan that called for an immediate cessation of hostilities and the withdrawal of Russian and Georgian forces to their preconflict lines. Of course the Russians had no intention of ceding their gains and allowing the Georgian army to return to Abkhazia and South Ossetia. But without Sarkozy's restraining influence, the Russians might have marched into Tbilisi, arrested Saakashvili on alleged war crimes, and forced Georgia to sue for peace on entirely different terms. For the Georgian president, accepting the loss of territories that had been de facto independent even before the conflict was the least ignominious choice.

The Russians got as far as Igoeti, a dusty junction on the main highway between Gori and Tbilisi. They parked their tanks and dug in as Georgia's shattered army accepted defeat. Three days after the ceasefire agreement, the Russians had not given up an inch of ground. With a dozen other Moscow-based journalists, I waited in Igoeti for a Russian military escort to take us first to Gori, then South Ossetia, and across the mountains into Russia.[55]

A haggard Georgian, unshaven and with bloodshot eyes, crossed over on foot from the Russian side carrying only a backpack and a child's violin case. His name was Jumber Garuzashvili, a driver from Gori trying to reunite with his wife and three children in Tbilisi. "The Cossacks and Ossetians are looting," he said. When I asked who was to blame for the fighting, he didn't hesitate: "Everyone." I pointed at the violin case. "My son must learn the violin," Garuzashvili said and trudged off.

The checkpoint consisted of a handful of Russian soldiers standing in the middle of the road. One of them stood out from the others by the white armband identifying him as a "volunteer." At their meeting during the Olympic opening ceremony, Putin had told Bush that such volunteers were pouring across the border to aid the South Ossetians. Letting irregular fighters loose was a calculated move to terrorize South Ossetia's ethnic Georgians without directly involving the Russian army. The volunteer at Igoeti was cradling a Kalashnikov and dressed in mismatched fatigues and tennis shoes. The U.S. Army cap on his head and the American helmet dangling from his belt were obvious booty from a Georgian military depot. He mumbled monosyllabic answers to my questions, and all I got out of him was that he came from Dagestan, an impoverished Russian region bordering Chechnya. I had just given up on an interview when the young officer in charge of the checkpoint approached. "Get lost! I don't want you mixing with my men," he shouted at the volunteer. "Fuck off," the Dagestani fighter replied. "You better watch out. I'll be waiting for you tonight. I'll fuck you up so bad." The Russian officer backed off. Irregulars from Dagestan did not fit into the Russian command structure.

Finally the Russian military escort arrived, and my colleagues and I clambered into the back of a giant Ural military truck with two soldiers wearing sunglasses and kerchiefs to hide their faces. From the tiny windows I could see burning fields and Georgian villagers returning to their homes. We got out of the truck on Gori's main square, across from a statue of Stalin. Although most residents appeared to have fled, a Georgian flag was still flying over the Gori town hall. Other than an apartment building that had been struck by a Russian bomb, I saw few signs of damage.

Tskhinvali, less than half an hour away over bumpy roads, bore evidence of a ferocious battle. Not a building had escaped damage: walls bore the pockmarks of machine-gun bullets; apartment blocks were blackened by fire; and decapitated tank turrets littered the streets. In the town center, the face of a statue of the South Ossetian linguist Vaso Abayti had been blown off. Shards of his head, collected by locals, lay in a pile next to the pedestal. Near the theater, a pink playbill for "The Three Little Pigs" still hung from a column. Atsamaz, a thirty-year-old local with a thick black beard, cursed the Georgians. "We'd like to be a part of Russia," he said. "It's our only defense."

At dusk my colleagues and I boarded a bus that took us up through the Roki Tunnel connecting South Ossetia to Russia. On the outskirts of Tskhinvali a billboard declared: "Putin is our president." We passed through a hamlet called Khenajabeti, once inhabited by ethnic Georgians. The houses were gutted, and stray dogs roamed the streets. The words "To Tbilisi" were painted on a gate. One house was still on fire, the flames licking the darkening sky.

For the Kremlin, Russia's first foreign armed engagement in twenty years was a liberation from the humiliation of watching helplessly as the United States projected its military might around the world. Bogged down in two unpopular wars under a lame-duck president, the United States was powerless to aid Georgia. If the West was unwilling to recognize that Russia had a sphere of influence in its former colonies, then the Kremlin would demonstrate by force of arms that it did. Revenge also played an important role—against the United States for its unilateralist foreign policy and against Saakashvili personally for defying the Kremlin and trying to lead Georgia into NATO.

After nine straight years of economic growth on the back of spiraling oil prices, Putin was at the top of his game when he handed the presidency over to Medvedev. The petrodollars flooding into Russia gave the Kremlin an exaggerated sense of its foreign policy possibilities. The price of crude oil hit an all-time high of $147 a barrel in July 2008. The volatile combination of hubris, envy, and rage exploded a month later.

Even before the Bucharest summit, Kosovo's declaration of independence in February 2008 inflamed the Kremlin. Days later Saakashvili met Putin outside Moscow in what would be their last face-to-face meeting. "You know we have to answer the West on Kosovo. And we are very sorry but you are going to be part of that answer," Putin said, according to the Georgian record of the meeting.[56] Saakashvili suggested that he was willing to revisit Georgia's application to join NATO if the Kremlin would negotiate on the status of South Ossetia and Abkhazia. But Putin's mind was made up. He repeated that Russia's response to Kosovo's independence would be directed at the United States and NATO, not at Georgia. And then he warned Saakashvili that NATO membership would turn his country into an American vassal state. "You think you can trust the Americans, and they will rush to assist you? *Nobody* can be trusted! Except me," Putin said.

Kosovo provided a flimsy precedent for the Kremlin. The former Serbian province's ethnic Albanians had first been subjected to a campaign of persecution and ethnic cleansing by the Serbian authorities, and only after more than eight years as an international protectorate did Kosovo declare its independence. Putin, however, was in a hurry. South Ossetia and Abkhazia called on Russia to recognize their independence in early March—Putin's promised "answer" to the United States. Then, in the aftermath of the war with Georgia, the Kremlin recognized the two territories as independent nations. Only Venezuela and Nicaragua, enamored with Russia's antagonistic stance toward the United States, followed suit. Putin and Medvedev constantly compared South Ossetia to Kosovo, but the comparison was weak. How could the Kremlin justify its recognition of South Ossetia on the precedent of Kosovo's independence, which Russia considered illegitimate? And why did Chechnya, which had suffered much greater death and destruction than South Ossetia, not have a right to break away from Russia?

The Kremlin was not troubled by logical fallacies and wanted to give the United States a taste of its own medicine. Russian officials peppered their explanations of Russia's war aims with the language of recent U.S. military campaigns: the invasion was a "peace enforcement operation" and a "humanitarian intervention" to prevent a "genocide" of the South Ossetian people. Medvedev's comparison of Saakashvili to Saddam Hussein was not coincidental. During Sarkozy's visit to Moscow to end the fighting, Putin told the French president that if the Americans could hang Saddam, he wanted to hang Saakashvili "by the balls."[57]

Saakashvili's crime was to ignore Putin's advice. After being elected Georgia's president in 2004 on the heels of the Rose Revolution, Saakashvili made his first foreign trip to the Kremlin, saying that Putin was an example for him. Already then, Putin warned him not to befriend the Americans, Saakashvili remembered later.[58] The Georgian president did exactly the opposite. He made joining NATO a cornerstone of his foreign policy and strove to prove Georgia's commitment to the alliance. Saakashvili ramped up Georgia's contribution to the "coalition of the willing" in Iraq to two thousand, the third highest behind the United States and Britain, and welcomed U.S. military advisers to train his soldiers. Bush rewarded Saakashvili with a visit to Georgia in 2005. The attention went to Saakashvili's head.

Again and again the Bush administration warned him that there would be no U.S. support if he tried to retake South Ossetia by force. Condoleezza Rice remembered receiving a memo from the Russian foreign minister Sergei Lavrov in spring 2008.[59] After reading the Kremlin's "grievances" with Georgia, she understood that "it was only a matter of time until a spark ignited open conflict in the area." Rice traveled to Tbilisi in July to try to persuade Saakashvili to sign a no-use-of-force pledge. Saakashvili insisted the Russians needed to give him something in return. "Whatever you do, don't let the Russians provoke you," Rice recalled telling him. "No one will come to your aid, and you will lose."

The next time Rice visited Tbilisi was on a scorching day a little more than a month later. Rice spent nearly five hours twisting Saakashvili's arm to accept the terms of the Sarkozy peace plan. Hundreds of people had been killed, tens of thousands displaced, and Russia had cut Georgia in half. This time Saakashvili had no choice.

The White House—and the Kremlin—realized that the U.S. options to help Georgia were limited. Besides ferrying Georgian troops in Iraq back to Tbilisi, there was little the world's largest military could do to stop a peer nuclear power from attacking a nontreaty ally. "Saakashvili kept calling the White House to say that his government was about to be overthrown," Rice wrote in her memoirs.[60] "After the second desperate call, we decided that our friends needed visible help." That assistance came in the form of humanitarian aid, delivered by giant U.S. Air Force C-17 Globemasters. Inside the White House, Vice President Dick Cheney and others were calling for tougher action.[61] Rice later recalled a National Security Council meeting where "everybody was getting all spun up" and "testosterone was flying around the table."[62] Stephen Hadley, the national security adviser, asked point-blank if anybody was recommending going to war with Russia. "To his credit, the vice president was the first one to say: 'No, I am not recommending use of military force against Russia,'" Hadley remembered.[63] To prevent any misunderstandings, Admiral Mike Mullen, the chairman of the Joint Chiefs of Staff, set up a special link with his Russian counterpart.

Given that the United States was not ready to risk escalation with Russia over Georgia, there was very little the Bush administration could have done. The Kremlin read the U.S. administration's unwillingness to stand up for Georgia as a tacit acceptance of Russia's self-declared "sphere of privileged interests"—and a genuflection before its awesome nuclear arsenal. From the Russian perspective, the deliveries of humanitarian aid on U.S. military planes, then warships, was less a sign of America's power than of its impotence. The special line opened by Mullen flattered the Kremlin by putting the Russian military on an equal footing with the Americans.

There was anger inside the State Department over the war. "You have an administration desperate for proof that the 'freedom agenda' is real. We over-stroked Misha wildly," a dissenting senior U.S. diplomat told me at the time, referring to the Georgian president by his nickname.[64] "Saakashvili acted unwisely. He took the bait." But Bush, who remained unrepentant about his decision to invade Iraq, also did not reflect on the role he played in the lead-up to Russia's invasion of Georgia. In his memoirs, Bush remembered "wondering" if Russia would have been so aggressive had Georgia been awarded a NATO Membership Action Plan in Bucharest.[65] It was much more likely that the Kremlin saw little difference between a MAP and a promise of future membership—and that the disunity displayed in Bucharest emboldened Russia to seize the first opportunity to wreck Georgia's aspirations to join the alliance. By prematurely raising hopes among Georgians and Ukrainians for NATO membership, Bush paradoxically ended up putting their applications on indefinite hold.

To many U.S. allies in Europe, Georgia's five-day war with Russia seemed to prove that rushing NATO membership was a bad idea. The Kremlin faced no pushback from the EU, which was not interested in disrupting burgeoning business ties with Russia because of a conflict on Europe's fringes. Russia faced no sanctions because the big European powers preferred to view the war as an aberration that required no further action. The same was largely true about the United States, where Barack Obama came into office promising a more peaceful foreign policy. Less than a year after the Georgia war the new U.S. administration embarked on a "reset" in relations with Russia. Few in the West were ready to see the paradigm shift that Russia's invasion of Georgia implied.

Bush's devil-may-care foreign policy showed Putin a brash new way to step out on the international stage. Abkhazia and South Ossetia were

miniscule territories, but their occupation was the beginning of the restoration of Russia's lost power. From the Kremlin's point of view, separatism was the worst thing that could happen to Russia's far-flung territories.
But when it came to Russia's enemies, separatism was exactly what they
deserved. Putin would reach for the South Ossetia playbook again.

The Kremlin took lessons from its experience in Georgia. During the
fighting, embarrassing inadequacies in the Russian military came to light:
vehicles broke down before they reached the combat zone; intelligence
was poor; and radio equipment was so shoddy that Russian soldiers communicated on their mobile phones, making themselves easy targets. Two
months after the war, the Russian Defense Ministry announced a major
military reform.[66]

Putin also learned that by conducting a quick assault and creating facts
on the ground, he could get away with a military intervention, especially
in a country not bound by NATO treaty obligations. The absence of any
financial cost in the form of sanctions may have given Putin a false sense
of security that he could repeat such an operation. About two weeks after
the ceasefire in Georgia, a German reporter asked Putin if Crimea could
become Russia's next target.[67] Irritated, Putin replied that Crimea was not
a disputed territory, there was no ethnic conflict there, and Russia had
long recognized Ukraine's borders. "I think that asking a question about
Russia's targets of this kind reeks of provocation," he said.

3

Moscow Uprising

On December 24, 2011, tens of thousands of antigovernment protesters packed a central Moscow thoroughfare named after Soviet dissident Andrei Sakharov. The crowd roared when Alexei Navalny, a thirty-five-year-old anticorruption blogger, took to the stage under a banner reading "Russia will be free!" Navalny, who had just served two weeks in jail for participating in an unsanctioned protest, shouted: "I read a little book called the Russian Constitution. It says the Russian people are the only source of power. We're not appealing to the powers that be. *We* are the power. Who's the power? We are!" Navalny, dressed in a wool coat, scarf, and jeans, spoke forcefully and freely. He seemed to build his speech on the protesters' enthusiastic cries of approval. "I see enough people here to take the Kremlin [seat of the presidency] and White House [prime minister's office] right now. But we're a peaceful force. We won't do that *yet*. But if those swindlers and thieves keep trying to cheat us and lie to us and steal from us, then we'll take it ourselves! It's ours!"

Three weeks earlier Navalny had called on people to take to the streets following reports of mass vote rigging in elections to the Duma, Russia's lower house of parliament. That spontaneous rally was followed by a demonstration on December 10 whose huge turnout surprised even its organizers. Opposition protests in past years had become exercises in futility, where diehard democrats and principled babushkas were outnumbered by riot police and reporters. Now anger over routine elections that nobody was supposed to care about was snowballing into a protest movement directed against Vladimir Putin.

Putin had served as president from 2000 to 2008. As his second four-year term came to a close, Moscow was awash in rumors over who his successor would be, since the Russian Constitution permitted only two consecutive presidential terms. Putin chose his young chief of staff, Dmitry Medvedev, who handily won the 2008 election thanks to Putin's endorsement and the government's formidable "administrative resources," including a monopoly on national TV stations. Medvedev appointed Putin as his prime minister, and the two reigned over Russia as a so-called tandem. In the final year of his first term, speculation arose over whether Medvedev would run again. The answer came at a convention of the ruling United Russia party in September 2011, when Medvedev nominated Putin for president and Putin accepted, openly admitting that the deal had been agreed on "several years ago." The highly choreographed performance disposed of any pretense of a succession and exposed the Medvedev presidency as a fraud. One of Medvedev's first legislative initiatives as president had been to extend a presidential term from four years to six, so Putin could now return to the Kremlin for twelve more years.

Cynicism was what Russians had come to expect from their leaders; apathy was all that their leaders wanted in return. It was a tiny minority of Russians who upset that balance in December 2011. The tens of thousands of middle-class Muscovites who took to the streets after the Duma elections finally realized that they enjoyed every freedom in the world except the freedom to choose their leaders. They watched videos of ballot stuffing taken on smartphones, fueled their outrage by reading opposition blogs, and signed up on Facebook for one demonstration after the other. Seeing that thousands upon thousands of others were planning to protest helped people overcome their fear of a violent police crackdown.

On December 24, prodemocracy demonstrators crowded onto Sakharov Prospekt in central Moscow, filling a space as big as five football fields. The journalist and prison rights activist Olga Romanova, one of the MCs at the rally, called for a moment of silence for Václav Havel. The Czech dissident, who helped overthrow Czechoslovakia's Communist dictatorship in the 1989 Velvet Revolution, had just died. The boisterous rally fell silent in honor of the Czech poet-president. The Kremlin had ignored

Havel's passing even as it publicly sent condolences to North Korea after the death of dictator Kim Jong Il, who had died a day earlier. The omission was not only a postmortem retort to Havel's criticism of the Kremlin but also a reflection of Putin's antipathy toward any kind of regime change via the street. As a KGB officer in East Germany in 1989, Putin had witnessed how mass demonstrations brought down the Berlin Wall and Communist regimes across central and eastern Europe. The impotence of the Soviet Union, which had more than three hundred thousand soldiers in East Germany alone, left its mark on him.

Fifteen years later the Orange Revolution in Ukraine shocked Putin and his entourage. For the Kremlin leadership, it was hard to believe that tens of thousands of ordinary Ukrainians, supposedly so similar to Russians in temperament, would suddenly take to the streets to make political demands. That protests were now breaking out in Moscow was Putin's worst nightmare. He accused Hillary Clinton, the U.S. secretary of state, of criticizing the Duma elections before receiving an official report from election observers. "She set the tone for some actors in our country and gave them a signal," Putin said after the first protest broke out. "They heard the signal and with the support of the State Department began their active work." In the Arab Spring and the Occupy movement, people were protesting the status quo in cities around the world. But for Putin, it was not possible that Russians had enough agency to demonstrate against blatantly falsified elections; it had to be an American conspiracy.

When Alexei Navalny called for a spontaneous protest the night after the Duma vote, I was no longer living in Moscow. Four months earlier, I had moved to Berlin to pursue new journalism projects after almost eight years in Russia. Hunched over my laptop in my rented attic room, I watched in disbelief as the number of people planning to go to the December 10 protest ticked up by the hundreds every time I refreshed the rally's Facebook page. I realized something huge was happening that could not be grasped from abroad. I flew back to Moscow the day before the demonstration.

I had first visited Moscow in 1991. The Soviet leader Mikhail Gorbachev was struggling to keep the Soviet Union from falling apart as independence movements in republics such as Lithuania and Ukraine tore at the threadbare Soviet empire. In Russia, the largest republic, Gorbachev also faced fierce opposition from democrats who opposed the continuation of

Communist rule. In March that year I found myself in a sea of people demonstrating against Gorbachev on Revolution Square, across the street from the Bolshoi Theater. There were speeches and chants and lots of pushing as the police chased us into the nearest metro station. I hardly understood a word of Russian, but I was thrilled to be a witness to history. Within less than a year, the Soviet Union collapsed and Gorbachev was out of power.

Twenty years later I was again heading to a protest on Revolution Square. Although the location of the rally had been changed to a more spacious location, many people were still gathering near a granite statue of Karl Marx. Police trucks and buses were parked nearby, and police officers lined the street up to Lubyanka Square and beyond. But instead of telling the crowds to disperse, the cops were directing them to make their way on foot to Bolotnaya Square, located on an island in the Moskva River. I joined the opposition leaders Boris Nemtsov, Gennady Gudkov, and his son, Dmitry, in a boisterous, impromptu protest march past St. Basil's Cathedral and across the Bolshoi Moskvoretsky Bridge. Just a week earlier such a scene would have been unimaginable.

A gigantic crowd was forming on the island despite the cold, wet December weather. The flags of Russia's marginalized liberal political parties were flapping in the wind, as were black-yellow-white czarist tricolors flown by Russian nationalists. People were holding homemade signs that read "Putin Go Away" or "Putin, burn in hell." It was clear that this protest was about much more than stolen elections.

Well-known Moscow liberals gave forgettable speeches, and the sound system was inadequate for the enormous crowd. But the significance of the rally was not in any of the speeches—it was in the turnout of thousands of people united in their disdain for Putin's brazen power grab. "Putin, resign! Putin, resign!" the crowd chanted. "Russia without Putin! Russia will be free!" Vladimir Ryzhkov, a liberal politician whose own political career had been stunted by impossibly harsh registration rules, took a symbolic vote on the protesters' demands: freedom for all "political prisoners," i.e., the hundreds of demonstrators locked up earlier in the week; the annulment of the Duma elections; the resignation of the elections commission chairman; the registration of all political parties; and free and fair elections.

At the time, it was unclear if this was the beginning of a people power revolution. But the peaceful demonstration set an important precedent for Muscovites, namely, that protest need not be accompanied by fear and violence. The civic spirit of the Bolotnaya rally was a strong antidote to the cynicism that had poisoned public life in Russia for so long.

I filled my notebook with notes and interviews. When the rally was over, I felt exhilarated, then depressed: I had no editor to call or headlines to dictate. I did not even understand how Twitter worked. The next day I wrote the first post of a blog that would become a chronicle of the burgeoning protest movement.[1] I canceled my ticket home for Christmas and spent that winter in Moscow going to protests and hammering out blog posts in a friend's kitchen in the company of his cat.

I first saw Alexei Navalny in the dead of night at a police station in a Moscow suburb. A crowd of supporters and journalists met him like a celebrity when he was released from a two-week jail sentence for disobeying police orders at the first rally after the Duma elections. A roar went up as Navalny walked through the gates into a lightning storm of camera flashes. Overnight he had turned into the hero of the Moscow protest movement and the greatest hope for Putin's enemies.

Before the Duma vote, Navalny had made a name for himself as a muckraker, attacking the rampant government corruption fueled by record-high oil prices. A corporate lawyer by trade, Navalny bought stock in state companies, making him a shareholder who could demand accountability from management. With gleeful zeal he went after the oil pipeline monopoly Transneft, the energy behemoth Gazprom, and state-owned VTB Bank for dodgy deals that were never meant for public consumption. A year before the protests broke out, Navalny founded a website where anybody could upload suspicious government contracts. He built a loyal following on the LiveJournal blogging platform. In 2010 he spent several months at Yale University on a fellowship for young leaders from around the world.

Politically, Navalny was hard to pin down, appealing to liberals, nationalists, and libertarians all at the same time. When he was in his early twenties, Navalny joined Yabloko, the first pro-Western liberal party in post–Soviet Russia. He soon came into conflict with Yabloko's leadership and was finally kicked out for espousing nationalist views. Navalny participated in the Russian March, an annual demonstration of far-right nationalists, and in 2007 he appeared in a video in which he called for the deportation of migrants, concluding that "we have a right to be Russians in Russia and we will defend this right." Navalny's argument was that nationalism should not be left to skinheads and neo-Nazis; his motivation appeared to be opportunistic as some of Putin's fiercest opponents were nationalists. A little more than a month before the antigovernment protests erupted in December 2011, Navalny spoke at a nationalist rally on Bolotnaya Square attended by several hundred people. His more moderate views clashed with those of the other speakers, including some of Russia's most notorious ultranationalists.[2]

Navalny's flirtation with Russian nationalism alienated many liberals who otherwise agreed with his criticism of the Kremlin. But Navalny's main audience were not Russian nationalists; they were young, educated urbanites who shared his blog posts and donated to his anticorruption projects. Navalny was different from the old-guard democrats from the 1990s who were incapable of organizing popular resistance to the Kremlin. Navalny was an early adapter of social media, blogged prolifically, and spoke in memes and other pop culture references. His language could be harsh and combative, but he was also very funny. Navalny popularized the designation "party of crooks and thieves" for United Russia, the highly unpopular ruling party. In the lead-up to the 2011 Duma elections, Navalny rejected calls by liberals to boycott the vote. Instead he exhorted citizens to vote for any party on the ballot except United Russia. Navalny's calculation was that if enough angry voters went to the polls, United Russia would lose its constitutional majority in parliament. He was right.

The party of crooks and thieves fell just short of 50 percent of the vote, losing seventy-seven seats in the chamber. The three other parties in the Duma—the so-called loyal opposition approved by the Kremlin—all saw significant gains. The extent of the authorities' desperation became clear as reports of vote rigging flooded in from independent election observers. Navalny called his followers into the street, and soon he and dozens of other protesters found themselves behind bars for "insubordination."

On the snowy night Navalny was due to be released from jail, a small crowd of supporters gathered to meet him. Alexander Sokolov, a burly thirty-year-old truck driver from Moscow, had written "Freedom Navalny" in English on the grime of his delivery truck parked across the boulevard. Sokolov had cast a protest vote for the Communist Party in the Duma elections—but he felt betrayed because the Communists later refused to boycott the results to force new elections. I asked Sokolov what his personal political convictions were. "I'm for freedom and justice," he replied.

Not wanting to create a media spectacle, the authorities kept Navalny's exact whereabouts a secret and released him in the middle of the night. At 2:30 A.M. on December 21, Navalny walked out of the Marinsky Park police station. "Something amazing has happened," he told the waiting scrum. "We served our fifteen days in one country and came out in a different one." The strategy of voting for anybody but United Russia had proven itself, Navalny said, and now the same thing must happen in the March presidential election. "Putin won't become the lawful president," he said. "It will be an illegal succession to the throne." Navalny thanked the crowd and tried to find his wife Yulia, who had come to pick him up. "What about the nationalist threat?" someone shouted. "There is no nationalist threat whatsoever," Navalny said. "The threat is that crooks and thieves usurped power in Russia. We need to fight against them, and not some mythical nationalists." The questions kept coming. "Aren't you afraid?" a voice asked. "I'm not afraid," Navalny answered. "These fifteen days strengthened my belief that there's nothing to fear. We are not at all alone; the majority is behind us. We are the majority. They're the ones who are scared, and we see and feel that."

Vladimir Putin was no longer the man he used to be. His announcement to return to the presidency was not met with widespread enthusiasm. United Russia, from which he had been studiously distancing himself, could not win half the vote in an unfair election.[3] Worse than that, a survey taken by a government polling agency after the Duma elections found that only 42 percent of Russians would vote for him.[4] Of course Putin was in no danger of losing the March election, but it was a shockingly poor showing for a politician who had always claimed to represent a majority of Russians. In the survey, Gennady Zyuganov, the colorless Communist Party leader, came in a distant second with 11 percent; Alexei Navalny, who had no intention of running and was banned from state television, polled at 1 percent. The same poll found that a mere 35 percent of voters supported United Russia, even less than the party's official result in the Duma elections. The growing protests and poor poll numbers showed the Russian public's fatigue with Putin. He was at his most vulnerable since first becoming president in 2000.

When Putin bestowed the presidency on Medvedev, oil prices were still climbing and the Russian economy was booming. Now a global economic downturn was taking its toll on Russia, which was still dangerously dependent on the export of natural resources. Had Putin retired from politics in 2008, he would have been remembered as one of Russia's greatest leaders, presiding over a period of unprecedented economic growth that raised millions out of poverty. But Putin could not retire. Medvedev, at forty-two, was weak and untested, and the "power vertical" Putin had constructed meant that one man with an iron fist controlled the factions vying for Russia's fabulous wealth. If Putin had retired at the tender age of fifty-five, his own system would likely have devoured him.

So Putin shared the limelight in the tandem, an arrangement in which Medvedev presided in the Kremlin as a kind of boy czar while Putin served as regent from the premier's office. Medvedev copied Putin's clipped speaking style and even started mimicking his mentor's "gunslinger gait."[5] Medvedev's main qualifications as Putin's protégé were his loyalty and his lack of ambition. The pair had worked together when Putin was a deputy mayor in St. Petersburg, and Medvedev followed Putin to Moscow as he rose through the Yeltsin administration.

A little more than a year into office Medvedev began to carve out his own space, raising hopes among younger, more liberal Russians that perhaps he was more than a junior partner to Putin. In September 2009, Medvedev published an extraordinary online manifesto assailing Russia's "primitive" dependence on natural resources. Simply by enumerating the problems facing Russia, Medvedev was challenging the central message of the Putin presidency: that the country enjoyed stability and was headed on the right track. Without apportioning blame to anyone in particular, Medvedev confessed that "we" had not done everything necessary in past years and that mistakes had been made. If Russians were to have any hope for a dignified future, he said, the country would have to reorient its economy to high technology, uproot corruption, and reawaken private initiative long stifled by a paternalistic state. Peace must finally return to the North Caucasus region, a cauldron of violence since the Chechen wars. Medvedev called for a multiparty political system and a proactive citizenry. "Society will become open and transparent like never before, even if the ruling class doesn't like it," he wrote. In international affairs, Russians must not show arrogance, oversensitivity, or distrust in dealing with the West, he said. It was time for a new foreign policy driven by national interests, not superpower nostalgia.

The global economic crisis made it easier for Medvedev to show humility about missed opportunities and to state the obvious: The country's oil addiction, corruption, and low-level insurgency in the North Caucasus threatened Russia's future, while a belligerent foreign policy was only speeding up the decay. The Putin-era social contract of trickle-down oil wealth in exchange for acceptance of the political status quo appeared to be over. Medvedev, in the Russian tradition of top-down reform, was trying to preempt social unrest with a recognition of the need for change. The president, who himself lamented the low level of individual initiative among Russians, presented no plan of how he would motivate a passive citizenry to heed his call. Medvedev's project to build a Russian "Silicon Valley" outside Moscow turned out to be a multi-billion-dollar boondoggle, and the essence of his law enforcement reform boiled down to renaming the Soviet-era *militsiya* (militia) to the more Western-sounding *politsiya* (police). Medvedev's part in the tandem was not to shake up the precarious political structure he had inherited from Putin—it was to take on a representative role like a European monarch, securing social peace at home while putting on a respectable face for the rest of the world.

The election of a new president in the United States helped Medvedev step out of Putin's shadow. Initially, the Kremlin reacted coolly to Barack Obama's victory. But Russian skepticism began to evaporate as the Obama administration actively pursued a "reset" in relations. American harping on Russia's democratic shortcomings was replaced with an appeal to the country's vanity as a nuclear power and a permanent member of the United Nations Security Council. The new administration was focused on winning Russian support for the priorities of Obama's foreign policy: creating enough stability in Afghanistan to begin withdrawing U.S. troops and preventing Iran from acquiring a nuclear bomb.

Medvedev presented a fresh face in the Kremlin that let the United States turn over a new leaf in relations. Obama grasped that Putin's hostility toward America was linked in a large part to the irrelevance the Bush administration had assigned to Russia. By focusing on areas of common interest and ignoring disagreements, Obama built up Russia's importance, automatically raising Medvedev's stature. When Obama visited Moscow in July 2009, Medvedev basked in the global attention.

Two weeks after Obama's Moscow summit, Vice President Joe Biden traveled to Ukraine and Georgia to reassure the countries of continuing U.S. support despite the "reset." During his visits with Viktor Yushchenko and

Mikheil Saakashvili, Biden limited his public statements to ritual phrases about backing young democracies and rejecting geopolitical spheres of influence. But on the flight back to Washington, Biden gave a newspaper interview in which he brushed off Russia as a has-been superpower that deserved more pity than fear.[6] "The reality is the Russians are where they are. They have a shrinking population base, they have a withering economy, they have a banking sector and structure that is not likely to be able to withstand the next fifteen years," Biden said. "They're in a situation where the world is changing before them, and they're clinging to something in the past that is not sustainable." Russians themselves will realize sooner or later that threatening neighbors is economically unsustainable and not in their own self-interest, Biden said. The United States should be sensitive to Russia's loss of empire and not grate the leadership unnecessarily. "These guys aren't absolute average-intellect ideologues who are clinging to something nobody believes in," he said. "They're pretty pragmatic in the end." Putin reacted angrily to Biden's words, saying they made him wonder who was really in charge of U.S. foreign policy—Obama or his vice president. It was a trademark Putin riposte, echoing chatter in Moscow about whether he or Medvedev was really running Russia.

In fact, Biden had far more international experience than Obama, having been a fixture on the Senate Committee on Foreign Relations for years. In February 2009, six months after the Georgia war, it was Biden who proposed the "reset" in relations with Russia—at the same security conference in Munich where Putin had railed against the West two years earlier. The "reset" was not without results. The crowning achievement was the 2010 signing of the New START arms control treaty, which set limits on strategic nuclear weapons. The Obama administration also secured Russian support for its efforts to keep Iran from developing a nuclear weapon and for resupplying U.S. troops in Afghanistan. In return, the United States worked to speed up Russian membership in the World Trade Organization (WTO) and remove Russia from the Jackson-Vanik Amendment, Cold War–era legislation that restricted trade with the Soviet Union because of human rights abuses.

In March 2011, Biden made his only trip to Moscow as vice president. With Russia's presidential election a year away, both Medvedev and Putin were withholding comment on which one of them would run as the Kremlin's candidate. Moscow found itself in a strange limbo when Joe and Jill

Biden arrived, and there was speculation that the U.S. vice president would use his visit to endorse Medvedev. In a speech to students at Moscow State University, Biden repeated many of Medvedev's talking points.[7] "History shows that in industrialized societies, economic modernization and political modernization go hand-in-hand," Biden said. "I urge all of you students here: Don't compromise on the basic elements of democracy. You need not make that Faustian bargain."

In Biden's meetings with Medvedev and Putin, the main agenda item was Russian membership in the WTO.[8] But the unresolved question of Russia's political direction loomed in the background. After visiting Putin, Biden met at the American ambassador's residence with leaders of Russia's democratic opposition, including Boris Nemtsov and Garry Kasparov, the former chess champion. (Alexei Navalny, who at the time was more of a gadfly than an established opposition figure, was not invited.) Biden told the group that if he were in Putin's place, he would not run for president again because it would be "bad for the country and for himself," Nemtsov said after the meeting.[9] According to Leonid Gozman, a leader of the Right Cause party, Biden also said that he told Putin he had looked into his eyes and seen "no soul"—a reference to George W. Bush's first encounter with the Russian leader.[10]

The backdrop of Biden's visit was the Arab Spring, which was rattling authoritarian regimes throughout the Middle East. Medvedev had expressed sympathy for the democratic aspirations of people in the Arab world, and Biden tried to convince him to support a UN Security Council resolution authorizing military intervention in Libya, where protests against the dictator Muammar Gaddafi were spiraling out of control.[11] Other countries, including France and Italy, also appealed to Medvedev. One week after Biden's visit, Russia abstained from the UN Security Council vote on Libya, effectively permitting Western powers to use "all necessary measures" to stop Gaddafi from attacking civilians in rebel-controlled areas. As Russia's president, Medvedev was formally in charge of foreign policy. His decision not to veto the UN resolution infuriated Putin, especially after NATO warplanes started bombing targets in Libya. In televised remarks during a visit to a missile factory, Putin lambasted the military operation as a "crusade" and called the UN resolution "defective and flawed." That same day Medvedev hit back. Wearing a bomber jacket embroidered with a double-headed eagle and the words "commander-in-chief," the president

told reporters that Russia's abstention in the UN Security Council was justified given "the Libyan leadership's absolutely intolerable behavior and
the crimes that they have committed against their own people." Medvedev
said that "talk of crusades" was inadmissible.

For the first time, a clear fissure appeared in the tandem. Medvedev's
choice not to thwart a Western military intervention was the most consequential decision of his presidency—and if there still had been a chance
that Putin would let Medvedev run for reelection, it was buried at that
moment. In May 2011, Medvedev held his first press conference after three
years in office.[12] He was incongruously sunny. Medvedev said that relations
with NATO had returned to normal following the Georgia war. Asked about
Ukraine's European integration, he called it "a perfectly normal choice"
and said that Russia, too, was on friendly terms with Europe. On the question on whether he would run again, Medvedev gave a tortured nonan-
swer, only promising an announcement "soon."

In August, Putin and Medvedev took a fishing trip in southern Russia.
The Kremlin published photos of the two men in matching beige outfits
angling off a motor boat. It was on the Volga Delta that Putin told Medvedev that he needed to relinquish the presidency because he could "lose
Russia," according to the journalist Mikhail Zygar.[13] There was no room for
debate. The next month the pair finally made Putin's decision public.

A year before the announcement, Putin had invoked Franklin Roosevelt's election to four terms as an oblique justification of his own ambitions. It was becoming a habit for Putin to justify something possibly
blameworthy he did by citing some American precedent. Although not
surprising, Putin's decision to return to the Kremlin came as a shock to
Russia's elites, especially those who had been hoping that Medvedev's
presidency signified a generational shift in power. Medvedev, who was
twenty-six when the Soviet Union fell apart, represented a generation of
Russians that had profited from the fall of Communism—not just in material terms but also in the ability to interact with the rest of the world
through travel and the internet. In many post-Communist countries, the
old apparatchiks had long been retired for more modern leaders. In Russia,
Putin's return signified a regression.

Putin had already blocked the way for the next generation when he
jailed Mikhail Khodorkovsky, an oil tycoon unafraid to challenge the Kremlin, in 2003. Forty at the time, Khodorkovsky was one of the oligarchs who

had become fabulously rich in the privatizations of the 1990s. But Khodorkovsky stood out for his interest in developing Russian civil society. Sentenced to lengthy terms in two Kafkaesque trials, Khodorkovsky became a
public intellectual in prison, publishing opinion pieces in leading Russian
and foreign newspapers. After Medvedev made his public call for modernization in 2009, Khodorkovsky responded in the liberal Russian daily
Vedomosti, warning that Generation M—the modernizing generation of
entrepreneurs, managers, engineers, and intellectuals—would only suc-
ceed in changing Russia if there was serious democratic reform.[14] Two
years later, after Putin announced his return to the Kremlin, Khodorkovsky wrote a prescient follow-up piece in *Vedomosti* urging Generation
M not to despair and to form a new "modernizing class."[15] "You need to
learn to step out of the internet into real life and break out of the shell
of habit and servile behavior," he wrote. "You need to stop telling your-
self that nothing depends on me. Things do depend on you!" Two months
later, Moscow experienced its biggest antigovernment demonstrations in
twenty years.

Both Medvedev and Khodorkovsky, separated by two years in age, were
talking about modernization as a process, but Russia's young urban elite
already were modern. They were connected via social media, spoke English, and considered vacations in New York or Goa completely normal. It
was the contradiction between free global citizen and disenfranchised
Kremlin subject that drove young Russians to take to the street. Medvedev failed in his job as a bridge between generations. Putin, then fifty-
nine, could not grasp the significance of the protests because he did not
go online himself. Putin said on national TV that he "did not have time"
to use the internet, and in 2007 he had told *Time* magazine that he had
never written an email. Putin's isolation from the modern world hobbled
his ability to understand what was happening beyond the Kremlin's walls.

Putin made his first public remarks on the growing protests on December
15, when he held his annual call-in show on Russian television. He did his
best to show how "normal" he thought things were in the country, saying
he had been taking ice hockey lessons as tens of thousands of protesters
rallied on Bolotnaya Square. Putin's nonchalance was supposed to calm his
supporters and remind his opponents of their insignificance. Putin said he
saw "young, active people" protesting on the TV news. "If that's the result

of 'the Putin regime,' that's good," he said. His sarcasm went even farther when he claimed to have at first mistaken the white ribbons worn by
protesters for unfurled condoms, perhaps as part of an AIDS awareness
campaign. While Putin hinted at a few liberalizing adjustments to his cen-
tralized power structure, the basic message was "stay the course."

One viewer asked Putin about a remark by U.S. Senator John McCain,
who after the first big protest had tweeted: "Dear Vlad, the Arab Spring is
coming to a neighborhood near you." Putin said that the decorated Vietnam War veteran had the blood of innocent civilians on his hands and must
have gone crazy during the years he spent as a prisoner of war. "Probably
he can't live without the horrible, disgusting scenes of Gaddafi's massacre,
when it was shown on TV screens around the world how he was killed,"
Putin said. "Is that democracy?"

To the hardliners around Putin, the United States was following a policy
of world domination by social media, nongovernmental organizations, and
smart bombs. With street revolutions in the Arab world spreading with the
help of Twitter and Facebook, Putin was waking up to the potential risks
that lurked in the Russian internet, a freewheeling space that he did not
know and, as a result, had largely ignored. Putin drew a straight line from
the Orange Revolution in Kyiv to the nascent protest movement in Moscow. It did not fit into Putin's understanding of the world that civil society
was an essential building block of democracy; to him it was just another
instrument of political influence used by the West. Russian nongovernmental organizations such as Golos had played a key part in documenting violations during the Duma election. Golos—which means both "vote"
and "voice" in Russian—had sent out thousands of election monitors and
set up an interactive map where people could upload reports of vote rigging. That the organization received funding from sources such as the U.S.
Agency for International Development cemented Putin's belief that his
regime was under siege by the West.[16] To Putin's clique, the outbreak of
protests in Moscow was not a troubling sign of discontent; it was confirmation that Medvedev was too weak to resist Russia's enemies and that Putin
was right to stage a comeback.

The liberals who organized the protests were sensitive about being
branded foreign agents and revolutionaries. After the first rally on Bolotnaya Square, one of the organizers, Vladimir Ryzhkov, brusquely turned
away on the stage when I introduced myself as an American journalist.

At another protest near the Kremlin, I spotted Maria Baronova, a spokeswoman for the protest movement, holding up a placard that read: "This is not Athens and not the Maidan," i.e., Moscow's middle-class protesters were not demonstrating for a social welfare state, as many Greeks had been, nor were they trying to repeat the 2004 Orange Revolution. The political upheavals of the twentieth century had made "revolution" a bad word in Russia—and explained why "stability" was such a winning slogan for Putin.

The exuberance and creativity of Moscow's antigovernment protesters reminded me of the high spirits I had experienced in Kyiv in the aftermath of the Orange Revolution. Both protest movements erupted after an unpopular government tried to rig an election. Both were peaceful and demanded democracy writ large. But while the police in Moscow mostly stood back during the winter rallies, the Russian authorities were determined not to permit the start of anything resembling a protest camp. To Putin, people in the street heralded the breakdown of public order, the loss of government control, and often enough, regime change.

The example of Gaddafi's grisly killing was fresh in Putin's mind. In an effort to normalize relations with the West, the Libyan dictator had accepted responsibility for the 1988 Lockerbie airplane bombing, agreed to compensate victims' families, and voluntarily surrendered his weapons of mass destruction. But when Gaddafi began a brutal crackdown on his opponents, NATO intervened and helped overthrow him. To Putin, the lesson of Libya was clear: weakness before the West had first cost Gaddafi his regime and then his life. Gaddafi's involvement in international terrorism and his ruthless repression of his own population were irrelevant.

Putin emerged from the Moscow protests as the defender of autocrats. On his watch, he had already seen the dictators of Serbia, Iraq, and Libya get chased from power and face ignominious deaths. None of them were particularly reliable Russian allies, but they had all distinguished themselves in their resistance to American domination. The first opportunity to protect a fellow strongman came in February 2012, when the UN Security Council voted on a resolution backing an Arab League peace plan that called for the Syrian leader Bashar al-Assad to end his assault on his opposition and step down. This time there was no wavering in the tandem, and Russia, together with China, vetoed the resolution. Russia's foreign minister, Sergei Lavrov, then traveled to Damascus to shore up the Assad regime as it continued its pitiless attack on its opponents.

Putin was contemptuous of appeals to democracy. For the Kremlin, power did not derive from the people as much as from the manipulation of the people: "the people" were not independent actors but a chaotic, unpredictable mass that needed to be channeled and controlled. Yet just because democracy was illusory did not make the *appearance* of democracy any less important to Putin. In fact, it was crucial for his legitimization.

Elections are the most vulnerable moment for any pseudodemocracy. Cooking the numbers is not the problem; it is the danger of getting caught and sparking protests. The Duma elections caught the Kremlin unawares because even with all the safeguards to guarantee victory for the ruling party, no amount of vote rigging could disguise United Russia's unpopularity. Going into the March 4 presidential election, Putin promised webcams in every polling station to forestall any new accusations of fraud. His victory was a foregone conclusion because the four strawmen the Kremlin had allowed on the ballot posed no threat to him. The candidates' only purpose was to make Putin look like the obvious reasonable choice, and none of them ran anything resembling an election campaign.

The campaign of Sergei Mironov, the colorless head of the Fair Russia party, was instructive. I was mystified why anyone would vote for Mironov, who had already run in the 2004 presidential election on the dubious platform that he supported the incumbent, Putin. As Fair Russia was holding a rally to protest censorship, I headed to the hulking headquarters of Russia's state-run Channel One on a frigid February afternoon. Waving yellow party flags and wearing yellow vests over their overcoats, a couple of hundred people had gathered in the bright sunshine. Speaking in his jowly warble, Mironov repeated a few stock phrases about bringing social justice to Russia. Then he vanished from the scene in a dark limousine.

I tried to interview Mironov's would-be voters, mostly older women, but they answered my queries in monosyllables. Finally an older gentleman, wearing a Fair Russia baseball cap, confessed that he would, in fact, be voting for Putin. He could not explain what he was doing at a Mironov rally. As the crowd dissipated, I noticed that many of the demonstrators were filing to a row of rickety buses with license plates from regions around Moscow: Ivanovo, Tula, Kostroma, and Tver. One bus had come all the way from the Kursk region, 250 miles away. At the nearby monorail station, I spotted a woman paying rally participants, including the Putin supporter I had just spoken to. At that moment it dawned on me to what extent Putin's democracy was a giant postmodern show. The rally I had attended was an elaborate charade with only one goal: providing footage of an "opposition" candidate's rally for the evening news.

Although Putin enjoyed genuine support, progovernment rallies were just as fake, with people bussed in from the provinces to wave flags and pre-printed placards. About a week before election day, on the Defender of the Fatherland holiday, Putin held his first and last campaign rally in Moscow's enormous Luzhniki Stadium. The contrast with the enraged citizens' protests of the previous three months was striking. Nobody was livestreaming the proceedings from their iPad, and there were no homemade signs with ironic texts. People walked in groups, not as individuals. It was a Soviet-style mobilization of workers' collectives on a public holiday. As I walked across the stadium grounds, I passed a long line of men in front of army field kitchens distributing free soup. The smell of *papirosy*, the pungent filterless cigarettes of another era, wafted through the air. An old man played an accordion as elderly ladies in flowered shawls swirled around him.

Inside the vast stands, I found myself sitting with workers from the GAZ car factory in Nizhny Novgorod, 250 miles east of Moscow. I struck up a conversation with the middle-aged autoworker sitting next to me. Only Putin offered the stability that Russia needed, he explained. There was no alternative. When I asked him for his name, the autoworker shook his head. "Suddenly it'll turn up in a newspaper," he said warily. He had said nothing controversial, but fear sat deep among Russians, especially when talking to a foreigner.

At last Putin appeared in the stadium, evoking the Battle of Borodino, a turning point in Napoleon's ill-fated invasion of Russia in 1812. Calling on Russians to resist the traitors in their midst, Putin promised certain victory. "People like us, who share our views, don't number in the tens of thousands but in the tens of millions!" he said. "We won't allow anybody to meddle in our internal affairs. We won't allow anybody to impose their will on us because we have our own will!" Putin's only campaign speech was over in ten minutes. The moment he stopped speaking, the participants streamed to the exits, eager to set off on the long way home.

Officially, Putin won the presidential election with 64 percent of the vote, with the Communist, Gennady Zyuganov, coming in second place with 17 percent, and the token liberal, Mikhail Prokhorov, taking a distant third with 8 percent. The conduct of the vote was free of the scandal that had marred the Duma elections, largely because Putin's popularity—unlike United Russia's—was indisputable.[17] Putin's electoral support was based on the fear of chaos and the absence of any viable alternative. Russians were not apathetic as much as they were apolitical, and Putin had become the default leader. After the polls closed, Putin appeared at a staged victory rally outside the Kremlin with tears in his eyes. (He later claimed his tears were caused by the wind.)

Putin had just survived the biggest challenge to his rule. But his showing was more than seven percentage points lower than in his first reelection in 2004. Putin failed to win even half the vote in Moscow. The day after the election, the protest organizers called for a rally on Pushkin Square in central Moscow. As police flooded the capital, the mood was edgy and depressed. The intoxicating feeling of solidarity and empowerment at previous demonstrations was gone. Putin's successful power grab jolted them back to reality. Alexei Navalny spoke to the crowd. "We know the truth. We're sure of our righteousness. And we know we'll prevail," he shouted. Navalny vowed to stay on the square. Riot police soon closed in, stormed the stage, and made hundreds of arrests.

The inevitability of at least six more years of Putin began to sink in. On May 6, 2012, the day before Putin's inauguration, the protest movement called for one more rally on Bolotnaya Square. Navalny later recalled that he advocated for escalation—and that the protesters were fed up with peaceful rallies and itching for "something more hard-core."[18] The protest descended into violence with more than four hundred arrests and dozens of injured, including police.

The next day the authorities turned the center of Moscow into a ghost town. Followed by multiple cameras for a perfectly shot TV spectacle, Putin left the premier's office in Moscow's White House for the last time. Accompanied by two boxy black Mercedes SUVs and a motorcycle escort, Putin's armored black stretch limousine sped through eerily empty streets to the Kremlin, less than two miles away. Putin had supposedly won a landslide, but there were no cheering crowds lining the way. An opposition activist might try to unfurl a banner, which would then be broadcast live around the world. Nothing could be left to chance. If Medvedev had bathed in the pomp of the presidency, Putin acted like it was old hat. He rattled off the oath of office partially by memory, and after a choir sang the national anthem, he produced his inaugural speech from his suit pocket. Putin spoke for five minutes, vaguely calling for unity and patriotism. Then he strode purposefully out of the Kremlin's gilded halls to retrieve the nuclear briefcase from Medvedev. The power transfer was complete.

The inauguration ceremony was not even over when a sweeping crackdown on the opposition began. Police raided Jean-Jacques, a popular French brasserie right off the motorcade's route, where journalists and antigovernment activists had gathered. In the following weeks and months, prosecutors launched investigations against dozens of protesters who had been caught up in the May 6 melee. Three criminal cases were opened against Navalny in 2012. A raft of new legislation raised fines for taking part in unauthorized protests, created the designation of "foreign agent" for organizations receiving funding from abroad, and expanded the legal definition of treason. The show trial of punk-rock performance group Pussy Riot became a symbol of Putin's new authoritarianism. After holding a "punk prayer" in Moscow's main cathedral before the presidential election, three of the group's participants were arrested and sentenced to two years in prison for "hooliganism."

A clash of civilizations came to a head in Russia's extraordinary winter of protests. On one side was the traditional authoritarian state, which for centuries had relied on coercion to perpetuate its rule. On the other was a modern citizenry that knew exactly what people in democratic countries could expect—and demand—from their governments. Putin ultimately prevailed because there was still no critical mass of Russians who had abandoned the Soviet mentality of acquiescence to the powers that be. This silent majority was the most inert part of Russian society, and their inertia allowed Putin to hold onto power.

Russia was still not ready for its Maidan. In Ukraine, a far greater proportion of the population had given up the Soviet mindset of reliance on the state for direction and livelihood. And now a critical mass of Ukrainians was ready to break with the Soviet past once and for all.

4

Massacre on the Maidan

Igor Girkin, a colonel in the FSB, Russia's Federal Security Service, was resigning after sixteen years. The formal reason was a bureaucratic reorganization. But in his own words, Girkin had personal conflicts with some of his superiors, and his dim view of Vladimir Putin's government was well-known within the agency.[1] A year had passed since mass demonstrations rattled the Kremlin. The protests had been led by liberals but also attracted ultranationalists like Girkin, who dreamed of restoring Russia's lost empire and despised a regime that held no beliefs beyond self-enrichment. As a young man, Girkin had fought in the wars that broke out as the Communist bloc dissolved—in places the rest of the world knew little about: Transnistria, Bosnia, and Chechnya. His hobby in peacetime became the reenactment of historic battles.

In November 2013, not long before his forty-third birthday, Girkin traveled to Ukraine for a reenactment of the liberation of Kyiv from Nazi occupation seventy years earlier. A notice on a city news site announced that more than one thousand participants were expected from across Europe and the United States. The Red Army's victories in World War II provided a never-ending loop of anniversaries. Nine years earlier, Putin had attended a parade in Kyiv marking the expulsion of the last Nazi invader from Ukraine. Just days before the reenactment of the battle for Kyiv, Viktor Yanukovych—now Ukraine's duly elected president—had watched a giant reenactment of the Red Army's 1943 breaching of the Dnipro River in eastern Ukraine. Yet as Putin turned the memory of World War II into an ideological crutch in Russia, the legacy of the war left Ukrainians deeply divided. People in eastern and central Ukraine largely saw the Soviet army as a liberating force from the Nazis, while many western Ukrainians were more ambivalent, viewing the Soviet Union as just as bad as Nazi Germany, if not worse. In Kyiv that November, both "Germans" and "Soviets" played their roles with glee. The reenactment included charging Cossacks on horseback, two airplanes, and a German tank. Wearing a Red Army *vatnik* (quilted jacket) and forage cap, Girkin fired a wheeled Maxim machine gun as his comrades stormed the Nazi lines.

Less than three weeks later, protests broke out in Kyiv after Yanukovych's government abruptly abandoned plans to sign an association agreement with the European Union. Yanukovych's about-face brought first hundreds, then tens of thousands of demonstrators onto Kyiv's Maidan Nezalezhnosti, Independence Square. The so-called Euromaidan protest turned into a second iteration of the 2004 Orange Revolution, with a tent city rising in central Kyiv to demand Yanukovych's resignation and Ukraine's European integration. Unwilling to repeat his defeat in the Orange Revolution—and with plenty of encouragement from the Kremlin—Yanukovych deployed riot police and paid thugs to break up the new Maidan. The violence only brought out more people and strengthened the determination of the demonstrators.

Two months into the protests, Colonel Girkin returned to Kyiv on another curious mission. This time he was in charge of security for a tour of religious relics to one of the holiest sites for Orthodox Christians, Kyiv's Pechersk Lavra, or Monastery of the Caves. The relics, part of the Gifts of the Magi, had left their repository in Greece for the first time in five hundred years to be displayed in Russia, Belarus, and Ukraine. Stored in an ornately decorated box, the relics were said to contain some of the gold, frankincense, and myrrh the Three Wise Men had given to Jesus after his birth. Kyiv was the last scheduled destination. But even before the Gifts of the Magi arrived in Ukraine, the tour organizers secretly planned to add one more stop: Crimea.[2]

The sponsor of the unusual tour was a Russian businessman named Konstantin Malofeyev, nicknamed "the Orthodox oligarch" for his close connections to both the Russian Orthodox Church and Putin's entourage.

A self-proclaimed monarchist since the age of sixteen, Malofeyev had made his fortune through an investment fund that benefited from his Kremlin ties. He was celebrated as a Russian version of the American financier George Soros, only Malofeyev—via his Russian Orthodox charity—was countering the prodemocracy projects funded by nongovernmental organizations such as Soros's Open Society.[3] "I don't believe in democracy," Malofeyev told a Russian newspaper.[4] "Democracy in its present form is show business." Monarchy was the only correct form of government for Russia, he continued, and the country was lucky to have Putin at its helm. Malofeyev believed that Russia was an empire in its essence and could not exist in any other form.[5]

After leaving the FSB, Girkin found a job providing security to Malofeyev and his family.[6] On the day Girkin and Malofeyev arrived in Ukraine, the Euromaidan mourned its first fatalities.[7] During the week he spent in Kyiv, Girkin found time to reconnoiter the protest camp. "I perfectly understood the people's dissatisfaction with Yanukovych, a stupid, greedy gangster," Girkin recalled later.[8] "After taking a look at the Maidan in Kyiv and talking to people there, I understood that in the near future, Ukraine would fall apart. That is, I was completely certain of the Maidan's victory."[9]

From Kyiv, the Gifts of the Magi traveled on to Crimea on January 30, 2014, ostensibly to meet the spiritual needs of local Orthodox believers. There was such a bad winter storm that Crimea's main civilian airport was closed and Malofeyev's plane had to seek permission to land at Belbek, a Ukrainian air base.[10] Girkin and Malofeyev established contact with locals who could help deliver Crimea to Russia if the Maidan prevailed. On the night of their arrival, Malofeyev met with the speaker of the Crimean parliament, raising the question of whether he was ready to take "more drastic action" in asserting Crimea's autonomy should Kyiv descend into complete mayhem.[11]

What was extraordinary about Girkin's and Malofeyev's undercover mission to Crimea was that Yanukovych was still firmly in control at the time. The "Maidan's victory" was anything but a foregone conclusion. In fact, the protesters had run into a deadlock with Yanukovych, whose office in Kyiv's government quarter was just a five-minute walk up a hill overlooking the square. By the middle of February, the standoff in the Ukrainian capital had lasted almost three months, and Maidan leaders feared that

Yanukovych would finally gather enough forces to seal off the protest camp and destroy it.[12] The opposition lawmakers and activists decided to seize the initiative. They planned a march on the Rada, Ukraine's parliament, to demand early presidential elections and a return to the 2004 constitution, which curbed executive power in favor of the legislature.[13]

On the morning of February 18, protesters set out from the Maidan to the Rada, a short walk away. The procession was led by members of the "Maidan self-defense," the protest camp's improvised security force, armed with wooden poles and wearing construction helmets.[14] As the protesters approached the parliament building, they were met by Berkut ("golden eagle") riot police. A clash between two very unequal sides erupted, with the Berkut making use of all the weapons at their disposal, including air guns and riot control grenades wrapped in nails. The Berkut was backed up by *titushky*, paid thugs. Oleksandr Turchynov, an opposition lawmaker and a Maidan leader, later said that an arson attack on the nearby headquarters of the ruling Party of Regions served as a pretext for Yanukovych to unleash the full force of the riot police, including the use of live ammunition.[15] Before February 18, he said, there had been no guns on the Maidan.[16] But after the violence at the Rada, people began bringing hunting rifles and other firearms to the square, said Turchynov, who himself started carrying a pistol.

After the Berkut chased them back to the Maidan, the protesters braced for one more attempt by government forces to clear the square. Yanukovych ordered eight thousand law enforcement personnel to the center of Kyiv, and another three thousand were deployed to the suburbs.[17] The Ukrainian president refused to take calls from the German chancellor Angela Merkel or the European Commission president José Manuel Barroso, but he did speak with Joe Biden, then the U.S. vice president.[18] Barack Obama's point man on Ukraine, Biden called on Yanukovych to pull back his forces from Kyiv and "exercise maximum restraint."[19] European and American officials had become trusted intermediaries for both the government and the opposition, but their influence on events unfolding on the ground was minimal. Biden's advice fell on deaf ears.

At 8 P.M. the feared attack on the Maidan began.[20] The protesters fought back with Molotov cocktails and paving stones. They set alight barricades made of tires, creating a defensive wall of smoke and fire. The battle raged all night, but miraculously the protest camp still stood in the morning. The hulking Trade Unions Building, which had served as the Maidan's head-quarters and field hospital, was a now smoldering black shell. Even though the protesters were bloodied and outnumbered, the Berkut had also run out of strength, having fought without interruption since the previous morn-ing. Investigators would later establish that in the bloodshed that began on February 18, thirty-six people, including eleven police officers, were killed, with hundreds more injured.[21] After the defense minister ordered paratroopers to Kyiv the next morning, the intervention of the military could no longer be ruled out.[22] Ukraine was in upheaval. Overnight, dem-onstrators in cities in central and western Ukraine attacked police stations and offices of the SBU, Ukraine's state security service. The SBU declared an "antiterrorist operation" across the whole country. The mayhem that Girkin and Malofeyev had anticipated was taking place.

On February 18, I stayed up half the night in a Berlin TV studio where I was providing commentary on the events in Kyiv. A stationary camera on the Maidan provided live footage of ambulance after ambulance arriving to pick up wounded protesters. I was in a state of shock. After my first visit to Kyiv following the Orange Revolution, I had returned many times, and to me the Maidan was a familiar landmark. I loved Kyiv for its sunny disposition and its architectural treasures; I nearly moved there instead of to Berlin after Mos-cow. That winter I observed the Maidan from afar. Now, as I watched a massa-cre unfolding in a European capital, I knew I had to return immediately, even without a concrete assignment. I instinctively understood that this story was no longer about an internal Ukrainian power struggle but about something much, much bigger. In the morning I bought a plane ticket to Kyiv.

On the way to the airport on February 20, I scrolled through the latest news from Kyiv on my phone: alarming reports were coming in that police had shot and killed dozens of protesters. When I arrived in Kyiv, I did not recognize the city anymore. It was dark and empty and full of fear. Titushky roamed the steep cobbled streets. I checked into a Soviet-era tourist hotel near the government quarter. I expected to stay for a few days at the most. I never imagined I would soon bear witness to the beginning—not the end—of Ukrainians' struggle to choose their destiny as a nation.

Viktor Yanukovych's moment of triumph came on February 7, 2010, when he beat Yulia Tymoshenko, one of the heroes of the Orange Revolution, in a presidential runoff vote, 49 percent to 45.5 percent.[23] The electoral map showed a familiar picture of a divided nation, with Yanukovych sweeping the southeastern half, including Crimea, and Tymoshenko holding the central and western regions. For Yanukovych, whose presidential aspirations had been thwarted by the Orange Revolution, it was a moment of sweet revenge. In the first round of the election, the incumbent, Viktor Yushchenko, came in fifth place, winning not even 6 percent of the vote. Voters punished Yushchenko for an economy gripped by recession and for the gridlock resulting from incessant infighting with his prime minister, Tymoshenko. Yanukovych came into office promising to cut taxes, secure an international bailout loan, and turn Ukraine into a bridge between Russia and the EU.

In his first one hundred days in office, Yanukovych went out of his way to improve ties with the Kremlin. The new Ukrainian president signed a decree abolishing a commission to oversee Ukraine's preparations for NATO and said he did not consider membership in the alliance realistic given low public support.[24] Echoing the official Russian version of history, Yanukovych said the Holodomor, Ukraine's great famine of 1932–33, had not been a genocide targeting Ukrainians but a tragedy that affected other peoples of the Soviet Union as well. Yanukovych wanted school textbooks to call World War II the "Great Patriotic War," as Russians still referred to it, and the return of Russian-language instruction to Ukrainian universities.

The clearest sign of a rapprochement between Kyiv and Moscow was an agreement Yanukovych reached with his Russian counterpart, Dmitry Medvedev, extending the lease for Russia's naval base in Crimea until 2042. In exchange, Ukraine would receive a steep discount on natural gas deliveries from Russia. The deal was emblematic of the bilateral relationship: for Kyiv, cheap energy was the top priority; for Moscow, the most important thing was its strategic outpost in Sevastopol, the Russian Black Sea Fleet's base for more than two hundred years. Signed in Ukraine's second largest city, just a half-hour drive from the Russian border, the so-called Kharkiv Accords were viewed as a breakthrough by the Kremlin. Yushchenko had been seeking the departure of the Russian Black Sea Fleet from Crimea once its lease expired in 2017.

Yanukovych refused to see Russia as a menace. He reversed a Yushchenko-era decision expelling FSB officers operating under the cover of the Russian Black Sea Fleet and revoked Moscow Mayor Yury Luzhkov's status as persona non grata in Ukraine. Luzhkov, who had supported calls for eastern Ukraine to go its own way during the Orange Revolution, was blacklisted in 2008 for saying that Sevastopol should be "returned" to Russia. In July 2010, he traveled to Kyiv to celebrate Yanukovych's sixtieth birthday.

Yanukovych, a Russian speaker from Donetsk, felt comfortable around Russians of his generation and could relate to them through their shared Soviet past. But he also enjoyed the prestige—and profit—of being the leader of an independent country. Yanukovych was "pro-Russian" to the extent that it brought financial benefit. He had the same mercantile approach to the EU. The first guests he received after his inauguration on February 25, 2010, were Catherine Ashton, the EU's top diplomat, and Štefan Füle, the EU commissioner in charge of enlargement, who presented Yanukovych with a paper outlining Ukraine's path to Europe.[25] To show his administration's interest, Yanukovych made his first foreign trip not to Moscow but to Brussels, the seat of the EU Commission. He had no intention to diverge from Ukraine's path to an association agreement with the EU.

By 2010, the European Union had gone through two waves of enlargement that granted membership to all the Soviet Union's former vassal states in central Europe, as well as the three Baltic nations. The EU, now at twenty-seven members, was a remarkable achievement, uniting erstwhile rivals in the world's most powerful economic bloc. In 2012, the EU won the Nobel Peace Prize for "the advancement of peace and reconciliation, democracy and human rights in Europe." Since the EU had no geopolitical ambitions of its own, its leaders could not imagine that the Kremlin might view their peaceable union as a threat.

When the EU first held out the prospect of an association agreement to Ukraine in 2008, it was more out of bureaucratic habit rather than any strategic vision. There was little appetite in Europe for offering Ukraine full-fledged membership. Wracked by poverty and corruption, Ukraine was seen as an economic basket case. For western European leaders, Ukraine's raison d'être was delivering Russian natural gas via its Soviet-era pipelines. Nevertheless, the negotiations that had begun during Yushchenko's presidency continued under Yanukovych, and in March 2012 the EU and Ukraine initialed the association agreement. There was just one major obstacle to finalizing the deal: the imprisonment of Yulia Tymoshenko, Yanukovych's chief political rival. After Yanukovych assumed the presidency, a number of criminal investigations were opened against Tymoshenko. In 2011, she was sentenced to seven years for overstepping her authority as prime minister when she negotiated a deal ending the 2009 cutoff of Russian natural gas deliveries. Tymoshenko's conviction became the symbol of Yanukovych's increasingly authoritarian tendencies. As long as she was in prison, European leaders refused to sign the association agreement.

Certain of the EU's righteousness, the Europeans failed to grasp the fury that the pending association agreement with Ukraine had ignited in the Kremlin. The conventional wisdom in Brussels was that a symbiotic economic relationship with Russia was the best guarantee of peace and stability on the continent. The EU was Russia's largest trade partner, even as Putin disdained it as a meddling, bothersome giant. He preferred to deal with the major European powers on bilateral terms, where he could leverage business interests and appeal to historical ties to get his way. The EU, on the other hand, gave a platform to smaller countries that had long been dominated by Russia. Bureaucrats in Brussels were accosting Gazprom, the Russian natural gas monopoly, over antitrust violations on the European market. And by negotiating an association agreement with Ukraine, the EU was treading on Russia's self-defined sphere of influence, just as NATO had done in 2008.

Putin's answer to the EU was the Eurasian Union, a grouping of former Soviet states based on an existing customs union between Russia, Belarus, and Kazakhstan. The Russian thinking behind an alternative union borrowed heavily from Eurasianism, an ideology that laid out and justified a unique, Russian-led civilization on the Eurasian landmass.[26] In an article published in *Izvestia* in October 2011, Putin denied that the Eurasian Union was an attempt to revive the Soviet Union, claiming that it was no different from other economic blocs such as the EU or NAFTA.[27] He criticized "some of our neighbors," i.e., Ukraine, for choosing European over Eurasian integration.

For the Eurasian Union to work, Putin needed Ukraine. With its rich agricultural lands and heavy industry, Ukraine had been the jewel in the crown of both the Russian Empire and the Soviet Union. "Without Ukraine, Russia ceases to be an empire," Zbigniew Brzezinski, the former U.S. national security adviser, wrote less than three years after the Soviet Union's collapse.[28] "But with Ukraine suborned and then subordinated,

Russia automatically becomes an empire." To the Kremlin, the West's open recognition of Ukraine's importance to Russian greatness seemed to confirm that the EU was trying to pry the country from its rightful master. The association agreement, which established a free trade area between the EU and Ukraine, was scheduled to be signed at a summit in Vilnius, Lithuania, in November 2013. But before that could happen, Yanukovych needed to free Tymoshenko and prove Ukraine's commitment to the rule of law.

In July 2013, Putin made what would be his last trip to Kyiv. The official occasion was the 1,025th anniversary of the baptism of Kyivan Rus, when a medieval ruler of Kyiv named Volodymyr, or Vladmir in Russian, converted to Christianity. Visiting the Monastery of the Caves and attending an outdoor prayer service with Yanukovych, Putin hailed Kyiv as the cradle of an eastern Slavic civilization shared by present-day Ukrainians and Russians. The next day the two presidents traveled on to Crimea, visiting the site in Sevastopol where Prince Volodymyr was believed to have been baptized. Yanukovych and Putin then reviewed a joint parade of Russian and Ukrainian warships to mark Navy Day, a Soviet-era holiday observed in both countries. "We have common roots, a common culture and religion," Putin told the sailors of the two Black Sea fleets.[29] "Our blood and spiritual ties are unbreakable."

During his two-day visit to Ukraine, Putin also showed up unannounced at a conference on "Orthodox-Slavic Values: The Foundation of Ukraine's Civilizational Choice," organized by Viktor Medvedchuk, the Ukrainian politician and oligarch whose daughter was Putin's godchild.[30] Medvedchuk, not Yanukovych, was Putin's trusted proxy in Kyiv. "We will respect whatever choice our Ukrainian partners, friends, and brothers make," Putin told the audience. "The question is only one of how we go about agreeing on working together under absolutely equal, transparent, and clear conditions."[31]

The answer to Putin's question came the day after his departure from Ukraine. Russia's consumer watchdog—which had been responsible for banning Georgian wine and mineral water during times of political tension—proclaimed that chocolates made by Roshen, a leading Ukrainian confectioner, suddenly did not meet Russian health standards and would no longer be imported. The chocolate ban was the opening salvo in a Russian pressure campaign on Yanukovych. For the Kremlin, the struggle for Ukraine was a zero-sum game: under no circumstances should it join either NATO or the EU.

Two weeks after Putin's visit, Russia closed its borders to Ukrainian exports as a warning of what could come. The Kremlin may have had legitimate concerns over European goods flooding into Russia once Ukraine joined a free-trade area with the EU. But Moscow was not interested in negotiating. Sergei Glazyev, an economic adviser to Putin, took on the role of Kremlin attack dog. Hardly a day passed without Glazyev, a hard-core Russian nationalist with Ukrainian roots, predicting impending catastrophe for Ukraine. In one interview, he said that the country risked becoming an "EU colony" whose fate would be dictated from Brussels. In another, Glazyev claimed that by forgoing Russia's Customs Union, Ukraine would lose up to $12 billion a year in discounts on natural gas and other trade privileges.

At an annual forum held in Yalta, Crimea, Glazyev made his most intimidating remarks. Hillary Clinton, who had recently resigned as secretary of state, was the conference's guest of honor. She praised Yanukovych's "guidance" in aligning Ukraine's government and opposition on European integration.[32] "We, the U.S.A., are for Ukraine's integration into Europe," Clinton said. "Closer relations between Ukraine and the European Union will be of benefit both for Ukraine and Europe, and the whole world." The next day, Glazyev warned that the exact opposite was true. Moscow would not reconcile itself with Kyiv's European choice, he said, and Ukraine would inevitably default on its debt as Russia was the country's largest creditor.[33] "We don't want to use any kind of blackmail. This is a question for the Ukrainian people," he said. "But legally, signing this agreement about association with the EU, the Ukrainian government violates the treaty on strategic partnership and friendship with Russia." Once that happened, Glazyev said, Russia would not be able to guarantee Ukraine's statehood and could even intervene on behalf of the country's pro-Russian regions.

Yanukovych felt pressure from all directions. With its economy stuck in a recession and insolvency looming, Ukraine was engaged in difficult negotiations with the International Monetary Fund (IMF), which was demanding that Kyiv slash consumer subsidies for natural gas and devalue the Ukrainian currency, the hryvnia. At the same time, the clock was ticking for Yanukovych to free his imprisoned political rival, Yulia Tymoshenko, before the EU summit in November. One compromise under discussion was for Yanukovych to let Tymoshenko receive medical treatment in Germany, where she would stay at least through the 2015 presidential election. At a meeting with Angela Merkel, Yanukovych brought up the possibility of receiving "compensation" for releasing Tymoshenko, to which the German chancellor responded: "She is not a cow, and we're not haggling at a bazaar."[34] Of course Yanukovych could simply have pardoned Tymoshenko, but that option would have required her to request it, thereby admitting her guilt. Ukrainian diplomats implored the Europeans—the Germans in particular—to drop their fixation on Tymoshenko as Putin tightened the screws on Yanukovych.

It was an irony of fate that Yanukovych, a rough-hewn boss from eastern Ukraine's coal country, had done more for European integration than any of his predecessors. Yanukovych may not have been motivated out of any deep feelings for Europe, but his political instinct told him that bringing home the EU association agreement would secure his reelection in 2015, when he would be able to add pro-European voters in central and western Ukraine to his loyal base in the east. In September, at a meeting with lawmakers from his Party of Regions, Yanukovych browbeat dissenters who were afraid of crossing the Kremlin.[35] He even had one particularly stubborn pro-Russian lawmaker from his party kicked out of parliament and jailed.[36] Yet with the EU digging in its heels over Tymoshenko's release and the IMF balking at new loans to bail out his government, Yanukovych began to cave to Putin's bullying.

In the month before the Vilnius summit, the two presidents met repeatedly. It is possible that Putin told the Ukrainian leader that the Kremlin had *kompromat*, or compromising information, on his dealings with the EU.[37] A little more than a week before the crucial summit, Štefan Füle, the EU commissioner for enlargement, visited Kyiv. Yanukovych told Füle that in their meetings, Putin had opened his eyes to just how intertwined the Ukrainian and Russian economies were.[38] The cost of lost business to Russia would total not $3 billion per year, as calculated by a group of German economists, but manyfold more, Yanukovych claimed. He appealed for financial help from the flummoxed EU commissioner, who answered: "Sorry, we aren't the IMF." On November 20, the IMF turned down Ukraine's request for a multi-billion-dollar loan.[39] The next day, Yanukovych's prime minister, Mykola Azarov, signed an order suspending talks with the EU and reviving "active dialogue" with Russia.

Instead of becoming Yanukovych's crowning achievement, the EU summit on November 28-29 turned into a fiasco. At the last minute, José Manuel Barroso, the president of the European Commission, withdrew the EU demand for Tymoshenko's release as a condition for signing the association agreement.[40] But it was much too late. Yanukovych was no longer haggling over Tymoshenko but staving off economic collapse—and the only lifeline was coming from Moscow. Angela Merkel drily remarked that she felt like she was at a wedding where the groom had suddenly gotten cold feet. "We expected more," she told Yanukovych.[41] "We have great problems with Moscow," he replied. "I have been left alone for three-and-a-half years in very unequal circumstances with Russia."

The European Union had sleepwalked into a brawl with the Kremlin and received a bloody nose. Viktor Yushchenko, the Ukrainian president who had most clearly articulated his country's European aspirations, later recalled running into Yanukovych before the EU summit.[42] When Yushchenko told his former rival that he, too, would be in Vilnius, Yanukovych said: "Please tell the Europeans not to close the door on Ukraine." It sounded like a message from a hostage to the outside world. Yanukovych was now in Putin's pocket.

The Euromaidan protests began with a Facebook post on November 21, the day Ukraine's prime minister officially stopped talks on the EU association agreement. To Yanukovych's critics, his EU course had always been suspect— and now they were exposed as an elaborate lie. "Who is ready to go out on the Maidan before midnight today?" Mustafa Nayyem, a well-known Kyiv journalist, asked his followers on Facebook. "Let's meet at 10:30 P.M. under the Independence Monument." A crowd of several thousand people showed up in the cold autumn rain, joined by politicians from the three main opposition parties represented in parliament: Yulia Tymoshenko's Batkivshchyna (Fatherland) party; UDAR, the party of retired heavyweight boxing champion Vitali Klitschko; and Svoboda (Freedom), a far-right party led by the Ukrainian ultranationalist Oleh Tyahnybok.[43] Nobody had any particular plan except to keep on protesting until the Vilnius summit.

Yanukovych's abrupt U-turn on EU integration was the trigger for the protests. But discontent had long been building over corruption, a skewed judicial system, and the government's increasing pressure on independent media and civil society. On Sunday, November 24, tens of thousands of protesters packed central Kyiv in the largest antigovernment demonstration since the Orange Revolution, which had started nine years earlier. After Yanukovych returned from Vilnius empty-handed, Berkut riot police stormed the Maidan, where a few hundred people, mostly students, had camped out. The brutal dispersal of the peaceful demonstrators, some of them minors, shocked the country. The following Sunday, December 1, even larger crowds took to the streets. After occupying the Trade Unions Building and City Hall, the protesters set up barricades on the perimeter of a new tent city.

Yanukovych's attempt to snuff out the Maidan had backfired colossally. But even as the protests in Kyiv ballooned, he was determined to keep up the image of business as usual. Yanukovych set off on a planned three-day trip to China, where he sought to show that Ukraine had other options besides the EU and the IMF. He had a meeting with Xi Jinping, China's new president, and oversaw the signing of a dozen agreements. Yanukovych claimed to have attracted $8 billion in investments, but the Chinese pointed out that they were not loaning Ukraine any money. On his way home, Yanukovych met Putin in Sochi, where workers were racing to prepare for the 2014 Winter Olympics. There were no official announcements following the talks, and both presidents' press services denied speculation that Yanukovych had agreed to join the Russian-led Customs Union. Ten days later, on December 17, Putin received Yanukovych in the Kremlin to announce their secret deal: Russia would bail out Kyiv by buying $15 billion worth of Ukrainian bonds and gradually reducing the price of natural gas deliveries by one-third.

Like the Orange Revolution before it, the Euromaidan seized global headlines. But if Ukrainians in 2004 had inspired people around the world with their peaceful revolution, the renewed Maidan protests were marred by violence almost from the start. Yanukovych, who did not need to be reminded of the danger of a protest camp in central Kyiv, deployed riot police, thugs, and provocateurs to crush his opponents. As the winter dragged on, activists were abducted, beaten, and even killed as the standoff grew increasingly bitter. The battles fought on the streets of Kyiv at times evoked medieval warfare: helmeted riot police wielded clubs and shields against protesters armed with improvised weapons, while black-robed Orthodox priests tried to intervene. At one point, demonstrators even used a catapult to lob Molotov cocktails at police lines.

The violence put the spotlight on the Maidan radicals who were spoiling for a fight. Pravyi Sektor, or Right Sector, was the most prominent ultranationalist group to emerge from the protest, even though its ranks on the Maidan numbered no more than a few hundred. Flying the red and black flag of the Ukrainian Insurgent Army—which during World War II had collaborated with the Germans against the Red Army—Pravyi Sektor fed into a caricature propagated by Russian state media of neo-Nazis running amok in downtown Kyiv. While Pravyi Sektor and other far-right groups played an outsized role during clashes with the police, they were in no way representative of the Maidan as a whole. Mustafa Nayyem, the journalist who had called protesters to the Maidan on Facebook, was born in Afghanistan; Serhiy Nihoyan, the first demonstrator to be shot and killed by police, was ethnic Armenian.

A survey of 1,300 people on the Maidan found that the "median protester" was male, between thirty-four and forty-five years old, with a full-time job, and not particularly partisan.[44] Their motives varied, but most demonstrators said they were less concerned about some formal relationship with the EU than about Ukraine embracing "European values." Although the use of nationalist slogans increased after the police used deadly force in January, they never became the dominant motive among protesters. Noteworthy, too, was the high level of self-organization and absence of any one leader. The Euromaidan was a grassroots, national movement that brought people out not just in Kyiv but also in cities across the country, including Lviv, Odesa, and Kharkiv. It was a motley coalition of entrepreneurs and soccer hooligans, civic activists and Afghan war veterans, liberal intellectuals and nationalists.

While Ukrainian nationalists exploited the growing polarization as the protest wore on, a sense of civic patriotism—direct citizen action—was the driving force behind the Maidan. Ethnic nationalism was no more prevalent in Ukraine than in other European countries; the ultranationalist Svoboda party's best showing in parliamentary elections was in 2012, when it won 10 percent of the vote. Ukrainian party politics was dominated by strong personalities—Yanukovych, Tymoshenko, Klitschko—not by ideology.

Maidan supporters gravitated toward the idea of Ukraine as a full-fledged member of the European family of nations. This European choice certainly meant a break with the Soviet past and a rejection of Russian-style crony capitalism. But it was not a rejection of Russia, where millions of Ukrainians still had family ties. In fact, the Maidan attracted participants from other former Soviet republics, including Russia. Russian democrats, who had watched their own protest movement peter out two winters earlier, envied Ukrainians for their fearlessness and endurance.

Unsurprisingly, Europeans and Americans were also not indifferent to the Ukrainians out demonstrating in the name of democracy. Although EU leaders were infuriated with Yanukovych for his about-face, they were not ready to slam the door shut on him after years of negotiations. Barack Obama, who had just won a second presidential term, took little interest in Europe as he sought to "pivot" U.S. foreign policy to China. Obama delegated his vice president, Joe Biden, to deal with the brewing crisis in Ukraine. Biden had met Yanukovych—at the time an opposition leader—during a 2009 visit to Kyiv. The two men began phoning frequently as the Maidan protest heated up. The Kremlin considered the West's outreach to Ukraine as interference in its sphere of influence. But Yanukovych welcomed the attention. As he hammered out a bailout with Putin, Yanukovych kept alive the idea that the EU association agreement had only been postponed. Western leaders believed that if they could rescue the deal, the impasse on the Maidan would end.

On December 10, 2013, Victoria Nuland, the top State Department official for Europe, and Catherine Ashton, the EU's chief diplomat, arrived in Kyiv for two days of talks to de-escalate tensions and nudge Yanukovych back to the association agreement. It was Nuland's third visit to Ukraine in a little more than a month. Halfway through the visit, just hours after Ashton met with protesters on the Maidan, riot police charged onto the square in an unsuccessful night raid to clear protesters from City Hall. When Nuland saw Yanukovych the next day, she condemned the violence but indicated that it was still not too late to "get Ukraine back into a conversation with Europe and the International Monetary Fund."[45] Mykola Azarov, the Ukrainian prime minister, told a government meeting that same day that Ukraine was seeking 20 billion euros in assistance from the EU if it signed the association agreement.[46]

Nuland also visited the Maidan, distributing food from a plastic bag to both protesters and police. "Nuland handing out cookies on the Maidan" would become an internet meme symbolizing American support for revolution in Ukraine. Within a matter of days, U.S. Senator John McCain turned up in Kyiv. Although he met with Yanukovych and other Ukrainian powerbrokers, McCain's speech on the Maidan grabbed the most attention. "Ukraine will make Europe better, and Europe will make Ukraine better," McCain said. "We are here to support your just cause, the sovereign right of Ukraine to determine its own destiny freely and independently. And the destiny you seek lies in Europe."

Days after McCain's visit, Yanukovych traveled to Moscow on December 17 to accept Russia's $15 billion aid package, effectively abandoning a return to the EU association agreement. With no clear way out of the standoff, Western diplomats took on an even greater role as mediators, and in early February Nuland was due in Kyiv for more talks with Yanukovych. Two days before her arrival, a four-minute recording of a phone call between Nuland and Geoffrey Pyatt, the U.S. ambassador to Ukraine, appeared on YouTube with the title "Puppets of the Maidan." The leaked recording, whose authenticity the State Department did not deny, quickly gained notoriety as proof that the United States was pulling the strings in Ukraine. Nuland and Pyatt discussed the possibility of opposition leaders "Klitsch" and "Yats"—Vitali Klitschko and Arseniy Yatsenyuk—taking ministerial posts, and they noted the friction between the two men. "I don't think Klitsch should go into the government. I don't think it's necessary; I don't think it's a good idea," Nuland said. Pyatt then encouraged her to phone Klitschko directly to help with "the personality management." Toward the end of the recording, after Nuland expressed the hope that the United Nations would throw its support behind a new Ukrainian cabinet, she added: "And you know, fuck the EU." Pyatt answered: "No, exactly. And I think we've got to do something to make it stick together, because you can be pretty sure that if it does start to gain altitude, the Russians will be working behind the scenes to torpedo it."

To the casual listener, the eavesdropped call between Nuland and Pyatt sounded like evidence of a conspiracy in which American officials were designating ministers in a future Ukrainian government while insulting their European partners. But placed into the context of events, the conversation was far less sensational. In late January, after the first killings on the Maidan, the opposition leaders Yatsenyuk, Klitschko, and Oleh Tyahnybok held a series of talks with Yanukovych. The Ukrainian president offered a number of concessions, including making Yatsenyuk prime minister and

Klitschko deputy prime minister, in return for an end to the protests. The political constellation that Nuland and Pyatt could be heard discussing would have kept Yanukovych in power, and in the end, the opposition rejected the offer, seeing in it a poisoned chalice designed to split the Maidan. As for Nuland's crude remark about the EU, it concisely, if undiplomatically, expressed American frustration with the Europeans' reluctance to threaten Yanukovych with sanctions if he did not end the violence.

As planned, Nuland returned to Kyiv to meet with Yanukovych on February 6, 2014. The same day, Sergei Glazyev, the Putin adviser who had become the Kremlin's main spokesperson on Ukraine, accused the United States of supporting a coup attempt in Kyiv. Without citing any evidence, Glazyev claimed in a newspaper interview that Washington was financing the Maidan to the tune of $20 million per week, including the arming of fighters and their training on the grounds of the U.S. embassy in Kyiv.[47] (Nuland, speaking at the U.S. embassy the next day, dismissed Glazyev's claim as "pure fantasy.") Ominously, Glazyev said that Yanukovych was in his right to disperse the Maidan with force, and that only the "federalization" of Ukraine could help prevent a division of the country and civil war.

Behind the scenes, Russian actors with vague or secret assignments were laying the groundwork to make good on Glazyev's threats. Rather than seek a mediated settlement between Yanukovych and his opponents, these players were working to suppress the Maidan and, if necessary, foment conflict. Under the cover of the Russian Orthodox Church, which Putin had completely subordinated to the Kremlin, the former FSB colonel Igor Girkin and the oligarch Konstantin Malofeyev probed the willingness of Crimean officials to secede from Ukraine. The tour of the Gifts of the Magi was a fishing expedition with no Russian government imprimatur, but its findings contributed to the Kremlin's contingency planning in the event that Yanukovych lost power.

While Glazyev was the public face of Russia's pressure campaign on Kyiv, Putin deployed a secret envoy, Vladislav Surkov, to meet directly with Yanukovych.[48] During Putin's first two presidential terms, Surkov had been responsible for creating Russia's decorative democracy. In 2013, he was officially put in charge of Abkhazia and South Ossetia, the two regions that Russia had occupied in its five-day war with Georgia. At the same time, Surkov was quietly given the Ukraine portfolio, making unpublicized visits to the country at some of the most critical moments of the escalating crisis.

In summer 2013, as the Kremlin was warning Ukraine of the economic consequences of the EU association agreement, a member of Yanukovych's inner circle recalled being told that "all business-related questions are now going to be discussed with Surkov."[49] In mid-August Surkov showed up in Kyiv to press the Kremlin's position before traveling on to Crimea. On the same day that Putin's envoy left Ukraine, August 14, Russia closed its borders to Ukrainian exports. The following winter, as Yanukovych increasingly used lethal force against the Maidan protesters, Surkov made at least four more trips to Kyiv, also visiting Donetsk and Crimea in early February.

High-ranking officers of the Russian Interior Ministry and FSB were also frequent guests. More than a year after the fatal shootings in February 2014, Ukrainian prosecutors announced that while they had found no evidence of Russian involvement in the violence, they had established that Russian security officials visited Ukraine three times during the Maidan protest.[50] Each of those visits followed especially violent clashes, suggesting that the Russians were advising their Ukrainian counterparts on what to do next. Besides words of advice, in January the Russian Interior Ministry sent thousands of stun grenades to Ukraine in a shipment labeled as "humanitarian aid."[51]

To the rest of the world, Putin continued to profess that Russia had only the best of intentions toward Ukraine and its people. Even after the Kremlin strong-armed Yanukovych from his European course, the EU held a scheduled meeting with Putin in Brussels in January 2014. The EU had been holding twice yearly summits with Russia since Medvedev's presidency, and European leaders plodded ahead with bureaucratic inertia. At the press conference following the summit, Putin said that "Russia has no intention of ever intervening" in Ukraine.

It would be Putin's last EU summit. The next meeting was scheduled to take place in June, right before the G8 summit in Sochi. But within a matter of months, Russia would invade Ukraine, be sanctioned by the EU, and get kicked out of the G8.

On February 20, 2014, fifty-three people, including four policemen, lost their lives in the Maidan massacre. It was the worst bloodshed Kyiv had experienced in a single day since World War II. The violence began that morning when the Berkut riot police reported they were being fired on from the Conservatory, one of the main buildings on the Maidan.[52] It was unclear who was doing the shooting—government provocateurs or demonstrators seeking revenge for the earlier killings. But when the Berkut retreated up Instytutska Street, which leads from the Maidan to the government quarter, protesters started following them. Dozens of activists were shot and killed as they made their way up the street holding metal shields and wearing plastic construction helmets. The nearby Ukraina Hotel became a makeshift field hospital, and its lobby's polished white floors were slick with blood.[53] Although many Ukrainians were tempted to believe that Yanukovych or even Putin had ordered the shooting, Maidan leaders including Petro Poroshenko and Oleksandr Turchynov later concluded that there had been no clear command to open fire.[54] After weeks and months of the standoff, the police's command structure was in disarray, and the officers besieging the Maidan were demoralized and worn out.

Turchynov, a leading lawmaker from Yulia Tymoshenko's party, called on his colleagues to meet for an emergency session of parliament, the Rada. It was a challenge to assemble 226 lawmakers to meet quorum, yet by 10 P.M. 239 deputies out of 450 showed up and passed a resolution condemning the violence.[55] The lawmakers also called for an end to the SBU's "antiterrorist operation" and the return of military units to their bases. Eighteen legislators from Yanukovych's Party of Regions quit the party. As Ukraine's executive began to teeter in the aftermath of the massacre, the legislature stepped up. The country's democratic institutions were still weak and untested, but just as during the Orange Revolution they carried out vital functions at a time of executive failure. Following the vote, the opposition party leaders went directly to the president's office. It was after midnight when they sat down with Yanukovych for talks mediated by the foreign ministers of Germany, France, and Poland.

The footage of demonstrators getting picked off and crumpling to the ground on Instytutska Street went around the world. Joe Biden once again phoned Yanukovych. The vice president urged Yanukovych to pull back his forces and reach an agreement with his opponents before it was too late.[56] It would be Biden's last phone call with the Ukrainian president.

Yanukovych was also talking to the Kremlin. He asked for a Russian representative to help mediate in the upcoming talks with the opposition;

Putin offered to send Vladimir Lukin, the Kremlin's outgoing human rights commissioner and a former Russian ambassador to the United States.[57] Lukin's marginal standing in the Kremlin reflected the extent of Putin's interest in a negotiated settlement. For Putin, dominance, not compromise, was the way to deal with political rivals. Lukin's job was merely cosmetic. The Kremlin emissaries who really mattered were Vladislav Surkov, the Kremlin insider assigned to Ukraine, and Sergei Beseda, the FSB general in charge of operations in the former Soviet Union.[58] They were met in Kyiv that day by Volodymyr Bik, the deputy head of the SBU, who took them to a guesthouse outside the city. Following the bloodshed on the Maidan, Yanukovych's entourage was in a state of panic. Dozens of charter jets took off from Kyiv that day as high-ranking Party of Regions officials evacuated their families and loot.[59]

In Moscow, Putin addressed a concert hall filled with members of Russia's armed forces celebrating the upcoming holiday, Defender of the Fatherland Day. "Russia is a peaceful democratic state. We are convinced that international problems and conflicts should be resolved by political rather than military means," he said, adding that Russia must remain prepared for any situation.[60] After delivering his remarks, Putin excused himself for having to return to work. He called Angela Merkel and David Cameron, the British prime minister, to voice his concern over developments in Kyiv. Putin also consulted with Yanukovych as the EU-mediated negotiations with the opposition stretched into the night.[61]

When I landed in Kyiv on February 20, I saw the government jets of the three European foreign ministers parked on the tarmac at Boryspil Airport. By the next morning, they had brokered a deal that offered a way out of the deadlock between Yanukovych and his opponents. I headed to the Maidan to gauge the mood. At the opening in the barricades where I entered, young men from the Maidan self-defense force were standing guard. They carried whatever weapon was at hand: a police club, a baseball bat, even a poker. I met a twenty-seven-year-old university instructor named Yuriy Kulynych, who had traveled all night on an overnight bus from Lviv, in western Ukraine. Like many of the demonstrators, he was wearing a construction helmet for protection. "It's important who signs what. We've had many compromises already," Kulynych said about the peace deal, the details of which were still unknown. Ukraine must return to the parliamentary system it had under Viktor Yushchenko, he said. And after so many deaths, Yanukovych had to go.

That morning the opposition leaders tried to drum up support for the agreement among their followers. Later Yanukovych received visitors at his office: Surkov and Beseda, accompanied by Lukin and the Russian ambassador to Ukraine, Mikhail Zurabov.[62] Beseda told Yanukovych that the protesters were planning to kill him and his family, and that he should use the military to crush the Maidan, Ukrainian intelligence officials said later.[63] That afternoon Lukin, Putin's representative at the talks, was conspicuously absent at the signing of the peace deal. He returned to Moscow, telling Russian state television that he had not signed the document because it was unclear what would happen next and who would be in charge in Kyiv in the coming days.

The agreement called for curbs on executive power and a national unity government, early presidential elections no later than December 2014, and investigations into the killings on the Maidan with international participation. Nobody was happy with the compromise: Yanukovych's opponents were angry because it did not remove him from power immediately; his supporters saw the deal as a capitulation before the protesters. More lawmakers from the Party of Regions defected. The security forces, the most important pillar of Yanukovych's regime, felt betrayed. Interior Ministry troops camped out on the square in front of the Rada departed with such haste that they left much of their equipment behind.[64] Police commanders withdrew their forces when they realized their own leaders were on the run, according to Arsen Avakov, an opposition lawmaker who dealt with security on the Maidan. Many Berkut units were asking Maidan leaders to grant them safe passage out of the capital. "At that moment Yanukovych completely lost control of the Rada, the police started running away, and the pyramid he had built collapsed," Andriy Parubiy, the head of the Maidan self-defense, recalled later.[65] "He lost all the support there was to lose."

The parliamentary opposition, together with Party of Regions lawmakers appalled by the violence, was determined to make the peace deal stick. Volodymyr Rybak, the speaker of the Rada and a founding member of the Party of Regions, convened the legislature to put the provisions of the agreement into law. Hours later, Rybak tendered his resignation because, as he said later, the Party of Regions had lost its majority and the government had collapsed.[66]

I returned to the Maidan in the late afternoon. A Party of Regions flag was lying on the ground for protesters to wipe their feet on. Activists were collecting money in big, transparent plastic boxes—and people were actively donating. Cossacks beat on drums, and a column of self-defense fighters marched by. I spoke to a group of seasonal workers from Ivano-Frankivsk in western Ukraine. Viktor Semkovych, age thirty-six, said he had come to the Maidan "for the people," not the opposition. His comrade Vasyl Tsekit, age thirty-eight, said: "If we leave the square, Yanukovych will turn Ukraine into North Korea." In the background, a woman was banging out a lively tune on a piano painted in the Ukrainian colors, blue and yellow. A hush fell over the crowd as a funeral procession for the fallen heroes passed by. Four caskets bobbed over our heads, held aloft by protesters.

The opposition leaders' problem was convincing the Maidan to accept their compromise with Yanukovych. In the evening, Arseniy Yatsenyuk, Vitali Klitschko, and Oleh Tyahnybok took to the stage on the square. Klitschko was booed when he sold the deal as a "small victory," and a young activist, twenty-six-year-old Volodymyr Parasyuk, burst onto the stage. Wearing a camouflage jacket, Parasyuk gave the most memorable speech of the three-month protest. "We're simple people, and we're telling the politicians standing behind me: Yanukovych will not rule for another year!" he shouted. "If by tomorrow morning at ten you don't tell us that Yanukovych is resigning immediately, we will storm the government with weapons in our hands! I swear it!"

By this time, Yanukovych was no longer in Kyiv. That afternoon Serhiy Larin, Yanukovych's deputy chief of staff, had watched as Berkut riot police hurriedly withdrew from outside the presidential administration.[67] Soon afterward, Yanukovych and his trusted chief of staff, Andriy Klyuyev, left for Mezhyhirya, the president's opulent residence outside the capital. For days security cameras had been documenting how trucks were loaded up with paintings, sculptures, and other expensive possessions. Late that night he took a helicopter to Kharkiv, the largest city in eastern Ukraine.

Kharkiv region was run by a Yanukovych loyalist named Mykhailo Dobkin, who had been calling for the capital to be moved to Kharkiv and for Ukraine to adopt a federal structure.[68] On February 22, a Saturday, Dobkin was due to host a gathering of lawmakers from southeastern Ukraine. After signing the agreement with the opposition, Yanukovych called Dobkin to say that he, too, would attend.[69]

Dobkin later recalled how he met Yanukovych at the airport.[70] Yanukovych's entourage included his mistress Lyubov Polyezhai, his younger son Viktor, and twenty-one bodyguards. As always, Yanukovych was traveling with his own supply of food and water. The airport staff received Yanukovych coldly, as if they could later be implicated just for being in his presence. There was a bomb threat at the airport, and Dobkin left via a back exit to take Yanukovych to a government guesthouse. "He didn't understand what was really going on and acted as if he still held power and everybody obeyed him," Dobkin said. Yanukovych believed that once the Maidan dispersed, he would go back to Kyiv, according to Dobkin. "He didn't make the impression of a man on the run. He 100 percent counted on returning," Dobkin said. "If he had known that he wouldn't return, he would have blown up, burned, and destroyed Mezhyhirya."

In Washington, Joe Biden kept dialing Yanukovych's cell phone—to no avail.[71] "Where the hell is this guy?" he asked. When Kyiv woke up the next morning, Viktor Yanukovych had vanished. There were rumors that he was in Kharkiv but there was no confirmation of his exact whereabouts. In the wake of the retreating security forces, the Maidan self-defense took control over key government buildings. When a group of TV reporters arrived at Mezhyhirya, the guards let them in saying they had found the estate empty earlier that morning. The Rada convened again. Following the overnight resignation of the speaker, Volodymyr Rybak, twelve more lawmakers quit the Party of Regions.[72] The Rada elected Oleksandr Turchynov—one of the main faces of the Maidan and a close ally of the incarcerated opposition leader Yulia Tymoshenko—as the new speaker.

In the afternoon, Yanukovych gave a sign of life in a bizarre, ten-minute video. Yanukovych declared that he had done everything in his power to prevent bloodshed, and that Ukraine was now experiencing a coup d'état reminiscent of the Nazis' takeover of Germany. Yanukovych displayed both defiance and helplessness, often speaking haltingly. "I don't plan to leave the country. I don't plan to resign. I'm the legally elected president," he said, expressing the hope that the European mediators would intervene on his behalf. Yanukovych said he wanted to travel through southeastern Ukraine to "meet people" and figure out what to do next. The decisions taken by the Rada were illegal, he said, and members of his party were being beaten and intimidated. Yanukovych said his own car had been fired on and that Rybak, the outgoing Rada speaker, had been attacked. Yanukovych's grasp on reality looked fragile. The next day Rybak himself called the story of the attack "absurd" and "made up."[73] No evidence would emerge that there had been an attempt on Yanukovych's life.

Parliament continued its work to fill the vacuum left by Yanukovych's flight. Turchynov, the new speaker, told lawmakers that he and Arseniy Yatsenyuk had managed to reach Yanukovych by phone—and that Yanukovych agreed to resign. Now, with the appearance of the video, it was clear the president had changed his mind. With 328 votes—more than the two-thirds needed to change the constitution—the Rada passed a resolution establishing that Yanukovych had removed himself from his duties as president. Yanukovych would later complain that the Rada had ousted him without following proper impeachment procedures. Yet the Rada did not even try to impeach him as that would have involved a lengthy process.[74] The situation was unprecedented, and the constitution offered no guidance on how to remove a president who had gone AWOL. With the executive branch in a state of dissolution, the Rada had to act fast and decisively.

New presidential elections were set for May 25. Under constitutional amendments restored under the Maidan peace deal, the Rada speaker—now Turchynov—became Ukraine's acting president, responsible for overseeing the formation of a new cabinet. Finally, the Rada passed a resolution calling for the release of Tymoshenko, who was being held in custody in a hospital in Kharkiv.

For the city of Kyiv, the disappearance of Yanukovych and his security forces was an unexpected denouement after months of tension and violence. Many residents headed to Mezhyhirya to check out Yanukovych's residence, an outsized, five-story peasant cottage with a jewel-encrusted private chapel, a Spanish galleon, and an ostrich farm. A monster traffic jam formed on the way to Mezhyhirya, so I decided to go back to the Maidan instead. Although the protesters appeared to have prevailed, they were not taking any chances. The first barricade I passed was being reinforced with a fresh load of tires. Two captured police trucks with water cannons were on display as trophies; someone had put a sign reading "to Moscow" in one of the windshields. Ukrainians of all walks of life packed the square. "Tribunal! Tribunal!" they shouted.

Every human emotion seemed bundled up on the Maidan: mourning and anger, celebration and relief. More than anything, people felt disbelief at the courage and cowardice they had witnessed in the space of two short days. I made my way up Instytutska Street, following in the footsteps of the protesters who had been picked off two days earlier. In the places where demonstrators had been shot and killed, mourners had made makeshift shrines with a stretcher, a helmet, or a single shoe. Passersby lit candles and sobbed silently. The concrete flower boxes on the side of the street were pockmarked with bullet holes.

I reached the government quarter at the top of the hill. The last time I had been there was in 2010, when I covered Hillary Clinton's visit to Kyiv as secretary of state. Now Maidan self-defense fighters in blue ponchos and hardhats were guarding the House with Chimeras and the presidential office. "Glory to the heroes!" they shouted when a group of fellow fighters marched past holding shields and wooden stakes. "Glory to Ukraine!" was the answer. When I returned to the Maidan, a sea of people surrounded the stage. They had come to greet Yulia Tymoshenko, who was on her way to Kyiv after more than two years in prison. Nobody on the Maidan that evening could have known how short-lived their triumph would be.

The dramatic events on the Maidan set off a chain of events that would eventually lead to an open war between Ukraine and Russia. The Kremlin's warnings of division and conflict became a self-fulfilling prophesy—not because Russian officials could foresee the future but because they were signaling a contingency plan should pro-Western forces return to power. A fierce battle for the Ukrainian presidency was expected no later than 2015, when Yanukovych was up for reelection. The Euromaidan moved up that clash.

Central to the official Russian narrative was that the Maidan was a coup d'état, disguised as a protest, executed by neo-Nazis, and planned by the United States. Everything else flowed from that: the "illegitimacy" of the new government and Moscow's imperative to intervene on behalf of Russian speakers supposedly facing persecution. The Kremlin storyline was faithfully retold in the 2016 film *Ukraine on Fire*, in which the American director Oliver Stone interviewed only three protagonists from the Maidan: Putin, Yanukovych, and his reviled interior minister, Vitaliy Zakharchenko. The message was simple and conspiratorial: the United States had directed the Maidan through the tried-and-tested practice of funding nongovernmental organizations that later spearheaded a pro-American putsch.

One problem with this version of events was that it denied the agency of the millions of Ukrainians who demanded that Yanukovych live up to his promise to bring Ukraine closer to the European Union. In a speech in December 2013, the U.S. diplomat Victoria Nuland boasted that the United States had invested more than $5 billion in building democratic institutions in Ukraine since the country's independence from Moscow. The Kremlin began citing this figure as evidence of a diabolical American plot. But divided over Ukraine's entire population, the U.S. investment in Ukrainian democracy amounted to a little more than $100 per Ukrainian over a period of more than twenty years. The presence of Nuland and other U.S. officials on the Maidan was used as further proof of an American conspiracy, even though they were all official guests of the Yanukovych government—in contrast to the Kremlin emissaries who visited Kyiv in secret. If the infamous tape of Nuland's opinion of a coalition government proposed by Yanukovych was the juiciest piece of evidence against the United States, it proved little more than a shocking disregard for communications security by top State Department officials. American and European diplomats never hid their sympathy for the protesters, and it was exactly their ability to talk to Maidan leaders that made them valued mediators for Yanukovych.

Perhaps most problematic with the narrative of a U.S.-engineered coup was that Ukraine, for all of its vaunted geopolitical importance, figured nowhere in Barack Obama's foreign policy. After George W. Bush's militant approach to global politics, including the push for Ukrainian NATO membership, Obama was trying to limit America's foreign entanglements. In eastern Europe, Obama's main goal was to paper over disagreements with Russia while seeking the Kremlin's cooperation on U.S. priorities such as arms control, the war in Afghanistan, and an agreement on Iran's nuclear program. Only after the Europeans helped negotiate a settlement between Yanukovych and his opposition did Obama pick up the phone—and he called Putin, not Yanukovych, to discuss the situation in Ukraine. Later Putin told an interviewer that Obama had asked him to persuade Yanukovych not to bring in the army and let the peace deal take effect. Putin said he agreed to do so and that the next day there was a coup in Kyiv. "Was it the first time they cheated us?" his interviewer, the Kremlin propagandist Vladimir Solovyov, asked. "So crudely and brazenly, probably for the first time," Putin replied.

Whether Putin approached Yanukovych on the matter was not even important. By the time the American and Russian presidents spoke, Yanukovych's power base was crumbling, the police had withdrawn from the center of Kyiv, and he had neither the will nor the authority to order the army to attack the Maidan. To his erstwhile supporters Yanukovych was a coward who had bowed to the protesters; to his opponents he was a bloody dictator who should step down and face justice. As his harebrained flight to eastern Ukraine would show, Yanukovych was no longer welcome even in his political home base.

Putin had never been particularly impressed by Yanukovych, ever since he emerged as the handpicked successor of Ukraine's second president, Leonid Kuchma. But now Putin had all the more reason to disdain Yanukovych: for allowing the Maidan protest to take root in the first place and then lacking the guts to destroy it. When Yanukovych signed the EU-brokered agreement with the opposition, it is possible that Putin had already given up on him. But once he fled Kyiv, Putin needed Yanukovych to disappear from the scene so that Russia could get on with the business of seizing Crimea.

5

The Gifts of the Magi

When Viktor Yanukovych flew to Kharkiv on the night of February 21, 2014, he was, by all appearances, still under the impression that he was fully in control. Upon arriving in Kharkiv, Yanukovych told Mykhailo Dobkin, the regional governor and a vocal Maidan opponent, that he planned to stay for a few days.[1] That night Dobkin was among a group of confidants who sat up with Yanukovych over whiskey in a government guesthouse. At first Yanukovych seemed completely relaxed, believing he had prevailed over the Maidan by signing the European-brokered peace deal with the opposition. But by the next morning, when Dobkin left, he said Yanukovych appeared to have aged by ten years.

Dobkin was planning a secretive congress in Kharkiv to which he had invited lawmakers from the Russian-speaking regions of southeastern Ukraine, including Crimea. Dobkin was an outspoken supporter of "federalization," which the Kremlin was aggressively promoting as a way to strengthen its influence over the eastern half of Ukraine. On Saturday, February 22, some 3,500 lawmakers from all levels of government convened in Kharkiv's Palace of Sport. The Kremlin dispatched the heads of the foreign relations committees of both houses of parliament, as well as the governors of four neighboring Russian regions, to the gathering. The big question was whether Yanukovych himself would show up.

Dobkin later insisted that he had not invited the president to the congress and that it was a "fucking coincidence" that Yanukovych showed up in Kharkiv.[2] The purpose of the meeting, Dobkin said, was to demonstrate that the Maidan was not representative of the whole country. Yet for many Ukrainians the Kharkiv convention was darkly reminiscent of a similar gathering in the town of Sievierodonetsk during the Orange Revolution, when Russian-speaking lawmakers threatened to split off and establish a "Southeast Ukrainian Autonomous Republic" with its capital in Kharkiv.

Yanukovych, who had attended the Sievierodonetsk congress in 2004, was determined to make an appearance at the Kharkiv convention to shore up his base.[3] But Dobkin said he feared that Yanukovych would humiliate himself and be booed from the stage. "On Saturday morning it was already clear that he wasn't completely legitimate as president, that it was already the end," Dobkin recalled later. The wily governor realized that by running from the Maidan, Yanukovych had managed to lose eastern Ukraine, once his political stronghold. Dobkin phoned the president to tell him his security at the congress could not be guaranteed. Yanukovych finally relented and asked for a TV camera to be sent to his guesthouse. Yanukovych recorded a video in which he claimed that he was the victim of a neo-Nazi coup and declared that he did not plan to resign. What he did plan to do was anybody's guess.

Kharkiv was in a state of upheaval. Maidan supporters, including soccer hooligans, were gathering outside the Palace of Sport in anticipation of Yanukovych's arrival. Inside, the delegates to Dobkin's congress passed a resolution taking responsibility upon themselves for securing Ukraine's "constitutional order." Despite the defiant words, the gathering failed to rally resistance to the revolutionaries in Kyiv. Dobkin escaped from the demonstrators outside the congress in a speeding car. Later that day he took his family to the Russian town of Belgorod, fifty miles away across the border. Dobkin's political mentor, the Kharkiv mayor Hennadiy Kernes, also left for Russia following the convention. The two rulers of Kharkiv openly flirted with separatism, but both of them returned to Ukraine almost immediately. Events may have played out very differently without the intervention of the Ukrainian oligarch Ihor Kolomoiskyi, who urged Kernes to take a clear stance against separatism.[4] Kolomoiskyi met with Kernes, persuading him not to align Kharkiv's fate—and his own—with Moscow.[5]

As Kernes and Dobkin ran to Russia, Yanukovych was trying to figure out his next move. Before the congress started that morning, Yanukovych's security detail informed Dobkin that two private jets were landing in Kharkiv.[6] Dobkin assumed they would take Yanukovych and his entourage to Crimea, which was too far to reach by helicopter. But then the Crimean prime minister, Anatoliy Mohylov, who was in Kharkiv for Dobkin's congress, learned that the Crimean branch of the state guard service was refusing to protect Yanukovych if he came to Crimea. The news was not only a sign of Yanukovych's loss of authority in Ukraine's most pro-Russian region; it also indicated that the Kremlin was beginning to exert its influence to force Yanukovych to flee the country.

In Kharkiv, Yanukovych still appeared determined to remain in Ukraine. He could have easily gone to Russia, just a few minutes' flight away. Instead, Yanukovych continued on by helicopter toward Donetsk, the industrial center where he had launched his political career as governor in the 1990s. There Yanukovych boarded a waiting business jet, but the airport authorities refused to give the plane permission to take off.[7] When Ukrainian border guards approached the aircraft, Yanukovych's bodyguards offered them a briefcase stuffed with cash.[8] The border guards stood firm, and Yanukovych had to accept the reality that even in his hometown, he was no longer in control.

Yanukovych headed to the Donetsk Botanical Garden, where the coal and steel baron Rinat Akhmetov had his residence. Ukraine's richest man, Akhmetov had helped finance Yanukovych's rise as a politician. Now the oligarch's only message to Yanukovych was to resign. With the airport closed to him and longtime allies such as Akhmetov telling him to give up, Yanukovych's options were narrowing. Driving to Crimea, 250 miles away, was a last resort. The local population was largely hostile to the Maidan, and Russia's Black Sea Fleet was docked in the port of Sevastopol. Accompanied by his chief of staff, Andriy Klyuyev, and a handful of bodyguards, Yanukovych set off into the night.

Several of Yanukovych's former bodyguards later testified before a Kyiv court about their nerve-wracking escape. Kostyantyn Kobzar, the president's chief of security, said that when he learned the motorcade was heading into an ambush outside the coastal town of Melitopol, he saw no other option but to appeal to colleagues from Russia's Federal Guard Service (FSO) for help.[9] Another bodyguard, Viktor Riznychenko, recalled how they turned off the main highway and drove up to a field.[10] When the cars shone their headlights on it, three Mi-8 helicopters with red stars on their fuselages landed in front of them. Yanukovych and his escort were flown to the town of Yeysk, on the Russian coast of the Sea of Azov, where they boarded a plane for Crimea. Because of a technical problem with the plane, they had to make one more stop in Anapa, Russia, before finally flying to the Russian Black Sea Fleet's air base outside Simferopol, the Crimean capital.[11]

When they landed in Crimea, Yanukovych discovered that a team of commandos from Kyiv had arrived to apprehend him. Again his bodyguards had to turn to the FSO for help with ground transportation and a safe place to stay.[12] Yanukovych huddled with what remained of his inner circle: Kobzar, Klyuyev, Viktor Pshonka, his prosecutor general, and Vitaliy Zakharchenko, his interior minister. According to Kobzar, they unanimously decided to leave Ukraine instead of putting up a fight and setting off a civil war. The choice was delusionary. Yanukovych had lost all credibility among his own base and was no longer welcome in what had been the bastions of his regime—Kharkiv, Donetsk, and Crimea. Only the Kremlin acted as if Yanukovych were still Ukraine's legitimate president, and on the night of February 23 he was spirited away to Russia aboard a Russian warship. Yanukovych's role as a Russian client was over; his remaining use to the Kremlin was as a "president-in-exile" to give the takeover of Crimea a sheen of legality.

In Kyiv, Yanukovych's furtive departure created a power vacuum. Most Ukrainians, whether they supported him or not, took the president's disappearance during a national crisis as an abdication. A day earlier the Rada, Ukraine's parliament, had enshrined into law the provisions of the peace deal facilitated by the European foreign ministers. Yanukovych accused the opposition of breaking the agreement, although it was his responsibility to approve the bills passed by the Rada. By failing to sign them, Yanukovych did not live up to his end of the deal. The Rada moved swiftly to oust Yanukovych and replace an executive branch that had completely disintegrated. As Rada speaker, Oleksandr Turchynov took on the responsibility as acting president—and until a new government could be formed, he embodied all executive power in the country.

Under no circumstances did Turchynov want to let the fugitive president slip away and escape justice.[13] When he learned that Yanukovych had left Kharkiv, Turchynov ordered him to turn around, threatening to use fighter planes to force his helicopter to land.[14] Yanukovych's pilot replied that they did not have enough fuel and continued on to Donetsk.[15] Although the border guards there stopped him from flying onward, most law enforcement agencies were taking a wait and see attitude. Ukraine's security forces, which just days earlier had tried to crush the Maidan, were unsure how they would be treated by the new regime. With Yanukovych and his top security officials on the run, the chain of command to Kyiv was broken. And even if Yanukovych could be found, it was not clear on what legal basis he should be arrested.

On the night of February 22, Turchynov sent Arsen Avakov, the freshly minted acting interior minister, and Valentyn Nalyvaichenko, the designated head of the state security service SBU, to Crimea to intercept Yanukovych with a dozen commandos. They were in for a bad surprise. "At that moment it turned out that the SBU in Crimea was already completely working for Russia," Andriy Parubiy, now Turchynov's top security adviser, recalled later.[16] "It turned out that information about our special operation was fully known to Yanukovych and the Russian security services."

In Moscow, Putin and four top security officials followed Yanukovych's helter-skelter road trip through eastern Ukraine. In a propaganda film broadcast on the first anniversary of Crimea's annexation, Putin recounted how he had personally overseen the extraction of Yanukovych. The central message of the faux documentary, *Crimea: The Way Home*, was that Putin had first saved Yanukovych and then Crimea from Ukrainian "fascists" and their American puppet masters. "We had never thought about seizing Crimea from Ukraine. Never," Putin said.[17] It was only after the night of February 22, he said, that "we were forced to start working on returning Crimea to Russia."[18] The assertion that Russia was simply reacting to events in Ukraine was at the core of the Kremlin narrative about Crimea's annexation. But it belied the open threats to Ukraine's unity by Putin's adviser, Sergei Glazyev, and the advance preparation for the peninsula's seizure by shadowy Russian emissaries.

Even before Yanukovych set off for Crimea from Donetsk, Putin said that Russian military units had been activated to bring him out "by land, by sea, and by air." After Yanukovych contacted the Kremlin from the road, the Russians were able to track the route of his forlorn motorcade by its radio signals, according to Putin. In the course of his Crimean docufiction, Putin repeatedly said that Russian intelligence had learned that Yanukovych was in danger of "physical destruction"—and delivered that message to Yanukovych's bodyguards. "According to our information, some heavy machine guns had been set up so they wouldn't have to have a long discussion," Putin recalled in the film.[19] "There's reason to believe they simply would have destroyed him."

Yanukovych and the bodyguards who fled with him to Russia later justified their actions with the story of an imminent ambush with "heavy machine guns." It was their alibi. In Putin's version of that night, the Kremlin warned Yanukovych of the impending attack and gave his team directions to where the Russian helicopters would pick them up. In other words, Putin frightened Yanukovych into Russian custody. Yanukovych's removal from Ukraine was not a spontaneous act of charity; it was a prerequisite for Russia's occupation of Crimea. With a power vacuum in Kyiv, Russia could claim to be restoring order in the name of Ukraine's "legitimate" president.

Putin's Crimea film inadvertently showed that Russian special forces did not rescue Yanukovych as much as they kidnapped him. In an interview from his Russian exile, the former Ukrainian president later revealed his passive role.[20] "The fact that Vladimir Putin took that decision, on the recommendation of his own special forces, that was his right and his business. He did not consult me," Yanukovych said. "I am of course grateful to him for giving the order and helping my security to get me out and save my life." Yanukovych was only able to thank Putin for his magnanimity by phone. Although Putin had offered to meet him after his flight from Kyiv, when Yanukovych arrived in Moscow two days later, the Russian leader no longer had any time to see him. The conquest of Crimea was now Putin's top priority.

The night Yanukovych set off for Crimea, I received a one-line email in my Kyiv hotel room. "Want to go to Crimea for us? Like, ASAP?" asked the foreign editor of *BuzzFeed News* in New York. Nobody knew exactly where Yanukovych was, but it was already clear that if there was going to be any trouble for the new authorities in Kyiv, it would likely start in Crimea. A peninsula the size of Sicily, Crimea did not become part of the Ukrainian Soviet republic until 1954. It was the only Ukrainian region with the status of "autonomous republic" and maintained close ties to Russia thanks to the Russian Black Sea Fleet and the hundreds of thousands of Russian tourists who visited every year. Many older Russians had nostalgic memories of Crimea as the southern summer playground of their youth.

I flew to Simferopol, Crimea's capital, the next evening.[21] On the way into town I asked my cab driver what he thought about Yanukovych, who owed his electoral victory in 2010 to Russian-speaking regions like Crimea. "I'm 1,000 percent against Yanukovych," he said. And what about Russia? "Ninety percent of people here are for Russia," he replied. Yanukovych's pathetic flight from Kyiv had eliminated any remaining popular support. But many Crimeans feared that the new authorities in Kyiv would seek retribution for their backing of the ancien régime. I checked into the deserted Hotel Ukraina, a few steps from the Crimean legislature.

I had stayed in the same hotel in 2007, when I first visited Crimea. Simferopol was a sleepy provincial town with crumbling architectural monuments to its time as a Russian imperial outpost. The town's oldest Russian Orthodox church bore a plaque to Catherine the Great, the Russian empress who wrested control over Crimea from the Ottoman Empire. Just up the street was a mosque that predated the Russian conquest by almost three hundred years. During my first trip, I explored the ruins of fourteenth-century fortresses built by traders from Italy. In Feodosiya, I slept in the same hotel room where Anton Denikin, a White Army general who fought the Bolsheviks, had stayed before fleeing aboard a British warship in 1920. In Yalta, I wandered through the Livadia Palace, where Franklin Roosevelt, Joseph Stalin, and Winston Churchill decided the fate of Europe at the end of World War II. Everywhere I went in Crimea I found the traces of history—military history. But the impression that lasted with me was of a place lost in time and eaten by neglect.

When I returned on February 23, 2014, Crimea was waking from its long slumber as a backwater. Crimeans of all political stripes were angry with Yanukovych for stuffing the provincial government with his Donetsk cronies. Especially for the Crimean Tatar ethnic minority, the Maidan's triumph promised a fairer distribution of power on the peninsula. During World War II, Stalin had deported the entire Crimean Tatar population to Central Asia, and they were not allowed to return until the last years of the Soviet Union. Making up more than 12 percent of Crimea's population, the Tatars were an important political force on the peninsula because of their group unity and allegiance to the Ukrainian state. On the day I arrived in Simferopol, thousands of Crimean Tatars had taken to Lenin

Square to mark the ninety-sixth anniversary of the killing of their national hero, Noman Çelebicihan. Some of the demonstrators called for tearing down the Lenin statue, an enduring symbol of the Soviet regime that dotted town squares across southeastern Ukraine. After a Lenin statue in Kyiv was toppled during the Maidan, monuments to the Soviet Union's founder became a target for Ukrainians protesting against Russia's continuing influence over their country.

Meanwhile in Sevastopol, thousands of anti-Maidan protesters took to the streets to mark the Defender of the Fatherland Day, a Soviet-era holiday celebrating the Red Army. Waving Russian flags and holding up signs saying "Putin is our president," the crowd chose local businessman Alexei Chaly as the "people's mayor" and denounced the change of power in Kyiv as a Western-backed putsch. Their anger was fueled by a bill in the Rada, which voted to repeal a Yanukovych-era law granting regional status to the Russian language. Although Turchynov did not end up signing the bill into law, it stoked fears among many Russian speakers that the new authorities in Kyiv were determined to discriminate against them.

Putin was keeping a close eye on events from Sochi, where he attended the closing ceremony of the Winter Olympics. Hosting the Olympics in Russia was supposed to be Putin's greatest moment of glory. But rather than recognize his achievement, world leaders such as Barack Obama and Angela Merkel stayed away to protest Russian anti-LGBTQ legislation. Western media focused on the waste, graft, and environmental damage behind the Sochi games. The cover of one American magazine depicted a fur-capped bear on skis in a Russia hockey jersey, gnashing a cigar, shouldering a machine gun, and clutching a suitcase full of cash. Putin was reaching the conclusion that no matter what he did, the West would never accept him.

Late on the night of February 23, Putin received word that Yanukovych and his retinue had been brought to the safety of a Russian warship. The next morning at an International Olympic Committee breakfast, Putin openly recognized the gamble that Russia—and the rest of the world—had taken with the Sochi games. "He who doesn't risk doesn't drink champagne," Putin said. Few could have guessed the double meaning of his toast.

On my first day in Simferopol, I headed to the Crimean Tatar assembly, or Mejlis, located in a sky blue, two-story house. There I met Refat Chubarov, the soft-spoken, bearded intellectual who headed the Mejlis. Like many Crimean Tatars of his generation, he had been born in exile in Uzbekistan. Chubarov expressed hope that Yanukovych's clan would finally be ousted from Crimean politics. "There is no domestic reason for conflict," he said. "But there is the danger of an escalation if there's external interference from Russia."[22] Across town, Chubarov's local rival, Sergei Aksyonov, sat in his office hidden from the street behind a garage door and up a couple of flights of stairs. In a previous life Aksyonov had been known as a smalltime crook with the nickname "Goblin." Now he was the leader of Russian Unity, a pro-Russian party. Aksyonov answered my questions calmly, without any nationalistic bluster. Russian speakers were simply reacting to events in Kyiv, he said, and would defend themselves if attacked. "There's no question of breaking off, no question of a split," Aksyonov told me. "The Tatars fear a split from Ukraine. But we say: don't look for problems where they don't exist."

The local politician most active in the Russian takeover was not Aksyonov but Vladimir Konstantinov, the speaker of Crimea's provincial legislature. In the previous months he had repeatedly traveled to Russia to lay the groundwork for the annexation. On February 20, the day of the Maidan massacre, Konstantinov was in Moscow visiting Russian lawmakers. He warned that if there was a change of Ukraine's "legitimate government," Crimea would broach the issue of secession.[23] Days later that hypothetical scenario was suddenly in play. On February 25, Konstantinov called for the provincial legislature, or Supreme Council, to convene the next day.

Outside the boxy parliament building, several hundred people gathered for a demonstration organized by an unknown group called "Crimean Front." Many of the participants displayed the orange-and-black St. George's ribbon, a symbol of the Red Army's victory in World War II that had become a badge of Russian nationalism under Putin. "Sevastopol! Crimea! Russia!" the protesters shouted. Konstantinov came out of the building to calm down the crowd. "We will fight for the autonomy of our republic to the end. Fascism won't come to Crimea," Konstantinov said, as the crowd interrupted him with chants of "Re-fe-ren-dum! Re-fe-ren-dum!" and "Ross-i-ya! Ross-i-ya!" The demonstrators were just as confused about their demands as I was. "We know about American-style democracy. Just look at Libya or Yugoslavia," one man said. He added: "We want democracy, not anarchy. We want stability, just like you have in America."

Another man told me bluntly that Crimea should be "returned" to Russia. A third said that he did not care if Crimea stayed in Ukraine or went to Russia, as long as conflict was avoided.

That afternoon two visiting Russian lawmakers, Leonid Slutsky and Oleg Lebedev, met with the local Russian community in the yellow mansion that housed Rossotrudnichestvo, the Kremlin's outreach agency for "compatriots living abroad." Slutsky, a disciple of the Russian ultranationalist Vladimir Zhirinovsky, declared that Russia still considered Yanukovych to be Ukraine's president. He vowed that Moscow would take "corresponding, appropriate measures" if needed, while insisting that "we're for the territorial integrity of Ukraine." Well-fed and wearing a fancy suit, Slutsky pretended to listen to the concerns of the dowdy locals, who were mainly interested in financial assistance from Moscow. Slutsky's vague and noncommittal words left me feeling that he was bluffing about a Russian intervention.

Chubarov, the Crimean Tatar leader, was not taking any chances. He suspected that Konstantinov was planning to use the special legislative session to petition Putin for help.[24] Chubarov called on Tatars to demonstrate. Aksyonov, the pro-Russian politician, announced a counterdemonstration. On the morning of February 26, Tatars from around Crimea descended on Simferopol. They were joined by other Crimeans who supported Ukraine's unity. The light blue banners of the Mejlis flew alongside Ukrainian flags above the growing crowd. "My mom is Russian, my dad is Polish, and I'm here with the Tatars," a local artist told me. "Russia will keep up the pressure. Things won't calm down here so fast."

A spindly line of police stood in front of the Supreme Council. Behind them was a boisterous pro-Russian counterprotest. When the first scuffles broke out, Chubarov was inside the building trying to stop Konstantinov from pushing through a vote on Crimea splitting off from Ukraine and joining Russia. He appealed to the legislators not to make any rash moves and demanded negotiations on the formation of a new Crimean government before reconvening the legislature. Rustam Temirgaliyev, Crimea's first deputy prime minister and one of Konstantinov's co-conspirators, later spoke candidly about that day in the Supreme Council.[25] He conceded that Konstantinov planned to force the issue of secession by bundling a vote on sacking the provincial government with the question of Crimea joining Russia. Temirgaliyev also admitted that he and Aksyonov had paid "a lot of money" to organize the pro-Russian rally outside the parliament.

When it was clear that no quorum had been reached, Chubarov and Aksyonov waded into the crowd to tell their people to go home. The remnants of the street battle were strewn on the ground: broken flagstaffs, the sole of a shoe, somebody's hat. There were reports of two deaths in the crush outside the Supreme Council. But the Crimean Tatars and their Ukrainian allies had prevailed in stopping Konstantinov from initiating Crimea's secession. "I was sure that we had saved Crimea, saved ourselves, and saved Ukraine," Chubarov remembered.[26]

That evening Aksyonov went on Crimean television. He blamed outside provocateurs on both sides—including people he called "professional Russians"—for sowing panic. Aksyonov denied rumors that trains filled with Ukrainian nationalists were on their way to take revenge on Crimeans. He called for calm and expressed the belief that Crimeans of all ethnicities were capable of compromise. On February 26, Aksyonov was still a bit player in a grand scheme he was only beginning to fathom. Less than twenty-four hours later, he would be the head of the Kremlin's puppet government in Crimea.

When I woke up the next morning in the Hotel Ukraina, I read the latest headlines on my phone. I could not believe my eyes: shortly after 4 A.M. heavily armed men had broken into the Supreme Council, sent home the security guards, and raised the Russian flag over the building. Around the same time, the Cabinet of Ministers, Crimea's seat of government, was stormed and occupied. I jumped out of bed, pulled on some clothes, and ran outside. The Crimean legislature, just a block away, was cordoned off by police. Simferopol was quiet, but a sense of dread hung over the city. Police blocked the main street to traffic, and government offices and many shops closed for the day. When Anatoliy Mohylov, officially still Crimea's prime minister, tried to go to his office at the Cabinet of Ministers, he was told by the armed men occupying the building: "Sorry, you are dismissed."[27]

Chubarov called an emergency press conference. It was no coincidence that armored vehicles belonging to the Russian Black Sea Fleet had been spotted outside Simferopol that morning, he said. Supposedly they had run into technical problems after returning to Sevastopol from guard duty at an inland base. Across the peninsula, checkpoints were popping up that did not display Ukrainian state symbols, Chubarov said. He called on Tatars to remain calm and not give in to any "provocations."

Konstantinov reconvened parliament in a building occupied by armed men, which the SBU later identified as troops belonging to Russia's Forty-Fifth Special Forces Guards Regiment based outside Moscow. Konstantinov's main goal was to fire Mohylov and set the date for a referendum on Crimea's future status. The Kremlin's choice to head the secessionist government was Leonid Grach, a well-known Communist politician and the former speaker of the Crimean parliament.[28] But because Grach had little support among the assembled deputies, Konstantinov nominated Aksyonov as an alternative candidate for prime minister. According to the official tally, fifty-three of sixty-four deputies in the one-hundred-seat parliament voted for Aksyonov that day. How many lawmakers were actually present was unclear because no journalists or staff members were allowed into the session, and the deputies who did show up were required to surrender their phones.[29] Igor Girkin, the former FSB colonel who played a key role in the Russian surprise attack, later said he had helped round up lawmakers and herd them into the Supreme Council.[30]

Aksyonov, the leader of a fringe party with only three seats in the Crimean legislature, was suddenly the region's prime minister. His election was problematic not only because the voting took place in a hall filled with gunmen without any witnesses; Aksyonov's nomination as prime minister also had to be approved by the Ukrainian president. Here Viktor Yanukovych's role as "president-in-exile" became useful to the Kremlin for the first time—he sent a fax from Russia signing off on Aksyonov's candidacy.[31]

If there was a foreign-backed coup d'état in Ukraine in February 2014, it took place in Crimea, not Kyiv. On February 27, following the armed takeover of the Crimean parliament by Russian troops, Kremlin proxies installed a puppet leader in a sham procedure. In Kyiv, on the other hand, opposition politicians were left scrambling after the unexpected collapse of the Yanukovych regime. Although the Rada acted quickly and appointed Turchynov acting president, the politicians in Kyiv were still haggling over cabinet posts when the Russian occupation of Crimea began. "Putin used the period between Yanukovych's flight and the formation of a new government," Andriy Senchenko, a political ally of Turchynov and native of Crimea, later recalled.[32] "There were no levers of power."

Turchynov ordered Interior Ministry troops based in Simferopol to free the occupied government buildings.[33] But the troops were unwilling to confront pro-Russian demonstrators surrounding the buildings and ill-equipped to attack the well-armed gunmen inside. Putin's special military operation had come as a complete surprise. Pro-Russian activists had been fomenting unrest across southeastern Ukraine, and with the security forces in disarray, Turchynov had received no intelligence reports on Russia's creeping takeover of Crimea. "Before February 27, Crimea was no different for me than Kharkiv, Donetsk, or Odesa," Turchynov remembered later.[34] He called for the coalition talks to end immediately and appointed a cabinet. Turchynov gave the new heads of Ukraine's military and law enforcement agencies until the next day to draw up plans on how to stave off Russia's aggression.

When Simferopol awoke the following day, there was a new surprise: soldiers without insignia had occupied the airport and were fanning out across the peninsula. The Russian flag was flying over the occupied Supreme Council for a second day. An art student had set up his easel and was painting the scene. I asked him if he would put the Ukrainian flag on the parliament building. "Don't ask me provocative questions," he replied. An older man standing nearby said: "Of course it will be the Ukrainian flag." The young artist concurred.

I set out to find the Russian army with a local driver. Only half a year earlier he had chauffeured Bill and Hillary Clinton during an annual international conference in Yalta sponsored by a Ukrainian oligarch. The strangest part of that job was keeping a case of Diet Coke in the trunk to keep Bill Clinton caffeinated. But stranger yet was to look for Russian soldiers with an American journalist. It did not take us long to find them.

On the outskirts of Simferopol, we spotted five olive drab Kamaz trucks with black Russian military plates trundling by. Outside Bakhchysarai, the historical capital of the Crimean Tatars, we encountered eight armored personnel carriers—two with the Russian tricolor painted on their ventilation pipes—and passed a checkpoint flying the Russian flag. Outside Belbek, Ukraine's main air base in Crimea, twenty ragtag militiamen guarded a makeshift barrier made out of pipes. One hundred yards down the road stood a giant Ural army truck and a dozen well-armed soldiers. Andrei Sitnikov, the head militiaman, told me the soldiers had not responded when he called out to them. His ignorance was a charade. We both knew we were looking at soldiers from the Russian army.

Ambiguity over the identity of the disciplined, heavily armed soldiers was key to Russia's lightning occupation of Crimea. The soldiers wore no insignia on their Russian-style uniforms and did not answer questions. Local militiamen from a hastily assembled "self-defense" force served as a screen for elite Russian troops. Rustam Temirgaliyev, one of the leading pro-Russian politicians in Crimea, later admitted to misleading journalists by saying that members of the "Crimean self-defense" had taken over the parliament building.[35] In fact, Temirgaliyev said, the self-defense forces on the peninsula numbered no more than five hundred people. To further cloud the picture, the Russian military flew in a plane-load of veterans from the Afghan and Chechen wars, "patriotic" athletes, and bikers to create the illusion that ordinary Crimeans were rising up to protect themselves from bloodthirsty Ukrainian nationalists from the mainland.[36]

Reporters on the ground could see that the Russian army was overrunning Crimea. But because of the Kremlin's strenuous denials, faraway editors added disclaimers that cast doubt on their correspondents' reporting. People started referring to the silent invaders as "little green men." Some Russian media euphemistically called them "polite people." I asked my driver what he thought about them. He had grown up in a Soviet military family and been in the first cohort of army conscripts that pledged allegiance to independent Ukraine. At first my driver said that he did not care because the Russian soldiers were not aggressive and maintained order. But as the reality sank in that they were not going to leave, he said no, the clandestine takeover of Crimea was not okay.

On February 28, Turchynov convened the National Security and Defense Council, now staffed with his new cabinet, to discuss what options Ukraine had to stop the Russians.[37] Turchynov was inclined to declare martial law and actively resist the covert invasion. But what he heard from his colleagues was sobering, if not alarming.

Arseniy Yatsenyuk, the new prime minister, argued that Ukraine lacked the resources to fight back—and that the Kremlin would use any Ukrainian military action as a pretext to intervene further. Yulia Tymoshenko, a close Turchynov ally, recalled how the Georgian president Mikheil Saakashvili had sparked a war with Russia after attempting to retake a breakaway region in 2008. "We don't have the right to repeat his mistakes,"

Tymoshenko said. "So I'm calling on each and every one of you to think seven times before taking a single step. If we had even a one in a hundred chance of beating Putin, I'd be the first to support active measures." Valentyn Nalyvaichenko, the head of the SBU, said that the Americans and Germans were asking Ukraine to refrain from any action that could trigger a full-scale Russian invasion.

Russia had arrayed a huge army along the border with Ukraine, the defense minister Ihor Tenyukh reported. "Their goal is not just a demonstration of strength but a real preparation to invade our territory," he said. "I'll speak frankly: today we don't have an army. It was systematically destroyed by Yanukovych and his entourage under the direction of the Russian security services." There were soldiers who had never shot a gun in their lives, the defense minister said, and the entire country could muster only five thousand combat-ready service members. If the Russians entered Chernihiv region in the morning, they would be in the capital by evening, Tenyukh warned.

"The biggest threat wasn't Crimea anymore, it was Kyiv," Turchynov said later, recalling the meeting.[38] He ordered a mobilization but was told by his military leaders that they had no record of draftees because of the neglect and corruption of the old regime. The military needed a month to salvage Ukraine's conscription system, and Turchynov made it a priority to win time for his army. The soldiers based in Crimea, surrounded and cut off from mainland Ukraine, were told to sit tight.

The meeting was interrupted by a call from Sergei Naryshkin, who at the time was the speaker of the Russian Duma. When Turchynov returned to his colleagues, he said that Naryshkin had passed on a message from Putin that if a single Russian died, the Ukrainian leadership would be declared war criminals and tracked down. "I replied that having started the aggression toward Ukraine, they were already war criminals and would answer before an international tribunal," Turchynov said.

Finally, when the National Security and Defense Council voted on Turchynov's proposal to declare martial law, he cast the only vote in favor. In retrospect, Turchynov acknowledged that martial law would not have solved the Crimean conundrum but would have limited the rights and liberties of Ukraine's citizens.[39] Crucially, the early presidential election scheduled for May 25 would have been suspended, bolstering the Kremlin narrative that a "junta" had seized power in Kyiv.

For Turchynov, the alarming news kept coming. He learned that the Russian embassy in Kyiv was urgently evacuating its staff, another sign that an invasion was imminent.[40] Late in the evening Turchynov was informed that the Russian general staff had given Ukrainian troops in Crimea until midnight to lay down their arms. When he attempted to call Putin, Turchynov was told that he was not Ukraine's legitimate president, so he ended up speaking again with Naryshkin, his equal as parliamentary speaker. In Turchynov's rendering, he warned Naryshkin that the Ukrainian units in Crimea would fight back if attacked—and that Russia's unprovoked aggression would then become obvious to the whole world. His gambit gave the Russians pause, Turchynov later said, delaying their original plan to complete the takeover of Crimea by March 1 before making a thrust to Kyiv to reinstall Yanukovych as Ukraine's "legitimate president."

On February 28, Yanukovych resurfaced at a press conference in the southern Russian city of Rostov-on-Don, sixty miles from the Ukrainian border. He tried his best to look presidential as he stood before four Ukrainian flags. "I wasn't just deceived, but cynically deceived," Yanukovych said. The West was to blame for the seizure of power by nationalist, fascist raiders. He had not run away. He was not afraid. He was just visiting an old friend in Rostov. Developments in Crimea were a "natural reaction" to events in Kyiv, Yanukovych said, although Ukraine should remain "whole and indivisible." Asked if he planned to seek help from the Russian army, Yanukovych replied that he considered any military actions "unacceptable" and would make no such request. "I believe that Russia should and must act. And knowing Vladimir Putin's character, I'm surprised that he's so restrained and quiet," Yanukovych said. "I haven't had a meeting with Putin. But as soon as it takes place, I'll understand his position."

Yanukovych cut a pathetic figure. Even as he insisted that he was still Ukraine's president, the Kremlin kept Yanukovych at arm's length. While he wondered aloud when Putin would find time for him, the Russian president was busy discussing Ukraine with leaders who mattered to him: Angela Merkel, the British prime minister David Cameron, and the European Council president Herman Van Rompuy. For the Kremlin, Yanukovych had only one more use: to sign off on the full-scale invasion of his own country.

On the morning of March 1, Sergei Aksyonov, the Kremlin's puppet leader of Crimea, appealed to Russia to help restore the "constitutional order" on the peninsula. Like clockwork, Putin then asked the Federation Council, Russia's upper house of parliament, to grant him permission to deploy troops to Ukraine to protect Russian citizens and ethnic Russians there "until the normalization of the social and political situation in that country."[41] The unanimous support of the Kremlin's rubberstamp parliament was a foregone conclusion. Yet by initiating the vote, Putin could give his actions an appearance of legality while piling the pressure on Kyiv. As Russian troops were already intervening in Crimea, the Federation Council's authorization raised the specter of an even wider military operation against the rest of Ukraine. As with Yanukovych's clandestine evacuation, Putin was making decisions in a tiny circle of advisers. Just days earlier, after a meeting of Russia's Security Council, Valentina Matviyenko, the head of the Federation Council, had ruled out that the Russian army would intervene in Ukraine. And at his press conference in Rostov, Yanukovych had declared that he would not ask for Russian military assistance. But now, as the Federation Council approved Putin's request, an influential lawmaker informed the chamber that Yanukovych had written a letter to Putin supporting Crimea's appeal for help.[42]

The Kremlin's disinformation campaign went into high gear. The Russian Foreign Ministry released a statement claiming that overnight "unknown armed people" sent by Kyiv had attempted to take over the Crimean Interior Ministry in Simferopol. Crimean "self-defense" forces had warded off the "treacherous provocation," the Russian ministry said, but not without casualties. I headed to the Crimean Interior Ministry to find out more. Across the street, a group of paunchy Crimean self-defense militiamen milled around a military field kitchen. They denied that there had been a nighttime attack on the building, as did four policemen I asked. When I said that I was going on information from the Russian Foreign Ministry, one policeman said: "If they say so, then that's how it was." Lies issued from Moscow were determining the reality in Crimea.

Putin's little green men had increased their presence in Simferopol and were patrolling the city center. As news of Aksyonov's appeal to Putin spread, a small crowd gathered in front of the Council of Ministers. One woman held up a pro-Russian sign, and babushkas thanked the silent gunmen. A noisy argument ensued when a man criticized the ongoing Russian occupation and voiced support for the provisional government in Kyiv.

It was hard to know what most Crimeans were thinking beyond that nobody wanted to go back to Yanukovych's rule. "If he returned, we'd take our money back and send him into retirement," a middle-aged Crimean militiaman told me. "He's a political corpse." Outside my hotel, I met a local entrepreneur, Oleg, out for a stroll with his wife, Anna. The couple had never supported Yanukovych but were also against the new authorities in Kyiv. Oleg blamed Viktor Yushchenko, the leader of the Orange Revolution, for splitting Ukraine over who should be considered heroes in World War II: the nationalists who had fought for independence or the Ukrainians who had served in the Red Army. Oleg's allegiance was clear. "Putin is great," he said. "He's our lifesaver."

Late that night, Obama called Putin in a futile attempt to win over the Russian leader with reason. It was a ninety-minute conversation between a lawyer and a gambler. The U.S. president brought up the treaties and charters that Russia's actions were violating and warned of the possible consequences, including the boycott of the upcoming G8 summit in Sochi. Putin responded that Russia had the right to defend ethnic Russians in Ukraine. Obama offered to help mediate any issues with Kyiv in the framework of international organizations. The U.S. administration would provide the Kremlin with more exit ramps in the coming months, but Putin was not lost. The takeover of Crimea was practically complete.

I lived in Russia for eight years before the annexation of Crimea. Not once did I hear anybody say that they missed Crimea or wanted it "back." Of course that did not mean that Russians, given the opportunity, would oppose the "return" of a region that played an outsized role in the Russian imagination. Russians flocked to Crimea in droves every summer. And the "loss" of Crimea loomed large in Russian pop culture. In the 2000 Russian crime classic *Brat 2* (Brother 2), one of the main characters shoots a Ukrainian mafioso in Chicago with the words: "You bastards will still answer for Sevastopol!"

In 1954, the Soviet leader Nikita Khrushchev transferred the peninsula from Russia to Ukraine in a move that made sense from an administrative point of view because Crimea was dependent on water and electricity from the Ukrainian mainland. The emotional consequence of that change only became clear more than three decades later, when the Soviet Union began cracking apart. Mikhail Gorbachev, the last Soviet leader, and Boris Yeltsin, Russia's first president, were bitter rivals. Yet they both threatened Ukrainians with territorial disputes over Crimea and other Russian-speaking parts of their republic if they chose independence.[43]

Conflict was avoided then because Russia was weak and Ukrainians were overwhelmingly for independence. In a referendum held on December 1, 1991, more than 90 percent of voters in Ukraine supported independence; in the Donetsk region almost 77 percent were in favor, and even in Crimea 54 percent backed the measure. That the referendum won a majority in every Ukrainian region demonstrated just how deep the disillusionment with the Soviet Union was. Given Ukraine's developed agriculture and industry, going it alone seemed to hold much more promise.[44]

The main bone of contention between Ukraine and Russia was the fate of the Soviet Black Sea Fleet based in Sevastopol. A 1997 treaty ended the dispute, with most of the fleet going to Russia, which was allowed to continue using the base in Sevastopol for the next twenty years. Another troublesome legacy of the common Soviet past was that Ukraine ended up with a huge nuclear arsenal. Under pressure from the West, Ukraine voluntarily gave up its Soviet-era nuclear weapons in exchange for security assurances enshrined in the 1994 Budapest Memorandum. Following Ukraine's independence, there were occasional calls by Russian lawmakers to lay claim to Crimea, but they were ignored by the Kremlin because they did not meet Russia's interests or capabilities at the time. Crying over Crimea became a pastime for second-tier politicians such as Moscow Mayor Yury Luzhkov or the nationalist firebrand Vladimir Zhirinovsky. Twenty years after the fall of the Soviet Union, most Russians appeared to have moved on. And for those who sorely missed Crimea, the peninsula was easily accessible and did not even require a passport to visit.

To be sure, enthusiasm for independent Ukraine was not particularly high in Crimea, and in the early 1990s there was a constant tug-of-war between Crimeans seeking greater autonomy and the central government in Kyiv. Almost a year before the referendum on Ukrainian independence, Crimeans voted overwhelmingly to restore the peninsula's status as an "autonomous republic," which it had lost after World War II. In 1992, Crimea adopted a constitution that established the territory as a sovereign state with its own president. A local politician, Yury Meshkov, promised to integrate Crimea into Russia and was elected president by a landslide in 1994. But when Meshkov clashed with the Crimean legislature, Kyiv stepped in, scrapping the region's constitution and exiling Meshkov to Russia.[45]

For the next two decades Crimean separatism was neutralized. The central government in Kyiv largely left Crimea alone, which also meant that it often neglected the needs of the people living there. Although Crimeans who identified as Russian did not necessarily harbor strong feelings for Ukraine, there was no majority supporting union with Russia either. One poll taken in 2013 found that 23 percent of Crimeans believed "Crimea should be separated and given to Russia."[46] In another poll taken that year, 36 percent of Crimeans supported the statement that "Ukraine and Russia must unite into a single state."[47]

Without the active intervention of the Kremlin and its agents, Crimea would never have broken off from Ukraine and joined Russia. There was no burgeoning Crimean independence movement or separatist underground that finally found its voice after the fall of Yanukovych. Instead, a handful of local conspirators, with no endgame of their own, carried out a Kremlin-planned putsch. Had there been no secret Russian emissaries or little green men, nothing would have stopped Crimeans from forming a more representative regional government, reestablishing ties with the new authorities in Kyiv, and continuing life as a sleepy Ukrainian province.

Given the swiftness of the Russian takeover, the seizure of Crimea appeared to be the Kremlin's Plan B for the event that Yanukovych capitulated to the protesters on the Maidan. Putin had learned his lesson from the Orange Revolution, when he was unprepared for Yanukovych to lose. This time the Kremlin was ready.

In January 2014, the tour of Orthodox religious relics to Ukraine provided the perfect cover for a reconnaissance mission to Crimea by the monarchist businessman Konstantin Malofeyev and the former FSB colonel Igor Girkin. Although Malofeyev later downplayed his role, he met with the local politicians who would help deliver Crimea to Russia: Vladimir Konstantinov, Sergei Aksyonov, and Rustam Temirgaliyev.[48] After Malofeyev and Girkin returned to Moscow, the Kremlin received an analytical report calling the Yanukovych regime "totally bankrupt" and without any future. As a result, the report urged the Kremlin to support secessionist movements in southeastern Ukraine, with Crimea and the Kharkiv region taking the lead. The Russian newspaper *Novaya Gazeta* published the entire document in February 2015, attributing it to Malofeyev as a possible author.[49] The Kremlin and Malofeyev denied any connection to the report, but it was startling how many of its recommendations became reality, including the specific slogans pro-Russian protesters used. In Girkin's own words, he returned to Crimea two more times following the Gifts of the Magi tour.[50] He was already in Simferopol when the takeover of the Crimean parliament building took place, and soon afterward he became an adviser to Aksyonov.

The actions of Malofeyev and Girkin, as well as legions of Russian bikers, Cossacks, and other patriotic "volunteers," let the Kremlin hide behind a shield of credible plausibility as these actors held no official positions and operated outside any chain of command. It was not public knowledge that Putin's aide Vladislav Surkov had been charged with Ukraine, and his visits to the country were shrouded in secrecy. According to an apparent hack of his email account published in 2016, Surkov started collecting information on Crimea's electoral system shortly after the Euromaidan protests began. Surkov visited Crimea on February 14, 2014, ostensibly to discuss building a bridge across the Kerch Strait separating the peninsula from Russia.[51] It is likely that Surkov used the occasion to try to recruit the Crimean prime minister Anatoliy Mohylov for the Russian cause. "I don't know what they talked about," Mohylov's deputy, Rustam Temirgaliyev, remembered later.[52] "I can only say that Mohylov was agitated and upset, and judging by his words, Surkov was also not satisfied with the meeting."[53]

The Crimean politician that the Kremlin was counting on was Vladimir Konstantinov, the speaker of the Supreme Council and a real estate developer with mounting debts. In December 2013, Konstantinov traveled to Moscow, where he met with Nikolai Patrushev, the head of Russia's Security Council and one of Putin's closest advisers.[54] Konstantinov told Patrushev that if Yanukovych were overthrown, Crimea would be ready to break off and become part of Russia. In Konstantinov's own telling, that same month he began holding brainstorming sessions on the legal basis for "returning" Crimea to Russia.[55]

At the end of January 2014, Konstantinov met with Surkov in Moscow.[56] Days later, on February 4, Konstantinov initiated an appeal to Putin to protect the region's autonomy and started preparing a "survey" of Crimeans on what its status should be.[57] The more violent Yanukovych's crackdown on the Maidan became, the louder the calls for Crimea's secession grew. On February 18, more than thirty people were killed and hundreds injured in the unrest in Kyiv. The next day, the sixtieth anniversary of Crimea's transfer to Ukraine, a Crimean lawmaker named Nikolai Kolesnichenko warned Yanukovych that if he failed to restore order, Crimea would be forced to consider joining Russia.[58]

On February 20, the bloodiest day on the Maidan, Konstantinov found himself in Moscow again, meeting with Russian lawmakers. After Russian news agencies quoted him as saying that a change in government in Kyiv could lead to Crimea breaking off, Konstantinov backtracked. He called talk of secession "harmful" and "premature" and said that Crimea was doing everything to support the central government and Ukraine's unity.[59] By linking Ukraine's territorial integrity with the regime's survival, Konstantinov betrayed his knowledge of a Russian plan to seize Crimea the moment Yanukovych vanished from the scene.

My editor in New York ordered me back to Kyiv. The Ukrainian capital was in a cloud of shock and gloom. The triumph of the Maidan had come at a bitter human toll, and now Crimea was being torn from Ukraine in real time. I flew on to Berlin for a rest. At the Kyiv airport duty-free shop, I looked for Ukrainian vodka to bring back to my friends, but all the vodka on sale was Russian.

Before the annexation of Crimea, most Ukrainians looked favorably on their giant eastern neighbor. A poll taken in November 2013 found that 82 percent of Ukrainians felt "positive" about Russia.[60] The sense that Russia was a friendly neighbor contributed to the surprise of the invasion—and also explained why so many Crimeans were ready to join the Russian side. Sergei Aksyonov and his accomplices, local and Russian, immediately began urging the Ukrainian troops based in Crimea to give up without a fight. The retired FSB colonel Igor Girkin later remembered appealing to Ukrainian officers' nostalgia for the past glory of the Soviet military.[61] "The complete wretchedness of the Ukrainian armed forces was visible to the naked eye," he said.

Oleksandr Turchynov, the acting Ukrainian president, found that he had almost no loyal forces in Crimea. More than 70 percent of the Ukrainian troops stationed there—most of them locals—ended up going over to the Russians, according to Turchynov.[62] Worse yet, 90 percent of the Crimean SBU and 99 percent of the region's police force joined the occupiers. Looking back later, Turchynov defended himself against criticism that he should have taken more decisive action. "You're asking: 'Why didn't you give those people orders?'" he said. "Russia had already given them their orders." Turchynov argued that by slow-walking its inevitable expulsion from Crimea, the Ukrainian military stopped Russia from seizing the initiative in other parts of Ukraine.

The appearance of Russian troops in Crimea shocked the rest of the world as much as it did the Ukrainians. Western Europeans, content to abdicate their defense to the American hegemon, lived under the illusion that they had banished war from their continent through the promise of trade and prosperity. The United States, under Barack Obama, was downsizing its global ambitions after the overreach of the Bush administration. Europe was not a priority, and Russia was considered a yesterday power. Putin's brazenness in Crimea defied the imagination of Western leaders, and it took them days to wrap their heads around what was happening. In the meantime, Russian troops were creating a new geopolitical reality on the ground. According to the Obama administration's estimation, Russia was already in "complete operational control" of the peninsula within four days of seizing the Crimean government buildings.[63]

After largely disappearing from public view, Putin finally met with reporters at his residence outside Moscow on March 4. For an hour, Putin was all bluster and obfuscation, denying that Russian troops were in Crimea or that he was considering the annexation of the peninsula. Unannounced military drills on Russia's western border, he insisted, had nothing to do with the situation in Ukraine. Putin was running circles around the rest of the world, even if he had not made a final decision on what to do with Crimea now that Russia controlled it.

After originally setting May 25 for a referendum on Crimea's future status, the puppet government in Simferopol moved up the date twice: first to March 30, then March 16. Crimea's new rulers at first insisted their referendum would be about wider autonomy, not secession. Their vagueness about exactly what would be at stake in the vote reflected deliberations in the Kremlin over Crimea's fate: as an unrecognized statelet like Georgia's rebel regions of Abkhazia and South Ossetia, or as a new Russian region.[64] Rustam Temirgaliyev, one of the Crimean politicians who facilitated the Russian takeover, later said that preparations for the referendum were made with Oleg Belaventsev, the right-hand man of Russia's defense minister Sergei Shoigu.[65] Belaventsev, who held the rank of vice admiral, arrived in Crimea several days before the little green men. "Honestly, his role in the reunification of Crimea with Russia was really very big," Temirgaliyev said. After the annexation, Putin rewarded Belaventsev for his efforts by appointing him as the Kremlin's envoy to Crimea.

On March 6, when the date of the referendum was abruptly moved to March 16, the final wording of the question on the ballot was published: voters would be able to choose between "reunification" with Russia or a return to Crimea's 1992 constitution, which had established the region's sovereignty. Even the second option implied a break with Kyiv, and there was no third option of retaining the status quo. The vote was problematic for other reasons too. With less than two weeks to prepare, there was no time for even the semblance of a serious campaign. The presence of armed foreign troops further called into question the legitimacy of the vote. Most significantly, the ballot violated the Ukrainian Constitution, which required any territorial changes to be determined by nationwide referendum.

The results of the slapdash plebiscite were wholly predictable. According to official results, 97 percent of voters elected to join Russia, with a turnout of 83 percent. A few days after the vote, Temirgaliyev visited Vladimir Konstantinov, the turncoat speaker of the Crimean parliament, in his office. Putin's portrait now hung on the wall instead of Yanukovych's, and a Russian flag had replaced the Ukrainian one. According to Temirgaliyev, the two men broke into a fit of hysterical laughter.[66]

The Kremlin and its allies would later say that Russia's annexation of Crimea was an act of self-determination as guaranteed by the United Nations Charter. But the vote was so flawed from the outset that international organizations, including the Russian-dominated Commonwealth of Independent States, refused to send election monitors to Crimea. After the referendum, Obama told Putin that the United States would "never" recognize its results, and a UN resolution declared the vote invalid.[67]

The last opinion poll taken before the Russian occupation, in February 2014, showed that 41 percent of Crimeans supported union with Russia.[68] Crimea's unhappiness with Kyiv was real. Most Crimeans were fed up with the rapacious rule of Yanukovych's boyars, and they did not trust Turchynov's provisional government to treat them better. Russian state television, which was a major news source in Crimea, railed against the "fascist junta" that had come to power in Kyiv. In the confusion that ensued after the Russian intervention, many Crimeans began to view Russia as a savior, although hardly in the numbers propagated by the Kremlin. In a report published a month after the referendum, a member of Putin's human rights council wrote that most Crimeans believed the true results of the vote to be 50 to 60 percent in favor of joining Russia, with a turnout of between 30 and 50 percent.[69] Moreover, the council member said, most Crimeans had voted less for becoming part of Russia than for ending the corruption of Yanukovych's "Donetsk henchmen."

Two days after the sham referendum, Crimea and Sevastopol, a legal entity of its own, were absorbed into Russia in a pompous Kremlin ceremony. Addressing Russian lawmakers in the cavernous St. George's Hall, Putin delivered a blistering defense of Crimea's annexation.[70] In Putin's version of events, the "return" of Crimea to Russia was the righting of an "outrageous historical injustice," because Russians as an ethnic group had suffered the most not just from Soviet repressions but also from the collapse of the Soviet Union. "It was only when Crimea ended up as part of a different country that Russia realized that it was not simply robbed, it was plundered," he said. There had been repeated attempts by Ukrainian politicians to deprive ethnic Russians of their rights, Putin fumed, and now Ukraine was being run by the "ideological heirs" of Stepan Bandera, the Ukrainian nationalist who had briefly collaborated with the Nazis in his struggle against the Red Army.

Putin did not appeal just to Russians, however. He asked Americans to understand Crimeans' desire for "freedom," and told Germans that Russia's annexation of Crimea was not unlike Germany's reunification in 1990. Putin even addressed Ukrainians, claiming that Russia had "always" respected Ukraine's territorial integrity and that the loss of Crimea was entirely the fault of Ukrainian nationalists. "I want you to hear me, my dear friends," Putin said. "Do not believe those who want you to fear Russia, shouting that other regions will follow Crimea. We do not want to divide Ukraine; we do not need that."

Putin's speech was full of menace and contradiction. Even as he seemed to say that Crimea was an exception, Putin pledged to defend ethnic Russians living in Ukraine. Ukrainians and Russians were "one people," he said, implying that the assertion of Ukrainian identity was an affront to that unity. At the same time, Putin coveted the cultural legacy of the medieval Kyivan Rus state, which predated Moscow by centuries. "Kyiv is the mother of Russian cities," he said. "Ancient Rus is our common source, and we cannot live without each other." Coming from Putin's lips, the words did not exactly sound like a declaration of fraternal love. His obsessive claim on Ukraine would now define the course of his regime. Those Russians who opposed it, Putin said, were "national traitors."

Before Putin could read the last lines of his speech, he was met with a standing ovation. Russian officials, who normally scowled, smiled broadly. The three Crimean figureheads of the Russian annexation—Sergei Aksyonov, Vladimir Konstantinov, and Alexei Chaly, the "people's mayor" of Sevastopol—had front row seats. A month earlier, they had been almost complete nobodies. Now they were signing agreements transferring Crimea to Russia. A trumpet fanfare, a Kremlin honor guard, and the majestic hall lent the ceremony an aura of historic gravitas. After the signing ceremony, Chaly punched the air as Putin, stone-faced, joined hands with his three beaming Crimean puppets.

The speed with which Russia seized Crimea was a humiliation for Ukraine, and many Ukrainians later blamed Turchynov for not having nipped the Russian invasion in the bud. In reality, there was little that he could have done. Turchynov's main problem was that there were very few forces he could count on. Following the Maidan, Ukraine's law enforcement officers were demoralized and reluctant to take orders from the provisional government. While many state security officers preferred to lie low, others actively collaborated with the Russians. "At the start, we didn't know whom we could count on and who was working for the enemy," Andriy Parubiy, Turchynov's security adviser, recalled.[71] "Most of the time we were being sabotaged."

Ukraine's military had been long neglected and was unprepared to fight. As the little green men fanned out across Crimea, they besieged Ukrainian military bases and cut their lines of communication. Speaking to commanders by Skype, Turchynov had only one message: hold out as long as possible. Defending Crimea was not an option as Russia massed its army along the border with mainland Ukraine, and the few forces available to Turchynov were needed to protect Kyiv. Parubiy remembered "constant psychological attacks": Russian helicopters would fly up to Ukrainian air space, hover for two minutes, then dart away; tank columns would approach the border, idle their engines for five minutes, then turn around. "We understood that an attack could come at any minute," he said.

Stealth and deception were key to the success of the Russian seizure of Crimea. The Russian Orthodox Church, which had long wielded control over the Ukrainian Orthodox Church, played its small part. While the Gifts of the Magi tour was a genuine religious event, it also provided an opportunity for its monarchist sponsor to gather intelligence in Crimea. When the occupation began, Orthodox priests on the peninsula provided refuge and support to the invaders.[72] The Russian Orthodox Church was only nominally independent from the Kremlin, as were other nongovernmental groups that participated in the invasion such as Cossacks and bikers. Four years before the annexation, Putin had famously ridden a Harley-Davidson trike at a "patriotic bike show" in Crimea organized by the Night Wolves, Russia's first motorcycle club. When the time came to reclaim the peninsula, the Night Wolves returned as hybrid warriors. Their most celebrated exploit was abducting a Ukrainian general who had come to meet with besieged Ukrainian border troops.

The audacity of the Russian intervention took the world by surprise. The 1994 Budapest Memorandum extended security assurances to Ukraine in exchange for the country giving up its nuclear weapons. But the document was vague on what the three signatories—Russia, the United States, and Britain—would do if Ukraine became the target of armed aggression. "The guarantor countries were fixed on paper, but all that we received was sympathy and field rations. That was it!" Turchynov said later.[73] Unfortunately for Ukraine, its security guarantees had been lost in translation. In the Ukrainian version of the Budapest Memorandum, the wording "security guarantees" was used, whereas in the English version, State Department lawyers had insisted on "security assurances"—exactly to avoid any unforeseen future entanglements.

When Russia, as a signatory, broke its promise to "refrain from the threat or use of force against the territorial integrity or political independence of Ukraine," the West was at a loss. The United States and the European Union imposed targeted sanctions on top figures in the Putin regime, and the G8 suspended Russia's membership in the organization. But Western leaders were loath to arm Ukraine for fear of provoking the Kremlin. It was a bitter irony for Ukraine: not only had the country's voluntary surrender of its nuclear weapons made it vulnerable to attack, but Russia was now using its monopoly on the Soviet nuclear arsenal to intimidate the West.

For Putin, the annexation of Crimea was a moment of glory and comeuppance. The 2008 invasion of Georgia had been a warning shot, but the country did not hold the same significance to the Kremlin as Ukraine. Ukraine was Putin's line in the sand. The Kremlin saw itself in a struggle with the West for control of Ukraine, which began as the Orange Revolution and continued as the Euromaidan. From Putin's point of view, it was impermissible to let a new pro-Western government in Kyiv take Ukraine out of Russia's orbit.

In his March 18 Kremlin speech, Putin referred to Crimea's geopolitical importance only toward the end, saying Russians would never have tolerated the peninsula, the historical home of the Russian Black Sea Fleet, becoming part of NATO. But the seizure of Crimea was much more than a preemptive strike to forestall Ukraine's NATO membership, which after George W. Bush's departure from the White House had found few advocates in the West. As Putin made clear in his speech, seizing Crimea was also a way of seeking recompense from the West after Russia lost its superpower status and had to watch the United States become the world's hegemon. The annexation of Crimea was one way for Russia to begin restoring the balance. That is why Putin evoked a mishmash of precedents, from German reunification to Kosovo's declaration of independence.

Putin spent a good part of his speech justifying Crimea's annexation with the misdeeds of the United States and its allies. "They have come to believe in their exclusivity and exceptionalism, that they can decide the fate of the world, that only they can ever be right," Putin said. "They act as they please. Here and there, they use force against sovereign states, building coalitions based on the principle: 'If you are not with us, you are against us.'" That Putin was quoting Bush, his role model and nemesis, was no coincidence. His seizure of Crimea exhibited the same brashness as Bush's invasion of Iraq.

The incorporation of Crimea into Russia was strictly legal, Putin insisted, whereas the United States had repeatedly flaunted international law to achieve its diabolical, short-sighted goals in places such as Yugoslavia, Afghanistan, Iraq, and Libya. The specifics of each case were unimportant. What mattered was the accumulated injury over so many years. "They have lied to us many times, made decisions behind our backs, placed us before a fait accompli," Putin spat. "They are constantly trying to drive us into a corner for having an independent position, defending it, and calling things by their names and not engaging in hypocrisy. But there is a limit to everything. And with Ukraine, our Western partners have crossed the line."

Putin was clearly enjoying the moment. The West, despite its fantastic military might, was powerless to stop Russia. In Ukraine, like in Georgia in 2008, the Kremlin was operating in familiar territory with virtual impunity. Putin later recalled his many phone calls with Western leaders: "I talked to my colleagues and told them openly, as I'm telling you now: This is our historical territory where Russians live. They're in danger, and we can't abandon them. We weren't the ones who carried out a coup d'état. Nationalists and extremists did that, and you supported them. Where are you located? Thousands of kilometers away? We're here, and this is our land. What do you want to fight for over there? You don't know? We know. And we're ready."[74]

As a military operation, the seizure of Crimea was a blinding success. The peninsula was occupied in a matter of days with practically no bloodshed. But the ease of the Crimean operation was not indicative of the rest of Ukraine. Most Ukrainians did not consider themselves to be Russian, and they would fight back.

6

Zombie Revolution

On the day the sky fell, Maria Butenko was tending to her flowers and vegetables. "When I heard the explosion, I lay down in my garden. When the noise stopped, I got back up," she said. The field near her house was ablaze with the remains of a passenger jet carrying 298 people. A surface-to-air missile had brought down Malaysia Airlines flight MH17 six miles over Butenko's home in eastern Ukraine. The Boeing 777, en route from Amsterdam to Kuala Lumpur, cracked apart in midair, with the main body crashing outside the hamlet of Hrabove and the cockpit landing several miles away. Passengers and crew members, together with their belongings and pieces of the plane, rained down on the undulating farmland below, the latest victims of a Russian-backed insurgency that had started three months earlier. By a miracle, nobody on the ground was harmed.

I met Butenko five days after the catastrophe on July 17, 2014. Dozens of villagers, mostly elderly women in headscarves, had gathered at the white wooden cross, etched with the words "Save and Protect," that stood at the entrance to Hrabove. They held flowers, candles, and well-thumbed psalm books as a bearded Orthodox priest in flowing black robes led the memorial service. The smell of incense wafted through the summer air. "There is only one God. We should pray to Him to resolve this conflict," said Butenko, age seventy-three, wearing a light green housedress and a yellow headscarf. "Our only weapon is the cross in our church." Butenko's neighbor Anna, a tiny babushka with thick glasses, said she had stopped counting her years upon reaching eighty. The only calamity comparable to the fighting between pro-Russian insurgents and Ukrainian government forces was World War II, when Anna and her family fled the Nazi invaders to Russia. "It's our biggest misfortune," she said about the crash. "Not just for a day but the rest of our days. Our whole church is praying."

Across the country road that led into Hrabove lay the scorched earth of the plane crash. Red-and-white tape tied to sticks partially marked the perimeter of the disaster site. Two armed rebels roamed in the distance but did not stop me from walking onto the field. Thousands of pieces of metal littered the charred ground. There were remnants of landing gear, an airplane seat, and hardened pools of melted aluminum. I saw a men's toiletry bag and a galley coffee machine. The bodies had been recovered, but an acrid smell and the buzz of flies indicated that human remains were still trapped under the wreckage.

The MH17 crime scene was now thoroughly contaminated. There were reports that valuables had been looted from the victims and their luggage. Somebody had propped up a crumpled sheet of fuselage with a row of windows against a wooden post. An empty pack of cigarettes with a Ukrainian warning label lay next to a burned running shoe. Villagers had brought stuffed animals, flowers, and votive candles to the site to honor the victims.

What complicated an orderly recovery was that the Ukrainian government was no longer in control of large swaths of the Donetsk region. Four months earlier ragtag bands of armed insurgents had started storming government buildings and declaring their independence from the new government in Kyiv. A month before the downing of MH17, the rebels began picking off Ukrainian military transport planes with surface-to-air missiles. In the space of a few short months, a peaceful, forgotten corner of eastern Europe had been turned into a war zone. An insurgency that many locals had hoped would end like Crimea's annexation was spiraling out of control.

On March 1 pro-Russian protests broke out simultaneously in a dozen cities located in a crescent stretching from Kharkiv in the northeast to Odesa in the south. That same day Russia's Federation Council granted Vladimir Putin permission to use force on behalf of ethnic Russians in Ukraine. Two days earlier armed men had seized Crimea's parliament and installed a

Russian puppet government. In that context, the wave of rallies appeared to be part of a larger plan to foment a secessionist uprising across Russian-speaking, southeastern Ukraine. There were reports that Russian "tourists" had been bussed in from across the border to help storm the regional administrations in Kharkiv and Donetsk and raise the Russian flag. Ukrainian prosecutors later published the recordings of intercepted phone calls made by Sergei Glazyev, a Putin adviser who half a year earlier had threatened Ukraine with dismemberment if it chose to align itself with the European Union.[1] In one call, Konstantin Zatulin, a nationalist Russian lawmaker, asked Glazyev to fund protests in Kharkiv and Odesa. In a later call, Glazyev instructed pro-Russian activists in Odesa to follow the examples of Kharkiv and Donetsk by taking over the regional administration, rounding up regional lawmakers, and forcing them to appeal to Putin for help. Those who resisted were to be branded traitors, fascists, and "Banderites," disciples of the Ukrainian nationalist hero Stepan Bandera. The leader of the Donetsk uprising, Pavel Gubarev, later wrote in his memoirs that he began thinking of seizing power after a phone call from Glazyev.

It was unclear whether Glazyev was acting on his own or carrying out orders. But either way, the hawks in the Kremlin felt empowered by Russia's lightning occupation of Crimea. The provisional government in Kyiv scrambled to prevent the same thing from happening in eastern Ukraine. The authorities arrested pro-Russian activist Gubarev—who had already proclaimed himself Donetsk's "people's governor"—as well as separatist leaders in Luhansk and Odesa. Rallies and counterrallies continued. In Donetsk, a pro-Ukrainian activist was stabbed to death after a demonstration for the country's unity.

I returned to Kyiv on March 18, the day Putin formally annexed Crimea in a grand Kremlin ceremony. As I checked into the Kozatskiy Hotel, the TV in the lobby was showing a speech to Ukraine's Russian speakers by the new Ukrainian prime minister, Arseniy Yatsenyuk. Speaking Russian, Yatsenyuk said Moscow was behind attempts to create an artificial conflict and provoke a military confrontation. "Nobody is attacking your right to freely use the Russian language," he said. "My wife Tereziya primarily speaks Russian. And she, like millions of other Russian speakers, doesn't need the Kremlin's protection." Yatsenyuk sought to address eastern Ukrainians' concerns directly: decentralization was one of his government's goals; the signing of the economic part of the EU association agreement would be postponed because of hesitancy in the industrial east; and the divisive question of NATO membership was not on the agenda for the sake of national unity.

Yatsenyuk's speech was a much-needed political declaration to the former supporters of Viktor Yanukovych, a solid third of Ukraine's electorate. But coming almost a month after Yanukovych's flight from Kyiv, the new government's outreach to Russian-speaking Ukrainians was too little, too late. The winners of the Maidan had unnerved many Russian speakers with a bill downgrading the status of the Russian language. In the immediate aftermath of the Maidan, none of Ukraine's new rulers had the largesse to take the concerns and fears of millions of their fellow citizens seriously. That vacuum in leadership created fertile ground for the distortions, caricatures, and lies beamed in by the Kremlin's TV channels.

I reached Donetsk a few days later. Compared to my first visit nine years earlier, the city was almost unrecognizable. Donetsk was still ringed by factories, coal mines, and mountains of mining waste. But after Donetsk was chosen as a venue in the 2012 European soccer championships, cohosted by Ukraine and Poland, the city of one million underwent a serious facelift. Under the patronage of Yanukovych and his powerful local ally, the oligarch Rinat Akhmetov, the city got a state-of-the-art stadium, a shimmering new airport terminal, and international hotels. There was a leafy pedestrian street in the city center, a cutting-edge contemporary art center in an abandoned factory, and a microbrewery named after the city's Welsh founder, John Hughes. Germany and the Czech Republic ran consulates in Donetsk, and Poland was about to open one. "Donetsk is calm, provincial, quite charming," I wrote in my diary. The only thing out of the ordinary were the rallies calling for union with Russia.

On a bright Sunday afternoon in late March, several thousand pro-Russian demonstrators gathered on Lenin Square under the dark, imposing statue of the founder of the Soviet Union. In the McDonald's across the street, teenagers looked up from their burgers as the malcontents with Russian flags started marching to the regional government building. "Ross-i-ya! Ross-i-ya!" they shouted. "Re-fe-ren-dum! Re-fe-ren-dum!" Their chants echoed those of the protesters I had met a month earlier in Crimea.

As I made my way to the front of the procession, I passed a billboard for a local beauty salon with a red hammer and sickle spray-painted on it. The marchers were the losers of Ukrainian independence: the people who had failed to adapt after the country's chaotic transition from Communism. It was a lumpen protest—the most active participants were aggressive young men whose faces were marked by poverty. Some had missing teeth, others were visibly drunk. A group of riot policemen guarded the boxy, eleven-story regional government building. They had propped their metal shields on the ground in front of them and pushed up the visors on their helmets. Demoralized after the Maidan and hostile to the new government in Kyiv, the police were doing their job with the utmost reluctance.

The protesters had never heard of the publications I was writing for, but they were convinced that I was an enemy combatant in an undeclared "information war." In all the conflicts I had covered, I had never encountered such hostility from a group that was supposedly facing persecution. The protesters I spoke with could not articulate their motivation beyond a few catchwords from Russian state television: the provisional government in Kyiv was an "illegitimate fascist junta," and the Donetsk region needed a "referendum"—on what, exactly, nobody could say. "Here's what the people think!" a young woman shouted in my face. "We don't need Europe. Fuck you, European Union! Got it? We want Russia!"

Outside the regional administration, I spotted a friend of a friend, a young Donetsk photographer named Misha. We had never met before, but he stood out with his goatee, wispy hair, and bell bottoms. He was as surprised as I was by the furious protest. We followed the strange procession to the mayor's office, where two men raised the Russian tricolor on a flagpole to cheers from the crowd. "Yanukovych is our president!" they shouted.

The authorities in Kyiv accused Russia of sending busloads of provocateurs across the border and suspected that Yanukovych was paying for the protests in his hometown. Still, I was determined to find an authentic demonstrator. Back on Lenin Square, I approached a middle-aged man who cheerfully gave Misha and me a piece of his mind. Sergei Savenkov had served in the Soviet air force, but when the Soviet Union fell apart, he refused to take a new oath to independent Ukraine. "One oath is enough," Savenkov said. He went into business and opened an auto shop. "We only want to be with Russia. I'm an opponent of Europe," he said. For Savenkov, the EU was nothing more than the coalition of countries—Germany and its former fascist allies—that had invaded the Soviet Union in World War II. He pointed at an airplane high above in the cloudless sky. "Khimtreil," he said in Russian. I looked at Misha for help, but he too had no idea what Savenkov was talking about. "Chemtrail," Savenkov repeated, gesturing at the white condensation trails streaking across the sky. That was an American plane, he said, and it was releasing clouds of poison on the people and soil of eastern Ukraine.

A couple of days later I returned to the regional administration. A row of riot police guarded the entrance, but there were no demonstrators. From the tenth-floor office of the new governor, Serhiy Taruta, Donetsk looked tranquil and orderly. Below his window, the Ukrainian flag fluttered over city blocks and green squares. Yes, a few weeks earlier protesters had briefly occupied the building and a pro-Ukrainian activist had been killed, but now things were returning to normal, Taruta assured me.[2]

Taruta was not a professional politician but a steel magnate. As pro-Russian protests started heating up, the provisional government in Kyiv offered Taruta the job as governor after Rinat Akhmetov declined. Taruta reluctantly accepted, viewing himself as a temporary crisis manager. In his horn-rimmed glasses, Taruta bore a passing resemblance to Woody Allen. He was gregarious and self-assured. Eastern Ukraine's challenges were economic, Taruta explained. Corruption was impoverishing the population, strangling entrepreneurship, and scaring off investors. Poland, not Russia, was the model for economic transformation and renewal. "With the right policy, reforms can be implemented without too much upheaval. There are problems, but they can be minimized," he said. "I think everyone who loves their kids will be ready to wait two or three years to be happy in the future."

I found Taruta's optimism blithe and unfounded. I brought up the demonstrators I had joined outside the regional administration, draped in Russian flags and calling for his head. Taruta politely told me that I was misinformed about the situation. Less than two weeks later pro-Russian protesters stormed his office, proclaimed the "Donetsk People's Republic," and called for a referendum on secession.

At the same time pro-Russian demonstrators seized the Luhansk regional headquarters of the SBU, Ukraine's state security service, gaining access to a large cache of weapons. In Kharkiv, protesters took over the regional administration building and declared the founding of the "Kharkiv People's Republic." On April 7, Oleksandr Turchynov, Ukraine's acting president, went on TV saying that Russia had started a "second wave" of a special operation designed to overthrow Ukraine's government, disrupt the May 25 presidential election, and "tear our country into pieces." Turchynov formed an "anti-crisis headquarters" and threatened "antiterrorist measures" against those who took up arms. The next day Ukrainian special forces succeeded in clearing the Kharkiv regional administration of pro-Russian protesters. But in the Donetsk region the Kyiv authorities were about to face their biggest challenge yet.

On April 12 a band of some fifty fighters appeared out of nowhere and overran Slovyansk, a town on the main highway between Kharkiv and Donetsk. They were led by Igor Girkin, the former FSB colonel who had played a lead role in the takeover of Crimea. After Russia annexed the peninsula, he stayed on as an adviser to Crimea's puppet governor, Sergei Aksyonov. But Girkin soon felt unneeded and began to recruit volunteers for a new mission.[3] There was not a single active Russian service member among his soldiers of fortune, and at least three-quarters of them were Ukrainian citizens, according to Girkin.[4] The group crossed on foot from Russia's Rostov region into Ukraine, where they were met by followers of the jailed Donetsk separatist, Pavel Gubarev.[5] To get to Slovyansk, more than eighty miles away, Girkin commandeered a truck from a logistics company to smuggle his fighters into the city.

Girkin later said that he had settled on Slovyansk after asking Gubarev's people to name a pro-Russian town willing to take up arms and support him.[6] When Girkin's heavily armed band arrived in Slovyansk, they were joined by three hundred local activists and together stormed the police station, the local SBU office, and city hall.[7] According to Girkin, the townspeople took his group to be the same "little green men," i.e., Russian special forces who had seized Crimea before the Russian annexation.[8] "The people very happily received us," Girkin said. "They believed that everything was being repeated like in Crimea." Girkin said he himself believed that he could nudge Donetsk in the same direction as Crimea by helping local separatists establish a "people's government," conduct a referendum, and join Russia. From his foothold in Slovyansk, he took over four neighboring towns.

Girkin denied being sent by Moscow. In fact, he took credit for starting the insurrection on his own. "I'm the one who pulled the trigger of war. If our squad hadn't crossed the border, it all would have ended like in Kharkiv or Odesa. There would have been a few dozen killed, burned, and arrested.

And that would have ended everything," Girkin later boasted to an ultranationalist Russian newspaper.[9] "Our squad set the flywheel of war in motion.
We reshuffled all the cards on the table." The one connection to Russian
officialdom that Girkin did not conceal was his relationship with Aksyonov.
Girkin said he turned to Aksyonov for support because his original sponsor
in Crimea, the Russian oligarch Konstantin Malofeyev, opposed his plan to
leapfrog to Donetsk.[10] Pavel Gubarev, the self-proclaimed "people's governor" of Donetsk, later said that by starting the armed uprising, Girkin had
"saved" the pro-Russian protests from being snuffed out.[11]

Girkin, who used the nom de guerre Strelkov, gleefully assumed the role
of triggerman in eastern Ukraine. For committed Russian imperialists such
as Girkin, who railed against the greed and corruption of Putin's elite, their
moment had come with the annexation of Crimea. Girkin believed that a
"revolution from the top" would follow in Moscow, resulting in the creation of a "union state" consisting of Russia, Ukraine, and Belarus.[12] For the
Kremlin, which valued cynicism over sincerity, Girkin was a freak whose
enthusiasm could be exploited or left to fizzle, depending on his success or
failure. After Crimea, Putin was taking a wait-and-see attitude, telling his
aide Sergei Glazyev that eastern Ukrainians needed to make the first move
before counting on any Russian help.[13] At the same time, Putin was sending threatening signals back to Ukraine. In a call-in show on April 17, Putin
for the first time used the term "Novorossiya" (New Russia), a czarist-era
designation for much of southeastern Ukraine favored by the separatists.[14]
"These territories were given to Ukraine in the 1920s by the Soviet government," Putin said, echoing the argument that Crimea had been mistakenly
"gifted" to Ukraine.

Freelancers and adventurists were playing an increasingly important
role in Russian foreign policy, granting the Kremlin plausible deniability
should they be discovered or things go wrong. Although Girkin may well
have planned the Slovyansk raid himself, he could not have gone very far
without the Kremlin's assistance. Girkin saw the mission of his fighters as
an advance guard paving the way for an intervention by the regular Russian army. According to Girkin, in April there was a sizable Russian military
contingent ready at the border, its vehicles freshly marked as belonging to
a "peacekeeping force."[15]

The day after Girkin took over Slovyansk, his fighters attacked a Ukrainian
reconnaissance team outside the town, killing an SBU captain. Later that

day Turchynov declared the start of an "antiterrorist operation." On April 16, Ukrainian army troops tasked with retaking the town of Kramatorsk from Girkin's men surrendered six armored vehicles and their weapons after being surrounded by local residents.[16] Unbeknownst to the Ukrainians, who did not understand exactly who their opponents were, Girkin's fighters were direly underequipped. "There was a catastrophic shortage of ammunition, especially at the beginning," Girkin later remembered.[17] "If the Ukrainian military had known that we had only one-and-a-half magazines per gun, I don't think we would have held out beyond the beginning of May."

The Ukrainian military was ill-prepared to deal with an uprising that involved unarmed, angry babushkas and shadowy, determined fighters. Officers were not ready to order their troops to fire on civilians and were unclear about the army's role in the absence of martial law.[18]

The authorities in Kyiv faced the exact same challenges as they had in Crimea: pro-Russian sympathy within the ranks and an unwillingness to fight. "Our biggest problem was finding one complete unit that could have carried out our orders," said Andriy Parubiy, Turchynov's top security adviser.[19] After pro-Russian militants stormed the regional SBU headquarters in Luhansk in early April, Parubiy remembered, Ukrainian Interior Ministry troops said they could not retake the building because locals were preventing them from leaving their base. When Parubiy arrived at the scene, he found six women sitting near the entrance—the troops themselves had called them to "block" the gate. Sabotage, resentment toward the new authorities, and extensive infiltration by the FSB stymied Kyiv's efforts to nip the rebellion in the bud.

Parubiy and others in the provisional government did not deny making mistakes during the chaotic months following the Maidan. But they were adamant that if Russia had not intervened, there would have been no insurgency. "Our political culture was such that we tried to resolve all conflicts by peaceful means," Oleksandr Lytvynenko, Parubiy's deputy, said.[20] "If there hadn't been Russian involvement, the crisis would have been solved without violence."

As the Russian-backed insurgency spread, the Ukrainian authorities were faced with a dilemma: provoking a Kremlin response through the use of force or showing restraint and ceding even more territory to rebel control. Turchynov's "antiterrorist operation," known as the ATO, predicated a fight. "The ATO was a trap and Ukraine fell into it," a European diplomat in Kyiv told me.[21] "The Russians wanted conflict in Ukraine, and they got it."

Skirmishes around Slovyansk continued during the spring, but the single biggest loss of life until then came on May 2, when pro-Russian protesters clashed with pro-unity activists in Odesa. A total of forty-eight people lost their lives that day, including forty-two in a fire in a building where pro-Russian protesters had barricaded themselves from pro-unity supporters. The grisly images of the fire's victims helped fuel the Kremlin narrative that Russian speakers were being persecuted by ruthless Ukrainian nationalists.[22] It was becoming difficult for Ukrainians to remain dispassionate as violence and hate begat more violence and hate.

A poll taken in early April 2014 showed that less than a third of respondents in the Donetsk and Luhansk regions were for joining Russia, while slim majorities were against it.[23] Another poll taken around the same time found that 77 percent of respondents nationwide believed Ukraine should stay united, with 14 percent saying regions should be permitted to secede.[24] Even in the Russian-speaking east, 70 percent of respondents were for unity, and only 18 percent supported the right to secession.

Reducing the growing conflict to a language issue was a gross oversimplification and reflected a misreading of Ukrainian society by outsiders—first and foremost by Russians. Although Ukrainian speakers did not support the pro-Russian cause, language was no predictor of the allegiances of Ukrainians who happened to speak Russian. In Ukraine there were not two separate communities speaking two different languages. Almost all Ukrainians understood both languages, and many mixed them freely depending on whether they were dealing with official bureaucracy, school, work, or home life. When I first started traveling to Ukraine, I thought locals were answering me in Ukrainian out of national pride. But after overhearing countless conversations where one person spoke Ukrainian and the other Russian, I realized that most people assumed I could understand Ukrainian the same way their Russian-speaking compatriots could.

The Kremlin erroneously assumed that Ukraine's Russian speakers, given the chance, would identify as Russians. Putin believed that Ukraine was an artificial construction that would fall apart like a house of cards. In fact, a new generation of Ukrainians, regardless of the language they spoke, had developed a distinct sense of national identity. Even in eastern Ukraine, young, educated people felt loyalty to the country of their birth, did not miss the Soviet Union, and had no interest in joining Putin's auto-cratic Russia.[25]

I returned to Donetsk in late April. I flew into Sergei Prokofiev Interna-tional Airport, a shiny glass box named after the region's most famous composer. That same day Ukraine's Interior Ministry announced it had launched a "special operation" in Slovyansk, killing five fighters and destroying three of their checkpoints. Putin, speaking in St. Petersburg, said that Ukraine's use of the military against its own population consti-tuted a "very serious crime" and warned of "consequences." The threat of a full-scale Russian invasion hung in the air.

The city of Donetsk existed in a strange limbo between humdrum nor-mality and apeshit anarchy. I checked into the Beatles-themed Liverpool Hotel in the center of town, next to a university dormitory filled with inter-national students.[26] The next day I headed over to the regional adminis-tration, which had become the power center of the self-declared Donetsk People's Republic, or DNR for short. At the entrance, thuggish young fellows in masks manned barricades of tires laced with razor wire. There were signs with blunt slogans such as "Ukraine against American-Fascist Aggression" and "No to USA-EU." From a balcony hung the Russian flag, the Russian Air-borne Forces' flag, and the black-blue-red flag of the DNR. Inside the build-ing, in the so-called press department, a cheerful woman named Klavdiya issued me my DNR press credentials: a slip of paper with a stamp on it.

The reception for foreigners was less welcoming in the rest of the DNR. One colleague was detained and beaten by Girkin's fighters in Slovyansk. Another was pistol-whipped by separatists in Kramatorsk. The day after I returned to Donetsk, the self-proclaimed "people's mayor" of Slovyansk had seven military observers from the Organization for Security and Coop-eration in Europe arrested.

I decided the best way to get into Slovyansk was in a press tour orga-nized by Oleg Tsaryov, a Ukrainian politician who sympathized with the pro-Russian separatists. It did not take me long to realize that Tsaryov's trip was merely a publicity stunt for Russian television. A reporter from St. Petersburg pretended to help load a truck with "humanitarian aid" as he recorded his stand-up. Not even half full, the small truck contained a few cases of bottled water and some sacks of onions and potatoes. Tsaryov's convoy trundled through a rust belt landscape of five-story Soviet housing blocks, smokestacks, and slag heaps. Low-rise cities thinned into villages that gave way to sprawling industrial sites. At a Ukrainian checkpoint, Tsaryov's cavalcade stopped and a group of women approached the officers singing hymns and holding signs saying "Don't shoot, soldier."

Except for the masked men manning barricades on the outskirts of town, Slovyansk felt sleepy and provincial. "These aren't terrorists, they are citizens of Ukraine," Tsaryov told the Russian TV cameras as he stood outside city hall on Lenin Square. After the press scrum disappeared, the truck with the fake humanitarian aid drove away. Two young men I spoke to on the square said they would welcome the Russian army if it intervened. "We want independence as part of Russia. All our relatives will be there," said a retired warrant officer who had served in both the Soviet and Ukrainian armies. I asked him what his nationality was. "De jure Ukrainian, de facto Russian," he replied. "But I hope soon de jure as well."

Supporters of Ukrainian unity were less vocal. One entrepreneur in Donetsk disdainfully confided in me that the only people who wanted to join Russia were the ragtag band in front of the regional administration. I listened in as several members of a district election board debated in all seriousness how they could still carry out the May 25 presidential election since Ukrainian law did not provide for armed men threatening voters. Even that meeting was an act of civic defiance, as most members of the election board were too scared to show up. Misha, the photographer I had befriended on my previous visit to Donetsk, was finding it more and more dangerous to do his work. Like other young people I talked to in Donetsk, he was frustrated with the Kyiv government's inability to stamp out the insurgency and restore order.

Pro-Ukrainian activists organized a march down Donetsk's main street to demonstrate against the rising tide of separatism. On social media, the separatists were calling on followers to bring "surgical equipment and instruments" to the rally to "cure" the demonstrators of their "Ukrainianness." I was late for the march, and when I got there, terrified people were fleeing the scene. They were followed by a horde of several hundred young men carrying baseball bats, clubs, and shields. "Ross-i-ya! Ross-i-ya!" they chanted victoriously. Behind them marched an almost equally large group of riot police, who had done nothing to protect the pro-unity protesters from the thugs. I stopped a middle-aged married couple rushing home.

"Tell the world the real fascists are the ones shouting 'Russia,'" said the man. "We're peaceful citizens. We never took up clubs or sticks." His eyes turned red, and he started crying. It was the last pro-unity rally in Donetsk.

The separatists used May 1, the traditional workers' holiday, to stage their own rally. Their march ended at the prosecutor's office, which they proceeded to storm. I found a crowd of young men and aggressive pensioners cheering as the Ukrainian flag was torn down. "Fascists!" the crowd shouted as a group of riot police filed out of a courtyard and vanished down the street. Building by building, the authorities in Kyiv gradually ceded Donetsk to a band of riffraff, Cossacks, and Russian provocateurs. Governor Taruta, who now governed out of a hotel room, posted polite videos, asking the rebels to lay down their arms and citing Dostoyevsky. Raw executive power lay in the hands of the separatists. They arrested their opponents and locked them up in the regional administration. That spring I watched the Ukrainian flag over the Donetsk mayor's office get smaller and smaller until one day it disappeared altogether.

For the separatists in the Donetsk and Luhansk regions, everything hinged on a slapdash independence referendum scheduled for May 11. They hoped to repeat the Crimean scenario by providing Russia with a legal pretext for annexation before Ukrainians even had a chance to elect a new president. Vladimir Putin, however, was in no big hurry. It was clear that the Russian-speaking regions were not falling like dominoes under a wave of pro-Russian euphoria. Clashes with the authorities were isolated and had failed to ignite a popular uprising. Moreover, Western governments were threatening new sanctions if Russia continued to destabilize eastern Ukraine. Four days before the separatists' planned referendum, Putin suggested that they postpone the vote and enter into a "dialogue" with the authorities in Kyiv.[27] He hinted that Ukraine's May 25 presidential election could be a step in the right direction.

Putin's comments were met with shock and dismay by followers of the DNR. On the plaza in front of the regional administration, a small crowd of long faces gathered that evening. I asked a middle-aged woman what she made of Putin's suggestion to delay the vote. "It's his personal opinion. He's the leader of another country," she said. "Our conscience won't permit a delay. There have been too many victims."

The separatists in Donetsk and Luhansk pushed ahead with their plans for a vote, even though they controlled only pockets of territory, had made no real preparations for a referendum, and were acting in direct violation of Ukrainian law. Roman Lyagin, the DNR's self-proclaimed election commissioner, boasted that more than four hundred journalists from around the world were accredited to cover the "referendum."[28] As Lyagin held forth, I realized that just by interviewing him I was taking part in a media circus that was legitimizing a patently illegitimate vote. To the casual news consumer halfway around the globe, an independence referendum in Donetsk may have seemed no different than one in Scotland or Catalonia. The problem was that in the Donbas, as Donetsk and Luhansk were known collectively, there was no nation to liberate. Russian speakers made up the area's overwhelming majority, Russian was spoken everywhere, and local bosses had been running the economy and regional political machine since Ukraine's independence.

On the day of the referendum, Misha and I drove out to his hometown of Dobropillya, about sixty miles northwest of Donetsk. The mining town of thirty thousand was in a corner of the region still under Ukrainian control, although the separatists had plenty of sympathizers. On one side of Victory Prospekt, at the base of the town's Lenin statue, a couple of hundred people—mostly middle-aged or elderly—had lined up to cast photocopied ballots into cardboard boxes with stickers of the DNR flag on them. "At first we wanted autonomy," a miner named Anatoly Gutnik told me. "But after they started killing us in Slovyansk, Odesa, and Mariupol, we don't want to live in this country anymore." On the other side of the street, a considerably smaller group of people was holding a poll for Ukraine's unity. "We'll answer a farce with a farce," said Mykola Strepochenko, a pro-unity activist and the owner of a large farm. The pro-Ukraine crowd sought comfort in numbers. "I'm tired of being afraid," said Mykhailo Zhelezov, a miner who said five generations of his family were buried in Dobropillya. "I grew up in Ukraine. How can I love Russia? Should I betray my ancestors?" He acknowledged the split in opinion over the DNR—but added that most of the townspeople were simply indifferent.

The self-proclaimed results of the two "referendums" were 89 percent for independence in the DNR and 96 percent in the LNR, as the "Luhansk People's Republic" was known. Not even Russia had sent election observers, but after the vote the Russian foreign minister Sergei Lavrov said that Moscow would "respect" the will of the Donbas people. Even while the Kremlin formally maintained its distance from the separatists, well-connected Muscovites were taking an ever-greater role in turning the DNR and LNR into quasi states to distract and harry the authorities in Kyiv. Less than a week after the referendum, the DNR's self-appointed leadership council named Igor Girkin "defense minister" and Alexander Borodai, a Moscow PR consultant, "prime minister." In July, Marat Bashirov, another consultant from Moscow, was appointed the "prime minister" of the LNR.

Before Borodai became the round, stubbled face of the Donetsk separatists, few people had ever heard his name. Borodai, age forty-one, had grown up in an academic family in Moscow and studied philosophy at Moscow State University. Like Girkin, he went to fight alongside pro-Russian separatists in Moldova, and the two men befriended each other in the ultranationalist circles that seethed at Russia's weakness before the West.[29] In 1993, Borodai took part in the failed uprising by nationalists and Communists against Russia's first president, Boris Yeltsin.[30] Borodai never forgave pro-Western liberals for supporting the use of force to put down the rebellion.

Borodai shared Girkin's fanatical belief in the heroism of war and the mortal threat posed to the "Russian world" by the United States. It was no coincidence that Borodai had worked as a consultant for the influential Russian Orthodox businessman Konstantin Malofeyev.[31] And after the annexation of Crimea, Borodai, like Girkin, advised the puppet government of Sergei Aksyonov.[32] Borodai denied that he represented the Russian government, claiming instead to be working in a "private-public partnership"—an apt description of the Kremlin's hybrid invasion of Ukraine. He first went to Slovyansk, then showed up in Donetsk in early May.[33] Borodai insisted that nobody had sent him, although he later admitted to being in contact with the Kremlin's shadowy point man on Ukraine, Vladislav Surkov, during his time in Donetsk.[34]

Officially, the Kremlin had nothing to do with Borodai or Girkin. Yet there was no way around the fact that the two top figures in the DNR were Russian citizens with high connections in Moscow. Their appearance in Donetsk was a triumph for a hardline ideology that until then had been the domain of Vladimir Zhirinovsky, the clownish Russian politician who assisted the Kremlin in channeling ultranationalist feeling into harmless bluster. Borodai, with his smirk and pot belly, and Girkin, in his moustache and camos, were preposterous figures as well, but their words and actions had consequences that were costing more and more lives.

The rise of Borodai and Girkin marked a Russian takeover of the separatist movement. In the past, elites in eastern Ukraine had wielded the cudgel of separatism to extract concessions from Kyiv. During the 2004 Orange Revolution, Russian-speaking lawmakers threatened to break off from Ukraine if their candidate, Viktor Yanukovych, was not declared the winner of the disputed presidential election. At the same time, the movers and shakers of the eastern regions understood perfectly well that Ukraine, as a sovereign state, protected their assets from voracious Russian businessmen.

In Donetsk, the backroom powerbroker was the oligarch Rinat Akhmetov. As the first pro-Russian protests broke out in Donetsk, Akhmetov played an ambivalent role, offering moral, if not financial, support to the self-proclaimed separatists.[35] The Donetsk protests were still primarily a Ukrainian game, in which Akhmetov and other members of Yanukovych's entourage sought to strengthen their position vis-à-vis the new regime in Kyiv—with no intention of splitting off and joining Russia. Akhmetov's steel business was dependent on exports to western Europe, and any change to Ukraine's borders would have cut him off from his customers.

Akhmetov first rejected Turchynov's offer to become the Donetsk region's governor. Then, after pro-Russian activists proclaimed the DNR in early April, he turned down their request to lead them.[36] By the time Girkin and Borodai became the figureheads of the DNR, Akhmetov was sidelined. What was supposed to have been a power play by Donetsk elites took on a life of its own, as the pro-Russian activists could no longer be bribed out of the regional administration building. Akhmetov fled Donetsk shortly before the Ukrainian presidential election on May 25. That same day separatists raided Akhmetov's mansion in the Donetsk Botanical Garden.

Akhmetov's maneuvering, despite his allegiance to Ukraine, contrasted with the decisive action of other Ukrainian oligarchs, in particular Ihor Kolomoiskyi, a magnate based in Dnipropetrovsk, a region bordering Donetsk to the west. Kolomoiskyi accepted Turchynov's offer to become Dnipropetrovsk's governor in March 2014, using his wealth and influence to stop the pro-Russian unrest from spreading to his region. Kolomoiskyi also convinced Hennadiy Kernes, the powerful mayor of Kharkiv, to end his flirtation with pro-Russian separatists and come down unequivocally on the side of Ukraine.

Where local Ukrainian elites grasped the risks of a Russian takeover, the separatist movement never had a chance. But the Donbas was different: it had a working-class ethos rooted in the region's glory days as the Soviet Union's industrial powerhouse. After the Soviet collapse, the coal miners of the Donbas saw their fortunes plummet. Many associated Ukrainian independence with poverty, banditry, and the rise of an oligarchic class.

Culturally and linguistically, the Donbas differed little from the neighboring regions of southern Russia. Politically, it also bore a striking resemblance to Putin's brand of authoritarianism. After his humiliating defeat in the Orange Revolution, Yanukovych signed an agreement aligning his Party of Regions with Russia's ruling party, United Russia. The Party of Regions borrowed from its Russian sister party, creating a similar political monopoly in the Donbas and using its power to protect loyal business interests.[37]

As in other depressed industrial regions in the former Soviet Union, there was little tradition of civic activism in the Donbas. Most people were not as supportive of Yanukovych as they were politically indifferent. The power vacuum that opened up in the Donbas after Yanukovych's fall created an opportunity for a group of bit players to revolt not only against Kyiv but also against the local business elite led by Akhmetov. Supporters of the pro-Russian cause were those who had lost the most—and gained the least—from Ukraine's independence. They did not want their own "people's republics" or even Putin's Russia. What they really wanted was a return to the Soviet Union. In Makiivka, an industrial suburb of Donetsk, an auto mechanic named Boris Dekhteryenko told me how much he missed the good old days. "We had advanced socialism," he said. "It was a happy childhood. Ice cream cost 20 kopeks, and a miner could earn enough in a month to buy a Lada."[38]

People nostalgic for the Soviet past were easily moved by the tropes of the Communist era, many of which had originated in the Soviet Union's existential struggle against Nazi Germany. Any enemy was a "fascist," no matter their actual ideology, and any proponent of a nation-state, especially one that the Soviet Union intended to swallow up, was a "nationalist." In the Ukrainian context, any supporter of Ukraine's independence became a "Banderite," or follower of Ukrainian nationalist Stepan Bandera, who fought against the Red Army by any means possible, including collaborating with the Nazis. The Soviet-era political vocabulary was ill-equipped to describe the complexity of contemporary Ukraine, but it evoked powerful associations among many Ukrainians and Russians. Pro-Russian activists—taking up arms against Ukraine and advocating union with Russia—protested being called "separatists," instead calling themselves *opolchentsy*, or "militiamen." In their view, they were not separating from Ukraine but "reuniting" with Russia. When the Soviet Union collapsed, "separatists" were those who had wanted to go their own way; Mikhail Gorbachev used the term to refer to supporters of Ukrainian independence.

Another way to describe the pro-Russian fighters in Ukraine could have been "counterrevolutionaries." They called their angry revolt an "anti-Maidan." But in a broader sense they were also rebelling against the peaceful revolutions of 1989 that had swept away Soviet puppet regimes in central Europe and heralded the end of the Soviet Union. By famously calling the fall of the Soviet Union "the greatest geopolitical catastrophe" of the twentieth century, Putin had placed himself at the head of the camp that lamented the collapse of a great empire—and was determined to save what bits of it that it could.

The peaceful protesters who took to the streets of Prague in 1989 or Kyiv in 2014 were taking back agency over their own destinies. The people on the Maidan demonstrated that they were no longer malleable Soviet citizens—cowed, indoctrinated, and dependent on the state. The anti-Maidan rallies that flared up in southeastern Ukraine were a parody of the Maidan. Protest leaders were fly-by-night characters that nobody had ever heard of. Demonstrators copied the tactics and optics of the Maidan, wearing balaclavas, storming government buildings, and building barricades out of tires. When asked what they wanted, they were surprisingly incoherent and confused.

The anti-Maidan was a top-down rebellion sponsored by scheming local elites and later hijacked by outsiders like Igor Girkin. Yet the pro-Russian uprising fed on real discontent among the local population. Perhaps the biggest tragedy of the escalating conflict was that the principal grievances of people in southeastern Ukraine—poverty, corruption, and government neglect—were exactly the same as those who had demonstrated in Kyiv. The protests in the Donbas, just like the Maidan, were fueled by anger against oligarchic clans. The principal difference, in the words of the journalist Sonya Koshkina, was that the Euromaidan was a bourgeois revolution, whereas the Donbas uprising was a proletarian revolt. The Maidan protesters saw their future in Europe; the separatists saw theirs in a revived Soviet Union. If their protest could be called a revolution at all, then it was a zombie revolution to resurrect a country that no longer existed. Putin's resurgent Russia was the next best thing.

The Kremlin portrayed the increasingly heavy fighting between Ukrainian government forces and separatists as a "civil war," warning that it would not stand idly by as "fascists" persecuted ethnic Russians. For fanatical Russian nationalists like Girkin and Borodai, the conflict was indeed a civil war because they did not consider Ukrainians a separate nation. For the Kremlin, calling the insurgency a civil war was a cynical ploy to deny being a party to it. Without Russian involvement, there would have been no war in the Donbas. Before 2014, many Ukrainians believed that they had achieved their independence from Moscow using completely peaceful means. Now they found themselves waging a belated war of independence—not only from Russia but also from the legacy of the Soviet Union.

The idea of the Donbas breaking off from the rest of Ukraine had its origins in the dying days of the Soviet Union. As national liberation movements gained strength in Ukraine and the Baltic nations, reactionaries in the Communist establishment struck back, supporting groups called "international movements," or "intermovements" (*interdvizheniya* in Russian), which advocated for the preservation of the Soviet empire.[39] The Donbas Intermovement, founded by the Donetsk historian Dmitry Kornilov in November 1990, drew its inspiration from the Donetsk-Krivoy Rog Soviet Republic, a short-lived, self-proclaimed entity that encompassed much of Russian-speaking Ukraine following the 1917 Russian Revolution. Kornilov's group actively agitated against Ukrainian independence—and for the Donbas's separation from Ukraine should Ukraine leave the Soviet Union.

In Ukraine's 1991 referendum on independence, solid majorities supported the measure in both the Donetsk and Luhansk regions. Given the Donbas's strong industrial base, most people believed that Ukraine would prosper once freed from the decrepit Soviet command economy. But it did not take long for disillusionment to set in as the region's inefficient industrial giants struggled to survive the transition to capitalism. In 1993 striking miners demanded autonomy for the Donbas. The following year Donetsk held a regional referendum on federalization that passed with a large majority. Leonid Kuchma, who was elected president several months later, paid no heed to the results. He was opposed to diminishing Kyiv's power, and in 1996 Ukraine's status as a unitary state was enshrined in the country's first constitution.

In the early 1990s, the so-called Slavic Party emerged in Donetsk with the declared goal of uniting Russia, Belarus, and Ukraine—the Slavic core of both the Russian Empire and Soviet Union. The party, which existed on the fringes of Ukrainian political life, was used by Viktor Yanukovych's allies as a blunt instrument against his pro-European rival, Viktor Yushchenko. The Slavic Party attempted to field a fake candidate named Yushchenko to draw votes from the real Yushchenko's party in the 2002 parliamentary election.[40] And when Viktor Yushchenko visited Donetsk in October 2003, Slavic Party activists tried to prevent him from leaving the airport and plastered the city with billboards showing the opposition leader in uniform throwing a Nazi salute.

Until the Orange Revolution, the pro-Russian separatists played a marginal role as spoilers. The turning point came when lawmakers from eastern Ukraine descended on Sievierodonetsk, in the Luhansk region, to threaten secession if Yanukovych's dubious election victory was not recognized. The cavalier way with which politicians attacked Ukrainian statehood reflected the casual feelings of many in the Donbas toward Ukraine as a country. Among a generation that had already seen the Soviet Union crumble, there was a lack of loyalty to Ukraine as a reborn nation.

An uptick in separatist activity followed Yushchenko's win in the second runoff vote. In 2005, Russian sympathizers founded an organization called Donetskaya Respublika (Russian for "Donetsk Republic"), the direct ideological predecessor to the DNR. The most radical of the separatist organizations, Donetskaya Respublika reached out to Russian right-wing extremist groups, including Russian ultranationalist thinker Alexander Dugin's International Eurasian Movement.[41] Andrei Purgin, one of Donetskaya Respublika's founders, would later play a leading role in the DNR.

Even as the Ukrainian authorities banned Purgin's organization, the political mainstream in Donbas was becoming more pro-Russian. Yushchenko, who envisioned Ukraine's integration into the EU and NATO, was a strong motivator. The Russian lawmaker Konstantin Zatulin, head of the revanchist Institute of CIS Countries in Moscow, became a frequent guest in the Donbas. Vladimir Kornilov, the brother of the founder of the original Donetsk separatist group, the Donbas Intermovement, headed the Ukrainian branch of Zatulin's institute. In 2009, the Russkiy Mir (Russian World) Foundation, founded by Putin as a cultural organization, opened a "Russian Center" in Luhansk. The center cultivated the pro-Russian activists who would seize power five years later.

Separatist activities in the Donbas did not end with Yushchenko's political demise in 2010. The criminal cases launched against Donetskaya Respublika were closed. The Party of Regions benefited from radical pro-Russians and Ukrainian ultranationalists on the political scene. The image of an unbridgeable chasm running through Ukrainian society helped Yanukovych's party look more respectable and moderate.[42] The many conferences held in the Donbas on the threat of "Ukrainian fascism" or the need for "federalization" generated widespread local media coverage, inflating the role of Ukrainian chauvinism in national politics. By the time the Euromaidan prevailed in February 2014, the Donbas was fertile ground for protests against the new "Kyiv junta." People's fears were real, even if the grounds for them were not.

Petro Poroshenko, known as Ukraine's "chocolate king" for the candy empire he built, won the May 25 presidential election with 55 percent of the vote. Yulia Tymoshenko came in second with 13 percent. Candidates from the Ukrainian far right, the bogeymen of Kremlin propaganda, fared miserably: Oleh Tyahnybok of the Svoboda party won a little more than 1 percent, and Dmytro Yarosh, head of the ultranationalist Pravyi Sektor, did not make even 1 percent. Poroshenko was an old hand in Ukrainian politics. He had helped create the Party of Regions but later became a close ally of Viktor Yushchenko. As a minister under both Yushchenko and Yanukovych, Poroshenko had consistently supported Ukraine's membership in the EU and NATO. His TV news network, Channel Five, had been one of the main sources of information about the Euromaidan protests.

Poroshenko's victory meant that Ukraine once again had a duly elected president—even if the election could not take place in occupied Crimea and only a small number of local election commissions were able to carry out the vote in the Donetsk and Luhansk regions. On June 6, a day before his inauguration, Poroshenko met informally with Putin during ceremonies commemorating the seventieth anniversary of D-Day in Normandy. The Kremlin begrudgingly began to refer to Poroshenko as Ukraine's new president. Within his first month in office, Poroshenko traveled to Brussels to sign the economic part of the EU association agreement that Yanukovych had rejected the previous November.[43]

Poroshenko promised to end the pro-Russian rebellion in the east of the country. The Donetsk separatists met his electoral victory with an attack on the city's gleaming airport, provoking a fierce response from Ukrainian forces and beginning a bitter struggle that would end with the terminal's complete destruction. Slowly but surely Donetsk was being cut off from the outside world.

I returned to Donetsk by train. By the end of July the city had become a ghost town. The streets were largely empty, and few shops and restaurants were open. According to the DNR authorities, 40 percent of the population had fled the spiraling violence. After being threatened repeatedly by separatist fighters, my friend Misha decided that working as a photographer was too dangerous and moved away. One shopkeeper furtively told me that she had boycotted the May "referendum" and was impatiently awaiting the arrival of the Ukrainian army. "My parents are from Russia. But I'm Ukrainian from the top of my head to the tip of my toes," she said.

People I met no longer expressed support for the separatists. The easy annexation by Russia that many had hoped for had not taken place. Instead, their city was run by newly minted warlords and old-fashioned gangsters. The silent majority caught in the middle was feeling increasingly abandoned by the authorities in Kyiv. I visited a neighborhood of Soviet-era housing blocks after five civilians had been killed and twelve injured in an exchange of fire between separatists and government forces. The shoes of an elderly woman and a patch of ground darkened by blood were evidence of the random brutality of war. In a ninth-floor apartment, I found a college professor, Oleksandr Lytvynenko, examining what was left of his home after a rocket had crashed into his living room. He sounded surprisingly conciliatory. "The solution I see is to stop the shooting," he said. "Nothing will be solved by force."

Alexander Borodai's consolidation of power brought a new order to the rebellion. In the second half of May, the reconstituted Vostok Battalion, a Russian militia born during Putin's pitiless war in Chechnya, began to impose a more streamlined command structure on the motley armed groups.[44] The insurgency was being professionalized with direct involvement from Moscow. The mastermind was the Kremlin aide Vladislav Surkov, who had instructions from Putin not to create two unrecognized states but instead to use the rebellion as a way to hobble Ukraine.[45] Sergei Glazyev and Konstantin Malofeyev—the Russian ultranationalists who had helped seize Crimea—were sidelined.[46] At the end of June, Russia's Federation Council withdrew its March 1 decree allowing the use of Russian troops in Ukraine, signaling that the Kremlin was not planning to occupy and annex the Donbas.

Girkin was feeling more and more vulnerable in his stronghold of Slovyansk, perched on the western edge of the DNR. His fighters faced a chronic shortage of weapons and supplies, and Girkin had so little money that he could pay his fighters only twice.[47] With Ukrainian forces closing in on the city, he angrily blamed officials and oligarchs back in Russia for sabotaging the "Novorossiya" project.[48] In early July Girkin cut his losses and retreated to the city of Donetsk.

As the fighting escalated, the Ukrainian military lost several transport planes to enemy fire, including an Ilyushin 76 with forty-nine people on board. On July 17, Russian state media reported that Donetsk separatists had downed a Ukrainian Antonov 26. But when it turned out that a Malaysian airliner had come down instead, the Kremlin propaganda machine abruptly changed its tune. Russia's Channel One suggested that a Ukrainian fighter plane had shot down MH17, citing an eyewitness, "Tatyana," who spoke to the broadcaster by phone. Another version suggested that the Ukrainian air force had tried to shoot down Vladimir Putin's plane as he returned from an overseas trip—after all, his Ilyushin 96 was about the same size as the Malaysian Boeing 777 and had similar blue and red stripes on its side. The most outlandish explanation held that Malaysia Airlines flight MH370, which had vanished over the Indian Ocean earlier that year, had in fact been abducted by the U.S. government, filled with corpses, and used to stage the downing of MH17.

Putin had just returned to Moscow from a feel-good tour of Latin America, including Nicaragua and Cuba. He found out about the shooting down of MH17 shortly before a scheduled call with Barack Obama. Putin had wanted to argue against a new round of U.S. sanctions on Russia. Now he found himself personally informing Obama about the shocking news from the Donbas. In the following days, Putin almost completely disappeared from public view. For someone who claimed to be no more than a concerned observer of the conflict in eastern Ukraine, Putin took an inordinate interest in MH17. He phoned the leaders of the Netherlands and Malaysia, the two countries with the most victims. Putin spoke twice with Angela Merkel, as well as with the leaders of Britain, France, and Australia. Four days after MH17's demise, the Kremlin posted a two-minute video statement in the middle of the night. Standing next to his desk, Putin indirectly blamed Ukraine by saying that if it had not resumed operations against the separatists, MH17 would not have been shot down. "Nobody has the right to use this tragedy for their own narrow political aims," he said.

Putin had good reason to worry. While his propagandists could obfuscate before a domestic audience, the rest of the world was now riveted on the pro-Russian rebellion in eastern Ukraine. Because Europe had far deeper economic relations with Russia than the United States did, the EU had only reluctantly followed Washington in sanctioning the Kremlin. The shooting down of MH17 provided new impetus for European sanctions against Russia.

A Dutch-led investigation spent years reconstructing the downing of MH17, confirming what had been the likeliest version from the start: that the separatists mistook the Malaysian Boeing for a Ukrainian military plane and shot it down. The investigation established that a Buk surface-to-air missile had been used from a system brought to the Donbas from Russia's Fifty-Third Anti-Aircraft Missile Brigade. In November 2022 a Dutch court found Igor Girkin and two others guilty for the murder of the 298 people aboard MH17. They were sentenced, in absentia, to life in prison. The investigation into further perpetrators continued, and in February 2023 investigators announced they had found "strong indications" Putin had approved the Buk delivery but that they lacked sufficient evidence to prosecute him. In any case, as a head of state, Putin enjoyed immunity from Dutch prosecutors.

The separatists' use of ever more powerful Russian weapons came as Ukrainian forces ramped up their offensive against the insurgency. At first caught off guard, the Ukrainians gradually regained their balance. The volunteer spirit of the Maidan helped fuel a patriotic movement to save

Ukraine. "Putin calculated everything: how to destroy our army and our security service," said Andriy Parubiy, the Ukrainian security adviser.[49] "But he clearly could not foresee that thousands of boys would go straight from the Maidan to the front line with weapons in their hands." One volunteer formation in particular, the Azov Battalion, drew attention for its far-right commanders and use of Nazi symbols. Just as during the Maidan protest, the presence of ultranationalist radicals in the ranks of the volunteers was undeniable, but they did not reflect the overall outlook of the pro-unity camp. Many of the volunteer fighters were Russian speakers from the Donbas, motivated by the desire to defend their homeland from a foreign invader.

For most Ukrainians, including those who wanted to join Russia, it was difficult to grasp that war was exploding into their lives. Ukrainians had believed they lived in a country surrounded by friendly nations, and the last war fought on Ukrainian soil—World War II—was seventy years past. All of present-day Ukraine, including the Donbas and Crimea, had been overrun by Nazi Germany. When the Red Army steamrolled the Germans back out, Ukraine suffered a second wave of devastation. As distant as World War II was in time, its memory was etched in battlefield memorials and passed on within families. For many Ukrainians, war was not an abstraction. When I asked people in the Donbas whether they preferred the Kyiv authorities or the separatists, I often heard one and the same plaintive phrase: *Lish by ne bylo voiny* ("As long as there's no war").

Ukraine's new war arrived in sporadic bursts of intense, localized violence. During the course of the summer, the Ukrainian offensive picked up momentum. By late August the Ukrainians were poised to encircle Donetsk. The Kremlin was walking a fine line, sustaining the rebellion while vigorously denying any direct involvement. In early August Borodai resigned and made way for a local militant, Alexander Zakharchenko, to replace him as head of the DNR.[50] Zakharchenko got the job after a meeting with Surkov in the Kremlin.[51] Borodai later said that Moscow was eager to prove to the West that the DNR was not a Kremlin project by replacing the separatist leadership with locals. Girkin, in his own words, was forced to resign as the DNR's "defense minister." A similar government reshuffle took place in the LNR, where a local militant, Igor Plotnitsky, took over all executive functions. Subsequently, Surkov held regular meetings with the puppet leaders of the DNR and LNR, both in Russia and in the separatist territories.[52]

Even as the faces of the rebel leadership became more local, Russian involvement deepened. On August 24, Ukrainian Independence Day, the Kremlin sent a stealth invasion of regular Russian troops to reinforce the separatists at Ilovaisk, a rail junction east of Donetsk.[53] When nine Russian paratroopers were taken captive and paraded in Kyiv, Putin insisted that they must have crossed into Ukraine by accident. As the plight of the Ukrainian forces in Ilovaisk became desperate, Putin publicly appealed to the separatists to provide a "humanitarian corridor" out of the besieged town. The next morning, when the Ukrainians withdrew, they were ambushed by Russian forces hiding in the woods. As many as four hundred soldiers and volunteer fighters were killed in the massacre.

While the Russian military was seeing its first major engagement with Ukrainian forces at Ilovaisk, reports were coming in of a second column of Russian armor that had crossed the border at Novoazovsk on the Sea of Azov.[54] Some twenty miles down the coastal highway from Novoazovsk lay Mariupol, the Donetsk region's second city and its only port. The Kremlin denied that the Russian army was fighting in Ukraine. In a phone call with Merkel, who had become the West's main interlocutor with the Kremlin, Putin said that any Russian soldiers in Donetsk were volunteers on leave.[55] When Merkel asked if Russian soldiers always take their vacations fully armed, Putin blamed corruption and said the weapons must have been stolen along the way.

Nobody believed Putin's ludicrous explanations, especially after his bald-faced lies that the Russian military had not seized Crimea. The Donbas separatists themselves euphemistically referred to the Russian troops as *otpuskniki* ("vacationers") after Zakharchenko told Russian state television that active-duty service members from Russia preferred fighting in Ukraine to spending their vacations on the beach.[56] Zakharchenko said that between three thousand and four thousand such "volunteers from Russia" had seen action alongside the separatists.

The Russian army's intervention tipped the balance in the rebels' favor. After the defeat at Ilovaisk, two-thirds of Ukraine's armor was destroyed, and Mariupol was under direct threat of falling.[57] Poroshenko had no choice but to sue for peace. A fragile ceasefire was hammered out in Minsk, the capital of Belarus, and signed on September 5. Both sides needed the agreement, not just Kyiv. The hardening Ukrainian resistance, as well as the West's unified response to Russia's aggression, had taken Moscow by surprise. Wary of new sanctions and body bags returning to Russia, the Kremlin took a pause.

The first Minsk agreement did not survive the winter. The violence ticked up again as the separatists took over the Donetsk airport, dislodging the Ukrainian government from its last toehold in the city. The rebels, with the backing of Russian troops, then turned to ousting the Ukrainians from the town of Debaltseve, which bulged precariously into separatist-held territory on the border of the Donetsk and Luhansk regions. Meanwhile in Washington, calls in Congress were getting louder for Obama to overcome his reluctance to supply Ukraine with defensive weapons. In Berlin, German officials feared that American military aid would backfire because it would be too little to help the Ukrainians prevail, give new fodder for the Kremlin's propaganda machine, and divide European allies. In a last-ditch effort to resuscitate the peace process, Merkel embarked on a week of shuttle diplomacy that took her to Kyiv, Moscow, Washington, and Ottawa, culminating in a summit in Minsk on February 11, 2015, with Poroshenko and Putin. The French president François Hollande, who had helped set up the so-called Normandy Format in June, played a supporting role.

As fate would have it, the marathon talks coincided with the seventieth anniversary of the end of the Yalta Conference, where Franklin Roosevelt and Winston Churchill haggled with Joseph Stalin over the fate of Europe at the end of World War II. Putin, who had left open his attendance to the last minute, used his trademark brinkmanship in the knowledge that Poroshenko, Merkel, and Hollande were expected at an EU summit in Brussels the next day. At the same time, the separatist assault on Debaltseve was intensifying. As the talks dragged into the night, Merkel asked Poroshenko: "Petro, do you really want to sign this? Can you sign this?"[58] The haggard Ukrainian president answered: "I need this, I need peace." The negotiations lasted almost seventeen hours, but the next morning there was a new agreement, a rehash of the original Minsk protocol with concrete deadlines and specifics as to its implementation.[59]

The deal was clearly to Kyiv's disadvantage. It stipulated that Ukraine would regain full control over its border only *after* the holding of local elections in the Donetsk and Luhansk regions, as well as the adoption of a new Ukrainian constitution "with the key element of decentralization"—both of which were to happen before the end of 2015. Putin forced the Minsk II agreement on Poroshenko literally at gunpoint as his troops besieged the Ukrainian forces in Debaltseve. If Poroshenko tried to fulfill the political points of Minsk II, he would risk a new revolution on the Maidan; if Poroshenko refused, Ukraine would carry the responsibility for the peace deal's failure. Either outcome promised Russia future dividends, including the possibility of a new Ukrainian government ready to bow to the Kremlin's will. In the meantime, Moscow would be able to resupply the separatists unhindered. The agreement obligated Putin to nothing since Russia was not formally a party to the conflict.

None of the signatories to Minsk II held any power on their own: the separatist leaders Zakharchenko and Plotnitsky; Russia's ambassador to Ukraine, Mikhail Zurabov; the former Ukrainian president Leonid Kuchma; and Heidi Tagliavini, a Swiss diplomat representing the Organization for Security and Cooperation in Europe. Minsk II was a piece of paper that Moscow could always use against Kyiv—and that the Western powers could hide behind as their "diplomatic solution" to a dirty little war on the edge of Europe.

For Russian ultranationalists such as Girkin, the Minsk agreement came as a bitter disappointment because it spelled the end of their dream of "Novorossiya" stretching from Kharkiv to Odesa. Once back in Russia, Girkin publicly criticized the Kremlin, Surkov in particular. Girkin also fell out with Borodai and lambasted the DNR leadership as a band of gangsters and fools. From the Kremlin's point of view, Girkin and Borodai had done their jobs and were no longer needed. But the nationalist genie was out of the bottle.

In his March 2014 speech celebrating the annexation of Crimea, Putin had spoken darkly of his domestic critics as "national traitors" and the West's "fifth column" inside Russia. Events in Ukraine became the subtext for everything that happened in Russia. For Putin's supporters, Ukraine had been too weak to resist the march of the United States to Russia's borders; for his liberal opponents, it was only a matter of time before Russians would be inspired by Ukrainians' civic activism and bring down their own corrupt government.

The Russian opposition leader Boris Nemtsov emerged as one of the loudest critics of Putin's military intervention in Ukraine. A former reformist governor and deputy prime minister in the 1990s, Nemtsov had once been seen as a possible successor to Boris Yeltsin. After his liberal Union of Right Forces party failed to get into the Duma in 2003, Nemtsov became a fixture at Moscow opposition rallies. Following the Orange Revolution, he served as an adviser to Yushchenko, earning the Kremlin's ire.

As the first anniversary of the annexation of Crimea approached, Nemtsov was organizing a protest march and putting together a report on Putin's covert war in Ukraine. Late on the night of February 27, 2015— exactly one year after the Russian takeover of the Crimean parliament— Nemtsov was gunned down below the Kremlin walls after having dinner with his girlfriend on Red Square. He died a few steps from the onion domes of St. Basil's Cathedral.

Boris Nemtsov became the first victim of the Ukraine conflict on Russian soil.[60] The March 1 protest that he had been planning in the days before his death turned into a memorial march attended by thousands. Some people carried the blue and yellow Ukrainian flag. Suddenly it was no longer just the national symbol of Ukraine but a banner of democratic change in Russia.

7

Yankee, Come Back!

Less than a month after Russian troops cemented their grip on Crimea and massed on the borders of mainland Ukraine, the USS *Donald Cook*, an American guided-missile destroyer, steamed into the Black Sea. The lightning occupation of the peninsula had taken the world by surprise, and the Pentagon was scrambling to reassure U.S. allies in the region. "The main thing is that the aborigines don't eat it," Dmitry Rogozin, Russia's pugnacious deputy prime minister, wrote on Twitter, referring to a song about explorer Captain James Cook's deadly encounter with Indigenous people in the South Seas. Two days later, on April 12, 2014, a Russian Sukhoi 24 attack plane made a dozen passes next to the American destroyer. The showdown was reminiscent of a 1988 incident in which two Soviet frigates "bumped" two American warships that had challenged Moscow's claim on waters off the coast of Crimea.[1]

The U.S. military downplayed the buzzing of the *Donald Cook*. The Pentagon said the Sukhoi had ignored queries by the American destroyer, describing the Russian action as "provocative and unprofessional." No shots were fired, and the Russian jet appeared to have been unarmed. A second Sukhoi was also spotted in the vicinity. "The *Donald Cook* is more than capable of defending herself against two Su-24s," a Pentagon spokesman said. Russian media told a rather different story. The official government newspaper boasted that the Sukhoi had jammed the *Donald Cook*'s

Aegis missile defense system, causing the warship to hightail it to Romania and twenty-seven traumatized crew members to resign.[2] If the Americans cannot pulverize a poorly armed enemy from a safe distance, they do not play, the paper wrote.

Almost a year later, Vladimir Putin commented on the incident in a documentary-style film. Putin recalled that Russia had deployed its Bastion antiship missiles to Crimea to forestall any U.S. military response.[3] "We deliberately rolled out those systems so they could be seen from outer space," he said. As the *Donald Cook* approached, the Crimean Peninsula came into the range of its Tomahawk missiles, the film's narrator said ominously. Yet when the crew realized that the Bastion missile system had locked in on it, the American warship abruptly turned around. As for the Sukhoi fighter, Putin said that he had not ordered it to buzz the American destroyer.[4] "They were just messing around," he said like an indulgent father brushing off a son's prank. "They didn't even tell me about it."

Putin could be confident that NATO would not lay siege to Sevastopol, as a coalition of European powers had done in the nineteenth century and Nazi Germany in the twentieth century. For most Westerners, Ukraine was on the periphery of Europe and hardly distinguishable from Russia. The Kremlin, however, regarded Ukraine as a vital buffer zone that Russia had controlled for more than two hundred years. With a noninterventionist president in the White House and most continental Europeans committed pacifists, Putin had little to fear. Ultimately, Putin's brazenness was backed up by the confidence of commanding the largest nuclear arsenal in the world.

After the collapse of the Soviet Union, the Kremlin withdrew its armies from Europe and scrapped much of its military machine. If both sides had planned for mammoth tank battles involving hundreds of thousands of soldiers during the Cold War, post-Communist Russia had neither the weapons nor the resources to prepare for such contingencies. In a Europe at peace, there was no need for vast conventional armies, and the nuclear arsenal inherited from the Soviet Union became the main guarantee of Russia's national security. When Barack Obama came into office talking about ridding the world of nuclear arms, the Kremlin was not interested. For Putin and his protégé, Dmitry Medvedev, Russia's nuclear arms were no longer just a deterrent against attack but also a shield for military adventures in neighboring states.

In January 2014 the United States quietly informed NATO allies that Russia had been testing a new ground-launched cruise missile in violation of a key arms control treaty.[5] After months of trying to resolve compliance issues with the Kremlin behind the scenes, the Obama administration finally went public in July, declaring that Russia was not upholding its obligations under the landmark 1987 Intermediate-Range Nuclear Forces (INF) Treaty. Moscow, for its part, countered that new U.S. missile defense systems based in eastern Europe would give the United States an offensive strike capability banned by the treaty.

The Kremlin did not want the world to forget Russia's nuclear potential. On the day of Crimea's fraudulent independence referendum, Russia's chief propagandist, Dmitry Kiselyov, went on his weekly news show suggesting that Obama had gone gray after multiple phone calls with Putin. Standing before the image of an orange mushroom cloud, Kiselyov said: "Russia is the only country in the world that is really capable of turning the United States into radioactive ash." Casual references to the Russian nuclear arsenal became commonplace in the Kremlin's rhetoric—not only to rattle the West but also to remind Russians of the mortal danger they faced every day. As Western resistance to Russia's aggression toward Ukraine stiffened, the Kremlin leaked plans for a sea drone packed with radioactive explosives; threatened to target Denmark's warships with nuclear weapons should the country join NATO's missile defense shield; and announced plans to deploy dozens of new intercontinental ballistic missiles.

In September 2015 the American TV host Charlie Rose asked Putin whether nuclear weapons made Russia "a force to be reckoned with." The Russian president laughed and replied: "I hope so, otherwise what are these weapons for?"[6] He added: "We proceed from the assumption that nuclear weapons and other weapons are the means to protect our sovereignty and legitimate interests, not the means to behave aggressively or to fulfill some nonexistent imperial ambitions."

Putin argued that the West's encroachment on Russia's western borders gave him no choice but to move on Ukraine. "Let me say too that we are not opposed to cooperation with NATO," he said in his March 18 speech justifying the Crimea annexation.[7] "We are against having a military alliance making itself at home right in our backyard or in our historic territory. I simply cannot imagine that we would travel to Sevastopol to visit NATO sailors.

Of course, most of them are wonderful guys, but it would be better to have them come and visit us, be our guests, rather than the other way round."

In reality, Ukraine was even farther from joining the Western military alliance than it had been right before the 2008 NATO summit in Bucharest. The Euromaidan protests that had swept Viktor Yanukovych from power were about Ukraine joining the European Union, not NATO. Even though many members of the new government in Kyiv supported NATO membership, the issue was still much too divisive among Ukrainians to put on the political agenda. Ironically, by seizing Crimea and starting a rebellion in the Donbas, Putin did more than any Ukrainian politician to drive Ukraine toward the West and away from Russia. Before 2014, most Ukrainians viewed Russia positively, and a majority felt ambivalent or negative about NATO.[8] But after the unprovoked Russian aggression, more and more Ukrainians saw Russia as an enemy and NATO membership as a sensible goal.

More importantly, Ukraine no longer had any powerful backers among Western powers. In the United States, George W. Bush's strident unilateralism had been followed by disengagement, particularly in regard to Europe. The former U.S. national security adviser Zbigniew Brzezinski—who had so pithily described Ukraine as the essential piece of any Russian empire—suggested on the eve of Crimea's occupation that the best geopolitical model for Ukraine was Finland, which maintained deep economic ties with both Russia and the West while remaining neutral.[9]

The Americans' lack of interest in Ukraine reflected their lack of interest in Europe as a whole. It was also a tacit recognition of a Russian sphere of influence or, at the very least, Moscow's disproportionate ability to influence the region. In 2008, even the hawks in the Bush administration had to concede that Georgia was too far away and indefensible. Despite Putin's land grab during the five-day Georgian war, the United States did not view Russia as a threat to NATO territory and continued its massive troop withdrawal from Europe that had begun after the Cold War. Obama, who inherited Bush's wars in Afghanistan and Iraq, was determined to shift U.S. foreign policy to the Pacific. There was a widespread opinion in Washington that Europe—rich, unified, and at peace—should take care of its own defense.

Europe at the beginning of 2014 was a deceptively tranquil place. Western Europe's great powers were now all democracies, trade partners, and allies. Centuries-old rivalries had been relegated to Eurovision song contests. In the Europe of the twenty-first century, national borders had evaporated, and territorial expansion was a thing of the past. Europeans no longer believed that Russia, which had threatened half of the continent during the Cold War, posed a military danger.

In the Kremlin, there was a growing sense of vulnerability that had little to do with the West's intentions or capabilities. The main source of this insecurity came from inside Russia, namely, the country's failure to become a democracy after the collapse of Communism. The more dictatorial Putin's rule became, the greater his fear of an uprising—sponsored and cheered on by the United States.

The lack of respect from Washington flustered the Kremlin. More than anything, Putin and his entourage craved recognition as the leaders of a select group of countries that would determine the fate of the world. The Soviet Union had achieved that status as a victor nation in World War II and shortly thereafter as a nuclear superpower. In the first decade after the Soviet collapse, Russia struggled just to stay together as a country. When Putin took power in 2000, he sought to restore the lost glory of the past and carve out a place as an equal partner to George W. Bush. Although the two men developed a warm personal relationship, Bush's aggressive foreign policy ran roughshod over Russian sensibilities.

Obama's approach to Russia looked like the opposite of Bush's: more pragmatic and flattering, less ideological and confrontational. But the "reset" faltered after Putin returned to the presidency in 2012—and finally crashed with Russia's seizure of Crimea. As different as Bush and Obama were, Putin reached the conclusion that the United States, regardless of its leader, was driven by its exceptionalism and determined to emasculate Russia. In the aftermath of Crimea's annexation, Putin bristled when Obama described Russia as a "regional power" that was acting "not out of strength but out of weakness." The Kremlin fumed again when Obama, speaking at the United Nations, named Russia as a global threat alongside Ebola and the Islamic State terrorist group.

Putin obsessively followed every U.S. foreign policy step with envy and anger—and every misstep with glee. For the Kremlin, the long hand of Washington was everywhere, including in Russia and in its most important neighbor, Ukraine. In Putin's version of events, it was the United States—and not the Ukrainian people—that had ousted a corrupt and hated leader.

In comments to journalists after Yanukovych's downfall Putin said: "I sometimes get the feeling that somewhere across that huge puddle, in America, people sit in a lab and conduct experiments, as if with rats, without actually understanding the consequences of what they are doing. Why did they need to do this? Who can explain this? There is no explanation at all for it."[10]

For Putin it was inconceivable that democracy and human rights could ever be the true motivation behind a foreign policy decision; America's wars and support for dictators were evidence of a double standard. Putin's disillusionment with the West, which he had still been striving to join at the beginning of the Bush presidency, mirrored a sentiment among a generation of Russians who decided that the United States and its allies used talk of democracy to conceal their own cynical goals. But calling out, even resisting, U.S. hypocrisy was not enough for Putin. He concluded that Russia now had a free hand to give the Americans a taste of their own medicine.

To counter what it regarded as America's reckless hegemony, the Kremlin laid out a set of tactics that became known as the "Gerasimov Doctrine."[11] In February 2013 Putin's newly minted chief of the general staff, Valery Gerasimov, published an article in a Russian military journal outlining his vision of war in the twenty-first century.[12] The paper became widely seen as Russia's blueprint for its "hybrid war" against Ukraine, although Gerasimov was describing what he viewed as the new *American* way of war and how Russia should respond to it. Gerasimov blamed the United States for fomenting the Arab Spring, whose consequences he compared with those of a real war. "The very 'rules of war' have changed," Gerasimov wrote. "The role of nonmilitary means of achieving political and strategic goals has grown, and, in many cases, they have exceeded the power of force of weapons in their effectiveness."

In Gerasimov's view, the United States was making use of political, economic, and "informational" levers in conflicts, as well as the targeted application of special forces and private military contractors. His article was an exhortation to take a page from the Americans and adopt similar "asymmetrical" means of fighting war. A year later the Russian military had its first chance to do so.

The United States, like its European allies, was in a state of denial after the annexation of Crimea. Russia's audacious seizure of its neighbor's territory shattered the illusion that Europeans had banished conflict to the history books. The occupation of Crimea suddenly recast Russia as an unpredictable, hostile force on Europe's borders. The Obama administration was caught flat-footed because Ukraine barely registered in its foreign policy. A year before the Maidan protests, the priority for most U.S. intelligence collection on Ukraine was ranked at level 4 or 5 on a five-point scale, where 1 was the highest.[13] Ukraine was not raised to the highest priority until February 28, 2014, the day after Russian special forces took over the Crimean parliament.

The Russian narrative that the CIA used the Maidan protests to install a "junta" of stooges was a caricature of American-backed coups of yore. The smoking gun for the Kremlin was a leaked phone call in which a top State Department official and the U.S. ambassador in Kyiv discussed their preferences for a national unity government that had been proposed—and would have been headed—by Yanukovych. That conversation paled in degrees of conspiracy compared to intercepted calls in which a Putin aide, Sergei Glazyev, instructed pro-Russian activists to start an uprising against Kyiv.

As the Kremlin ramped up its military involvement in Ukraine during the spring of 2014, the Obama administration proceeded gingerly. As a signatory to the 1994 Budapest Memorandum, the United States was committed to undefined "security assurances" to Ukraine, or in plain language, absolutely nothing. The Obama administration was reluctant to share intelligence on Russian troop movements with the Ukrainians and at first limited its military aid to Ukraine to three hundred thousand field rations.[14]

Ukrainians understandably felt abandoned by the West. The plodding predictability of the Western democracies worked in Putin's favor. A former senior Ukrainian diplomat I knew in Kyiv was blistering in his evaluation. In the past, his contacts in Washington were always willing to dispense advice to Ukraine like to children, he said.[15] Now, all those people could say was "It's a mess." The former diplomat looked up from his cup of coffee with a look of disgust: "We don't have a Churchill, only a whole range of Chamberlains."

The United States, together with the EU, sought to rein in Russia's behavior with largely symbolic sanctions. But the Obama administration's caution, as maddening as it was for Ukrainians, also had its logic. Ukraine was not a treaty ally and had never been considered an area of vital

American interest. Moreover, Putin was effectively wielding the threat of a nuclear escalation to force Washington to weigh its meager options very, very carefully.

Obama did not underestimate the weightiness of the Ukraine conflict, but he was happy to delegate Angela Merkel to lead the West's response to Russia's aggression. In office for more than eight years, Merkel was Europe's elder stateswoman and one of Putin's most frequent interlocutors. "The Georgia war taught the U.S. to coordinate with the Germans," a senior State Department official remembered later.[16] "We said to ourselves: Next time we're arm-in-arm with the Germans."

Inside the Obama administration, Joe Biden kept the Ukraine brief. The vice president was one of the most experienced foreign policy hands in Washington, given his many years on the Senate Foreign Relations Committee. Obama first sent Biden to Ukraine in 2009 to assure Kyiv that the United States still stood with Kyiv despite the "reset" with Moscow. Biden returned in April 2014, after Crimea had fallen into Putin's hands and the pro-Russian insurgency in the Donbas was picking up steam. With his trademark folksiness, Biden began a speech to Ukrainian lawmakers by quoting his mother.[17] He pledged continued American support for Ukraine but pleaded with the legislators to fulfill the bold reforms demanded by the Euromaidan protesters. "You have to fight the cancer of corruption that is endemic in your system right now," he said.

Less than a month later, a little-known Ukrainian oil company called Burisma announced that Biden's son, Hunter, had joined its board of directors.[18] At the time, I was wrapping up a reporting trip to Donetsk. Although I had never heard of either Hunter Biden or Burisma, I was flabbergasted by the news. I knew that the appointment would cause smirks in Russia because it had the exact same appearance of something a Russian or Ukrainian politician's son would do. Nobody could have imagined what consequences Hunter Biden's new job would have for American politics five years later.

If U.S. political leaders were unprepared for Russia's seizure of Crimea, the American defense establishment was hardly in a better position. While the CIA did warn U.S. policymakers of a possible Russian military intervention before the takeover, the Pentagon's Defense Intelligence Agency did not consider such a scenario likely.[19] Twenty-five years after the fall of the

Berlin Wall, most people found it inconceivable that troops from one European country would simply march into a neighboring country and occupy its territory. The 2008 Georgian war was widely considered a one-off that Mikheil Saakashvili, Georgia's mercurial leader at the time, had played no small role in bringing on himself. The seizure of Crimea, in contrast, came without warning or provocation.

Following the dissolution of the Soviet empire, the United States had begun drastically cutting its forces in Europe. U.S. Army Europe, based primarily in western Germany, shuttered almost six hundred military installations. In 2013, the U.S. Army announced plans to bring European troop levels to below thirty thousand, down from 213,000 soldiers at the end of the Cold War.[20] That year the Pentagon disbanded two armored brigades in Europe, symbolically removing its last M1 Abrams tank from German soil.[21]

The question of a U.S. military intervention on Ukraine's behalf was never under discussion. But Pentagon planners immediately began to calculate how they would defend a remote NATO member such as Estonia if Russia launched a stealth attack on it. The three tiny Baltic nations were connected to the rest of NATO by a forty-mile-wide bottleneck surrounded by Russian territory on one side and Russia's ally, Belarus, on the other. After the Baltic nations joined NATO in 2004, alliance members began a rotating air-policing mission over their airspace as none of the Baltic states had their own fighter planes. But otherwise, there were no plans to base personnel from Western militaries in countries that once had been part of the Soviet empire, except for small contingents of U.S. troops to man missile defense sites in Poland and Romania.

In January 2014, when Yanukovych was still firmly in power and Putin's main headache was pulling off the Sochi Olympics, NATO held a routine meeting of defense chiefs in Brussels. A special guest was Valery Gerasimov, the chief of the Russian general staff and the author of the article on asymmetrical warfare. Gerasimov laid out his views on improving military cooperation with the alliance and hosted his American counterpart, General Martin Dempsey, at the Russian mission to NATO. The Russian general, stone-faced in official photographs, smiled broadly as he presented Dempsey with a gift. The Russians expressed interest in gaining access to American technology for countering improvised explosive devices to prevent a terrorist attack during the Sochi games.[22] The United States also took the threat seriously. Obama and Putin discussed it during a phone call that same day, and the Pentagon sent two warships to the Black Sea to assist in the event of an attack.

Hardly a month had passed after Gerasimov's congenial meeting with Dempsey when Russian forces occupied Crimea. The Olympics were over and forgotten, and a rawer sort of competition was returning to Europe. In an effort to reassure its new NATO allies in central and eastern Europe, the Pentagon expanded previously planned air exercises in Poland to include fighter jets and sent additional warplanes to take part in air patrols over the Baltic countries.[23] At the time only one U.S. warship from the Sochi support mission, the USS *Taylor*, remained in the Black Sea, and it was moored in a Turkish port after having run aground.[24] As the Kremlin's proxies in Crimea prepared to break off from Ukraine, the U.S. Navy dispatched the USS *Truxtun*, a guided-missile destroyer, to participate in "scheduled" drills with the Bulgarian and Romanian navies. The *Donald Cook* took its place in April.

Just as in the aftermath of Russia's invasion of Georgia—when the United States sent warships bearing humanitarian aid into the Black Sea—the display of U.S. naval power during the takeover of Crimea failed to impress. The *Taylor* had to be towed to Greece because of a damaged propeller, and its captain was relieved of his duties.[25] The *Truxtun* was subjected to constant attacks by Russian electronic warfare.[26] And the *Donald Cook* was buzzed by a Russian fighter jet in an incident reminiscent of Cold War face-offs.

The Kremlin portrayed the appearance of the *Donald Cook* in the Black Sea as proof that the United States was a hostile, meddling power—and, at the same time, as validation of Russia as a power worthy of America's respect. The Pentagon had intended for the destroyer to show the flag in the face of Russian aggression. But rather than demonstrate American power, the *Donald Cook* incident underscored the United States' limitations in confronting a peer nuclear power with no qualms about brandishing its deadliest weapons.

The overriding concern in Western capitals was to prevent what was still a regional conflict from escalating into a global conflagration. The Kremlin's frequent references to nuclear weapons were deliberate and effective. Deterrence, once the underpinning of the power balance between the United States and the Soviet Union, was now working only to Putin's advantage. While leaders in the West repeated the mantra that there was "no military solution" to the conflict, the Kremlin kept all its options on the table.

Even if the alliance could not stop Putin from carving up Ukraine, NATO military planners decided that at least he could be deterred from attacking the thinly defended NATO members on Russia's doorstep. The revival of deterrence represented a sea change in Western strategic thinking. The concept was an affront to the privileged pacifism of western Europeans, who did not wish to recall that Europe's liberation from fascism had come from the barrel of a gun, and that the credible threat of force had held back the Soviet Union for more than forty years. Spoiled by the certainties of their rules-bound societies, Europeans were convinced of the universality of their liberal democracies. As institutions, NATO and the EU had viewed enlargement as a logical—even inevitable—process as long as there were still willing and eligible candidate countries. The underlying assumption in the West was that Moscow had a shared interest in the countries of central and eastern Europe turning into stable, flourishing democracies, as Russia would gain a secure western border for the first time in its history. In fact, the Kremlin preferred weak, dysfunctional states that it could easily control.

In the wake of Crimea's occupation, NATO suspended all cooperation with Russia. In June 2014, Obama introduced the European Reassurance Initiative, later renamed the European Deterrence Initiative, which committed the funds and forces to enhance the U.S. military presence across central and eastern Europe.[27] American and other NATO troops started rotating through the Baltic nations and Poland as the alliance began contemplating the permanent stationing of Western forces in the region.

The status quo was hard to give up. Even as France joined its allies in imposing sanctions on Russia, French officials insisted they would honor a $1.6 billion contract to deliver two Mistral-class amphibious assault ships to the Russian navy. The Mistral was capable of carrying helicopters, armored vehicles, and hundreds of troops. In June 2014, the first ship, the *Vladivostok*, began sea trials, and four hundred Russian sailors arrived in the French port of Saint-Nazaire for training ahead of the vessel's imminent delivery.[28] A second ship, the *Sevastopol*, was due to be completed in 2015. The deal was illustrative of Putin's way of doing business: while gaining access to Western technology, the Kremlin was simultaneously increasing France's reliance on Russia as the shipyards in Saint-Nazaire had fallen on hard times.

YANKEE, COME BACK! 167

The French president François Hollande held out until September 3, 2014, when the Russian military's direct involvement in Ukraine became undeniable. Hollande froze the Mistral deal and the next day traveled to Wales for a summit of NATO leaders. There they pledged to spend 2 percent of their countries' GDP on defense and beef up the alliance's presence in eastern Europe. Ukraine, which NATO described in its final statement as a "long-standing and distinctive partner," received words of moral support.

On his way to the Wales summit, Barack Obama stopped in Tallinn, the Estonian capital, to reiterate the U.S. commitment to Article 5 of NATO's founding treaty: an attack on one was an attack on all. "In this alliance, there are no old members or new members, no junior partners or senior partners. There are just allies, pure and simple. And we will defend the territorial integrity of every single ally," Obama said.[29] Two days after the U.S. president left, an Estonian security officer named Eston Kohver was detained by the FSB on the border between Estonia and Russia. The Estonians claimed that Kohver had been abducted from Estonian territory, while the Russians accused him of espionage. The timing of his arrest hardly seemed like a coincidence.[30]

Obama had just delivered a lofty speech with references to democracy, freedom, and shared values. But as committed as the United States might have been to its Baltic allies on paper, the issue remained of how they would be defended in practice. Estonia was more than a thousand miles away from the U.S. military bases clustered in southern Germany. Typically, it could take fifteen days or more to get diplomatic clearance to transport military equipment from one NATO member state to another. For NATO generals, the nightmare scenario was that Vladimir Putin would send "little green men" into a Baltic country before its allies could react, exposing NATO as a paper tiger.

The U.S. Army got its first opportunity to test out the logistical challenges of defending an eastern NATO ally in June 2016, when Poland held Anakonda-16, its largest military exercise in more than a decade. Only five years had passed since Poland hosted the first joint NATO-Russian counterterrorism exercise, involving fighter planes from both sides. Now the idea of military cooperation with Russia was a distant memory. Even so, the Obama administration and other Western governments were concerned that Moscow could view Anakonda-16 as provocative, especially coming less than a month before a NATO summit in Warsaw. As the U.S. Army moved more than one hundred convoys from Germany to Poland, it faced mountains of paperwork, a shortage of rail cars, and clogged roadways.

The Anakonda-16 exercise involved thirty thousand troops from more than twenty NATO and partner countries, with the United States contributing almost half of the soldiers. On the second day of the exercises, I watched as German and British engineers built a pontoon bridge over the Vistula River in central Poland.[31] Less than an hour later, a column of Strykers—the U.S. Army's eight-wheeled, twenty-ton fighting machines—trundled over the bridge to link up with a beachhead secured by Polish, British, and U.S. paratroopers. As he observed the river crossing, a German first lieutenant muttered about American "saber rattling" under his breath.

The divisions inside NATO were real, with Germany and France far slower to see a Russian threat than Poland and the three Baltic nations. In a newspaper interview published the day after Anakonda-16 ended, the German foreign minister Frank-Walter Steinmeier lamented NATO's "saber rattling" and "symbolic tank parades" on Russia's borders.[32] He called for dialogue with Moscow instead of deterrence. Steinmeier, a Social Democrat, was clearly playing to the pacifist voices in his own party, which shared power with Merkel's Christian Democrats.[33] In fact, Germany had played a key role in planning and carrying out Anakonda-16, and the German military leadership was largely in step with its NATO allies. Few remembered that it was a German defense minister, Volker Rühe, who had given the initial push for NATO enlargement in the early 1990s.[34]

The NATO summit in Warsaw took place under a cloud of uncertainty. The United States was distracted by problems at home, with the Republican candidate in the looming presidential election, Donald Trump, calling NATO "obsolete." The Merkel-Steinmeier tandem emitted conflicting signals on how to approach Moscow. And Hollande arrived in Warsaw saying that Russia was "not an adversary, not a threat" for France. "Russia is hyped up on testosterone while Europe is filled with self-doubt," Ivanna Klympush-Tsintsadze, Ukraine's deputy prime minister for European integration, told me at the summit.[35] "Russia wants to be great again. It doesn't measure greatness by the well-being of its people but by the greatness of its enemies. It wants to be feared, and it's getting what it wants."

Despite the dissonant voices, NATO agreed to base four multilateral battalions in the Baltic region, with the United States leading the battalion in Poland. In addition, the Pentagon committed to rotating an armored brigade through eastern Europe. NATO military planners were once again speaking in Cold War terms, only their frame of reference had shifted significantly eastward: the "tripwire" role that West Berlin used to play was filled by the three Baltic nations, and the "frontline" position of West Germany was now occupied by Poland. American troops were once again returning to Europe and taking on a permanent presence in new NATO member states. After the Russian aggression against Ukraine, the Kremlin's fears of U.S. forces being based on Russia's borders became a self-fulfilling prophesy. A Lithuanian vice defense minister, Giedrimas Jeglinskas, later told me that the annexation of Crimea had "saved" NATO.[36] "Events in Ukraine really show us that the bear hasn't gone anywhere," he said.

The threat perceptions of Russia were not just a function of geography but also of history. The small countries of central and eastern Europe, which had been dominated by the Soviet Union after World War II, generally took a dim view of the Kremlin's motives. Following Russia's attack on Ukraine, they were frustrated by the reluctance of large European powers to reconsider their stance toward Moscow. Germany in particular had a long, recurring history of ignoring the interests of smaller nations in favor of reaching a great power accommodation with Russia. The former leader of Lithuania's independence movement, Vytautas Landsbergis, called Kremlin offers of dialogue "gimmicks" meant to distract and divide. "Does Putinist Russia want to speak? No, they want to get us to listen and obey," Landsbergis said at a talk in Berlin to commemorate the twenty-fifth anniversary of the Baltic states' independence.[37] Many Germans still clung to the vision of a "common European home" proposed by the last Soviet leader, Mikhail Gorbachev. "Do you prefer to have a common house with a robber?" Landsbergis asked a former German ambassador to Moscow. "This neighbor is constantly planning how to destroy our membership in the EU. The first goal is to build a gap between Europe and America."

Slowly it dawned on western Europeans that they too had become targets in a wider Kremlin campaign against the West. The "hybrid" methods Russia had first employed in Ukraine—the financing of pro-Kremlin media and political parties or the planting of fake news stories—were now also being put to use in western Europe. In spring 2015, the IT network of Germany's lower house of parliament, the Bundestag, was subjected to a cyberattack that affected the email accounts of several lawmakers, including Merkel. German investigators later blamed the GRU, Russia's military intelligence agency, for the hack.

Rather than mark a new set of tactics, Russia's clandestine operations seemed to have been taken straight out of a KGB playbook on "active measures," according to the journalist Catherine Belton.[38] Many in the West believed that Russians were simply funneling stolen cash into the West; they did not see the money as a giant slush fund to implement a strategic agenda. Konstantin Malofeyev, the Russian businessman who had helped bankroll the Crimean uprising, now started promoting far-right parties across Europe—from France and Italy to Greece and Bulgaria. In December 2016, one senior German lawmaker told me that he was very concerned about Russian election interference.[39] He recalled how without any warning a flash mob of hundreds of members of Germany's Russian-speaking community, together with far-right activists, had descended on a town in his district to protest against migrants. The source of their outrage was a false story spread by Russian state media about the gang rape of a thirteen-year-old Russian girl in Berlin.[40]

A 2015 poll taken in eight NATO countries revealed gaping differences in the readiness to defend an ally if it came under attack by Russia.[41] Americans were the most willing to intervene militarily, with 56 percent for defending an ally and 37 percent against. In Germany, where respondents were the most reluctant to use force, the numbers were almost the exact inverse: 38 percent of Germans said their country should defend an ally against Russia, while 58 percent said it should not. Germans also stood out for a low level of support for arming Ukraine (19 percent vs. 46 percent among Americans) and their opposition to Ukraine's NATO membership (57 percent opposed it whereas 62 percent of Americans supported it).

Germany was an outlier in part because of its bloodstained history in eastern Europe. Several generations of Germans had internalized the guilt for Nazi atrocities committed in the Soviet Union, which in the popular imagination was equated with Russia. The suffering inflicted by the Nazis on the peoples of the Baltic nations, Belarus, and Ukraine was largely overlooked. Germans' penance for Nazi crimes, combined with economic assistance, paved the way for Gorbachev to bless Germany's unification in 1990. A sense of guilt for the past and gratitude for the peaceful resolution of their country's Cold War division colored Germans' view of post-Communist Russia. So did a vein of anti-Americanism that ran deep on both ends of Germany's political spectrum.

In Berlin a split opened up between the Chancellery and the Foreign Ministry. Merkel, who had grown up in Soviet-occupied East Germany, was wary of Putin's KGB past and clear-eyed about his subversion of Ukraine. "Every death in Ukraine can be blamed on Putin. He's responsible," a senior Merkel adviser told me as the Donbas insurgency dragged into its third year.[42] "We have to get used to being prepared. We will need to increase military spending even if we don't like it." Putin had made a grave miscalculation if he believed that Russia's close relations to Germany—embodied by his friendship with Merkel's predecessor, Gerhard Schröder—would confuse and neutralize the West. Instead, Merkel became the unlikely standard-bearer of the free world, overcoming internal divisions in the EU over sanctions and standing side by side with the Obama administration.

Meanwhile, Merkel's foreign minister, Frank-Walter Steinmeier, and her economy minister, Sigmar Gabriel, did not tire of traveling to Russia to preach the prospects of closer cooperation. Both men had risen up through the Social Democratic Party as disciples of Schröder, who continued to cast an outsized shadow on his party. Schröder's affinity for Russia had its roots in West German Chancellor Willy Brandt's *Ostpolitik*, the Cold War policy of rapprochement with the Communist bloc based on economic ties. While many Americans later credited Ronald Reagan's arms buildup for bringing the Soviet empire to its knees, many Germans believed it was *Ostpolitik* that had created the right conditions for regime change in central and eastern Europe. Schröder, who was convinced that integrating Russia into the European economy would help democratize it, found a willing partner in Putin. In 2003, when the United States invaded Iraq over the objections of Germany and Russia, the two men became even closer, united in their opposition to American hegemony.

Less than a month after handing over power to Merkel in 2005, Schröder landed a job as "chairman of the shareholders committee" of Nord Stream, a natural gas pipeline he had signed off on while he was still in office. Even after Russia invaded Ukraine, Schröder literally embraced Putin. In April 2014, on the same day that the EU slapped new sanctions on the Kremlin, the ex-chancellor celebrated his seventieth birthday in St. Petersburg at an opulent party attended by the German ambassador to Russia, the CEO of the Russian energy company Gazprom—and Putin, whom Schröder met with a hug and a smile.[43]

Schröder's retirement package was the crassest example of Putin buying influence in Europe, but it was not unique. The Kremlin handed out board positions on Russian state companies to former prime ministers of Austria, Finland, and France in the expectation that they would advance Russian interests in their countries. Some retired officials, such as Romano Prodi, the former Italian prime minister, or Donald Evans, a former U.S. commerce secretary and close friend of George W. Bush, turned down the honor.

Snagging Americans was less important for the Kremlin given the United States' relatively small share of Russian trade compared to Europe's. Yet even without financial incentives, part of the American establishment was still resistant to accepting the paradigm shift after Russia's military intervention in Ukraine. This faction was not blind to the injustice of the Kremlin's actions but believed that managing the fraught relationship with Russia, a rival nuclear power, took priority over a territorial conflict in a nonaligned country. Before Ukraine exploded in its face, the Obama administration was seeking Russian assistance in ending Syria's civil war and reining in Iran's nuclear program. Those efforts continued after the annexation of Crimea. In 2015 alone, the U.S. secretary of state John Kerry met with his caustic Russian counterpart, Sergei Lavrov, eighteen times. One former senior U.S. diplomat I knew despairingly compared Kerry to "a bowl of Jell-O" when it came to Russia.[44]

A small minority of Americans sympathized outright with the Kremlin. "Vladimir Putin rocks," a retired U.S. military officer who had served in Germany told me. "I know he's crooked, but he speaks his mind. We need more of that."

Understanding Putin's motives and agreeing with them were two very different things. It was entirely possible to comprehend Putin's territorial claims and sensitivity toward NATO enlargement without endorsing his surprise attack on an unsuspecting neighbor. Much of Russia's rise from land-locked principality to empire was driven by an expansion to the seas. When Catherine the Great annexed Crimea, a former Turkish possession, in the eighteenth century, the peninsula became Russia's strategic gateway to the Black Sea and beyond. The 1997 treaty that divided up the Soviet Union's Black Sea Fleet set up the arrangement by which Russia would lease its Crimean bases from Ukraine. For the Kremlin, loss of access to those bases was unacceptable.

A major irritant for Russia were the regular Sea Breeze exercises cohosted by Ukraine and the United States. The naval drills took place in the framework of Partnership for Peace, a NATO program to help prepare future members and build trust with nonmembers, first and foremost Russia. Sea Breeze 1997 was the first exercise of its kind. Only three years had passed since a Crimean leader, Yury Meshkov, came to power promising to join Russia. The script for the exercise was eerily prescient: after separatists backed by a neighbor try to take over a fictional "country orange," U.S. Marines deploy to rescue the legitimate government.[45] As the landing was supposed to take place on a Crimean beach, locals took to the streets to protest "American imperialism." Boris Yeltsin, Russia's pro-Western president, was still in office, but the scenario for the exercise was too much even for his administration. The Russian military angrily rejected an offer to take part in the exercises, and the script was quickly rewritten to have the Marines deliver humanitarian aid after an earthquake. The following year, Sea Breeze 98 stayed away from Crimea, and Russia sent two warships for its first joint exercise with the U.S. and Ukrainian navies.[46]

The next time Ukraine tried to hold Sea Breeze in Crimea was not until 2006, with the planned participation of 3,500 service members, ten ships, and twelve aircraft from the United States.[47] Viktor Yushchenko, the hero of the 2004 Orange Revolution, was mired in gridlock with his rivals and unable to get parliamentary approval to host foreign troops, as required by the Ukrainian Constitution. When an advance party of U.S. reservists arrived to do construction work at one of the training sites, they were met with protesters who confined the Americans to their quarters. The rallies were organized by Ukrainian parties opposed to Yushchenko, including Viktor Yanukovych's Party of Regions. But they were also joined by activists from Russia such as the revanchist Russian lawmaker Konstantin Zatulin. Unable to secure last-minute approval for the exercise from parliament, Yushchenko was forced to cancel Sea Breeze 2006. Amid the uproar, George W. Bush postponed his first visit to Ukraine planned for later that summer.[48]

Even before Sea Breeze 2006 was supposed to begin, an ultranationalist Russian lawmaker, Nikolai Kuryanovich, called for Crimea's "return" to Russia on the floor of the Duma, basing his claim on the 1774 treaty in which Turkey essentially ceded Crimea to Russia.[49] Kuryanovich was a marginal politician who advocated the annexation of Ukrainian regions by means of "referendums," followed by the restoration of Russian claims on all its former territories, including Kazakhstan and Alaska. Although Kuryanovich's views were fringe at the time, he gave voice to a Russian sense of possessiveness over Ukraine.[50]

Russia's FSB, and its head Nikolai Patrushev in particular, played an indispensable role in subverting the Sea Breeze exercises, according to Leonid Grach, a Communist politician and the Kremlin's initial choice as Crimea's puppet leader in 2014.[51] During Sea Breeze 2008, Grach led a group of protesters who successfully disrupted a landing exercise at the Donuzlav naval base. "Without Moscow, we would not have won Donuzlav," he said later. According to Grach, Patrushev began providing support to the separatist cause in 2005 following the Orange Revolution.

In 2009 Yushchenko again found himself faced with political paralysis amid infighting in his ruling coalition—and just as in 2006, he had to cancel the Sea Breeze exercise after failing to secure parliamentary approval for it.[52] Yet even after Yushchenko's defeat in a presidential election the following year, his successor, Yanukovych, continued with the joint naval exercises. Sea Breeze 2013 was overseen by the Ukrainian rear admiral Denis Berezovsky. A few months later, he was one of the first Ukrainian service members to defect to the Russian side during the occupation of Crimea.

In 2014 Ukraine held the Sea Breeze exercise in a reduced format. Ukraine's main naval base had been in Sevastopol, next to the Russian Black Sea Fleet base, and the annexation of Crimea cost the Ukrainian navy more than 80 percent of its assets.[53] The Black Sea port of Odesa became the home for what was left of Ukraine's navy. The Ukrainian armed forces as a whole were a shambles, the result of years of underinvestment and corruption, as well as the widely held belief that the country had no enemies. The Ukrainian military was slow to rise to the new challenge of fighting a Russian-backed insurgency. But ordinary citizens, who had come to expect little of their often dysfunctional government, stepped up, not just filling the ranks of volunteer battalions but also collecting food, sleeping bags, body armor, and other essentials for service members in eastern Ukraine.

In March 2014, when there were fears of a full-scale Russian invasion, I visited Ukrainian troops digging in at the border in the Kharkiv region. A stream of civilian cars arrived at the encampment to deliver supplies. It was there that I tried the tastiest slab of *salo*, Ukrainian cured pork fat, donated by farmers from the next village.

Even as the Ukrainian military increased its troop numbers and spending, it was poorly equipped to take on pro-Russian fighters who had access to a constant supply of Russian arms across an open border. Obama resisted the advice of those on his national security team, including Biden and Kerry, who recommended sending lethal aid to Ukraine.[54] Obama feared a spiral of violence that Russia would always be able to outmatch—and then blame on the United States. Antony Blinken, Obama's deputy secretary of state, shared that view. "Anything we did as countries in terms of military support for Ukraine is likely to be matched and then doubled and tripled and quadrupled by Russia," Blinken said after the Minsk II agreement was signed.[55] Obama's adamancy caused rifts within his administration, but as long as he was in office Ukraine received only "nonlethal aid" from the United States, such as Humvees and counterbattery radars for tracking enemy fire.

Perhaps the most consequential nonlethal aid Ukraine received was a joint training center in western Ukraine. The Yavoriv training ground, less than ten miles from the Polish border, had hosted a number of joint exercises with NATO in the past. In 2015, military instructors from the United States and Canada began training Ukrainian personnel heading to the Donbas. The goal was to help the Ukrainian army break out of its Soviet mold and adopt NATO standards. One Canadian officer recalled that Ukrainian troops would sometimes show up for training without enough food, ammunition, or boots, and that tanks occasionally ran out of fuel during drills.[56] Thousands of Ukrainian soldiers passed through Yavoriv, taking crash courses in the Western gear that did reach them. Whereas American troops typically spent a year learning how to use a counterbattery radar, the Ukrainians had only five weeks. Ben Hodges, the commander of the U.S. Army in Europe at the time, remembered being "astounded" by how fast Ukrainian soldiers mastered new technology.[57]

But the Ukrainians also had something to teach NATO. Even as the Kremlin dissembled about its military presence in the Donbas, the personnel that Russia did have on the ground put the latest Russian tactics and arms on full display. The Ukrainians shared what they saw on the battlefield with the Americans. "We learned so much from them that it changed our training model," Hodges said. "It helped jerk us out of the Iraq-Afghanistan mindset."

The annexation of Crimea was welcomed by an overwhelming majority of Russians.[58] But the countries with which Putin measured Russia's power and prestige condemned the move. As the conflict in eastern Ukraine escalated, Western leaders became increasingly frustrated with Putin. He had lied to them about the presence of Russian troops in Ukraine and equivocated about his aims. After the downing of Malaysia Airlines flight MH17, Putin became a pariah.

Before the G20 summit of the world's largest economies in November 2014, the host of the meeting, the Australian prime minister Tony Abbott, vowed to "shirt-front" Putin, referring to a tackle in Australian rules football.[59] As a precaution, four Russian warships steamed to Australia before the summit in Brisbane, but Putin was still subjected to a "psychological attack," as one Moscow tabloid huffed.[60] The Australians gave the Russian leader a chilly welcome, and the other participants largely avoided him at public events. For the official photo, Putin was placed on the far edge with the South African president Jacob Zuma and then ushered away from the gaggle of Western leaders, according to the paper. Putin cut short his visit, skipping breakfast on the last day to fly home early.

Putin was not used to international isolation, and it took him almost a year to find his way back into polite company. In September 2015 Putin traveled to New York to speak at the UN General Assembly, where he had not been seen in ten years. He read his speech from a sheaf of papers because he was afraid the Americans would manipulate the text if he used the teleprompter.[61] Putin evoked the victory of the "anti-Hitler coalition" that seventy years earlier had founded the UN.[62] Comparing the Islamic State to the Nazis, he proposed forming a new multinational coalition to fight the terrorist organization in Syria. It was not a new idea. In the aftermath of 9/11, Putin had pitched the idea of an "antiterrorist coalition" that would guarantee Russia's place in the new global order.[63]

Obama, predictably, turned down the Kremlin's warmed-up proposal. Two days later Russian warplanes started punishing bombing raids in Syria, although the targets were not the Islamic State but rebels fighting the regime of the Syrian dictator Bashar al-Assad. One of the first victims of the Russian campaign was a commander of the U.S.-backed Free Syrian Army, a senior State Department official told me later. Putin forced himself back onto the world stage by becoming both part of the problem and part of the solution in Syria.

Russia's first military operation beyond the borders of the former Soviet Union was a risky escalation that put Russian personnel in the same volatile battle space as U.S. troops. The Pentagon immediately renewed contacts with the Russian Defense Ministry to avoid accidental clashes. Almost overnight, Russia became the deciding factor in a conflict that had bedeviled the international community for years. Putin had studied the Soviet Union's lessons from Afghanistan and kept a small footprint in Syria. Limiting operations largely to the air, the Russian military mimicked the U.S. invasion of Iraq, publishing videos of seaborne cruise missiles fired at night—on Putin's sixty-third birthday—and grainy footage of precision strikes on enemy targets. The cruiser *Moskva*, the flagship of the Russian Black Sea Fleet, demonstratively appeared off the coast of Syria. The Kremlin even deployed its own version of the Blackwater private military contractor, the so-called Wagner Group, which had first seen action in Ukraine. Donning wraparound sunglasses, khakis, and baseball caps, Wagner's soldiers of fortune did the dirty work that the Russian army would not touch. Once again the West ignored Russia at its own risk.

Putin accomplished two main objectives by going into Syria. First, his intervention changed the conversation about Russia. For Europeans the Syrian war had overshadowed the simmering conflict in eastern Ukraine as hundreds of thousands of Syrian war refugees made their way into the EU. At the same time, France was enduring devastating terrorist attacks by Islamic extremists. The Kremlin saw an opening: a senior Russian diplomat visiting Berlin expressed interest in reviving the NATO-Russia Council and even establishing an EU-Russia security council.

Second, Putin wanted to keep Assad in power. By intervening on his behalf, the Kremlin was not just reasserting Russia's role as a Middle East powerbroker but also exacting posthumous revenge for deposed dictators Muammar Gaddafi and Saddam Hussein—victims, in Putin's eyes, of American perfidy.

On New Year's Eve 2015, Putin signed a new national security strategy that called NATO enlargement a threat and said the United States was targeting Russia with a policy of containment because of Moscow's independent course.⁶⁴ Russia had come full circle from 2000 when Putin, fresh in office, declared that he would not rule out Russia joining NATO.⁶⁵

When he returned to the presidency for a third term amid mass protests, Putin concluded that there was just one power that could unseat him: America. Yet the United States was more than Putin's fundamental antagonist. It was also an essential sparring partner that built him up at home and gave Russia a sense of purpose in the world. This dependency was a recipe for never-ending confrontation. For Putin, confrontation guaranteed his political survival.

8

Make Russia Great Again

Alexei Navalny never shied away from a fight, especially when his bona fides as a Russian nationalist were under attack. During the summer of 2017, the feisty anticorruption campaigner was building a nationwide network to run against Vladimir Putin in the upcoming presidential election. The gusto with which Navalny took on opponents was part of his appeal in a political field otherwise occupied by stuffed suits and automatons. When Igor Girkin, the former commander of the Donetsk separatists, challenged him to a debate, Navalny gleefully accepted.

After the Kremlin forced him to leave Donetsk in August 2014, Girkin found a niche for himself back in Moscow, organizing aid for the separatists and pillorying the Kremlin for abandoning the "Novorossiya" project. As Navalny ramped up his quixotic presidential campaign, Girkin proclaimed in a YouTube video that he could prove Navalny was neither a patriot, a nationalist, nor even a real opponent of Putin's regime. Russian liberals assailed Navalny for agreeing to engage with Girkin, the prime suspect in the downing of Malaysia Airlines flight MH17. But Navalny, who had started his political career by organizing debates, saw an opportunity to recruit Girkin's followers to help him oust Putin.

On July 20, 2017, Navalny and Girkin met across a wide table in the offices of Navalny's Anti-Corruption Foundation, located in a nondescript

Moscow business center. The breezy opposition leader and the dour war veteran made an odd couple. What united them was their contempt for Putin and his entourage. Since both men were banned from state television, their showdown was broadcast online.[1]

Girkin, who supported the reestablishment of an "autocratic monarchy," claimed that after the collapse of the Soviet Union the West had established a "colonial administration" of oligarchs to control the flow of Russia's natural resources. For more than three hundred years the West had been trying to keep Russia weak and divided, Girkin said. "The West is categorically against the reunification of the Russian people, which was torn to pieces in 1991 along the borders drawn by the Bolsheviks."[2] One-third of Russians ended up living in newly independent states, Girkin said, and once the process of "reunification" began with the annexation of Crimea, the West naturally opposed it.[3]

Navalny, who viewed Europe's parliamentary democracies as a model, responded that it was "a bit childish" to blame foreigners for Russia's misfortunes and argued that Russians' main enemy was not the West but their own avaricious leadership. The country could ill afford to fight a war in the Donbas when twenty million Russians lived in poverty at home, he said. Three years into the insurgency, the conflict had degenerated into a grinding, low-level war. Navalny said that it needed to end according to the Minsk II agreement, which foresaw the eventual return of the Donbas to Ukraine.

An hour into the debate, Girkin pronounced his verdict: "I'm drawing the conclusion that you never were a nationalist, and you're definitely not one right now based on what you've said."[4] A few minutes later Girkin declared that Navalny was "much worse than Putin" because Putin was at least leaving open the possibility of the Donbas's "reunification" with Russia, whereas Navalny would give it back, betraying the Russians who had died for it. And once the Donbas was returned to Ukraine, Girkin said, the next issue on the agenda would be the status of Crimea. Girkin's words sounded like a curse: "There will be no reconciliation with Ukraine. War in one form or the other is inevitable."[5]

Sitting across from Girkin, the face of Russian nationalism run amok, Navalny struggled to prove that he, too, was worthy of being called a Russian nationalist. All those years that Girkin had obediently served in Putin's FSB, Navalny had been penning nationalist manifestos and supporting nationalists persecuted by the government, he said. To Navalny, Girkin's idea of patriotism was old-fashioned and unrealistic. "I'm a real person from the real world, and that's why I plan to solve the problems that exist. I don't want to live in the chimera that we need to unite with Belarus right away, grab something over there, and annex it," he said.[6] "Helping people right now is not about war, but the fight against corruption and improving the economy."

The debate was a flop. Political commentators called it boring and lackluster, and it was unlikely that Navalny gained anything other than a few days of online outrage. Girkin's endorsement was wholly unimportant to Navalny as Girkin had a fringe following—and Navalny had no real chance of running for president. If the debate succeeded in doing anything, it was to highlight the importance of nationalism in any open discussion on Russia's future.

The Navalny-Girkin debate barely touched on some basic issues. It was the online audience, not Navalny, that raised questions about Girkin's role in the shooting down of Malaysia Airlines flight MH17. Girkin robotically maintained that his fighters had not possessed the weapons capable of bringing down the plane and declined any further comment on the matter. When viewers wrote in to ask if he considered Girkin a war criminal, Navalny wriggled out of a clear answer by saying that only a court of law could determine that. Navalny wheeled out economic arguments for opposing the war in the Donbas but did not mention the political and moral problems of Russia attacking one of its closest neighbors. The fate of Crimea came up only fleetingly.

Navalny was walking a fine line. He wanted to demonstrate his credentials as a nationalist without scaring off his liberal base. Navalny obviously was not a Russian nationalist of Girkin's ilk: bitter, fanatical, and ready to kill for the cause. But Navalny also did not shun the label of Russian nationalist. He actively courted it.

As a young man, Navalny had been drawn to Yabloko, one of post-Communist Russia's oldest political parties with a liberal, pro-Western orientation. In Putin's first two terms, Yabloko lost its representation in the Duma and gradually drifted into irrelevance. A number of liberals, including Navalny's political mentor, the journalist Yevgenia Albats, believed that the Putin regime could only be brought down by forming a coalition with nationalists.[7] Navalny split with Yabloko in 2007 and cofounded a group called NAROD, the Russian word for "people" and an acronym for National Russian Liberation Movement.

In their manifesto, the founders of NAROD warned that Russia risked disappearing from the map as the country's parasitic leadership squandered the nation's natural resources.[8] They called for a "national rebirth," democratic rights, and a unifying nationalism that would bring together all Russian citizens, regardless of ethnic origin. The 1,100-word paper was a jumble of ideas, some of them contradictory, that reflected the views of its eleven authors. At the time, the most prominent signatory was not Alexei Navalny but Zakhar Prilepin, a writer who would become an ardent supporter of the war in Ukraine. Among NAROD's "principles" were individual gun rights, the reversal of the privatizations of the 1990s, and a "sensible migration policy." The manifesto also called for recognizing the independence of Russia's "historical allies," such as the breakaway Georgian regions of Abkhazia and South Ossetia, but it did not advocate territorial expansion. Part vision and part fantasy, the NAROD manifesto was driven by the same rage against Putin that would motivate Navalny in the future.

In a 2011 interview with Albats—published five months before he became the leader of antigovernment protests in Moscow—Navalny mocked the debate over whether he was a nationalist.[9] Navalny said that he was seeking the support of people from across the political spectrum, from Communists to democrats to nationalists. He said he wanted to take on the problems that concerned "85 percent" of Russians, including illegal migration and "ethnic violence." Ignoring those issues only yielded the discussion on nationalism to the most aggressive, marginal elements, Navalny said. Although he acknowledged that NAROD had failed as a movement, Navalny said he stood by its original platform.

In his debate with Girkin, as in the NAROD manifesto, Navalny unapologetically referred to Russians as the "largest divided people" in Europe—a belief held not only by Girkin but also by Putin. In a 2005 address to the nation, Putin called the Soviet collapse the "greatest geopolitical catastrophe" of the twentieth century. "As for the Russian nation, it became a genuine drama," Putin continued.[10] "Tens of millions of our co-citizens and compatriots found themselves outside Russian territory. Moreover, the epidemic of disintegration infected Russia itself."

Estonians, Georgians, and Ukrainians may finally have achieved self-determination and independence in 1991, but the new Russia that emerged was only a shadow of its former empire. If there was one thing that Navalny, Girkin, and Putin all could agree on, it was that Russians had suffered a great historical injustice when the Soviet Union fell apart. As different as the three men were in their outlook, postimperial trauma was at the root of their worldviews. Each of them saw himself as a nationalist and a savior of the long-suffering Russian people.

In 2008 Navalny cheered on Russia's short, victorious war against Georgia that turned the separatist regions of Abkhazia and South Ossetia into Russian client statelets. He later apologized for calling Georgians "rodents"—the two words are alliterative in Russian—but he did not retract his support for the invasion as such. Less than six years later, as Russian troops fanned out over Crimea, Navalny took a much more nuanced position.

In a lengthy blog entry posted on the eve of Crimea's "independence referendum," Navalny argued against the peninsula's impending annexation.[11] Russia's most important strategic advantage was not its natural resources or nuclear weapons, he wrote, but its close relations with its two fellow East Slavic neighbors. "With Ukrainians and Belarusians, we are like brothers living in different apartments and not simply neighbors," Navalny said. Before Russia's stealth occupation of Crimea began, most people in Ukraine and Belarus would probably have agreed with that statement. Now, Navalny warned, Putin was destroying that strategic advantage by seizing Crimea on the false pretext of defending Russians.

As an anticorruption campaigner and protest leader in Russia, Navalny welcomed the popular uprising in Kyiv that had ousted the corrupt Yanukovych regime. Navalny clearly stated that any change of borders by force was unacceptable, and that Russia should live up to its international obligations as a guarantor of Ukraine's territorial integrity—even if the 1954 transfer of Crimea to Ukraine had been "wrong, unfair, and insulting to any normal Russian citizen." Instead of annexing Crimea, Navalny said, Moscow should demand a number of concessions from Kyiv, including greater autonomy for the peninsula, a guarantee that Ukraine would not join NATO, and the indefinite, rent-free use of Crimean naval bases by the Russian Black Sea Fleet.

A little more than half a year later, Navalny appeared to accept the annexation of Crimea as a fait accompli. In an interview with the liberal radio station Ekho Moskvy, Navalny said that even if Crimea had been seized in violation of international law, it would de facto belong to Russia for the "foreseeable future."[12] Asked if he would return Crimea to Ukraine if he became president, Navalny replied: "What is Crimea—a ham sandwich that you can take and give back?" It would be only fair to conduct a "normal referendum," even if the final result would likely not differ from that of the Kremlin's fake plebiscite, he said.

Navalny took a controversial position and stuck to it. Years later he still insisted on the idea of a second referendum, disregarding the fact that the first one had been carried out in violation of Ukraine's constitution and that Crimea's population had changed significantly since the annexation, with pro-unity Ukrainians leaving and Russian citizens moving in.[13] However, Navalny was right that pro-Russian sentiment in Crimea had always run high, and that returning it to Ukraine would be fraught with complications for the people living there.

For Navalny, relations with Ukraine were a deeply personal issue. Like millions of other Russians, Navalny had roots in Ukraine; his father came from a village near Chernobyl, site of the 1986 nuclear disaster.[14] Pressed in the Ekho Moskvy interview on whether he viewed Russians and Ukrainians as one people, Navalny responded that as a person who had spent a lot of time in Ukraine he saw "no difference" between them. His viewpoint was shared by many, if not most, Russians.

The seizure of Crimea was wildly popular in Russia, and Putin's ratings showed it. In June 2014, 86 percent of Russians approved of Putin's performance as president, while only 13 percent disapproved, according to the independent Levada Center.[15] A year earlier Putin's approval rating had been just 63 percent—a low number by Kremlin standards—with a record 36 percent of Russians disapproving of his performance. The annexation of Crimea sowed confusion among Putin's domestic opponents. On Facebook, activists I had met at antigovernment protests two years earlier were rejoicing. In October 2014, when I traveled to Moscow for the first time after the Russian invasion, I met for beers with a former protest leader. She condemned Putin for the spiraling violence in eastern Ukraine, but she called the conflict a "civil war" and the Donbas "our land." In Ukraine, people began to repeat the saying that "a Russian liberal ends where Ukraine begins." In fact, few Russian opposition figures took a categorical, principled stance against the war. Boris Nemtsov was a notable exception, and he was assassinated in 2015.

Postimperial trauma permeated all of Russian society. In terms of territory, the Soviet Union had been a continuation of the Russian Empire, and when it fell apart in 1991, the colonizers were left unmoored and disoriented. For centuries, Russians had seen themselves as the civilizational center of a multiethnic land empire encompassing their neighbors. In the nineteenth century, most peoples of Europe experienced a national awakening and striving for their own nation-state. Russians did not. Their home was an empire, and it continued to be one for most of the twentieth century.

Following the disintegration of the Soviet Union, the term "Russian nationalist" was commonly used to describe someone who wanted to reestablish Russia's control over its former colonies. Navalny tried to return the term to its original meaning—more in line with the nation-building, exclusionary nationalism of a nation-state than the hungry expansionism of the Russia of centuries past. "Imperialism is stupid and evil. It harms the interests of the Russian people," Navalny warned as Putin's "little green men" were occupying Crimea.[16] Navalny said that Russians should focus on raising living standards inside their own country and turn it into a modern European democracy. "Russians' main interest is not the seizure of land, but the normal management of the land we already have. Take a look at a map, there is quite a lot of it," he wrote.

Putin probably would have agreed with Navalny at the beginning of his rule. In his first year in office, Putin set a goal for Russia to reach Portugal's per capita GDP in fifteen years, which on the back of rapidly rising oil prices seemed completely realistic. Yet as Russia's oil revenues grew, so too did Putin's nostalgia for the Soviet Union's superpower status. By the time he began his third term in office, Putin had abandoned the idea of accommodating the West and instead set out to challenge it. When he annexed Crimea in 2014, Putin turbocharged ultranationalists like Girkin, who had been thirsting for the expansion of post-Communist Russia's borders. Putin's nationalism was morphing from a quest for national revival into a march to imperial restoration.

For the Kremlin, the matchup between Navalny and Girkin was a storm in a teacup. If an event was not shown on state television, then it did not happen for the vast majority of Russians. Navalny posed no real threat to Putin's grip on power because the Kremlin had erected insurmountable barriers for independent candidates to take part in elections. Negative or no media coverage took its toll. Although 55 percent of Russians said that they had heard of Navalny in March 2017, only 18 percent of that number were ready to vote for him, whereas 72 percent were not, according to a Levada Center poll.[17] Girkin was even more marginal. In a Levada poll taken in September 2014, following Girkin's unceremonious removal as commander of the Donetsk separatists, only 21 percent of respondents said they had heard of him.[18]

Putin ruled supreme. He ignored all his opponents, whether they were from the Kremlin-approved "systemic" opposition or representatives of the "nonsystemic" opposition such as Navalny. Putin cultivated the image of a statesman who decided war and peace in the world while his opponents squeaked and squabbled in their kitchens. The presidential election that Putin cared about was not the predetermined Russian race scheduled for 2018, but the bitter contest in the United States to become Barack Obama's successor. Amazingly, the Republican candidate, Donald Trump, prevailed in the November 2016 election, singing Putin's praises and promising to improve relations with Russia. Trump's victory was especially sweet for the Kremlin because his Democratic rival, Hillary Clinton, had made no secret of her animosity toward Putin.

It was at this turning point that National Public Radio hired me as their Moscow correspondent. As I bid Berlin farewell, German officials were voicing concern that Trump would pull the United States out of NATO and make some kind of grand compromise with Putin behind Europe's back. A week after the election, Obama paid one last visit to Angela Merkel, lingering in Berlin for two days to celebrate a friendship forged during Russia's invasion of Ukraine. When Obama was gone again, the Germans were left with a sense of impending doom.

Moscow, in contrast, eagerly anticipated the inauguration of Trump, who had said during the campaign that he would "look into" recognizing Crimea as Russian territory and lifting sanctions against Russia. In a congratulatory message to Trump, Putin expressed the hope that the new U.S. president would lift bilateral relations "out of the current crisis" and establish a "constructive dialogue."[19] Vladimir Zhirinovsky, the head of the Kremlin-backed ultranationalist party, toasted Trump's election with champagne in the Duma.[20] "To the new domestic and foreign policy of the United States and an improvement of relations with Russia," said Zhirinovsky, who himself had a reputation as a "Russian Trump" for his politically incorrect pronouncements and nonstop showmanship. There was even more jubilation in Moscow when Trump announced that he would nominate ExxonMobil CEO Rex Tillerson as his secretary of state. Tillerson had engineered ExxonMobil's strategic partnership with the Russian state oil company Rosneft, and in 2013 Putin had personally awarded him Russia's Order of Friendship.

At his annual press conference in December 2016, Putin openly disparaged the outgoing Obama administration—and showed surprising leniency toward the president-elect. Just a day earlier Trump had tweeted that "the United States must greatly strengthen and expand its nuclear capability," but Putin shrugged off the comment, saying "there was nothing new here."[21] Instead he lashed out at Obama, who in a routine speech to U.S. military personnel had called on them to remain "the strongest fighting force the world has ever known." Putin reminded "representatives of the current administration" of Russia's modernized nuclear arsenal and boasted that his country was "stronger than any aggressor." Asked about the Obama administration's accusations that the Kremlin had been behind hacking attacks on the Democratic Party to influence the U.S. presidential election, Putin scoffed. The Democrats were sore losers, he said, and Trump was right that anybody—even someone lying on their bed—could have hacked the party's leadership.

I moved back to Russia one month after Donald Trump had been elected president. NPR rented a three-bedroom apartment for its correspondents in central Moscow, managed by the Russian Foreign Ministry. On the gray December morning after my arrival, a neighbor, another American reporter, greeted me with the words: "Isn't it depressing?" We had last seen each other on the Maidan in Kyiv, where he had asked me the same question. The NPR apartment was spacious and comfortable, but every time I left the building I had to swipe myself out and pass a guard booth. Soon I felt like I was living in a gilded cage.

In a similar way, Moscow had become a gilded cage for its residents. The city had undergone an enormous transformation since I last lived there. Facades were renovated, handsome granite flagstones replaced undulating asphalt sidewalks, and the parks were manicured and well-lit. Moscow's sanitized, austere appearance was the face of Vladimir Putin's new authoritarianism. Like the picture of Dorian Gray, the city was looking better than ever while the regime ossified behind the Kremlin walls.

Putin was in his seventeenth year in power. In 2011, when I had left for Berlin, nobody imagined Russia would become an international pariah, saddled with Western sanctions like Iran or North Korea. Reversing those sanctions and ending Russia's isolation were Putin's top priority, and no means were off-limits to achieve that goal.

The U.S. presidential election gave the Kremlin a unique chance to take revenge on Hillary Clinton. When she was the secretary of state, Putin had accused Clinton of interfering in Russian politics, and during the presidential race Russian state media portrayed her as a deranged warmonger. Trump's rise presented the Kremlin with a tantalizing opportunity: an American president who promised to upend U.S. foreign policy and set relations with Russia on an entirely new course. The Kremlin's means to influence the outcome of the U.S. election were very modest, but if the Russians could tip the scale ever so slightly, the benefit far outweighed the risk.

Hints of Russian interference emerged during the summer before the election. In July, U.S. spy agencies determined that Russian military intelligence had hacked into the Democratic National Committee to steal emails and documents that were later published online.[22] In September the Trump campaign had to distance itself from one of its foreign policy advisers, Carter Page, following a news report that Page was being monitored by U.S. spy agencies for his contacts to the Kremlin. Two weeks before Trump's inauguration, the U.S. intelligence community published a report that accused Putin of personally ordering an influence campaign to undermine public faith in the U.S. electoral process and hurt Clinton.[23] The Kremlin, the report found, had developed "a clear preference" for Trump. The new American president entered office with a cloud hanging over his head. Four months later Trump's Justice Department appointed Robert Mueller III, a former FBI director, to investigate the ties between Trump's campaign and the Kremlin.

Russian election interference had three parts, according to Vladimir Frolov, an expert on Russia's intelligence services.[24] The first part he called "legitimate hacking," the collection of information that any intelligence agency engages in. The second part was taking hacked information and leaking it to online resources such as WikiLeaks. "When intelligence gathering went to an influence operation, that was crossing the red line," Frolov said. Whether the release of the information influenced the election is debatable, he said, but it contributed to negative news about the Democrats. The third part consisted of social media campaigns on platforms such as Facebook, which Frolov said were largely meaningless except in battleground states such as Michigan or Wisconsin, where Clinton lost to Trump by a few tens of thousands of votes. "It was about discrediting Hillary and creating chaos," Frolov said. "Nobody expected Trump to win."

As the lid came off on the extent of Russian interference, Putin retorted that Russia never intervened in other countries' politics, and that all the accusations were baseless rumors. The Kremlin propaganda machine duly parroted Trump's defense that he was the victim of a witch hunt by his political opponents to undermine the legitimacy of his election. Russian state media did not downplay the story. On the contrary, the allegations of Russian interference fed into the narrative that Trump's domestic enemies were whipping up "Russophobia" to prevent a U.S.-Russian rapprochement. America was a basket case, and democracy did not work.

The U.S. intelligence community's January 2017 report on Russian election interference focused on the actions of state actors, such as the Kremlin's English-language news channel RT. It largely overlooked the world of freelance operatives who—like Igor Girkin and Konstantin Malofeyev in Ukraine—gave the Kremlin the shield of plausible deniability. During the U.S. election campaign, Nataliya Veselnitskaya, a Moscow lawyer, met with Trump's son, Donald Jr., promising dirt on Clinton. When Veselnitskaya could not deliver the goods, her fishing expedition to Trump Tower ended quickly. In the words of security analyst Mark Galeotti, Russia had become an "adhocracy" of informal actors vying for the Kremlin's favor.[25] Putin himself nodded to his army of willing helpers when he suggested that "patriotic hackers" had taken it upon themselves to launch cyberattacks on the United States when they felt that Russia was being slighted.[26]

For the Kremlin, the ends justified the means. Ironically, those ends included an improvement in U.S. relations, which had plunged to new depths after the 2014 invasion of Ukraine. There was no question that a Hillary Clinton presidency would have meant a continuation of American hostility, but a Trump administration at least held out the promise of a normalization, if not renaissance, of bilateral relations. From the outside,

Russia looked like a contrarian nation, cheering on an American presidential candidate whose victory most of the world dreaded. Asked in a November 2016 poll who they thought would be better for Russia, 60 percent of respondents chose Trump, 5 percent picked Clinton, and 36 percent said they did not know.[27] But even discounting months of inculcation by state television, Trump represented a positive change for many Russians. After years of fraying ties, finally there was an American politician who spoke about improving relations—something most Russians supported.

One of the most persistent myths about Russia that I encountered was that Russians were anti-American. On the level of government propaganda, of course, the United States made a convenient bogeyman responsible for the world's ills and the Kremlin's failings. Old Soviet tropes were still effective at mobilizing public support for the regime. But on a human level, I found that Russians were as enamored of the United States as they were conflicted about it. Once, after a weekend trip to a provincial town, I boarded a train back to Moscow. When the elderly man in my compartment learned that I was American, his eyes widened as he slowly uttered the words: *"Nash samy strashny . . . drug!"*—"Our most terrible . . . friend!"

In the twenty-five years that I was based in Berlin and in Moscow, I witnessed more anti-American sentiment in Germany than I ever did in Russia. During the height of the Iraq War, a friend from Berlin visited me in Moscow. I tried to explain to him the difference between German and Russian opposition to the U.S. invasion: while Germans condemned the war out of a sense of moral outrage, Russians were angry that they lacked the capabilities to do the same.

After the Cold War, many Russians had naive, inflated expectations of what the West had to offer and how fast Russia could become, in their words, a "normal country." When Washington stopped treating Moscow as an equal, hopes for partnership turned into resentment. Yet because Russians—unlike Germans—had not been defeated by Americans on the battlefield, they refused to bow to their former rival. And for that reason, most Russians continued to have grudging respect for America. Their sense of national pride, although dented, was very much intact.

At the same time, Russians who had experienced the end of Communism carried in them a deep sense of shame. When Putin called the breakup of the Soviet Union the "greatest geopolitical catastrophe" of the century, he was referring to much more than the dispersion of ethnic Russians across new borders. Putin was lamenting the fall of an empire that had stretched from Prague to Pyongyang, the absolute zenith of Russian power. For Russia, the end of the Soviet empire meant the loss not only of half of Europe, but also of Ukraine and Belarus—nations that after centuries of domination, many Russians hardly distinguished from their own. An economic crash accompanied the fall of the empire, adding hardship to humiliation.

I did not understand how Russians' shame could coexist with their deep sense of pride until I visited Kuvshinovo, a forgotten town about two hundred miles northwest of Moscow. I set off for Kuvshinovo one summer morning with the goal of bringing back a story about life in a "monocity," one of the hundreds of factory towns in Russia built around a single industry. Kuvshinovo was home to one of Russia's oldest paper mills, which after the end of Communism had been sold off to private investors who bought foreign machinery and fired most of the staff. With a population of more than twelve thousand in the 1980s, the town lost more than a quarter of its residents in the following thirty years. I visited the paper mill, but the workers were busy and the owners indifferent to the fate of the town. The mayor was unavailable for an interview; the priest in the churchyard was in a hurry; and the two women who ran the city-owned newspaper brushed me off. Ramshackle Kuvshinovo was not the kind of place that outsiders visited—it was a place that people fled. I felt the locals were united in a wall of silence.

By a stroke of good luck, I made the acquaintance of the town archivists, two cheerful women who set about looking for someone who had witnessed the town's change of fortunes. They called Ivan Paramonov, a sprightly eighty-five-year-old who soon pulled up in front of the archives in his Lada. Paramonov was the former Communist Party boss in the paper mill. He spoke with pride about the honors that the factory had once won and complained that now there was nothing left to be proud of. Paramonov vented about Russia's yawning wealth gap and the Kremlin's disregard for small towns like his. But when he realized that his words would be broadcast on American radio, Paramonov retracted every word he had just said. The archivists energetically vouched for my integrity as a journalist, and he reluctantly gave his consent.

My visit to Kuvshinovo was a revelatory moment. Paramonov was both proud that he had been part of a great country and ashamed of the hard times that had befallen it. When he found out that he was speaking to a foreigner—and an American at that—Paramonov clammed up. That strange mixture of pride and shame helped explain how Putin was able to overcome discontent at home and consolidate public sentiment against outside threats. For Putin, engagement with the United States raised Russia's status as a world power and legitimized his leadership. By extolling Russian greatness, Putin instilled many Russians with a sense of pride that masked their shame for the privations they had to endure in daily life.

The Soviet collapse left a scar on the Russians who lived through it. Vladimir Putin's career as a KGB officer came to an abrupt finish, and he later said that for a time he worked as an unlicensed cab driver to make ends meet. Many men of Putin's generation fell prey to alcoholism, depression, and early death, unable to find their way when their world turned upside down.

A quarter century after the fall of the Soviet empire, however, a new generation of Russians was coming of age that had little or no memory of the Soviet Union's demise. Alexei Navalny was fifteen years old in 1991, and his rebellious outlook reflected his coming of age during Russia's freest decade. Corruption had always been a reality in the Soviet Union, where scarce goods and long lines were part of daily life. But when the strictures and controls of the Communist system fell away, corruption reached an altogether new order of magnitude. During Putin's first two terms as president, the greed of officials ballooned with the price of oil.

Navalny first rose to prominence blogging about corruption in state companies and skewering the ruling United Russia party as the "party of crooks and thieves." In 2011 he founded the Anti-Corruption Foundation to investigate and publicize the graft that had become an endemic part of Putin's power structure. The organization gave him a platform when he announced his presidential run in a YouTube video in December 2016. Sitting behind a desk in a Moscow skyscraper, Navalny looked and talked like a new kind of politician. Flanked by a Russian flag and photos of his wife and two children, Navalny promised to bring back real competition to a presidential election for the first time in twenty years. It was not his first political race. Three years earlier Navalny had run for Moscow mayor against a Putin apparatchik, winning more than 27 percent of the vote despite a state media blackout and attempts by the government to disqualify him with a fraud conviction. After the European Court of Human Rights ruled that Navalny's rights had been violated in that case, prosecutors sought to convict him again in a new trial.

When he was retried and handed a five-year suspended sentence in February 2017, Navalny complained that prosecutors had used the same evidence and the judge had issued the same verdict as in the original trial. Even though it seemed that the conviction's only purpose was to stop him from running for president, Navalny was undeterred and started traveling around Russia building a campaign network. Less than a month after his conviction, Navalny published an investigation alleging that Dmitry Medvedev, Putin's stand-in president and the serving prime minister, owned a secret real estate empire of luxury properties, including two yachts and a Tuscan vineyard. In the accompanying YouTube video, Navalny showed how the colorful sneakers Medvedev wore in an Instagram post were the vital clue to a convoluted scheme of fake charities funded by some of Russia's richest men.[28] Part investigative journalism, part agitprop, the short film was an internet blockbuster. Navalny called for a day of nationwide protests.

The rallies on March 26, 2017, were the largest show of dissent since the antigovernment demonstrations five years earlier. In dozens of cities, thousands of people turned out, many of them teenagers. It was a national debut for Russians who had been schoolchildren during the last protests. Some brought rubber ducks with them, a reference to Navalny's allegation that Medvedev kept a dedicated duck house at one of his estates. More than 1,500 protesters were arrested, including Navalny. Medvedev, unused to public scrutiny, awkwardly compared the investigation to fruit compote and accused Navalny of dragging children into the street to achieve his political goals.

The biggest surprise of my return to Russia was not the hardening of Putin's regime, but the appearance of a new generation of Russians ready to challenge it. Having grown up with open borders and the internet, these young people were unburdened by the inferiority complexes of Russia's ruling class. They measured their quality of life by that of their peers abroad, not by the impoverishment following the fall of the Soviet Union. Their values were informed by what they saw in the West, and they did not understand why Russians should live any differently. For this new generation, Putin was not a hero but the head of a rotting, archaic political system built on cronyism and repression.

I found these young, free Russians not just in Moscow but everywhere I traveled. They listened to rebellious Russian rap, sported tattoos, and cut and colored their hair the way they wanted to. They questioned traditional gender roles and were outraged by their country's glaring economic disparities. I started calling them "New Russians," reappropriating a pejorative term once used to describe the gaudy nouveaux riches of the 1990s.

Navalny addressed young people directly in their language and on their social media. He also met them in person as he set up campaign offices in dozens of cities. In May 2017 I caught up with Navalny's campaign in Tula, one hundred miles south of Moscow. A crowd of mostly twenty-something men greeted Navalny with cheers when he arrived at the new two-room campaign office. Navalny shook every volunteer's hand, then gave a spirited stump speech before fielding questions on everything from the army draft—he would abolish it—to LGBTQ rights—people's private lives were nobody else's business.

The sincerity and enthusiasm of Navalny's supporters in Tula impressed me. A few months later, when one of them invited me to hold a talk in a new art space in the town, I readily accepted. A city of half a million, Tula encapsulated the many sides of Russia: it was famed for the manufacture of guns and gingerbread, and just outside of town was the ancestral home of the writer Leo Tolstoy. On subsequent visits, I discovered a run-down industrial town undergoing an urban revival that mirrored Moscow's. Old factories were being turned into cutting-edge cultural centers, and garages where the Soviet army had once parked tanks now housed shops, bars, and restaurants. Many of the young people who hung out in Tula's renovated industrial sites had been born after Putin came to power. "We want to move forward. We don't want to stay in one place. We're getting sick of this tunnel vision," a nineteen-year-old university student, told me. "We want something new—and that's why we look at what's going on in other countries and sometimes wonder why we can't have the same thing."

I also met Yelena Agayeva, the mother of a local Navalny volunteer named Filipp Simpkins, in a muddy Tula suburb. Because of his political activism, Simpkins had been kicked out of vocational school where he was studying to be a train engineer. When the authorities threatened to lock him up, Simpkins, then twenty, fled Russia and received political asylum in Switzerland. Agayeva did not expect her son to return any time soon. "I hope that in many, many years he can come back as a visitor—and that he'll at least be a little homesick for Russia," she said.

Navalny reintroduced politics into Russian life. He was remarkable because he was doing something nobody had tried before in Putin's Russia: create a nationwide political organization fueled by grassroots enthusiasm. Unlike other regime critics, Navalny did not limit his political activism to angry Facebook posts and the occasional protest rally. Instead, he broke out of the Moscow bubble and went out into Russia. Twenty-four years younger than Putin, Navalny was everything the aging Russian leader was not—informal and witty, unscripted and self-deprecating. Unlike Putin's carefully stage-managed meetings with citizens, Navalny's campaign stops were spontaneous and energizing. His vision was of a "wonderful Russia of the future"—a country that would protect civil liberties, uproot corruption, foster entrepreneurship, and not be in eternal conflict with the West. Putin, in contrast, focused on the past. He reminded voters of Russia's troubles before his ascent to power and basked in the glory of the Soviet victory over Nazi Germany. Now as then, Putin warned, Russia was surrounded by enemies and subverted by traitors.

Putin, who shunned email and smartphones, was slow to grasp the power of the internet. But the internet helped Navalny break the news monopoly of state television and bring together like-minded people from across Russia's vastness. In April 2017, as his campaign was picking up steam, Navalny started a weekly news show that seemed to be inspired by the American comedian Jon Stewart's *The Daily Show.* Every Thursday evening, Navalny grilled Russia's powers that be with righteous outrage and a sense of the absurd. Often attracting more than one million views per episode, the show was livestreamed, allowing Navalny to field questions in real time. Thanks to the internet, Navalny's campaign was able to create a database of supporters, sign up tens of thousands of volunteers, and raise hundreds of millions of rubles in donations.

Having watched hours of his show and followed him on the campaign trail, I finally met Navalny in person in February 2018. Navalny had been officially barred from the presidential race because of his fraud conviction and was now calling for a boycott of the March election. I found Navalny in a cramped corner office at the headquarters of the Anti-Corruption

Foundation, which police had raided just a few days before to search for an imaginary bomb.[29] Even though I arrived early, Navalny did not make me wait. Just as in his videos, he was easygoing and funny, speaking to me almost twice as long as had been scheduled.

My first question was about what motivated him, as Navalny had been physically attacked and repeatedly jailed, and his brother, Oleg, was in prison on another fraud conviction. "I want to live in a normal country and refuse to accept any talk about Russia being doomed to being a bad, poor, or servile country," Navalny said. "I want to live here, and I can't tolerate the injustice that for many people has become routine." His first priority if he came to power would be a complete overhaul of the judiciary, he said. The second priority would be to move closer to a European-style parliamentary system to dilute Russia's overly powerful presidency. In foreign policy, Navalny viewed an end to the war in Ukraine as crucial to restoring relations with the West. His vision of Russia was as a leading European power that would join the European Union and cooperate closely with NATO. The strategic interests of the United States and Russia were largely aligned, he said. There was no doubt in his mind: "We're a Western country."

Navalny was fuzzy on his own political affiliation, saying Western labels did not translate well to Russia. A Russian Communist was more like a right-wing conservative in the U.S. context, whereas a liberal in Russia might be seen as a libertarian in America. Navalny said that political labels were meaningless in an authoritarian system. His idea was to form a broad coalition that could agree on basic democratic values and the common goal of ousting the regime. Navalny told me that the label of nationalist did not bother him, although he rejected the imperialist thinking behind Putin's war in Ukraine.

Navalny refused to be viewed as "some kind of dissident." He saw himself as a mainstream politician: "If you take any of my anticorruption investigations or any points from my political platform, I'm sure the majority of Russian citizens would support me—and that's why I wasn't allowed to run." Other Putin opponents such as Mikhail Khodorkovsky, who had spent ten years in prison, now found themselves in exile, and the 2015 assassination of Boris Nemtsov was still fresh in people's minds. Yet Navalny was determined to stay in Russia. When I asked him if he believed that his life was in danger, Navalny said that he tried not to think about it: "If you think about it constantly, you won't be able to do anything."

Even for Putin's autocracy, a presidential election was a vulnerable moment when the incumbent could be lawfully challenged and a transfer of power was at least theoretically possible. Elections created extreme nervousness up and down the vaunted "power vertical." Local bosses were worried about delivering satisfactory results from their districts, while Kremlin officials fretted about keeping up the appearance of a democratic procedure with a minimum of scandal. The fundamental weakness of authoritarianism is that without fair elections, free media, public protests, and open discourse, no regime can be sure about what its people really think.

In 2018 Putin faced seven preapproved rivals who had no chance—or desire—to become president. Putin was essentially running against himself in a referendum on his rule; his only task was to demonstrate that he had become even more popular since the last vote. Polls, even by independent organizations, consistently showed that Putin was far more popular than Navalny.[30] In our interview, Navalny argued that Putin's high approval ratings existed in a vacuum with no competition, and that only free and fair elections would reveal his true popularity.

There was a logic to denying Navalny's candidacy, even if the Kremlin did not consider him a threat. Russia was a "managed democracy," and Navalny was unmanageable. Allowing him to run would have not only thrown a wildcard into the mix but also legitimized Navalny as a politician and an alternative to Putin. After the State Department expressed concern that Navalny was being kept off the ballot, Putin shot back that the United States was interfering in Russia's elections by revealing its preferred candidate.

Putin wanted to claim that he was democratically elected, but he was not ready to go through the trouble of campaigning. For Putin, elections were a ritual, not a contest. He did not dignify the straw men running against him by taking part in debates. His annual state-of-the-nation address doubled as his only campaign speech.

In an exhibition hall next to the Kremlin, Putin rattled off his domestic agenda to top government officials, some nodding, others nodding off. An hour into his speech, Putin finally began to enjoy himself, presenting video animations of Russia's newest nuclear weapons as they snaked and weaved their way around U.S. missile defense systems. "Nobody wanted to talk to us about what really matters, and nobody listened to us. So, listen now," he said as the hall erupted into thunderous applause and a standing ovation.[31] Then, in reference to the Trump administration's plans to introduce so-called low-yield nuclear weapons into the U.S. arsenal, Putin upped the ante. "We will consider the use of any nuclear weapons—short, medium, or any range at all—as a nuclear attack on our country. Our response will be instantaneous, with all the ensuing consequences," he said to another round of applause. There were two audiences for Putin's nuclear-tipped speech: the Americans, whom he was telling to stay away; and his fellow Russians, whom he was telling to vote for him as he alone could defend them from the United States.

On the weekend of the election, I traveled to the Ural Mountains, nine hundred miles east of Moscow. In Yekaterinburg, I met Anton Volkhin, age thirty-six, the regional distributor for a national sausage company. Volkhin was more succinct in identifying the secret of Putin's success than any political analyst in Moscow. "We Russians just don't want things to get any worse. You Americans always expect things to get better," he told me. "Too many people have too much to lose. Those who don't are still in the minority."[32] Volkhin moonlighted by driving his Toyota Camry for a ride-hailing app and took me the eighty miles to Nizhny Tagil, an industrial town nicknamed "Putingrad" because of Putin's affection for its giant tank factory. There I met Yelena Okhotenko, age thirty-six, a military service member and mother of two. "This president did very much for Russia and my town and personally for me and my family," she said, standing on Putingrad's refurbished river embankment. "He raised up our country, and he raised our quality of life." Putin's message that Russia was under siege had gotten through to her. "Honestly, I'm afraid, very afraid, that war will break out," she said. "There's constantly this aggression toward us, and we're constantly holding back. I don't know how long our country can hold out."

Election day was on March 18, the fourth anniversary of the Crimea annexation. Putin, who was obsessed with anniversaries, had the election law changed especially so that the 2018 vote would fall on this special day. According to the official results, Putin received 77 percent of the vote, with his closest rival, the Communist Pavel Grudinin, barely making it out of the single digits with 12 percent. Putin had significantly improved over his showing in the 2012 elections, when he won 64 percent of the vote amid mass protests. Even if the process was neither free nor fair, Putin's popularity among a significant portion of the population was undeniable. What struck me when speaking to voters was that they simply did not see any viable alternative to Putin. A paradoxical situation was strengthening his position: the longer Putin clung to power, the more upheaval his departure promised to bring. For many Russians, Putin was the default candidate but, significantly, not the beloved candidate.

Putin's regime had no base of supporters who would take to the streets for him unless they were coerced or paid. He ruled by inertia and the fear of change. Young Russians were struggling to find a place in that reality. At a polling station in Yekaterinburg, I met a first-time voter named Grigory Dementyanov. "I've had a dream since I was a kid to put a check mark next to a candidate's name, but it hasn't come true," he said. The twenty-one-year-old music student said that he had intentionally spoiled his ballot so that nobody else could use it. I asked if that meant he supported Navalny. No, Dementyanov replied. Navalny was right about Russia's problems, but he was not up to the task of solving them.

Following the Russian election, Donald Trump wanted to phone Vladimir Putin. Before the call, White House advisers wrote "DO NOT CONGRATU-LATE" on Trump's briefing materials.[33] Given Putin's open hostility toward the West, the conversation was supposed to be businesslike and curt. The British government had just expelled twenty-three Russian diplomats in retaliation for a nerve-agent attack on Sergei Skripal, a former Russian spy living in England. The Mueller investigation was in full swing, new sanctions against Russia were being crafted, and the U.S. president was under intense scrutiny for any signs of collusion with the Kremlin. But when he got through to Putin, Trump congratulated him on his reelection. Trump mentioned neither the Skripal poisoning nor the 2016 election interference, focusing instead on "shared interests" such as North Korea and Ukraine.[34] "We had a very good call," Trump said afterward. "We will probably be meeting in the not-too-distant future." Two weeks later, the Kremlin's top foreign policy adviser deciphered those words, saying Trump had invited Putin to the White House during the congratulatory call.[35]

Trump's embrace of Putin contrasted with the wariness of his advisers. Trump lamented that U.S.-Russian relations had never been worse, yet his point was not to blame Putin for his growing aggressiveness but to argue for more dialogue or, more precisely, a presidential summit. Trump was right that the bilateral relationship was in the dumps. Putin had initially held off from a tit-for-tat response when Barack Obama, in one of his final acts as president, expelled thirty-five Russian diplomats in response to Russia's election interference. But when there was little change in American policy despite Trump's warm words, the Kremlin cut U.S. diplomatic staff in Russia by more than 750, making it practically impossible for ordinary Russians to get visas to the United States. Less than a week after Trump called to congratulate Putin, his own administration kicked out sixty Russian diplomats to show solidarity with Britain over the Skripal poisoning. The Russians reciprocated by sending home sixty Americans, including the embassy spokeswoman and the ambassador's interpreter.

Trump's three predecessors—Bill Clinton, George W. Bush, and Barack Obama—had each held a full-scale summit with his Russian counterpart in the first six months of his first term. Given the level of outrage over Russian election interference in Washington, Putin was lucky to meet Trump on the sidelines of a G20 summit in Germany in July 2017. By that time, Trump had already managed to host the leaders of China, India, and Turkey. Much to the Kremlin's frustration, a split had opened up inside the U.S. administration, with key members frantically backpedaling as Trump continued to gravitate toward Putin. Jim Mattis, Trump's defense secretary, had no illusions about Putin's efforts to undermine the West, and Rex Tillerson, despite his Russian medal, turned out be a disappointment for the Kremlin.

The one tiny patch of bilateral cooperation was counterterrorism. In December, Putin publicly thanked Trump for a CIA tip that had supposedly foiled a terrorist attack in St. Petersburg. Weeks later, in January 2018, the CIA director Mike Pompeo secretly met with the heads of Russia's intelligence agencies in Washington, raising new questions about the White House's true intentions.[36]

To patch up relations with Russia and get a summit with Putin, Trump appointed Jon Huntsman, a moderate Republican and former Utah governor, as his ambassador to Moscow. Trump had briefly considered Huntsman, who had served as Obama's ambassador to China, for the job of secretary of state. When he presented his credentials to Putin in October

2017, Huntsman found open doors in Moscow and established a direct line
to the Kremlin. Recognizing that much of the resistance to a thaw in relations was coming from Congress, Huntsman began organizing a visit to
Russia by American lawmakers.

The first sign of a breakthrough was the arrival in Moscow by John
Bolton, Trump's new national security adviser, in June 2018. It was surreal
to see Bolton, an avowed Russia hawk, being received by a smiling Putin in
the Kremlin. A year earlier, before his appointment, Bolton had accused
Putin of lying to Trump, called Russian election interference "a true act
of war," and said that the United States negotiated with Russia at its own
peril. Now, in Moscow, Bolton disavowed his past warnings and insisted
that the mere fact of a summit between the presidents would be an accom-
plishment. Days later the first congressional delegation since the annexation of Crimea arrived in Russia. The delegation of seven senators and a
congresswoman—all Republicans—were feted in the Foreign Ministry and
Federation Council, Russia's upper house of parliament. "We know that we
need a new beginning, that we can go over recriminations on both sides for
days in," said Senator Richard Shelby, the head of the delegation.[37] "But I
believe Russia and the United States and the world will be a lot better off if
we improve our relationship. Perhaps it won't be a utopia. Most marriages
are not utopia. But an improvement, gosh, I hope so." The eight lawmakers
avoided publicity, and none of them tweeted from Russia about their trip.
They spent July 4 eating hotdogs and tacos at the garden party at the U.S.
ambassador's residence in the heart of Moscow.

Even before the Helsinki summit took place, the Kremlin celebrated it
as an achievement. Putin had not made a single concession, yet Trump
agreed to give him the prestige of standing on the world stage next to a
U.S. president again. The Finnish capital was going through a heat wave
that made its sunbaked waterfront feel like a Mediterranean city. But the
overall climate in U.S.-Russian relations was very chilly, and the conditions
for a thaw were absent. Three days before the summit, Robert Mueller
indicted twelve Russians for interfering in the 2016 election, but Trump
remained stubbornly oblivious. After a NATO summit in Brussels sparring
with the United States' closest allies, Trump retired to his Scottish golf
resort for the weekend before his meeting with Putin.

The summit on July 16, 2018, took place in the Presidential Palace in
Helsinki. The first meeting was almost an hour behind schedule because

Putin, who was known to make world leaders wait, arrived late. After a one-on-one meeting between the presidents, they had lunch with a small group of advisers in the appropriately named Hall of Mirrors. The summit's highlight was the infamous closing press conference. After repeating his standard line that Russia never interfered in domestic American politics, Putin offered to help Mueller with his investigation, saying Russian officials would interrogate suspects in Russia—in return for the United States tracking down Americans suspected of illegal activities by Russia. Trump did not even seem to realize he was being trolled, calling the snide proposal "an incredible offer." As for election interference, the U.S. president suggested that Putin's denials were more persuasive than the assessment of his own intelligence agencies.

The Kremlin was triumphant. "Better than super" was how the Russian foreign minister, Sergei Lavrov, described the meeting. After Putin returned to Moscow, he cryptically referred to "useful agreements" reached during the summit, although nothing had been signed, not even a joint communiqué. Putin had received the recognition that he had been missing since Obama called Russia a "regional power" in the wake of Crimea's annexation. But the summit did not lead to any improvements in the U.S.-Russian relationship, nor to a second summit. Two months after Helsinki, the Kremlin invited China to take part in what it called the largest war games since the Cold War. In October, John Bolton returned to Moscow to inform Putin that the United States was withdrawing from the 1987 Intermediate-Range Nuclear Forces (INF) Treaty because of Russian violations first brought up by the Obama administration. As the year closed, the FSB arrested Paul Whelan, an American citizen, in a Moscow hotel and accused him of espionage. The Kremlin was retaliating for the detention in Washington of a Russian national, Maria Butina, who had been arrested the day before the Helsinki summit on charges of secretly interfering in the 2016 election on behalf of Russia.

The Trump reset was dead.

9

The Education of Volodymyr Zelensky

Volodymyr Zelensky, unshaven and wearing a Muhammad Ali T-shirt, appeared on Ukrainian television as Russian forces massed on the border. The presenter introduced him in Ukrainian, but Zelensky preferred to speak in his first language, Russian. "Dear Vladimir Vladimirovich. Do not allow even the hint of an armed conflict," Zelensky said, addressing Vladimir Putin.[1] Russia and Ukraine are fraternal nations of the same blood, he said. "If you need me to, I'm ready to beg you on my knees. Just don't bring our people to their knees."

It was March 1, 2014, and Russian troops were fanning out across Crimea as Russia's parliament authorized Putin to attack Ukraine. After the Maidan protests had ended in a massacre and the flight of their detested president, Viktor Yanukovych, Ukrainians were waking up to the new threat of a war with Russia. For the first time, Zelensky, one of Ukraine's most popular entertainers, went on TV not looking for a laugh. He advised Yanukovych, whom he knew personally, to accept the reality that nobody in Ukraine considered him to be president anymore. "Move aside," Zelensky said. "Don't give separatism a chance." Turning to the provisional government, which was trying to assert its authority after a week in power, Zelensky told Ukraine's new rulers to leave Russian speakers like himself alone. "Language will never divide our country. I have Jewish blood and speak Russian, but I am a citizen of Ukraine. I love this country and don't want to be part of another country," he said. Finally, Zelensky addressed his fellow Ukrainians, appealing to their sense of unity. "If God can't help us today, then may reason and love help us," he said. "I love you." He spoke the last three words in Ukrainian and smiled.

Zelensky's reaction to Russia's creeping aggression was heartfelt and spontaneous, although he would later be attacked for it. At the time, Zelensky was just a comedian who joked about politics and had no political ambitions of his own. Unwittingly, Zelensky's four-minute monologue on a news program turned out to be his first political speech. In his anger and confusion, Zelensky gave voice to a view widely shared by Russian speakers who had grown up in independent Ukraine and considered themselves proud Ukrainians. They were angry with Yanukovych, wary of the new government, and in complete disbelief that Russia had revealed itself to be an enemy.

Zelensky owed his success as a comedian more to Russian than to Ukrainian audiences. A little more than a year earlier, he had emceed a New Year's Day gala show on Russian state TV attended by Russian celebrities such as Vladimir Solovyov, who would later become one of Putin's most vociferous war propagandists. Zelensky's slick, vacuous rom-coms were filmed in Russian, and his movie *Love in Vegas* had just opened in Russia.

The millions of Ukrainians whose personal or professional lives were intertwined with Russia struggled to grasp the enormity of the 2014 invasion. Zelensky was no exception. He was on tour with his comedy group, Kvartal 95, when armed pro-Russian rebels started taking over towns in eastern Ukraine. Even though separatists had stormed the town of Horlivka, Kvartal 95 performed there on April 17, the same day that a local councilman, Volodymyr Rybak, was abducted after trying to raise the Ukrainian flag over the town hall.[2] Rybak was later found dead in a nearby river, one of the first victims of the spiraling violence in the Donbas.

The next month Zelensky was back in Moscow, where his production company had a Russian branch. Posing as a TV reporter for a satirical news show, Zelensky delivered gags from central Moscow about Putin, Russian cars, and drunk Russian tourists. The main news, he reported on May 22, was that the Russians were finally withdrawing their forces from the Ukrainian border. But rumor had it, Zelensky added, that the Russians were not going anywhere and were moving the border instead.

The battle for the Donbas had not yet begun, but it took a good dose of black humor to laugh at the looming Russian threat. Zelensky was getting into arguments about Crimea with his Russian friends, and people showed up at a Moscow premiere holding signs calling Zelensky—a Jew—a "fascist" and a Banderite."[3] Zelensky found doing business in Russia untenable and closed his Moscow office later that year. He declined to go to a family gathering hosted by his wife's cousin, who lived in the Russian capital. But his father-in-law did attend, and the party ended in a family feud over Russia's aggression against Ukraine. In an October 2014 skit, Zelensky read an imaginary letter to his relatives in Russia, ridiculing the caricatures of Ukraine in Kremlin propaganda. "I'm learning English now so I can forget Russian," he said. "American mercenaries, who are everywhere, are helping me." As usual, Zelensky was performing in Russian, not Ukrainian. "Please send me a copy of Hitler's *Mein Kampf*," he said. "It's flying off the shelves here."

Zelensky's weapons were his words and wit. As the fighting in the Donbas escalated, Zelensky received four call-up notices and ignored them all.[4] That Zelensky the funnyman would become Ukraine's next president—and a wartime president at that—would have seemed beyond belief.

Zelensky's rise was all the more remarkable given his modest beginnings in Kryvyi Rih, an industrial city in central Ukraine. For much of its history, Kryvyi Rih had been part of the Pale of Settlement, the area in the Russian Empire where Jews were allowed to live, and the city once boasted nine synagogues.[5] Following the Russian Revolution, a giant metallurgical factory was built in Kryvyi Rih, part of the coal and steel belt that stretched across southeastern Ukraine into the Donbas. Many of the workers came from Russia, embedding Russian language in the local culture. During the Nazi occupation of the region during World War II, Zelensky's grandfather, Semyon, lost his parents and three bothers when the Germans razed their village.[6] Semyon, in a twist of fate, was saved from the Holocaust by joining the Red Army, where he led an artillery platoon.[7] After the war, he served in the Kryvyi Rih police force.

Zelensky was born in 1978, when the Soviet Union was still a superpower that projected influence around the world. Zelensky's parents were both engineers, and his father, Oleksandr, was sent to Mongolia to help build a copper mining plant. When Zelensky was a small child, his family lived in Erdenet, Mongolia, but after four years he returned to Kryvyi Rih with his mother, Rymma, as the harsh climate was taking a toll on her health.[8] Oleksandr continued working at the Mongolian plant, and young

Volodymyr did not see much of his father. Later Oleksandr took a position as a computer science professor at the technical university in Kryvyi Rih.

As a child, Zelensky demonstrated a talent for singing and dancing.[9] He also learned English and dreamed of studying at MGIMO, the elite diplomatic school in Moscow.[10] When he was sixteen, Zelensky won a competition to study in Israel for free, but his father was opposed. Oleksandr wanted his son to be a lawyer, and Volodymyr ended up earning his law degree in Kryvyi Rih. His father was so fastidious about what he believed was right and wrong, Zelensky later said, that he would not even accept a box of sweets from a former student who visited from America.[11] Even after Zelensky hit the big time, his parents stayed in their modest apartment in Kryvyi Rih and refused to take presents from their celebrity son.

A strong family was important in the Kryvyi Rih of Zelensky's childhood. In the chaos after the collapse of Communism, drug use was rampant and gangs ruled the city's streets. Volodymyr learned how to wrestle and lifted weights for self-defense. Even so, Zelensky said that he loved his hometown and owed it everything he had accomplished in life.[12] Although Kryvyi Rih was hardly associated with song and dance, Zelensky found friends in his neighborhood who shared his passion for the stage. They got their inspiration from KVN, a comedy show that would open the doors to fame and fortune.

KVN, which stood for "Club of the Cheerful and Resourceful" in Russian, started in the Soviet Union as a televised contest among teams that competed against each other with skits, improvisations, and musical numbers. Zelensky was a natural for the KVN format and made his debut at the KVN festival in Sochi in 1997, shortly before his twentieth birthday.[13] A few months later he was back with a new team, which became known as Kvartal 95 (Quarter 95), the name of his neighborhood in Kryvyi Rih. It was the beginning of a cooperation with Russia's premier comedy show that would last for six years.

Zelensky moved to Moscow, where he shared a studio apartment with the brothers Serhiy and Borys Shefir, fellow comedians and natives of Kryvyi Rih.[14] The Russian capital was still the economic and cultural center of gravity for the post-Soviet world, and Ukrainians pursuing their dreams in Moscow were no different from Canadians trying their luck in New York or Belgians seeking their fortune in Paris. Off screen Zelensky put on shows for Russia's high and mighty, including the country's prime minister, a former KGB officer named Vladimir Putin.[15] Zelensky later remembered that the future Russian president did not laugh at his jokes.[16]

In 2003 Zelensky was offered a permanent job at KVN, but the promotion would have come at the cost of disbanding Kvartal 95.[17] Instead, Zelensky decided to take his team of friends back to Ukraine and start their own production company. It was a fateful decision. Studio Kvartal 95 broadcast its first show in March 2004 and launched one successful production after the next.

Before moving to Kyiv to set up his new company, Zelensky married Olena Kiyashko, a native of his old neighborhood in Kryvyi Rih. A trained architect, she became a scriptwriter at Studio Kvartal 95.[18] While Volodymyr rose to stardom, Olena preferred to stay out of the limelight with their two children. Zelensky called his wife his "closest friend" and said that he took the most important decisions together with her.[19]

Political satire is possible only in a free country, and even though Ukraine was far from an ideal democracy, it was free. Across the border in Russia, however, the space for freedom of expression was shrinking. When Putin came to power in 2000, the satirical political show *Kukly* (Puppets) soon vanished from TV screens. Even as Putin tried to export his soft brand of authoritarianism to Ukraine, Ukrainians were still laughing at their leaders. Before the violence on the Maidan, Viktor Yanukovych was a source more of mirth than of fear. Zelensky did a bitingly funny impression of Yanukovych's oafish way of speaking, and after a wreath fell on the Ukrainian president's bowed head during a ceremony with the Russian president Dmitry Medvedev, Kvartal 95 duly parodied the event.

Even so, Zelensky later said that Yanukovych was the Ukrainian president whom he got to know the best. Zelensky recalled giving a private performance for Yanukovych and Medvedev, who for some reason were both wearing nothing but bathrobes.[20] Another time, Zelensky said, he was invited to Yanukovych's kitschy residence Mezhyhirya, where the Ukrainian president plied him with alcohol. At the time, Zelensky was the general producer at one of Ukraine's biggest TV channels. In Zelensky's telling, Yanukovych offered him a $100 million budget in exchange for his loyalty—but Zelensky declined "because I'm not sick in the head." Encounters with politicians and oligarchs gave Zelensky insight into how Ukraine was run, and in 2016 he began considering his own foray into politics.[21]

Before the Russian annexation of Crimea, political satire was only a small part of Kvartal 95's repertoire. The company's movies and sitcoms, filmed in Russian, were marketed to a wide audience in both Ukraine and Russia. Zelensky had the universal appeal of a "Ukrainian Tom Hanks," David Dodson, an American filmmaker who worked on a number of movies for Kvartal 95, remembered.[22] Dodson classified Kvartal 95's brand of comedy as "Borscht Belt humor," well beyond the bounds of Western political correctness and very often below the belt. In one sketch, Zelensky pretended to play a Jewish folk song on the piano with his penis.[23]

The 2014 Russian invasion of Ukraine made Zelensky much more political—as it did most Ukrainians. Rather than just ridicule politicians, Zelensky began to take a political position of his own. Putin barbs were easy. The reason the Russian leader could not keep his hands off Ukraine, Zelensky joked, was because he liked the country more than his alleged mistress, rhythmic gymnast Alina Kabayeva. Zelensky got into trouble when he attacked the Ukrainian president Petro Poroshenko. At a comedy festival in Latvia in 2016, Zelensky impersonated Poroshenko asking European donors for yet another tranche of financial aid for Ukraine. Zelensky portrayed Poroshenko as a huckster who compared Ukraine to a German porn actress "ready to take it in any quantity from any side." The sketch caused a hail of criticism back in Ukraine.[24] For many people, Zelensky's humor was not patriotic enough. Some remembered an off-color joke Kvartal 95 had made at the expense of Maidan protesters who were beaten by the police. Zelensky was unrepentant. "We are a proud nation, not beggars," he wrote in a Facebook post. "This is a joke about the actions of our top officials, our government, not about the people or about our country."

A year earlier, the first season of Zelensky's hit series, *Servant of the People*, had been released. It told the story of a high school teacher, played by Zelensky, who accidentally becomes Ukraine's president after his students record him ranting about the country's unabated corruption. The show's hero turned into Zelensky's medium for expressing his fury and frustration with Ukraine's political class. For a second time in a decade, the promise of a Maidan revolution had ended in shady deals in the back rooms of Kyiv. Asked in a December 2018 interview if *Servant of the People* had been made with a future presidential campaign in mind, Zelensky laughed and threw up his hands. "Of course not," he said.[25]

At the end of 2018, as Zelensky was contemplating a run against Poroshenko in the upcoming presidential election, Ukraine found itself in a tough spot. Ukraine fatigue, a recurring condition, was again afflicting the powerful countries that Kyiv relied on for economic and moral support. Donald Trump, who did not conceal his admiration for Putin, was singularly uninterested in Ukraine. In the tug-of-war inside the Trump administration, Russia hawks such as the defense secretary Jim Mattis managed to push through the delivery of lethal defensive weapons to Ukraine. But as a foreign policy priority, Ukraine did not matter to the Americans. Meanwhile in France, a new president, Emmanuel Macron, was courting Putin. Like Trump, Macron believed that he could find a common, manly language with Putin to defuse the very crises that the Russian leader had created.

The Donbas was stuck in a stalemate, with occasional flare-ups of violence but no significant military engagements. According to the United Nations, about thirteen thousand people had been killed in the fighting, a quarter of them civilians, since 2014.[26]

I tried to return to the "Donetsk People's Republic," but the separatists denied me entry because their higher-ups in Moscow had deemed me "anti-Putin" and "anti-Russian." Few, if any, foreign reporters who had witnessed the violent creation of the DNR were allowed to visit. I watched from my perch in Moscow as one rebel warlord after another was killed in targeted assassinations. The separatists blamed the Ukrainians; the Ukrainians said Russian special forces were purging the separatist leadership to establish stricter control over their proxies.[27] Russian state television lionized the dead warlords as Russia's new heroes.

In early 2018, I traveled back to Crimea. I could have taken a direct flight from Moscow, but the authorities in Kyiv would have blacklisted me for entering Ukrainian territory without formally crossing the border. So I first flew to Kyiv, received special permission to visit the occupied peninsula, and traveled by overnight train to a small town near the border crossing with Crimea. It was my third visit to the peninsula.

The main complaint I heard was that prices had doubled because Crimea, cut off from mainland Ukraine, could only be supplied by sea. At the same time, many people said that things would only have been worse had Crimea remained in Ukraine—and that at least there was no war as in the Donbas. Four years earlier, Crimeans' grievances about neglect by Kyiv had been a significant reason so many were ready to join Russia. Putin poured billions of dollars into the annexed region, and even opponents of the Russian occupation told me that schools, hospitals, and the power grid were being upgraded. Putin's main infrastructure project was a twelve-mile-long bridge linking Crimea to the Russian mainland.

Again I tracked down Sergei Aksyonov, the Kremlin's puppet leader of Crimea, whom I had first interviewed in February 2014, days before he was plucked out of obscurity to head the separatist government. This time he met me in the prime minister's office in the capital, Simferopol. "Not one Ukrainian president devoted as much attention to Crimea as Vladimir Putin does now," he said.[28] Aksyonov was defiant. "Crimea will never return to Ukraine, and it's senseless to set any conditions to that end," he said. The peninsula had become an "impenetrable fortress" capable of facing down any threat. When I asked about the dozens of Crimeans who found themselves behind bars in politically motivated cases, Aksyonov bristled. "We don't have any political prisoners, not a single one," he said. "Crimea has returned to Russia forever. Anyone who advocates resistance is advocating bloodshed; of course we can't accept that and will react."

In terms of repression, Crimea was only second to Chechnya among Russian-ruled territories. There was a palpable sense of fear on the streets of Simferopol. One young man, who identified ethnically as Ukrainian, told me that he had voted for Russia in the 2014 "referendum." Now, disillusioned by the lack of political freedom and economic opportunity under Russian rule, he planned to emigrate to Europe.

"The biggest change has been that in Ukraine we lived freely, while in Russia today, freedoms have been severely limited or in some cases, simply banned," said Nariman Dzhelyal, one of the few remaining leaders of the Crimean Tatar minority who was not in prison or exile.[29] "Only that small group of people who are completely in love with Putin feel comfortable saying what they think. Anybody with a critical viewpoint will be rather afraid."[30]

On May 7, 2018, Vladimir Putin was inaugurated to a fourth term in office in a grand Kremlin ceremony. About a week later Putin opened the bridge connecting Russia with Crimea by driving an orange dump truck over it. For the Kremlin, the road and rail link over the Kerch Strait was a monument to Russian dominance that would cement Crimea to Russia once and for all. For the Ukrainian leadership, the bridge was a further injury to Ukraine's sovereignty and territorial integrity. More than just plugging Crimea into Russia's transportation network, the bridge served as a physical gateway to the Sea of Azov, where the strategic Ukrainian port of Mariupol was located. Six months after the bridge's opening, Poroshenko sent three Ukrainian naval vessels into the Sea of Azov, challenging Russia's claim to the Kerch Strait. The Russian coast guard intercepted the Ukrainians, ramming a tugboat, firing on the gunboats, and taking two dozen crew members prisoner.[31]

With a presidential election just four months away, Poroshenko was struggling in the polls, lagging behind political evergreen Yulia Tymoshenko and Volodymyr Zelensky—although Zelensky had not even declared his candidacy.[32] Disillusionment with Poroshenko was widespread as his promises to restore peace to the Donbas and make a dent in corruption had gone unfulfilled. According to one poll, 47 percent of young Ukrainians aged eighteen to thirty-five said they were considering emigrating to find work.[33]

As he flirted with a run for president, Zelensky said in December 2018 that his fourteen-year-old daughter talked about moving to a "calm" country.[34] "I love this country, and she loves it, but her generation has a different attitude toward it," he said. "Now we have a chance to change something so our children won't want to leave." Zelensky said that finding personal happiness was not enough for him: "You can't be happy among people who are having a very tough time. That won't work." Zelensky the successful businessman exuded a healthy self-confidence in his abilities to run the country. He said that a president should serve only one five-year term and predicted that if he was elected, people would first sling mud at him, then learn to respect him, and cry when he left office.

Zelensky did not hide that his family was opposed to his running for president. But on New Year's Eve 2018, before the president's traditional New Year's message, Zelensky went on TV to announce his candidacy. He spoke for a minute, beginning in Russian and continuing in Ukrainian. Fortunately for Zelensky, a party called Servant of the People had been registered a year earlier by his childhood friend from Kryvyi Rih, Ivan Bakanov.[35] In January 2019, the pop-up party nominated Zelensky for president.

Petro Poroshenko had come into office on the slogan "live in a new way," even though he was an old-school politician who had been a fixture in Ukrainian public life for two decades. As he ran for reelection in 2019, Poroshenko's new slogan was "army, language, faith." He presented himself as the only Ukrainian leader who was tough enough to stand up to Putin. Nikolai Patrushev, the head of Russia's Security Council, called Poroshenko an American puppet and warned that if he was reelected, Ukraine could fall apart.[36]

For Poroshenko, the appearance of Zelensky as a candidate was literally a joke. The incumbent portrayed his new rival as a lightweight who would crumple before Putin. Poroshenko repeated unsubstantiated rumors that Zelensky was a drug addict.[37] "He's hardly a threat, but he's a serious competitor because there are enormous media and financial resources behind him," Ihor Hryniv, Poroshenko's campaign manager told me.[38] "Zelensky was never engaged in politics and was never interested in it. This looks more like a project of Ihor Kolomoiskyi." One of Ukraine's richest men, Kolomoiskyi was in an open conflict with Poroshenko. He also owned 1+1, the TV channel that broadcast Kvartal 95's shows. Zelensky, for his part, denied taking orders from anybody, including Kolomoiskyi.

Zelensky was an enigma. His campaign was largely virtual, taking place on social media, and the candidate studiously avoided journalists. Zelensky's promises were so broad that they were practically meaningless: end the war, slash red tape, defeat corruption. Zelensky's very candidacy made a mockery of Poroshenko's pompous slogan of "army, language, faith." Zelensky had never served in the military; he used Russian in his public appearances; and he was a nonpracticing Jew in a majority Orthodox Christian country. His logo was simply "Ze!" on a green background. For Zelensky, as for most of his compatriots, language was not a controversial issue. "Ukrainian is the state language, and you speak the language you want to," Zelensky said.[39] There was no need to amend the constitution to make Russian a second official language, just as there was no need to restrict the use of any language, he said.

In a rare pre-election interview with 1+1, Zelensky found himself defending his words in 2014 about genuflecting before Putin.[40] Zelensky said that he had meant he would do anything to save Ukraine—and that he was still ready to do so. The Minsk agreement was clearly not working, so the United States and Britain should join it to provide new impetus to the peace process, he said. As for Crimea, its return to Ukraine was only possible after a change of power in Russia.

Instead of campaigning in a conventional sense, Zelensky kept dancing and goofing around on TV with the comedians from Kvartal 95. In one stand-up routine, Zelensky made a self-deprecating pitch for the presidency, joking about Jewish mothers, fad diets, and accusations that he was in Kolomoiskyi's pocket. Zelensky's aides said that he was unavailable for interviews because he was busy working on shows, as if his presidential campaign was just a side gig.

I visited Zelensky's campaign headquarters in a townhouse in an upscale part of Kyiv. Dmytro Razumkov, a top campaign adviser, rejected my suggestion that Zelensky was a protest candidate. "He is the only candidate who can unite the country in today's conditions," Razumkov said.[41] In a glass room, a dozen young people were taking orders for bright green Ze! campaign stickers and responding to questions submitted via Facebook. "I'm glad I could join something that will change my country for the better," said Nadezhda Tereba, age twenty-three, a campaign worker. "As a student, I want my future to be in my own country, here at home."

In the first round of the election on March 31, Zelensky won 30 percent of the vote, trouncing heavyweights Poroshenko, with 16 percent, and Tymoshenko, with 13 percent. Since none of the thirty-nine candidates on the ballot had won an outright majority, Zelensky and Poroshenko moved on to a runoff. Poroshenko was confident that he could expose Zelensky as a fraud if only he could lure him into a debate. But when he finally accepted the challenge, Zelensky turned the showdown into a show, demanding it be held in Kyiv's Olympic Stadium and that Poroshenko agree to take a drug test beforehand. Zelensky was a polished performer, and he held his own against Poroshenko's attacks. When the dust had cleared, the most memorable line was Zelensky's zinger: "I am not your opponent, I am your verdict."

Two days after the debate, on April 21, Zelensky buried Poroshenko in a landslide with 73 percent of the vote, beating even the election result of the hero of *Servant of the People* by six percentage points. Zelensky won in every part of Ukraine except the western Lviv region. Zelensky had channeled the disillusionment of Ukrainians as the Donbas war ground on and the fruits of the Euromaidan protests withered away. Zelensky's vague promises ended up helping more than hurting him. He presented voters with a blank slate, and they projected whatever they wanted on it.

The election of a complete outsider revealed the level of Ukrainians' desperation, but it also demonstrated the resilience of their oft-maligned democracy. Poroshenko, despite the bitter campaign, conceded. Ukraine still had the ability to renew itself. Zelensky was neither a former protest leader nor a Ukrainian nationalist. In his outlook—and in his humor—he was representative of most people I had met in Ukraine, people who wanted to live in peace and have leaders worthy of their respect. Zelensky personified what Putin could not comprehend about Ukraine: for one, that it was a democracy; and second, that a Russian-speaking Jew could identify as Ukrainian. Contrary to Kremlin propaganda, independent Ukraine had forged a civic identity that went beyond ethnicity, language, or religion. On the night of his victory, Zelensky thanked his family, his team, and his supporters. Then he said: "Since I am not officially the president, I can say as a citizen of Ukraine to all countries of the post–Soviet Union: Look at us, everything is possible."

Russians, who knew Zelensky well, were looking. Russian state media celebrated Poroshenko's spectacular downfall, although there was deep apprehension about what to expect from Zelensky and who stood behind him. For the Kremlin's propagandists, Ukraine's rough-and-tumble election was not an example of democracy but of anarchy. Putin remained silent, declining to congratulate the new president. Alexei Navalny was more diplomatic. On the day of the vote, the Russian opposition leader congratulated Ukrainians on holding fair and competitive elections. "May Ukraine prosper," Navalny tweeted. "Russia can only benefit from it."

Zelensky's inauguration took place on May 20, 2019, a cloudless spring day in Kyiv. The ceremony contrasted with Putin's quasi coronation in the Kremlin a year earlier. Zelensky arrived at the Rada, Ukraine's parliament, on foot, beaming and shaking the outstretched hands of supporters who lined the way. As he entered the Rada, Zelensky flexed his arms in triumph.

Zelensky's inaugural address was an appeal to unity and a call to action.[42] He said all Ukrainians, even those who had not voted for him, were now also president—meaning they shared not only power but also responsibility for what happened in the country. Europe, the goal of Ukraine's civilizational path, was not a place "somewhere out there" but right here, Zelensky said, pointing at his head. Lawmakers gave Zelensky a standing ovation after he said that his top priority was ending the war: "History is unfair. We are not the ones who have started this war. But we are the ones who have to finish it." Zelensky pledged that peace would not come at the price of territory. Turning to Ukrainian officials, Zelensky told them not to put up his portrait in their offices. "Hang your kids' photos instead and look at them each time you are making a decision," he said.

Zelensky spoke for less than twenty minutes. At the end of his speech he called on lawmakers to pass legislation giving up their parliamentary immunity and to dismiss the defense minister, the SBU chief, and the prosecutor general. Then he said he was dissolving the Rada and calling snap parliamentary elections in two months. Zelensky closed by saying that he had spent his life trying to make Ukrainians laugh—and now he would do his best so at the very least they would no longer have to cry.

The presidents of a number of eastern European countries attended the inauguration. Donald Trump dispatched Rick Perry, the energy secretary, as the head of the U.S. delegation. Sensing an opportunity in Zelensky's election, Trump's allies made no secret of what they expected of Ukraine's new leader. Special Counsel Robert Mueller's investigation into Russian election interference had just ended, finding insufficient evidence to charge anyone in the 2016 Trump campaign with criminal conspiracy. Now Trump's supporters decided to turn the tables on the Democratic opposition with a counternarrative of *Ukrainian* interference on behalf of Hillary Clinton's campaign.[43] They took interest in the 2016 leak of damaging material concerning Paul Manafort, Trump's former campaign manager. Manafort had previously served as an adviser to Viktor Yanukovych, and when documentation of secret payments to Manafort emerged in Kyiv in August 2016, he was forced to quit the Trump campaign.[44] Another line of attack was against Joe Biden, Trump's most likely Democratic rival in 2020. Trump's allies wanted Zelensky to initiate an investigation into Biden and his son, Hunter, who had served on the board of a Ukrainian oil company while his father was Obama's point man on Ukraine.

Even before Zelensky's inauguration, Rudy Giuliani, Trump's personal lawyer, said in a newspaper interview that he planned to travel to Kyiv to urge Zelensky to investigate the Bidens and the Manafort document leak.[45] Giuliani did not disguise the purpose of his trip. "We're not meddling in an election; we're meddling in an investigation, which we have a right to do," Giuliani said. "There's nothing illegal about it," he said, conceding that "somebody could say it's improper." Later Giuliani said on Fox News: "I guarantee you: Joe Biden will not get to Election Day without this being investigated."[46]

The next day Giuliani canceled his Kyiv trip amid an uproar over his attempt to drag a foreign government into America's widening political divide. Giuliani said he had changed his plans after learning that Zelensky was surrounded by "enemies" of Trump. In Kyiv, Giuliani's statements disconcerted the president-elect's team. The last thing any Ukrainian leader wanted to do was to risk the broad bipartisan support Ukraine enjoyed in the U.S. Congress. But the Trump administration's interest in Zelensky's political value had only been piqued. Once Zelensky took office, Trump himself would seek a way to persuade the Ukrainians to go after the Bidens.

Trump first reached out to Zelensky on the night of the Ukrainian election on April 21. After spending the Easter weekend in Florida, Trump called Zelensky from Air Force One as he flew back to Washington. Trump congratulated Zelensky on a "fantastic election," to which Zelensky responded by calling Trump a "great example" and inviting him to his inauguration.[47] The U.S. president said that if he could not make it himself, he would send someone "at a minimum at a very, very high level." Trump went on to invite Zelensky to the White House. "We'll have a lot of things to talk about, but we're with you all the way," Trump said.

Putin, meanwhile, was not sure he had anything to talk about with Zelensky. The days of direct Russian political influence on the Ukrainian leadership were a thing of the past. Although a fierce critic of Poroshenko, Zelensky had made uncompromising remarks about the return of Russian-occupied territory to Ukraine. He had also cracked more than one joke at the Russian leader's expense. Ironically, by annexing Crimea and creating two separatist statelets in eastern Ukraine, Putin had removed the most pro-Russian elements from the Ukrainian electorate. The low-level war in the Donbas was draining much of the remaining sympathy Ukrainians had for Russia.

Almost three weeks after Zelensky's inauguration, Putin hosted an annual investment forum in his hometown, St. Petersburg. As Putin participated in a panel discussion with the Chinese president Xi Jinping and the United Nations secretary-general António Guterres, the moderator asked Putin why he had still not congratulated the new Ukrainian president. Putin replied that Zelensky, like his predecessor, had called Russia an "enemy" and an "aggressor."[48] Although he did not rule out a future meeting, Putin said that Zelensky first needed to articulate what he wanted. "Judging by everything I've seen, he is a good specialist in the area he has worked in until now. He is a good actor," Putin said to laughter. "But it is one thing to play someone and another to be someone." Zelensky, he said, still needed to prove that he had the qualities of a statesman such as "bravery and strength of character."

Zelensky's election reframed the conflict between Russia and Ukraine as one between an aging, wooden autocrat who mourned the fall of the Soviet empire and a youthful, irreverent leader who was a teenager when Ukraine gained its independence. Zelensky had much more in common with Alexei Navalny, another upstart with zero experience in public office. The two forty-somethings were well-versed in the use of social media, devastating in their takedowns of opponents, and populistic and vague in their promises. Nevertheless, Navalny was almost as laconic as Putin following the Ukrainian elections. Only after Zelensky's inauguration did Navalny comment on the new president in his weekly YouTube show.[49] Navalny praised Zelensky's inaugural address as "outstanding" but said that he would have to be judged by his actions. Zelensky would have a tough time uprooting corruption because Ukraine's oligarchic clans were even more entrenched than Russia's, Navalny said. "I'm neither positively nor negatively inclined toward him," he said. "I'm looking at what he'll do. It will be great if he helps Ukraine because the strategic interest of my voters is that Ukraine prospers."

Navalny was not wrong about Zelensky's challenge of fighting corruption in Ukraine. But he completely ignored the much bigger challenge of restoring Ukraine's territorial integrity. Even if Navalny opposed Putin's covert war against Ukraine, it was not a position that would have widened his base of support. Postimperial trauma, inflamed by years of Kremlin propaganda, still colored the worldview of most Russians.

During the election campaign, Zelensky had promised to turn Ukraine into a meritocracy and end nepotism. After he was swept into the presidency, however, Zelensky filled the top ranks of his administration with old friends and business associates. Most controversially, Zelensky appointed Andriy Bohdan as his chief of staff. Bohdan, who had helped nudge Zelensky into politics, was the former personal lawyer of the oligarch Ihor Kolomoiskyi.[50] Bohdan throttled Zelensky's contact with the news media and pushed the idea that the president's social media posts made journalists superfluous.[51]

Zelensky's first move was to capitalize on his popularity and bring his supporters into the Rada. His party, Servant of the People, was an empty shell that still needed to be filled with people and ideas before the early parliamentary elections on July 21. Zelensky expected the party to win about 80 of the 450 seats in the Rada.[52] Instead, the Zelensky brand was so strong that Servant of the People took 254 seats, becoming the first party in Ukraine's history to win an outright parliamentary majority. People with no political experience—and often little vetting—became the new servants of the Ukrainian people. By the end of 2019, more than 150 bills were passed with the goal of turning Ukraine into a modern market economy.[53] Zelensky's first prime minister, Oleksiy Honcharuk, led a cabinet in which the average age was between thirty and forty.[54] His government set in motion programs to liberalize the land market, overhaul Ukraine's decrepit roads, and streamline routine bureaucratic procedures through a smartphone app.

Not surprisingly, Zelensky's team of political newcomers also brought chaos into the halls of power. The head of the National Security and Defense Council, Oleksandr Danylyuk, lasted four months. Andriy Bohdan, Zelensky's controversial chief of staff, made it until February 2020. A month later the Rada dismissed both the prime minister, Honcharuk, and the prosecutor general, Ruslan Ryaboshapka.

If Zelensky's introduction to Ukrainian politics could be called a rollercoaster ride, his foray into foreign policy was a baptism by fire. The new president was in a hurry to find a resolution to the grinding war in the

Donbas. When the fighting first broke out in 2014, the Obama administration had left conflict resolution to Germany and France. Zelensky believed that the United States could reinvigorate the peace process, so he was eager to win Trump's backing before dealing with Putin. What Zelensky discovered was that the United States was far more unpredictable as a friend than Russia was as an adversary.

Zelensky was confident that he would be able to charm the mercurial American president if given the chance. Commentators drew comparisons between the two leaders: they were both well-known TV personalities, businessmen, and outsiders turning the political establishment on its head. Even before he declared his candidacy, Zelensky said he could imagine holding talks with Trump—after all, they were both from the world of show business.[55] Zelensky said that as long as he was talking to a "normal person" and not a "windbag," he could find a common language with anybody. A few months later, as he stormed into the first round of the presidential election, Zelensky seemed cocky about winning over Trump. "We'll figure it out," Zelensky told the journalist Simon Shuster.[56] "I'm sure we'll get along."

A consistent challenge for Ukrainian presidents was asserting Ukraine's interests while commanding the respect—and attention—of the rest of the world. For Trump, the fighting in Ukraine was primarily a problem for the Europeans. At the Republican convention in August 2016, the Trump campaign—still led by Paul Manafort—watered down language in the party platform on assisting Ukraine. After Trump finally met Putin on the sidelines of a G20 summit in Germany in July 2017, the secretary of state Rex Tillerson announced the appointment of Kurt Volker, a former ambassador to NATO, as the U.S. special envoy for Ukraine "at the request of President Putin." Presumably Putin had reminded the Americans that the Kremlin was still waiting for the appointment of an official to conduct behind-the-scenes talks on Ukraine.[57]

After Zelensky's election, Volker increasingly found himself acting as an intermediary between the new Ukrainian administration and Rudy Giuliani instead of the Kremlin. Giuliani may have been forced to cancel his trip to Kyiv in May, but he did not give up trying to persuade Zelensky to launch investigations into the Bidens and "Ukrainian interference" in the 2016 U.S. election. Even if they went nowhere, the mere fact of investigations would avenge the Mueller probe and create an aura of impropriety around Biden ahead of the 2020 presidential race.

The gist of the Biden story was that, while he was vice president, Joe Biden had intervened to oust Poroshenko's chief prosecutor, Viktor Shokin, to prevent an investigation into Burisma, the Ukrainian oil company where Hunter Biden sat on the board. In fact, the United States, together with other Western donors, was openly pushing for Shokin's resignation exactly because he was doing so little to fight corruption. The accusations of wrongdoing against Burisma predated Hunter Biden, and he had been appointed to the board as part of an effort to clean up the company's image.

Giuliani became obsessed with the Bidens. One of his main sources of information was Shokin's successor, Yuriy Lutsenko, who was hoping to keep his job as chief prosecutor in a future Zelensky administration.[58] Lutsenko further ingratiated himself with Giuliani by attacking the U.S. ambassador in Kyiv, Marie Yovanovitch, a career diplomat who potentially stood in the way of Giuliani's machinations against the Bidens. Giuliani spread rumors that Yovanovitch was disloyal to Trump, and in May the State Department announced her premature departure from Kyiv. Giuliani's freelance foreign policy was taking place in plain sight of administration officials. "Giuliani's a hand grenade who's going to blow everybody up," John Bolton, the U.S. national security adviser, told an aide.[59]

Zelensky, in the meantime, continued to pursue a meeting with Trump. When two of the Ukrainian president's closest advisers, Andriy Yermak and Oleksandr Danylyuk, visited the White House on July 10, they were told that Zelensky would be invited only after the Ukrainians announced "investigations." Eight days later, top U.S. national security officials learned on a call that Trump had frozen almost $400 million in military aid, including everything from Humvees and night vision goggles to patrol boats and Javelin antitank missiles. The U.S. assistance made up a tenth of Ukraine's defense budget and was due to expire at the end of the fiscal year, on September 30.

When the Ukrainian and American presidents finally talked on the phone on July 25, each man had a very different goal. Zelensky needed Trump to show Putin that he had the American president's support; Trump needed Zelensky to help damage Biden's presidential prospects. According to a reconstructed transcript later released by the White House, Zelensky was cringingly obsequious, calling Trump a "great teacher," agreeing that the Europeans were not doing enough to help Ukraine, and mentioning that he had stayed in Trump Tower during his last visit to New York.[60] Trump was blunt about what he wanted. "I would like you to do us a favor," he said, referring to the investigations that Giuliani had been demanding. "Whatever you can do, it's very important that you do it if that's possible." Zelensky promised that his prosecutor general would look into the Burisma case. Trump replied that Giuliani and the U.S. attorney general William Barr would be in touch.

By early August, it became clear to the Ukrainians that U.S. military assistance had been frozen.[61] At the same time, the Trump administration was pressing Zelensky's government to make a public statement about the start of investigations. Volker, in his own words, helped draft a statement with input from Giuliani.[62] In September, Gordon Sondland, Trump's ambassador to the European Union, explicitly told the Ukrainians that the release of the military aid was contingent on a public announcement.[63] Zelensky had little choice left but to schedule an interview with CNN.

Fortunately for Zelensky, U.S. lawmakers found out about the frozen military aid to Ukraine, raising questions about why it had been delayed. Then a whistleblower in the CIA filed a complaint questioning the propriety of Trump's July 25 call with Zelensky. The White House finally released the military aid, and the Ukrainian president canceled his CNN interview. On September 24, the House of Representatives launched an impeachment inquiry to determine whether Trump had abused his presidential powers by seeking the aid of a foreign government to undermine a political rival.

As fate would have it, Trump and Zelensky met the very next day during the UN General Assembly in New York. As they took questions from journalists in a hotel meeting room, the Ukrainian president spoke in not completely fluent English and at times seemed to struggle to understand what was being said. Zelensky again invited Trump to Ukraine and, with reporters as his witnesses, tried to get the U.S. president to commit to a date for his White House visit. Zelensky denied that Trump had put him under pressure during the July 25 phone call and vouched for the independence of his new prosecutor general. It was not the meeting with Trump that Zelensky had hoped for. Nobody cared about Ukraine's lonely fight against Russian aggression. Zelensky was interesting to Americans only in how much he had been played by their unscrupulous president.

I flew to Kyiv in the midst of the brewing scandal. People in the government did not want to talk for obvious reasons: there was zero upside to commenting at a time when American support was on the line. Ordinary Ukrainians, however, were always happy to share their opinions on politics. Outside the Golden Gate, a Kyiv landmark, a retired chemist named Taisa Sukhan told me that Zelensky's performance in the infamous phone call had been "shameful," and that the "old wolf Trump" was leading him on. Yet most people I spoke to did not care about American impeachment intrigue. Zelensky's approval ratings were still above 70 percent thanks, in part, to a recent prisoner exchange with Russia that had resulted in the release of the sailors captured during the 2018 naval clash in the Kerch Strait.

Much more important to Ukrainians were Zelensky's efforts to end the war in eastern Ukraine. On October 1, Zelensky announced that Ukrainian troops would be pulled back from two locations in the Donbas as a sign of goodwill. More controversially, Zelensky agreed to hold local elections in the Russian-occupied parts of the Donetsk and Luhansk regions—one of the thorniest points in the Minsk II agreement. Zelensky insisted that the elections would not take place until *after* Russian-backed forces had been withdrawn and Ukraine had restored full control over its border with Russia. But for the quarter of the population that was dead set against Zelensky as president, his readiness to compromise was already a betrayal. Protesters took to the Maidan chanting "no capitulation."

Zelensky had a mandate from a majority of Ukrainians to stop the fighting. Now that a summit with Trump was off the agenda, Zelensky set his sights on a meeting with the one man who could call off the Donbas war, Vladimir Putin. By agreeing to fulfill key provisions of the Minsk process without spelling out exactly how he would do it, Zelensky created the conditions for a gathering of the leaders of the "Normandy Format"—Ukraine, Russia, Germany, and France. All four sides repeated the mantra of the indispensability of the Minsk agreement, but each had its own motive. For the Germans and French, the agreement was an alibi that they had done their part in seeking a peaceful resolution; for the Russians, it was a way to pressure Ukraine; and for the Ukrainians, it was a piece of paper that staved off all-out war, although the political points of Minsk II were impossible for any Kyiv government to fulfill without risking its own downfall.

Putin was satisfied with the unexpected turn of events. "Thank God nobody is accusing us of intervening in elections in the United States anymore. Now they are accusing Ukraine," Putin told a group of international investors.[64] "Let them figure this out among themselves." The Russian leader criticized the CIA whistleblower and defended Trump's phone call,

THE EDUCATION OF VOLODYMYR ZELENSKY 223

saying any leader would want to know if "former employees" of the previous administration had been engaged in corruption.[66] As for the Ukrainians, Putin advised them not to seek their fortune "overseas" but to learn to live with their neighbors.[66] As the Normandy Format summit loomed, the Kremlin had the much stronger hand: if the Minsk agreement failed completely, Moscow could blame Kyiv for noncompliance. And if Ukraine did try to reintegrate the Donbas according to the Minsk plan, civil strife would be sure to follow—while Russia, having foisted the Donetsk and Luhansk statelets back on Kyiv, would be eligible for sanctions relief.

Zelensky's meeting with Putin was set for December 9, 2019, in Paris, with Macron and Merkel acting as mediators. On the eve of the summit, Zelensky gave a rare interview to U.S., German, and French media. The Ukrainian president made an appeal for major powers not to view Ukraine as a piece on a chess board but a player in its own right.[67] It was a plea for agency by the leader of one of Europe's largest nations. Zelensky said that even if his talks with Putin went nowhere, he would still not resort to force. "I will never go for that because my position in life is to be a human being above all," Zelensky said. "How many of them will die? Hundreds of thousands, and then an all-out war will start, an all-out war in Ukraine, and then across Europe." Before his run for president, Zelensky had expressed a breezy certainty that he would be able to reach an understanding with Putin. Now, after the humbling experience with Trump, Zelensky sounded much more guarded. "I don't trust anyone at all," he said. "Everybody just has their interests."

Twenty years after the budding comedian Volodymyr Zelensky performed for the budding politician Vladimir Putin, the two men crossed paths again in the French capital. Zelensky arrived at the Élysée Palace in a Renault minivan, followed by Putin in a lumbering, Russian-built limousine. Three years had passed since Putin last met Poroshenko. Zelensky was visibly nervous, but he stood his ground in the six hours of talks. As expected, there were no breakthroughs. But the two leaders agreed to meet again in four months, and more prisoner exchanges would follow.

In a bitter coda to the Paris meeting, the Ukrainians had to watch as the Russian foreign minister Sergei Lavrov, who had accompanied Putin to the summit, flew on to Washington. The next day Donald Trump received Lavrov in the White House. Trump tweeted a picture in which he was sitting behind his Oval Office desk grinning while Putin's foreign minister stood beside him. In the post, Trump mentioned trade, arms control, and nuclear nonproliferation as topics of discussion—but not Ukraine. It was Lavrov's second White House meeting since Trump's election. Zelensky, by comparison, had failed to get even a date. The same day as Lavrov's meeting, Democrats in the House of Representatives announced articles of impeachment against Trump, charging him with abuse of power by pressuring Ukraine to investigate Biden and obstructing Congress in its subsequent investigation.

For Zelensky, Lavrov's visit to the White House was a final slap in the face. Nobody in Kyiv harbored illusions anymore about where the Trump administration's true sympathies lay. In January 2020, Mike Pompeo paid his first visit to Ukraine, almost two years after replacing Rex Tillerson as secretary of state. A few days before his trip, Pompeo abruptly broke off an interview with an NPR colleague when she asked him about his treatment of Marie Yovanovitch, the U.S. ambassador in Kyiv who was fired during the pressure campaign against Ukraine. "Do you think Americans care about fucking Ukraine?" Pompeo shouted.

NPR's State Department correspondent was not allowed on Pompeo's plane, and as a result, I ended up flying to Kyiv to cover the visit. Ukrainians were frustrated by the way their country was being treated by the United States, which an entire generation, including Zelensky, had grown up admiring. After their meeting, Zelensky and Pompeo held an awkward, perfunctory press conference, taking only two questions. Pompeo pledged that America's commitment to support Ukraine "will not waver." Considering the unannounced freeze on U.S. military aid during the previous summer, Pompeo's assertion sounded unconvincing at best. Under Pompeo's watch, Trump's personal lawyer had managed to upset years of established U.S. policy toward independent Ukraine.

Pompeo brought only pompous words to Kyiv—and none that the Ukrainians had been waiting to hear. He named neither a replacement for Kurt Volker, the special envoy for Ukraine who resigned during the impeachment scandal, nor a date for Zelensky's long overdue White House visit. The message from Washington was loud and clear: as long as Trump was president, Ukraine would not be able to count on the United States as an ally.

10

Grandpa in the Bunker

Five minutes before midnight on December 31, 2019, Vladimir Putin appeared on national TV with the fabled Kremlin towers illuminated behind him. New Year's Eve was Russia's most important holiday, and the president's traditional greeting, followed by the chiming of the Kremlin bells, was the official New Year's countdown for millions of Russians. The "true magic" of New Year's Eve transforms the world with joy and smiles, Putin said without smiling. Twenty years earlier to the day, he had come to power after Boris Yeltsin abruptly resigned as Russia's first president and anointed Putin, his inexperienced prime minister, as his successor. In his first New Year's Eve address in the last minutes of 1999, Putin seemed as surprised by his new job as everyone else. Two decades later, Putin had completely embodied the role of Russia's stern patriarch. "Our personal plans and dreams are inseparable from Russia," Putin said tellingly.[1]

Putin had big plans for 2020. The so-called 2024 Problem—the conundrum of what would happen after Putin's fourth presidential term, when he would be constitutionally barred from running again—would be solved once and for all. The year 2020 would also mark the seventy-fifth anniversary of the end of World War II. Perhaps Donald Trump and other Western leaders would attend the giant military parade on Red Square. Maybe they could even be convinced to come together for a summit to determine the fate of the world, just as the Allies had done toward the end of World War II in Yalta.

Putin did not waste any time getting down to business. With Russia barely over its holiday hangover, Putin announced the urgent need for constitutional changes to meet, as he put it, society's demand for change. Putin promptly fired the government of Prime Minister Dmitry Medvedev, who had become a target of popular ire following the 2017 investigation into his secret real estate empire by opposition leader Alexei Navalny. On the surface, Putin appeared to be reshuffling his government. But his opponents suspected the new appointments and calls for amendments were a smokescreen to extend his rule indefinitely.

After sacking his government, Putin traveled to Israel for a commemoration of the liberation of the Auschwitz death camp by Soviet soldiers in 1945. Representing the successor state of the Soviet Union, Putin spoke alongside leaders from the United States, Britain, and France.[2] He used the occasion to propose a summit of the five permanent members of the United Nations Security Council, which would elevate Russia back to the place the Soviet Union had held at the end of World War II.[3] Yet even as Putin voiced Russia's global ambitions, an invisible new enemy was invading the world.

The danger posed by the COVID-19 virus was not fully understood as Putin pushed changes to the constitution including a ban on same-sex marriage and an affirmation of Russians' faith in God. As the Duma gathered to approve the bundle of amendments in early March, a senior lawmaker theatrically proposed the most significant constitutional change of all: resetting Putin's term limits to let him stay in power until 2036, when he would turn eighty-four. As always, Putin applied the sheen of legality to his new set of tricks. Within less than a week, he rammed the amendments through Russia's rubber-stamp regional legislatures and won the Constitutional Court's approval to exempt him from the limit of two consecutive presidential terms. Although it was not required by the constitution, Putin planned to legitimize his latest power grab through a nationwide plebiscite. And then, on May 9, he would preside over a parade that would celebrate not only the Soviet victory in World War II but also his personal victory as the undisputed leader of a resurgent Russia.

The coronavirus upset Putin's grandiose plans. As the silent killer swept around the globe, the world went into lockdown as scientists raced to stop the virus. Reluctantly, the Kremlin first postponed the plebiscite, then the parade. Putin retreated to a germ-free bubble at his residences out-side Moscow. The Kremlin spent $85 million to provide accommodation for presidential support staff and visitors who had to quarantine for days, even weeks, before being allowed near Putin.[4] The Federal Guard Service set up special tunnels that sprayed visitors with a mist of disinfectant.[5] Putin mostly spoke with his ministers by videoconference, and his January visit to Israel turned out to be his last foreign trip for more than a year.

Yet even as Putin observed a strict regime of self-isolation, his lieu-tenants were under pressure to end the lockdown and hold the delayed parade and plebiscite. The mayor of Moscow rolled back most of the city's COVID restrictions by June 23, and the next day the parade on Red Square finally took place. For Putin, who obsessed over anniversaries, even this date was chosen to coincide with the Soviet Union's first victory parade on Red Square on June 24, 1945. Putin appeared on a stage with dozens of World War II veterans who had spent two weeks in quarantine for the honor. Neither he nor the fourteen thousand Russian service members who paraded past him wore protective masks that could ruin the spectacle. The only foreign guests who attended were the leaders of half a dozen for-mer Soviet republics and Serbia—countries that could ill afford to offend the Kremlin. Putin's idea of a "Yalta-2" conference among the World War II victor nations remained a fantasy.

The day after the parade, six days of early voting began in the plebi-scite, ostensibly to avoid overcrowding at polling stations but also provid-ing endless opportunities to stuff ballot boxes. Images appeared on social media of people casting their votes on tree stumps, out of a car trunk, and inside a city bus. The ballot itself was questionable because voters were being asked to give a single "yes" or "no" answer to a package of 206 con-stitutional amendments. For the authorities, the result was a foregone conclusion, and copies of the amended constitution appeared in Moscow bookstores even before voting started. On Twitter, Navalny mocked Putin as the "grandpa in the bunker" who hid at the end of a disinfection tunnel while herding voters to the polls to risk their health in a farcical vote. The plebiscite was not required by law, did not follow the rules of a referen-dum, and had no legal precedent; its sole purpose was to give the appear-ance that a vast majority of Russians supported the extension of Putin's rule. Predictably, the Central Election Commission duly announced that 78 percent of voters had approved the new amendments.

Putin's triumph was short-lived. Less than two weeks after the crowning plebiscite, tens of thousands of people began demonstrating in Khabarovsk, a provincial capital seven time zones east of Moscow on the border with China. Locals took to the streets after masked federal officers arrested the popular regional governor, Sergei Furgal, and flew him to Moscow to face charges of having organized contract killings fifteen years earlier. Putin only inflamed the protesters when he fired Furgal and dispatched a clownish politician to replace him as governor. "People go out every day without any kind of organization," Artyom Mozgov, a political activist, told me over the phone from Khabarovsk.[6] "I'm really happy that people from my region have finally taken responsibility for their lives, understand what's happening in our country, and go out and protest." At age twenty, Mozgov was one of the "New Russians" I had discovered in my travels across Russia—politically aware, outspoken, and unafraid.

Khabarovsk, a city of 600,000, is the last major stop on the Trans-Siberian Railway before the terminus, Vladivostok. What had struck me on visits to Siberia and Russia's Far East was how different the locals were from people in central Russia. Serfdom had never taken hold in the eastern reaches of the Russian Empire, and locals displayed an independent streak not unlike people in the American West.

Even before the 2020 protests, the Khabarovsk region had rejected the ruling United Russia party. Furgal, a member of the Liberal Democratic Party of Russia (LDPR), trounced the Kremlin-backed incumbent in 2018, and the LDPR almost completely swept United Russia out of the regional assembly a year later. Although the LDPR was nominally a nationalist party, many Russians voted for it primarily as a legal way to protest against the government. In Khabarovsk, the LDPR had served its function as a "systemic" opposition party by channeling discontent with the government in a controlled fashion. But once Moscow revoked their choice of governor, locals took to the streets. The Khabarovsk protests were remarkable for their peacefulness and their duration. And while the demonstrations eventually fizzled out, they showed that Russians were not passive and mute. Given the right circumstances, Russians—especially young Russians—were ready to protest.

A month after the Khabarovsk protests began, mass demonstrations broke out more than five thousand miles away to the west in Belarus, which alongside Russia and Ukraine had formed the Slavic core of the Soviet Union. The Belarusian protests were even more unexpected than those in Khabarovsk. Belarus was widely seen as a placid nation that had accepted its eccentric dictator, Alexander Lukashenko, in exchange for a modicum of economic stability. But in August 2020, when Lukashenko sought to extend his reign by five more years, he set off the biggest crisis of his quarter-century rule—and presented Putin with a unique opportunity to increase Russian control over Belarus.

For Russians, Belarus was practically indistinguishable from the rest of Russia. The two countries were bound together in a loose "union state," and most Belarusians spoke Russian as a first language and lacked a strong sense of national identity after centuries of Russian domination. From the Kremlin's point of view, Belarus, together with Ukraine, formed a cordon sanitaire against the West. Over the centuries, Swedish, French, and German invasions of Russia had all barreled eastward through the territory of Belarus, and the Kremlin was determined to keep the country in its sphere of influence. Control of Belarus gave Russia a strategic outcrop that jutted not only into central Europe but also across Ukraine's northern border.

A former collective farm manager, Lukashenko ran Belarus like a Soviet republic, wholly uninterested in its development as a democracy or a market economy. Although he was a testy partner who periodically lashed out at Moscow, the Kremlin tolerated Lukashenko because he kept Belarus isolated and reliant on Russian energy supplies. Still, the mustachioed Belarusian strongman pushed the limits of his independence, refusing to recognize Russia's annexation of Crimea. Belarusian neutrality allowed Lukashenko to position himself as a mediator in the Donbas conflict and play host to negotiations in the Belarusian capital that led to the Minsk peace agreement.

At the beginning of 2020, Putin cut oil deliveries to Belarus in an effort to force Lukashenko into closer integration with Russia. Lukashenko responded with his old tactic of flirting with the West to extract concessions from the Kremlin. Russia hawks in the Trump administration saw a chance to weaken the Kremlin's grip on Belarus. In February 2020, Lukashenko warmly received Mike Pompeo as the first U.S. secretary of state to visit Minsk in more than twenty-five years. Pompeo told Lukashenko that American energy companies could provide "100 percent" of Belarusian oil needs and promised to send a U.S. ambassador back to Minsk after more than a decade of frozen relations. In March, as the coronavirus was becoming a global pandemic, twenty-eight British Royal Marines conducted a rare joint exercise with Belarusian commandos near the border with Russia.[7]

Washington and London assumed that Lukashenko was the all-powerful dictator that he made out to be. But in the lead-up to the presidential election that summer, he faced a number of serious challengers who had widespread support. Belarusians were angry at the regime's cavalier response to COVID: there were no restrictions on public gatherings, and Lukashenko had downplayed the risks of the disease, saying it could be fought off with vodka and steam baths.[8] The economic hardship caused by the pandemic fueled public discontent. After Lukashenko jailed or exiled his main rivals, the wife of one of them, Sviatlana Tsikhanouskaya, stepped up as the united opposition's candidate. She did not voice any political ambitions of her own. Instead, Tsikhanouskaya promised to hold free and fair elections with the participation of all opposition candidates, including her jailed husband, Siarhei. Tsikhanouskaya's unassuming, authentic style brought out enthusiastic crowds around the country. "In our euphoria, we underestimated Lukashenko's brutality," she remembered later.[9]

Lukashenko, then sixty-five, represented the anachronistic Soviet way of doing things; Tsikhanouskaya, almost thirty years younger, symbolized the hopes of a generation fed up with the vagaries of a personalist regime they had known all their lives. After Lukashenko declared a landslide in the August 9 election, mass protests broke out in Minsk and other Belarusian cities. Police cracked down on protesters, arresting thousands. When reports surfaced of indiscriminate beatings and torture, more people took to the streets. The huge prodemocracy demonstrations that brought Minsk to a standstill were the belated Belarusian iteration of the peaceful protests in East Germany and Czechoslovakia in 1989 or Ukraine's Orange Revolution in 2004. The crucial difference was that in Belarus, the old regime responded with overhwelming violence and prevailed.

The KGB, as the Belarusian secret police was still known, pressured Tsikhanouskaya into exile by threatening her family. "I regret that I didn't have the courage to stay," she told me.[10] "In that moment, my sense of responsibility for my children—for what was mine—outweighed my responsibility for something bigger." Lukashenko ignored Tsikhanouskaya's calls for a dialogue under international mediation. Claiming that NATO was planning an invasion to help the antigovernment protesters, Lukashenko turned for support to the Kremlin, which was more than happy to oblige. Putin offered loans and pledged to send in a rapid-reaction force if the situation became "uncontrollable."[11]

Just like Ukrainian opposition politicians who had avoided criticizing Putin at the time of the Orange Revolution, Tsikhanouskaya and her allies recognized the importance of Russia to their country and rejected the notion that democratic change in Belarus was directed against Moscow. In an address to European Union lawmakers after her exile, Tsikhanouskaya said that the protests were neither anti-Russian nor pro-EU but an act of political self-determination.[12] Putin, however, did not want to see another client overthrown in a street revolution. With his regime on the line, Lukashenko became fully dependent on the Kremlin for political, economic, and military support. Lukashenko's prostration before Putin was a key pre-condition for Russia's full-scale invasion of Ukraine. And Lukashenko's ruthless repressions inside Belarus were a harbinger of things to come in Russia.

The outbreak of protests first in Khabarovsk and then in Belarus filled the Russian opposition with hope. The Kremlin's surprise constitutional reform had disillusioned and divided Putin's opponents. Then, in two places hardly known as hotbeds of dissent, people plucked up the courage to demonstrate against the powers that be. Although their causes were not directly related, protesters separated by thousands of miles understood that they shared a common struggle against autocracy. *"Zhive Belarus!"*— Long live Belarus!—Khabarovsk demonstrators shouted, waving the white-and-red flag used by the Belarusian opposition. In Minsk, people replied with banners and chants in support of the Khabarovsk protests.

Alexei Navalny cheered on both protest movements, even as the Kremlin put him under increasing pressure. In summer 2019, a number of Navalny's allies had been barred from running in the Moscow city council elections, setting off a new wave of antigovernment rallies in the Russian capital. The Kremlin understood that registering independent candidates would legitimize the "nonsystemic" opposition, leading to unforeseen consequences. Navalny struck back at the regime's greatest vulnerability: widespread disgust with United Russia.[13] He believed that the best way of breaking the Kremlin's monopoly on power was to challenge the ruling party through a system of "smart voting," namely, voting en masse for the one candidate who had the best chances mathematically of defeating the United Russia candidate in local and regional elections. When United Russia barely kept control of the Moscow city council and was almost shut out in Khabarovsk, Navalny's team declared victory. After the elections, the authorities branded Navalny's Anti-Corruption Foundation a "foreign agent" and conducted raids on the homes and offices of its activists across Russia.

COVID set political life into slow motion in countries around the world. In Russia, the government used restrictions on public gatherings as a way to ban practically any form of political protest. Navalny exhorted Russians to ignore Putin's dubious constitutional plebiscite. Instead, Navalny called on his supporters to apply the "smart voting" strategy in upcoming regional elections in September—and to keep the pressure on the regime by taking to the streets.

If Khabarovsk was an example of the protest potential of a provincial Russian city, then Belarus was an example of a national uprising in a country with a shared culture and history. On August 13, five days into the Belarusian protests, Navalny devoted most of his weekly YouTube broadcast to Belarus.[14] The videos he showed were scenes from Putin's worst nightmares and the Russian opposition's wildest dreams: riot policemen dumping their uniforms into the garbage; burly workers walking off the job on factory floors; and ordinary people standing up for their rights in towns large and small. Navalny celebrated the heroism of Tsikhanouskaya and all the women of Belarus who formed the backbone of the prodemocracy protests.[15] "Whatever success they have will be our great success—and our honest, sincere happiness for our Belarusian brothers," he said.[16] Navalny signed off from the almost three-hour broadcast saying he would be back in a week.

Navalny was in a coma by the time he was supposed to make his next YouTube broadcast. Earlier that day he had fallen violently ill as he was flying back to Moscow from Siberia after filming an investigation and meeting with local activists. The captain of the plane made an emergency landing in the city of Omsk. Doctors there put Navalny on a ventilator, but they gave contradictory information about his condition and said that it was too dangerous for him to travel to Europe for medical treatment. Only after Navalny's wife Yulia publicly appealed to Putin was Navalny allowed to be medevaced to Berlin. Navalny gradually recovered, and the German government announced that he had "without a doubt" been poisoned by a variant of Novichok, the same banned nerve agent used in the 2018 assassination attempt on Sergei Skripal, a former Russian spy living in England. Laboratories in Sweden and France, as well as the Organisation for the Prohibition of Chemical Weapons, confirmed the German findings.

The circumstantial evidence was damning because Russia was the only country in the world with the know-how and the capability to produce Novichok. But exactly how the Russian government had attempted to assassinate Navalny remained a mystery until Bellingcat, a digital investigative group, took up the case. Using leaked databases, Bellingcat had already identified the two main suspects in the Skripal attack as Russian military intelligence officers. Now, cooperating with Navalny and an international team of journalists, Bellingcat tracked down the government hit squad that had tried to kill Navalny. Bellingcat published its report in December 2020, identifying a group of FSB officers with training in medicine and chemical weapons who had started trailing Navalny around Russia following his announcement to run for president. Asked about the Bellingcat report at his annual press conference a few days later, Putin confirmed that the FSB had followed Navalny, suggesting that he was a CIA agent.[17] If the FSB had really wanted to finish Navalny off, Putin chortled, they would have. Navalny responded to Putin's awkward denial with his most sensational YouTube investigation. Posing as an aide to Nikolai Patrushev, the head of Russia's Security Council and one of Putin's closest confidants, Navalny phoned one of his would-be assassins. The unwitting FSB operative reported that Navalny's underwear had been laced with Novichok, and that Navalny likely would have died had his plane not made the emergency landing in Omsk.

If the Kremlin had gained anything from the bungled mission, it had at least chased Navalny out of Russia. To make him stay there, the Russian prison service announced that Navalny had violated the probation terms of a 2014 conviction and would be jailed if he did not return to Moscow immediately.[18] Exile guaranteed his relative safety, but Navalny understood that it also meant his eventual irrelevance as a Russian political figure. Navalny had always insisted that his place was in Russia, and on January 17, 2021, he defiantly flew back to Moscow, where he was arrested before he even passed through airport immigration.

A wave of protests rolled across Russia, with human rights activists reporting a record four thousand arrests in 125 cities.[19] On Moscow's

Pushkin Square, I met a business student who was at his first rally ever. "There is a certain point where you say, OK, now I have to go beyond my own insecurities and just step up," he said. A young corporate lawyer told me she hoped that at least her children would one day be able to live in a better country. The following weekend the police cracked down even harder. I had been reporting on demonstrations in Russia for more than a decade, but none felt as threatening as the Moscow protest on January 31. A young architect told me that although she was afraid and did not support Navalny as a politician, she felt a duty to demonstrate her disapproval with the Putin regime. As I walked on, a group of riot police stormed toward me, snatched an unsuspecting young man on the sidewalk, and bundled him into one of the waiting police trucks lining the street. Police detained almost six thousand protesters across Russia that day, and in Moscow the jails ran out of space.[20] When I later reached out to the young architect, she said that her boyfriend had been arrested and sentenced to thirteen days in a squalid detention center for undocumented migrants.

On February 2, a Moscow court granted the Russian prison service's petition to send Navalny to prison for more than two years on probation violations. Prosecutors began fabricating new cases against Navalny to lock him away for decades to come. Protesters were met with brute force, detention, and the threat of criminal prosecution. Thirty years after the collapse of Communism, Russia had once again become an unapologetic dictatorship, using the blunt tools of the truncheon and the show trial to crush dissent. For Putin, the elimination of Navalny as an opposition leader was another key precondition for the full-scale invasion of Ukraine.

Navalny's arrest came days before the inauguration of Joe Biden as the new U.S. president. Biden's antipathy toward Putin was well-known in Moscow, and Putin waited more than a month to congratulate Biden on his victory in the November election. The new administration came into office focused on four issues in relations with Russia: a massive cyberattack on U.S. government servers in which the Russian state was the prime suspect; reports that Russia had paid bounties to Afghan militants to kill U.S. service members; continuing Russian interference in U.S. elections; and Navalny's poisoning and imprisonment. The festering, low-level Russian war in Ukraine was of no greater importance for the incoming U.S. administration than it had been for the outgoing one. China was Biden's foreign policy priority, and the new American president was intent on minimizing Russia's role as a spoiler on the global stage. Within two weeks of Biden's inauguration, the United States and Russia extended New START—the last bilateral arms control agreement—shortly before it was due to expire. Although positive, the treaty extension was a formality that kept the floor in U.S.-Russian relations from dropping out completely.

The fragility of the relationship became clear in March, when Biden was asked in a TV interview if he thought that Putin was a killer. "Mm-hmm, I do," Biden replied. The Kremlin reacted with fury. The Foreign Ministry recalled the Russian ambassador to Washington, and Putin's spokesman lambasted Biden's "very bad" remarks as a clear sign that the U.S. president was uninterested in improving relations. Putin himself responded during a videoconference with Crimeans to mark the seventh anniversary of the peninsula's annexation. "It takes one to know one," Putin said about Biden's "killer" comment, adding that the playground taunt had a "very deep psychological meaning."[21] Putin suggested that Biden was projecting American guilt for the genocide of Native Americans, slavery, and even the nuclear bombs dropped on Hiroshima and Nagasaki. Putin was so agitated that he went back on state television to challenge Biden to a live debate the very next day.

The insult from the new U.S. president came amid rising tensions with Ukraine and the largest NATO exercise in Europe in more than twenty years. Both the United States and the EU had just sanctioned senior Russian officials over Navalny's persecution, and Biden promised that the Kremlin would "pay the price" for U.S. election interference and cyberattacks. Putin's response was the largest military buildup along Ukraine's borders since 2014. At the end of March, fighting flared up again in the Donbas region. As Russia continued massing troops near Ukraine, U.S. European Command raised the threat level to "potential imminent crisis," the highest level.[22] Putin's spokesman insisted that Russian forces were moving around on their own territory, threatened nobody, and should not concern anyone. Then Dmitry Kozak, the Kremlin official now in charge of the Ukraine brief, warned Kyiv that a hot war would mean "the beginning of the end of Ukraine."[23] That same day, Volodymyr Zelensky, wearing a flak jacket and helmet, visited Ukrainian troops on the front line in the Donbas.

Biden tried to defuse the crisis with a phone call to Putin. In exchange for a de-escalation on Ukraine's borders, Biden offered Putin a summit meeting.[24] Although there was precious little the two leaders could agree on, Biden's calculation was that he would finally get a chance to inject a degree of stability into the battered bilateral relationship. A week after Biden's call, Zelensky made a video address, rallying his nation in the face of all-out war.[25] "Does Ukraine want war? No. Is it ready for it? Yes," he said. At the end of the speech, Zelensky switched to Russian, inviting Putin to meet him "anywhere" in the Donbas to end the conflict. Zelensky had been trying to talk to Putin for almost a month without success.[26] Putin finally replied that he was prepared to meet with Zelensky but only to discuss "bilateral" issues—sticking to the duplicitous Kremlin line that the fighting in the Donbas was an internal Ukrainian conflict that Kyiv needed to settle with Russia's proxy statelets, the DNR and LNR.

Putin was far more interested in a meeting with Biden. But the Russian leader did not immediately accept the offer of a summit to show his displeasure with the U.S. administration. In his annual state-of-the-nation speech, Putin accused Western powers of plotting to assassinate Alexander Lukashenko, and he cautioned the West not to cross Russia's "red line"—without defining what it was.[27] The next day the Russian defense minister, Sergei Shoigu, announced the successful conclusion of a series of military maneuvers and ordered troops to return to their bases by May 1. But after that deadline passed, the Pentagon noticed that only a few thousand troops had been withdrawn from the border area—and that many of those units had left their armored vehicles and trucks behind.[28]

Putin had made his point to the U.S. administration: Russia's red line runs around Ukraine's western border. And if necessary, Moscow could turn the screws on Kyiv again.

During Trump's chaotic presidency, the Kremlin watched with glee and disbelief as an American president pilloried long-standing allies and questioned the utility of NATO. Trump's open disregard for Ukraine meant that there was no chance he would champion Ukrainian membership in the alliance. Biden, on the other hand, was a well-known Atlanticist and Barack Obama's former point man on Ukraine. Russia's massive military buildup was meant as a warning to the new American president. Yet it was also intended as an explicit reminder to Zelensky: you are still at Russia's mercy, and nobody will defend you. Ukrainians, however, drew the exact opposite conclusion. For Ukraine, the threats emanating from Russia only underscored the urgency of getting into NATO.

Following Russia's military intervention in 2014, a plurality of Ukrainians began to support NATO membership, although a third of the population remained consistently opposed to it.[29] In December 2014, the Rada voted to abandon Ukraine's nonaligned status that had been adopted under Viktor Yanukovych, and in February 2019, the parliament enshrined the country's EU and NATO aspirations in the Ukrainian Constitution. That spring, Zelensky ran for president saying Ukrainians themselves should decide on EU and NATO membership in a referendum.[30] Yet once Zelensky took office, he soon realized Ukraine's need for allies in its lonely struggle with Russia. In June 2020, Ukraine joined a NATO program to increase interoperability with the alliance; in September of that year, Zelensky approved a national security strategy that unambiguously called NATO membership "the strategic course of the state."[31] Zelensky then began actively lobbying NATO to grant Ukraine a Membership Action Plan (MAP)—the same issue that had divided the alliance at its Bucharest summit in 2008.

If the United States had been the main backer of a MAP for Ukraine back then, it was now firmly in the camp of the skeptics. No U.S. president after George W. Bush had any interest in bringing Ukraine into NATO. Although Biden was sympathetic to Ukraine's westward drive, he was not prepared to tip the delicate strategic balance with Russia by giving Ukrainians a clear path into the alliance. Biden was going to meet Putin right after the first NATO summit of his presidency, and the White House did not want to upset the Kremlin again. Ignoring Ukrainian objections, the State Department waived sanctions on Nord Stream 2, the second line of a Russian natural gas pipeline to Germany that would bypass Ukraine and increase Europe's energy dependence on Russia. As the two big summits loomed, Zelensky struggled to make his voice heard. In his desperation to meet with Biden before the Putin summit, Zelensky said he was ready to sit down with the U.S. president "at any moment and at any spot on the planet."[32] Biden was too busy. He phoned Zelensky and invited him to the White House later in the summer.

Before he embarked on his foray into politics, Zelensky had said that he supported Ukraine's NATO membership but did not want to have to beg for it like an uninvited guest.[33] Yet as the 2021 NATO summit in Brussels approached, anger was boiling over in Kyiv that Ukraine had not even been invited as an observer. As NATO leaders met, Zelensky told reporters in Kyiv that he expected a "yes" or "no" answer from Biden on a MAP.[34] He was bitterly disappointed. "It remains to be seen," Biden said about Ukraine joining NATO, and the final communiqué merely reiterated the alliance's 2008 compromise wording that Ukraine and Georgia would become members at some undetermined point in the future.[35] On his first overseas trip since taking office, Biden was on a mission to restore America's image as a status quo power after the drama and disruption of Trump's presidency. Embroiled in a territorial conflict with Russia, Ukraine had zero chance of joining the alliance in the foreseeable future. For Biden, raising the question of Ukraine's NATO membership would have needlessly tested the alliance's unity and aggravated the Kremlin.

On June 16, two days after the NATO summit, Biden and Putin met in Geneva. After Trump's bizarre encounter with Putin in Helsinki in 2018, the Geneva meeting was an old-fashioned, choreographed summit with no surprises. Both leaders later characterized their talks as a pragmatic attempt to make a difficult relationship a little more predictable. A terse joint statement reaffirmed the lowest common denominator in U.S.-Russian relations: "that a nuclear war cannot be won and must never be fought." At the top of Biden's agenda were continuing cyberattacks traced back to Russia, including a ransomware attack that had just shut down a major U.S. fuel pipeline. While Putin ridiculed American accusations of Russian hacking, he also hinted that cyberattacks were one way to pressure the United States to sign a treaty on cybersecurity.[36]

The fate of Alexei Navalny interested reporters covering the summit more than the fate of Ukraine. Biden warned that Russia would face "devastating consequences" if Navalny ended up dying in prison.[37] Without pronouncing his name, Putin said that Navalny had "deliberately decided to get arrested" by returning to Moscow.[38] Asked about the sweeping crackdown on dissent inside Russia, Putin called his domestic opponents foreign stooges and implied that the rioters detained after the storming of the U.S. Capitol in January were American political prisoners. Putin rebuffed every critical question with a blast of whataboutism, claiming that Russia was being assailed for sins that the United States committed on a far greater scale. In response to a question about whether he and Biden had talked about Ukrainian NATO membership, Putin said: "This issue was touched upon in passing. I suppose there is nothing to discuss in this respect." A mere six months later, that very issue would suddenly become so pressing for Putin that he would issue an ultimatum demanding that NATO renounce its intention to accept Ukraine as a member.

The Geneva summit did little to reduce tensions between Russia and the West. Less than a week later, one of Britain's most modern warships, HMS *Defender*, called on the Ukrainian port of Odesa. Aboard the destroyer, British officials signed an agreement pledging to the Ukrainian navy two minesweepers and assistance in building new naval bases on the Black Sea and the Sea of Azov, the inland sea shared by Ukraine and Russia.[39] The *Defender* then continued on its way across the Black Sea to Georgia, demonstratively passing near the coast of Crimea. The Russian military said that it fired warning shots and dropped four bombs in the path of the warship to force it to change course.[40] The British Defense Ministry downplayed the incident, denying that Russian forces had fired directly at the *Defender* or dropped any bombs.

For months Russian officials had been warning that the United States and its allies were goading Ukraine into attacking Crimea.[41] Putin later called the incident involving the British warship a "provocation" with full U.S. participation.[42] But what alarmed him most, he said, was a creeping foreign military presence on Ukrainian soil.

Relations between Ukraine and Russia had completely unraveled since the Zelensky-Putin meeting in December 2019, when the two leaders agreed to meet again. In February 2020, Putin fired Vladislav Surkov, his adviser on Ukraine. Surkov, who had taken an uncompromising stance toward Kyiv, was replaced by Dmitry Kozak, a native of Ukraine with a reputation as a level-headed, competent Kremlin aide. Unlike Surkov, Kozak was interested in resolving the Donbas conflict, which he viewed as a drain on resources and an obstacle to normalizing relations with the West.[43] Kozak's appointment was the last hope for the Minsk agreement, which—despite its built-in booby traps for Kyiv—was the only peace deal on the table. Zelensky's idea of a breakthrough was to persuade the Kremlin to allow Ukraine to regain control of its borders at an earlier point than stipulated in the agreement. "Time is ticking," Zelensky said in March 2020.[44] "The government can spend one year on the entire agreement. Then it should be implemented. Any longer is prohibited."

Kozak and Zelensky's closest adviser, Andriy Yermak, agreed to set up an advisory council including representatives from the DNR and LNR. Zelensky's domestic foes immediately attacked the decision as a tacit recognition of Russia's proxies and a traitorous concession to the Kremlin. Zelensky was forced to scrap the idea of the advisory council—and recognize the Minsk agreement for the ticking time bomb Putin had designed it to be. After Biden came into office, the Ukrainian president made one more attempt to salvage the Minsk deal. Since he had not signed it, Zelensky argued that the agreement should be revised, and that the United States, Britain, and Canada should be brought into the peace process.[45] The problem for Zelensky was that Putin had no incentive to back down. The Ukrainians, not the Russians, were balking at implementing an internationally brokered peace deal. Moreover, the incoming U.S. administration showed little interest in taking up a new initiative on Ukraine. In his only public remarks about Ukraine at the Geneva summit, Biden said the United States would "pursue diplomacy related to the Minsk agreement," which was rapidly becoming a meaningless incantation.

Two years after Zelensky's landslide victory, the magic was gone. There was no easy way to end the war in the Donbas, and in the meantime COVID had taken a heavy toll on Ukrainians. Zelensky did not hide his frustration that he had failed to secure COVID vaccines from the West, even as Putin was offering to share the Russian-made Sputnik V vaccine with Ukraine. For the Kremlin, Zelensky's vaccine quandary was a propaganda coup, proving the West to be an unreliable ally and Russia to be Ukraine's only true friend. Zelensky's sky-high popularity was slumping amid scandals and infighting within his government. In February 2021, two polls showed Zelensky's party, Servant of the People, slipping into second place behind the pro-Russian Opposition Platform—For Life party, which had about a fifth of the electorate's support.[46]

The Opposition Platform was led by Viktor Medvedchuk, who remained one of Ukraine's most influential political figures. In October 2020, Medvedchuk had appeared on Russian state TV meeting Putin outside Moscow. Always trim and manicured, Medvedchuk heaped praise on Putin for the development of Sputnik V before humbly asking him to make the vaccine available to Ukraine. Putin replied that he would consider the idea only if Zelensky's government submitted a formal request. As Zelensky resisted the poisoned chalice from Moscow, Medvedchuk condemned the Ukrainian government's "criminal actions" in denying its own citizens Sputnik V. In February 2021, Ukraine finally received its first batch of Western vaccine—made under license in India.

Viktor Medvedchuk was the ultimate insider, with a web of connections in Ukraine and Russia. He had served as the chief of staff of Ukraine's second president, Leonid Kuchma, and had asked Putin to be the godfather of his daughter. As the Donbas conflict escalated in 2014, Medvedchuk participated in peace talks and negotiated prisoner exchanges. Even after Zelensky removed him as an intermediary with the Kremlin, Medvedchuk retained his influence, representing the Opposition Platform in the Rada and overseeing a business empire including three TV channels.

On February 2, 2021, Zelensky signed a decree shutting down those three channels on the grounds that they spread Russian disinformation and threatened Ukraine's national security. Less than three weeks later, Zelensky sanctioned Medvedchuk and his wife for sponsoring terrorism and seized their assets. The U.S. embassy in Kyiv applauded Zelensky's efforts "to counter Russia's malign influence" and welcomed the sanctions against Medvedchuk, who had been blacklisted by the United States in 2014 for "violating Ukrainian sovereignty." But Zelensky's decision to go after Medvedchuk was controversial even among the president's allies, raising questions about executive overreach and cutting off a valuable, if self-serving, channel to Putin.[47] Two days after the sanctions against Medvedchuk were announced, Russia began its spring military buildup on Ukraine's border.

Even as Russian troops threatened his country, Zelensky was unapologetic about targeting Medvedchuk and his TV channels. "I consider them devils," he said in April 2021.[48] "Their narratives seek to disarm Ukraine of its statehood." Weeks later Medvedchuk was charged with treason and put under house arrest in Kyiv. Medvedchuk's role as Putin's Ukrainian proxy was officially over.

The day after Medvedchuk was confined to his home, Putin met by videoconference with officials from Russia's Security Council. In comments broadcast by state television, Putin said that Ukraine was being turned into an "anti-Russia" as domestic forces friendly to Russia were being "cleansed" from Ukraine's political landscape.[49] He blamed the West for encouraging the Ukrainian government in its actions and said that Russia would respond to the new threats in due course. Putin often made dire warnings, so his remarks may not have seemed notable at the time. But Zelensky's crackdown on Medvedchuk was a turning point. For the Kremlin, the Ukrainian oligarch and his TV channels had represented a narrow path to a political resolution with Kyiv. But once they were gone, Putin lost his last levers of political influence over Ukraine.[50]

If Putin suspected that Zelensky's targeting of Medvedchuk was somehow linked to the start of Biden's presidency, he was not wrong. In the words of Oleksandr Danylyuk, Zelensky's first national security adviser, the decision to go after Medvedchuk was "calculated to fit in with the U.S. agenda" on fighting corruption globally.[51] Following Trump's disastrous pressure campaign on his administration, Zelensky had great expectations for Biden, who knew Ukraine better than any U.S. president before him. Biden's priority, however, was to establish a modus vivendi with Putin that would curb the Russian leader's ability—and appetite—to cause trouble. Biden spoke to Putin within a week of taking office but waited until April, when Russian troops were threatening Ukraine, to reach out to Zelensky. Ukraine slipped down Biden's to-do list as tensions eased and Putin agreed to the Geneva summit.[52] Biden even met Sviatlana Tsikhanouskaya, the exiled Belarusian prodemocracy leader, before he finally found time to host Zelensky on September 1, 2021, following the calamitous American withdrawal from Afghanistan.[53]

For Zelensky, who had waited more than two years to visit the White House, the results of his meeting with Biden were underwhelming. The United States promised the release of $60 million in a military aid package that included Javelin antitank missiles and other small arms but none of the air defense, coastal defense, and other high-end weapons systems that Ukraine most wanted. Zelensky was unable to convince Biden to reverse his tacit approval of Russia's Nord Stream 2 pipeline or extract from the U.S. president a clear declaration on Ukraine's NATO prospects. Biden also dropped no hints as to the naming of a new U.S. ambassador to Kyiv or a new special envoy for Ukraine—two positions that had been left vacant since Trump's 2019 pressure campaign.

Zelensky did his best to keep Ukraine from vanishing from the headlines. A week before his White House visit, Zelensky opened the so-called Crimea Platform, an initiative to rally international support for the peninsula's peaceful return to Ukraine. The Ukrainian president's renewed focus on Crimea angered the Kremlin. Dmitry Peskov, Putin's spokesman, said that Zelensky's insistence on discussing Crimea's status made a meeting between the two leaders unlikely in 2021.[54] As for Zelensky's trip to Washington, Peskov said, the Ukrainian president's "anti-Russian rhetoric" created the impression that "the goal of Ukrainian-American friendship is to be friends against Russia."

At the end of August 2021, I left Moscow with my family and moved back to the United States. I had been covering Russia with little interruption for close to eighteen years, watching the country go from a state of freewheeling, consumeristic euphoria to angry, fearful austerity. I had been more or less confined to Moscow for almost a year and a half because of the pandemic. My last foreign trip had been to Ukraine to cover Mike Pompeo's first and only visit to Kyiv. Almost all of my reporting had to be done over the phone, and I felt claustrophobic and myopic. After dutifully renewing my Belarusian press credentials year after year, I could not cover the prodemocracy protests in Belarus because of travel restrictions on foreigners. Alexei Navalny agreed to meet with me following his return to Moscow, but instead I ended up reporting on the demonstrations following his arrest.

From my kitchen table in Moscow, I could look straight down on the Garden Ring, one of the concentric ring roads radiating out from the Kremlin. After the protests against Navalny's imprisonment, it seemed to me that there were many more boxy prisoner transport vehicles and black sedans of Russia's Investigative Committee speeding below my window. "They're catching criminals," my wife would say, not believing her own words. Russia had turned into a full-blown police state. There was no more opposition and no more protests, and the government was branding the last independent media outlets as "foreign agents."

I was happy to leave Russia. It had become a very dark place, and the only news to report was of tightening repressions and new injustices.

11

Killer in the Kremlin

fter trying to reason with Vladimir Putin as his troops were seizing Crimea in March 2014, Angela Merkel famously remarked that the Russian leader seemed to be living "in another world."[1] Out of fear of being surveilled, Putin already inhabited a parallel reality without internet or mobile phones. He relied on a tightening circle of advisers to make decisions, and the longer he ruled, the more he was surrounded by sycophants. The COVID pandemic increased Putin's isolation as he withdrew into a shell where only his closest confidants were allowed to see him.[2]

One of Putin's main sources of information on Ukraine was none other than Viktor Medvedchuk. The Russian leader's old friend reassured the Kremlin that Ukrainians still supported Putin and that pro-Russian sentiment remained strong in Ukraine.[3] Medvedchuk was hardly an objective source of information. For one, he received Russian money to fund his political machine in Ukraine.[4] Moreover, Medvedchuk, who had harbored his own presidential ambitions since the 2004 election, had an interest in positioning himself as the pro-Russian leader the Kremlin wished to see running Ukraine. Of course the idea that Medvedchuk—not to mention Putin—was popular among a majority of Ukrainians was ludicrous. Even though Medvedchuk ran the second largest party in the Rada, it could count on the support of a fifth of the electorate at the most.[5]

In his isolation, Putin was heavily influenced by his old friend Yury Kovalchuk, a billionaire whom the U.S. Treasury had designated as the Russian leader's "personal banker." To avoid having to quarantine, Kovalchuk practically moved in with Putin, becoming his closest adviser during the pandemic.[6] Together the two men hatched plans to bring back Russia's lost glory.[7] Inside the Kremlin, Kovalchuk was seen as playing the lead role in Putin's decision to launch a full-scale invasion of Ukraine.[8]

Putin had long taken an interest in Russian history, especially in the backers of the Russian monarchy who went into exile after the 1917 Communist revolution.[9] In May 2009, Putin laid flowers at the graves of the czarist general Anton Denikin and the philosopher Ivan Ilyin, whose remains had been reinterred at the Donskoi Monastery in Moscow. Denikin's diaries were worth a read, Putin told reporters at the cemetery, because the general had written that nobody should be allowed to interfere in relations between Russia and Ukraine.[10] Ilyin shared that sentiment. In 1938 he wrote that "Ukrainian separatism"—i.e., Ukraine's existence outside Russia's borders—was "an artificial phenomenon" that arose from the ambitions of its leaders and foreign conspiracies.[11]

Putin's obsession with the past became plain to see in a five-thousand-word treatise he published less than a month after the Geneva summit with Joe Biden.[12] Citing a millennium of shared history, Putin argued that Russians and Ukrainians were "one people" and that modern Ukraine had no basis for statehood. The West, he wrote, was turning Ukraine into an "anti-Russia," whipping up Ukrainian nationalism and ripping Ukrainians apart from Russians. Putin completely ignored the most important reason most Ukrainians were turning away from Russia: his own decision to invade Ukraine in 2014. In Putin's view, Ukrainians' choice to integrate with the West was not a result of their own agency but "a forced change of identity" imposed by foreigners. Channeling Medvedchuk, Putin wrote that "millions" of Ukrainians regarded Russia with "great affection" and found the "anti-Russia project" unacceptable.

Putin's article was full of menace. He compared "the forced assimilation" of ethnic Russians in Ukraine with the use of weapons of mass destruction. Although Putin said that there was still no alternative to the Minsk agreement, he accused Zelensky of lying about wanting peace and blamed NATO for militarizing Ukraine. In closing, Putin wrote ominously: "I am convinced that the true sovereignty of Ukraine is possible only in partnership with Russia."

The radicalization of Vladimir Putin was complete. By July 2021, Putin had fully adopted the language and worldview of Igor Girkin, the ultranationalist FSB colonel who set off the violent uprising in the Donbas believing he was "reuniting" Ukrainians with Russians. In 2000, when Putin was first thrust into the Russian presidency, he sounded much more like Alexei Navalny, pledging to democratize Russia and measure its success by its Western peers. Now, after two decades in power, Putin had devolved into a paranoid dictator who was convinced the West was out to get him. Putin was turning seventy the following year, and he was increasingly concerned with his historical legacy. He had everything to lose by becoming the Russian leader who "lost" Ukraine—and everything to gain by reconquering it.

In Putin's mind, there was a strong case for delivering a quick, decisive blow to reestablish Russian domination over Ukraine. Russia's currency and gold reserves were swelling to record amounts of more than $600 billion. Europe's reliance on Russian oil and gas deliveries appeared to guarantee a steady stream of income. In August 2021, Russia began throttling supplies of natural gas to Europe via Ukraine, driving up prices and increasing the pressure on Berlin to commission the controversial Nord Stream 2 pipeline. Germany and France were both distracted by domestic affairs, with Angela Merkel retiring from politics after the September election and Emmanuel Macron running for reelection in April 2022. The Biden administration had demonstrated that it did not seek to antagonize Russia and was interested in supporting Ukraine only to the extent required by decorum. After two years in office, Zelensky was facing growing discontent among Ukrainians. Meanwhile in Russia, Putin had crushed any organized opposition to his never-ending rule.

Following the momentary illusion of détente at the Geneva summit, U.S. intelligence agencies soon observed a new Russian military buildup on Ukraine's border that was even bigger than the one in the spring.[13] By mid-October, Paul Nakasone, the U.S. Army general who headed the National Security Agency, was convinced that Russia would attack Ukraine.[14] On October 27, Biden met with his top national security officials, who laid out the evidence pointing to a possible Russian invasion in early 2022.[15] General Mark Milley, the chairman of the Joint Chiefs of Staff, told Biden that the Russians were preparing "their version of 'shock and awe,'" shorthand for the use of overwhelming military force by the United States in the 2003 invasion of Iraq.[16] Biden decided to try to deter the Kremlin from attacking Ukraine while marshaling European allies to form a unified front if the Russians did invade.

The following week, the CIA director William Burns traveled to Moscow to lay out in detail what the Americans knew and to warn Putin of the consequences Russia would face in the event of an attack. Burns spoke to Putin by phone from the Kremlin as the Russian leader was in self-isolation in Sochi amid a new wave of COVID infections. Putin did not try to deny the U.S. intelligence.[17] "I came away with a very strong impression that Putin had just about made up his mind to go to war," Burns remembered later.[18] "He was convincing himself that strategically the window was closing on his opportunity to control Ukraine."

Secretary of State Antony Blinken personally informed Zelensky of the growing danger. On the flight home from Moscow , Burns called the Ukrainian president to describe his conversation with Putin. Zelensky was skeptical, as the Americans' warnings were not specific and raised the question of why the United States was not ramping up arms deliveries if the threat was so serious.[19] Washington would continue sending mixed signals to Kyiv, pledging "unwavering support" for Ukraine's sovereignty and territorial integrity while betraying an almost fatalistic resignation that Russia would prevail. The sudden collapse of a U.S.-backed government in Afghanistan that summer loomed over the Biden administration's deliberations, as did the perennial fear that a confrontation with Russia could blow up into World War III. The schizophrenic U.S. approach to Ukraine was encapsuled in a visit to Washington in early November by the Ukrainian foreign minister Dmytro Kuleba, who was greeted at the State Department with a smile and the words: "Guys, dig the trenches."[20]

Kuleba and Blinken signed a "charter on strategic partnership" that trumpeted a new era of bilateral cooperation.[21] At the same time, the flagship of the U.S. Sixth Fleet, the USS *Mount Whitney*, conducted maneuvers in the Black Sea. The exercise only fed the Russian narrative of American encirclement without providing Ukraine with any more security. Despite gestures of solidarity, the White House slow-walked military aid to Ukraine in the belief that U.S. weapons could hardly deter Putin—and might even precipitate a Russian attack.[22]

Even if Biden deemed arming Ukraine largely futile, he was determined to rally U.S. allies to punish any new Russian aggression with the toughest possible sanctions. At the end of October, he first sounded the alarm at a meeting with the leaders of Britain, France, and Germany during a G20 summit in Rome.[23] Biden's director of national intelligence, Avril Haines, presented the U.S. findings on the likely Russian attack to NATO allies in Brussels.[24] The intelligence was based on sources inside Russia's political leadership, its spy agencies, and its military. But the skeptics among the European allies—notably Germany and France—questioned the logic behind an all-out invasion and suggested the Kremlin could be bluffing once again. Furthermore, the United States had a record of spectacular intelligence failures, not just in Iraq in 2003 but also as recently as the fall of Kabul in August. The U.S. intelligence community went public. At best, the Americans' disclosures would change Putin's behavior; at the very least, they would deprive him of the element of surprise. "We were going to act," Jake Sullivan, Biden's national security adviser, recalled later.[25] "In Crimea, they created a fait accompli before the world had really fully woken up to what they had done. We wanted to make sure the world was wide awake."

For most Ukrainians, the possibility of a full-scale Russian invasion was an abstraction compared to the problems they faced at the end of 2021. According to one poll, Zelensky's approval rating dipped to 28 percent amid widespread disillusionment with his government.[26] A vast international document leak known as the Pandora Papers revealed that Zelensky had benefited financially from a network of offshore companies.[27] The Ukrainian government was in a constant state of churn, and in November Zelensky appointed his fifty-first cabinet minister. The Ukrainians that I spoke to that autumn said that people's top concerns were COVID and rising energy costs. "Everybody is in survival mode," Tanya, my old friend in Kyiv, told me. Less than half a year later, she and her family would be fleeing the Russian army.

As the Biden administration publicized Putin's secret war plans, the Kremlin responded with blanket denials, blaming the United States for inflaming tensions far from its borders while Russia was simply conducting military exercises on its own territory. Putin had not spoken by phone with Zelensky in more than a year, and Moscow pinned responsibility for the breakdown in relations with Kyiv on Washington.[28] In October 2021, Dmitry Medvedev, now the deputy head of Russia's Security Council, published a screed attacking Zelensky.[29] Medvedev, who as president had styled himself as a Western-leaning liberal, spewed the toxicity festering in Putin's entourage. He described Zelensky as a despicable, corrupt leader who had betrayed his Jewish roots by collaborating with Ukrainian neo-Nazis. Since Zelensky took his marching orders from the United States, Medvedev wrote, it was pointless to talk with Ukraine. Moscow, he said, need negotiate only with Washington.

In an annual meeting with foreign experts, Putin reiterated the idea of Ukrainians as a hijacked nation who were being denied their true will by an ultranationalist minority. "This is such a dead end. I don't really know how to get out of it," he said.[30] "Let's see what happens on Ukraine's domestic political scene in the near future." Putin went on to say that even if Ukraine never joined NATO, the alliance was already posing a threat to Russia by extending its "infrastructure" to Ukrainian territory. Putin appeared to reference the Yavoriv training center in western Ukraine, where NATO countries had begun instructing Ukrainian troops after the 2014 Russian invasion. "What should we do if missiles appear outside Kharkiv tomorrow?" Putin asked rhetorically, making a wild extrapolation with no basis in reality.[31]

Biden attempted to mollify Putin in a two-hour videoconference on December 7.[32] Putin demanded "legally binding guarantees" that NATO would not accept Ukraine as a member or deploy offensive weapons in countries bordering Russia.[33] Biden repeated his warning of devastating sanctions should Russia attack—but offered diplomatic talks on European security as a way out of the impasse.[34] The following week Karen Donfried, the top U.S. diplomat for Europe, traveled to Moscow, where she was handed two documents: one concerning Russia's relations with the United States, the other regarding relations with NATO as a whole. The U.S. ambassador to Russia, John Sullivan, later called the documents "slapdash drafts" that the Russians wanted to start negotiating in forty-eight hours.[35]

After the two days had passed, the Russian Foreign Ministry made the draft treaties public, adding to the sense among American diplomats that the Russian offer was perfunctory and not serious.[36] The Russians' key demands were obvious nonstarters: a commitment to end NATO's eastward enlargement and the removal of the alliance's troops and equipment deployed to Poland and the Baltic states. With the massive Russian buildup on Ukraine's border, the Kremlin was not proposing peace—it was issuing an ultimatum.

On Christmas Eve, Putin announced the "successful, flawless" test of a new hypersonic missile. On December 30, he phoned Biden to threaten that any additional sanctions could lead to the complete rupture of bilateral relations. Biden reassured Putin that the United States had no intention of deploying offensive weapons to Ukraine.[37] In fact, the American weaponry that was making it to Ukraine were mostly small arms and shoulder-fired Javelin antitank missiles, hardly enough to deter Putin from attacking.[38] But as the Biden administration hesitated to arm Ukraine, it was actively bolstering NATO's eastern flank. That winter the number of U.S. military personnel in Europe increased by a third to 100,000, with double the number of surface vessels and a third more air power than before the Russian buildup.[39] Even if Putin overran all of Ukraine, he was not to go an inch farther.

As 2022 began, the Biden administration tested the Kremlin's seriousness about diplomacy by engaging on some of the issues raised in the draft treaties. The deputy secretary of state, Wendy Sherman, met with her Russian counterpart, Sergei Ryabkov, in Geneva, where she offered to hold talks on missile deployments and the size of military exercises if Russia de-escalated.[40] Ryabkov said the situation was much more urgent than the Americans realized and that Russia could not wait for weeks or months for a resolution.[41] Antony Blinken and the Russian foreign minister, Sergei Lavrov, soon held a follow-up meeting in Geneva. Blinken asked Lavrov point-blank whether Russia's security concerns were at stake or the mounting confrontation was really about Putin's conviction that Ukraine was part of Russia.[42] Lavrov left the room without answering.[43]

On January 26, Ambassador Sullivan, delivered the American response to the draft treaties, repeating the offer to negotiate on individual points of dispute but insisting on the right of sovereign nations to choose their own security arrangements.[44] Three weeks later the Russian Foreign Ministry faulted the Americans for failing to reply constructively. "Moscow will have to respond, including by implementing certain military-technical measures," the ministry said.[45]

In the middle of January, the CIA director William Burns flew to Ukraine to update Zelensky on the latest U.S. intelligence, which foresaw Russian troops swooping down from Belarus to seize Kyiv, overthrow the government, and install a pro-Russian puppet regime.[46] Burns said that he understood Zelensky's predicament: the Ukrainian president was loath to create an economic panic, and a full military mobilization could have given Putin a pretext to attack. Zelensky later said that a war scare would have cost the Ukrainian economy $7 billion a month and caused people to flee the country.[47] "Our inner sense was right: if we sow chaos among people before the invasion, the Russians will devour us," he said. In Zelensky's view, the massive Russian buildup was designed to break the Ukrainians' will to fight even before the invasion started. Had Ukrainians panicked, Zelensky insisted, "we would have been a rag, not a country."

In contrast to the certitude of U.S. officials, Ukrainian intelligence agencies were more doubtful. Following Burns's visit, Zelensky received a briefing from his own intelligence chiefs, who foresaw a more limited Russian attack that they assessed was as likely to happen as the CIA's scenario.[48] Biden created confusion a week later when he suggested that "a minor incursion" by Russia might not warrant the same Western response as a full-scale invasion. Zelensky responded angrily on Twitter, writing that "we want to remind the great powers that there are no minor incursions and small nations." The White House quickly clarified that any Russian military action would be considered an invasion, but Biden's gaffe and Zelensky's sharp reaction revealed the prickliness in U.S.-Ukrainian relations. Despite Washington's dire warnings, American weapons were not forthcoming. None of the Western leaders he spoke to believed that Ukraine would survive a Russian onslaught, Zelensky said later, and some of them thought it would be better to get it over with as fast as possible.[49]

On February 11, Jake Sullivan announced that the Russian attack was imminent and told U.S. citizens to leave Ukraine immediately. The next day Biden made what would be his last personal appeal to Putin to call off the invasion. After the phone call, Putin's foreign policy adviser accused the Biden administration of whipping up "hysteria" and feeding the media false information about Russia's intentions.[50] That same day the Biden administration evacuated most of the staff from the American embassy in Kyiv and withdrew U.S. military trainers from western Ukraine. Defying fate and the alarming U.S. intelligence reports, Zelensky declared February 16 a "day of unity," calling on Ukrainians to display the flag and sing the national anthem in unison.

Amid the increasingly urgent warnings from Washington, western European leaders made a last-ditch diplomatic effort. Emmanuel Macron, who had been trying to forge a special relationship with Putin since the beginning of his presidency, met the Russian leader in the Kremlin on February 7. The two men sat at opposite ends of an absurdly long table, symbolizing not only Putin's fear of COVID but also the unbridgeable gap between Russia and the West.[51] For six hours Putin held forth on Russian history and Western hypocrisy following the Cold War.[52] Later that week the British government dispatched Liz Truss, the new foreign secretary, and Ben Wallace, the defense secretary, to the Russian capital. Wallace, the first British defense minister to visit Moscow in more than twenty years, later said that Sergei Shoigu, his Russian counterpart, had lied in his face, stating that Russia had no plans to invade Ukraine.[53] Olaf Scholz, who had recently been sworn in as Angela Merkel's successor, visited Putin on February 15. The German chancellor fared no better than the French president, having to endure Putin's same litany of grievances from the end of the same long table. When Scholz asked if it was possible that Russian warplanes would take off for Ukraine as soon as he left, Putin did not answer with a "no."[54]

The Russian army had drawn up a huge strike force, with units from as far away as Siberia and the Pacific region. But the military was only playing the supporting role in an operation in which intelligence officers were the stars. In July 2021, Ukrainian intelligence watched as the FSB team dedicated to Ukraine was ramped up to two hundred officers.[55] Sergei Beseda, the FSB general in charge of the former Soviet Union, was interested in building up a network of potential collaborators—and drawing up lists of locals who would resist a Russian occupation. The FSB's infiltration of the Ukrainian security services was one reason Ukraine had been so defenseless in 2014. But eight years later Ukrainian intelligence officials still suspected that many of their colleagues were Russian informants or sympathizers.[56] On the eve of the full-scale invasion, the Ukrainians estimated that two companies of Russian covert special forces were operating in Kyiv.

The FSB commissioned polls to gauge public sentiment in Ukraine. Although there were clear indications that Ukrainians would not view Russians as liberators, the Kremlin's political exigencies skewed the interpretation of the data.[57] Polling for the FSB in February 2022 showed that Ukrainians were pessimistic about the future and disillusioned with their politicians.[58] The Russians' assumption was that after the decapitation of their unpopular government, Ukrainians would be unwilling to resist in the face of overwhelming force.

Ukrainian military intelligence later determined that the initial Russian plan was to take Kyiv in three days and the whole country in ten.[59] The Crimean scenario would be repeated on a grand scale. Just as in 2014, the names of the puppet leaders were of secondary importance. Viktor Medvedchuk, held under house arrest in Kyiv, was seen as one prospective leader. According to one plan later uncovered by Ukrainian intelligence, Medvedchuk would first be elected speaker of the Rada and then acting president—the same sequence of events following Viktor Yanukovych's flight from Kyiv eight years earlier. Another plan involved Yanukovych himself returning to power on the basis of lawsuits that had been filed in a Kyiv court challenging his removal from power. A third possible puppet leader was Oleg Tsaryov, a former ally of Yanukovych who had fled to Russian-occupied Crimea.[60] Even before the invasion started, there were repeated reports of coup plots.[61] A swift Russian victory seemed inevitable, and Western governments urged Zelensky's team to consider a plan for a government-in-exile, possibly in Warsaw or London.[62]

For the FSB, the planned military intervention was a "special operation" that would dispatch a president who was struggling in the polls. The Russian military, however, was aware of the risks of a multipronged attack—but lacked the influence of Putin's hardline advisers.[63] Only a couple of retired military officers dared to criticize the looming invasion publicly. In a newspaper commentary published in early February, Mikhail Khodaryonok, a retired colonel who had served on the Russian General Staff, predicted that there would be "no Ukrainian blitzkrieg" and ridiculed the notion that Ukrainians would not defend their country.[64] A few days later, Leonid Ivashov, a retired general and the head of a veterans' association, wrote an open letter demanding that Putin resign because the unprovoked invasion of Ukraine would cost tens of thousands of lives, turn Russia into an international pariah, and threaten its very statehood.[65]

It was unlikely that the criticism ever got through to Putin. In fact, the arguments for a quick strike on Ukraine only seemed to be growing. The Russian military, which had been undergoing a lavish modernization, chalked up its recent interventions in Georgia, Ukraine, and Syria as unqualified victories. In January 2022, a Russian-led force propped up a friendly regime during mass protests in neighboring Kazakhstan. All these engagements had been limited in scope and could not compare to the invasion of a country the size of Ukraine. But for Putin's inner circle, the clock was ticking for Russia to take on a mission that would rewrite history.

Russia had few friends it could count on other than China, a strategic partner, and Belarus, a tactical ally. On February 4, Putin traveled to Beijing to attend the opening ceremony of the Winter Olympics. At their first meeting since the pandemic, Putin and Xi Jinping signed a statement declaring a "no limits" partnership against the West.[66] Two weeks later, Putin hosted Alexander Lukashenko in Moscow. Putin told journalists that massive joint military exercises in Belarus were "purely defensive" and would be over in a matter of days.[67] The next day he took Lukashenko into the Kremlin's situation room where the two men observed an exercise of Russia's nuclear forces on a giant screen.[68]

Fifteen years after Putin's "Munich's speech" assailing American hegemony, it was Zelensky's turn to criticize the world order from the same podium. Delivering the keynote speech at the annual Munich Security Conference, Zelensky accused the West of appeasing Putin's Russia and criticized NATO for not laying out a clear path to membership.[69] Zelensky's visit to Munich on February 19 was not a forgone conclusion. The day before, Biden had told reporters that he was "convinced" that Putin would attack, and the White House questioned the wisdom of Zelensky leaving his country when war seemed imminent. In Moscow, the Duma had just asked Putin to consider recognizing the DNR and LNR as independent countries. Tensions were rising in the Donbas amid renewed shelling along the front line. The Kremlin's puppet leaders in Donetsk and Luhansk had ordered the evacuation of civilians to Russia, making the improbable claim that Ukraine was planning an attack even as a vast Russian army stood poised on its borders.

Emmanuel Macron made one final attempt to stop the wheels of war after securing Biden's agreement to meet with Putin.[70] On February 20, the French president tried to coax Putin to a second Geneva summit with Biden. At the end of their conversation, Putin said that he was in the gym and wanted to play hockey but that he would first consult his advisers.[71] Macron thought he had clinched a deal, yet he was in for a bad surprise.

The next day Putin assembled his Security Council in St. Catherine's Hall in the Kremlin, turning the ornate hall into Russia's biggest echo chamber.[72] The topic on the agenda was whether to recognize the independence of the DNR and LNR. Putin sat behind a desk at a safe distance from his top advisers, who were arrayed before him like schoolboys—and one schoolgirl, the Federation Council speaker Valentina Matviyenko. Putin listened to his ministers with arched eyebrows, tapped his fingers absently on his desk, and told them to sit down when they were finished speaking. Putin was hearing a regurgitation of what he had said on numerous occasions: that Ukraine was run by extremists who were turning the country into an American beachhead against Russia. It was impossible to watch as Ukraine's "neo-Nazi regime" committed "genocide" against Russians, one speaker after the other said.[73] The Minsk process was dead. Putin needed to recognize the DNR and LNR to protect Russian lives.[74]

Still, it was clear from their statements that most of the speakers did not fully understand what Putin planned to do next. The foreign minister Sergei Lavrov said he would continue talking with the Americans and the French. Dmitry Kozak, the Kremlin's point man on Ukraine, offered his opinion on the outright annexation of the DNR and LNR before Putin cut him off.[75] And Sergei Naryshkin, head of the SVR foreign intelligence agency, sputtered awkwardly until Putin supplied the words he wanted to hear: "Yes, I support the proposal to recognize the independence" of the two Donbas republics.

The meeting was televised to force Putin's entourage to show their fealty and share responsibility for the coming invasion. When Putin invited anyone with a dissenting view to speak up, there was silence. In the estimation of the CIA director Burns, "no more than three or four people around Putin" made the decision for a full-scale invasion.[76] Not only was Putin trying to keep the West guessing about his true intentions, he also left his inner circle in the dark, including Lavrov, his spokesman Dmitry Peskov, and Sergei Kiriyenko, the official in charge of domestic policy.[77] The whole world was now awaiting Putin's next move.

Hours after the Security Council meeting, an urgent announcement interrupted Channel One's 9 P.M. newscast. Sitting in a wood-paneled Kremlin office, a grim-faced Putin launched into an hour-long tirade that borrowed heavily from his summer treatise.[78] He claimed Ukraine as an "inalienable part" of Russia's history, culture, and "spiritual space" and blamed Vladimir Lenin for creating an artificial Ukrainian state when he founded the Soviet Union.[79] Putin described postindependence Ukraine as a failed state held hostage by oligarchs, ultranationalists, and corrupt leaders who took their orders from foreign masters. Without citing any evidence, Putin claimed that Ukraine was planning a "blitzkrieg" on the Donbas and intended to build its own nuclear weapons.[80] Putin railed against a U.S.-built maritime operations center for the Ukrainian navy and called the Yavoriv joint training center a "foreign military base."[81] NATO had "cheated" Russia in the past, Putin complained, and Ukraine's membership in the alliance was all but inevitable. "This is not about our political regime or anything else," he said. "They just do not need a big and independent country like Russia around. This is the answer to all questions." Russia reserved the right to ensure its security, Putin said, and had no other choice but to recognize the independence of the DNR and LNR.

Putin's rant provided a rare glimpse into his state of mind, revealing his isolation and distance from the concerns of ordinary Russians. He cited Communist Party documents and dwelled on ideological disputes between Stalin and Lenin. The situation in the Donbas, the ostensible reason for Putin's speech, was not even directly connected to NATO enlargement. The only connection was the Minsk agreement, which, if implemented as written, would have given Russia's proxies the power to veto Ukraine's path into NATO. By recognizing the DNR and LNR as independent states, Putin was abandoning the Minsk agreement and any hope of a political settlement. Now Moscow's only option was to bring Kyiv to heel by force of arms. After Putin's speech was over, Channel One went straight to St. Catherine's Hall, where a few hours earlier the Security Council had convened. The Kremlin-backed heads of the DNR and LNR, Denis Pushilin and Leonid Pasechnik, were seated behind two desks, while Putin was ensconced behind his own desk at a very safe distance. Putin signed "treaties of friendship" with the two fake countries and nodded to his puppets. There was no trumpet fanfare. The Russian leader simply got up, smoothed his tie, and uttered a single sentence: "I congratulate you."

In Washington, Biden called Russia's recognition of the Donbas republics "the beginning of a Russian invasion" and promptly announced new sanctions against Russia. In a show of unity among Western capitals, the European Union began preparing its own sanctions package, and Germany suspended certification of the Nord Stream 2 pipeline. That day Biden demonstratively received Dmytro Kuleba, the Ukrainian foreign minister, in the Oval Office—in contrast to Trump, who twice had hosted Lavrov in the White House. Even from the sidelines Trump could not help declaring his admiration for Putin and contempt for Ukraine. Speaking in a radio interview, the former U.S. president called Putin's recognition of the separatist statelets "genius" and boasted how "very, very well" he knew the Russian leader.[82]

Kuleba also visited the Pentagon, where he asked the defense secretary Lloyd Austin for Stinger antiaircraft missiles.[83] Austin pledged American assistance but pressed Kuleba on what the Ukrainians would do if the government had to flee Kyiv. Kuleba responded that "we're not even going to talk about that or think about that." The Ukrainian foreign minister later recalled that it was only during this visit that the Americans started offering specific intelligence on the Russians' war preparations.[84] The United States had its reasons for holding back what it knew: internal rules did not allow U.S. intelligence agencies to share information that the Ukrainians could then use to attack Russian formations, and it was well known that Ukraine's security services were riddled with Russian informants. Conversely, the Ukrainians were reticent about sharing their own military plans with the Americans.[85]

In Kyiv, Zelensky was sending mixed messages, reflecting the combination of dread and denial gripping the Ukrainian government. Following Putin's recognition of the DNR and LNR, Zelensky addressed the nation saying that Ukraine was ready to defend itself but adding that there was "no reason" for Ukrainians to lose any sleep. Zelensky's advisers were dubious that Russia's recognition of the two separatist republics was the opening move of an all-out invasion. Oleksiy Reznikov, the defense minister, said in an interview that "Putin would not dare to bomb the 'second Jerusalem,' the city of Kyiv."[86] On the evening of February 22, Zelensky invited the heads of the Rada's parliamentary factions to a security briefing. Reznikov and Ivan Bakanov, the SBU chief, said that Russia was likely engaging in psychological operations and would limit any escalation to the Donbas region. Only Kyrylo Budanov, the head of military intelligence, soberly presented the possibility of a full-scale attack from multiple directions.

As Ukrainian officials often pointed out, their country had been under Russian attack since 2014. Bluffs were nothing new in the Kremlin's efforts to destabilize Ukraine. Having duly ratified the "treaties of friendship" with the DNR and LNR, Russia's Federation Council granted Putin permission to deploy the armed forces abroad, the same legal cudgel the Kremlin had wielded during the Crimea annexation. Putin then met with reporters, accusing Kyiv of "killing" the Minsk peace process and suggesting that it was pointless to reach any new agreements with Zelensky.[87]

The next day was Russia's Defender of the Fatherland holiday, originally known as Red Army Day. Putin laid a wreath at the Tomb of the Unknown Soldier at the Kremlin walls. In the afternoon, he phoned the Turkish president Recep Tayyip Erdoğan, his closest partner in NATO. According to the Kremlin readout of the call, Putin explained the "objective necessity" for Russia to recognize the separatist republics and expressed his "disappointment" with the Americans' response to his ultimatum.

February 23 was not a holiday in Ukraine. At a meeting of the National Security and Defense Council, Zelensky's top security officials could not agree on whether Putin would content himself with the DNR and LNR, break out of the Donbas to secure the elusive land bridge from Russia to Crimea, or start a full-scale invasion.[88]

Later that evening Zelensky recorded a nine-minute speech addressed to the citizens of Russia, one last attempt to penetrate the wall of Kremlin propaganda. Zelensky said he had initiated a phone call with Putin earlier in the day, only to be met with silence. Ukrainians did not need to be "liberated," Zelensky said, because they were already free. Zelensky mocked the idea that he was a Nazi, recalling that his grandfather had served in the Soviet army for the entirety of World War II. "We're different, but that's not a reason to be enemies," he said.

Zelensky was the embodiment of the alienation most Ukrainians felt toward Russia after eight years of Russian aggression. Zelensky had come into office accused by his rivals of being a Russian tool. He was moderate and open to dialogue with the Kremlin. But Putin was uninterested in renegotiating the Minsk agreement; the only peace that the Kremlin could accept was Ukraine's submission. When his overtures were rejected, Zelensky became hardened and defiant. "This is our land. This is our history. What will you be fighting for? And against whom?" Zelensky asked Russians. He warned that if they were attacked, Ukrainians would fight back. "You will see our faces, not our backs," Zelensky said.

On the morning of February 24, shortly before 5 A.M. in Kyiv, Putin announced the beginning of a "special military operation" against Ukraine on Russian state television.[89] Putin appeared to have recorded the speech at the same time as his February 21 address: he wore the same suit and tie, sat in the same office, and rested his hands in the same position on his desk. That Putin's declaration of war was recorded in advance underscored that his attack on Ukraine was premeditated, just as the Americans had predicted.

There was nothing new in Putin's rantings, which hearkened back to his 2007 Munich speech, although his language was rawer and angrier. After the Cold War, the United States had become "an empire of lies," unfettered by international law and hostile toward Russia's legitimate interests. The "Western bloc" had left a trail of destruction across the Middle East and had now arrived in Ukraine. Stalin had unsuccessfully tried to appease Hitler before the Nazi invasion of the Soviet Union; Putin would not make the same mistake. A clash was unavoidable, so Russia was forced to act. "For our country, it is a matter of life and death, a matter of our historical future as a nation," Putin said.

As with the annexation of Crimea or the cancellation of his constitutional term limits, Putin adorned his decision to attack Ukraine with a fig leaf of legalism. According to the "treaties of friendship" Russia had just signed with the DNR and LNR, Putin said he was simply helping them defend themselves as laid out in Article 51 of the UN Charter. To protect the people of the Donbas, Russia was setting out to "demilitarize and denazify" Ukraine. "It is not our plan to occupy Ukrainian territory," Putin said. He appealed to Ukrainians to "work together with us to turn this tragic page as soon as possible and to move forward together, without allowing anyone to interfere in our affairs and our relations." Putin promised Ukrainian soldiers that they would walk free if they laid down their arms, and he assigned responsibility for any bloodshed to the "ruling Ukrainian regime." Addressing external actors tempted to assist Ukraine, Putin threatened "consequences as you have never seen in your entire history."

Putin's half-hour speech was a collection of distortions and exaggerations to justify an unprovoked attack on a country that posed no threat to Russia. Putin's criticism of U.S. foreign policy was not entirely unwarranted, but the conclusions he drew were contradictory if not outright nonsensical. Rather than heed the lessons of American hubris that had come at such a devastating human toll, Putin's response was to imitate the United States' worst follies. It was telling that Putin cited the reckless U.S. invasion of Iraq as part of his case for the reckless Russian invasion of

Ukraine. The unapologetic unilateralism of George W. Bush's presidency had both fascinated and infuriated Putin—and it served as the inspiration and precedent for the Russian leader's own military adventures.

Bush's unilateralism also had fateful consequences for Ukraine long after he left office. Bush, the only U.S. president to advocate NATO membership for Ukraine, wanted to reward the country for its participation in the "coalition of the willing" in Iraq. Although joining NATO enjoyed little public support among Ukrainians, the alliance's 2008 promise of eventual membership put Russia and Ukraine on a collision course. The Kremlin had an incentive to take preemptive military action to make sure that promise would never come true. As a result, Ukrainians found themselves the target of increasing Russian aggression, which in turn made NATO even more reluctant to grant Ukraine membership.

Bush's successors demonstrated a total lack of interest in Ukraine and tacitly accepted Russia's traditional dominance in the region. Obama, Trump, and Biden were all determined to wind down America's disastrous military adventures in the Middle East and refocus on the challenge of a rising China. Before 2014, the U.S. military in Europe was drawing down, not building up. The rotation of troops and prepositioning of weapons on NATO's eastern flank came only after the annexation of Crimea. The United States deployed even more forces to eastern Europe once Russia began its buildup in autumn 2021.

Putin said the United States had crossed a "red line" by militarizing Ukraine. But in fact nothing had changed significantly on the ground compared to a year or two earlier. The biggest challenge to the status quo was Russia's massive military buildup on Ukraine's borders, followed by the decision to recognize the separatist republics and ditch the Minsk peace process. The urgency to attack Ukraine was linked to Putin's perception of his own waning opportunities to rewrite history rather than any concrete threats emanating from Ukraine.

In Putin's telling, Russian goodwill following the Cold War was met by duplicity and blackmail from NATO, which despite Russia's objections continued to add new members in central and eastern Europe. When Putin first came to power, he had openly entertained the idea that Russia, too, could join the alliance. Although the idea seemed far-fetched even then, it was not unthinkable given that the Kremlin claimed to be following a democratic path. An alliance of democracies would not threaten a democratic

Russia and could conceivably include it. NATO became an adversary only as Putin steered Russia toward dictatorship. NATO's eastward enlargement did not force Putin to attack Ukraine. It was Russia's failure to become a democracy and the revival of imperial ambition that lay at the root of Putin's invasion of Ukraine.

Russia had effectively stopped NATO from accepting new members from the former Soviet bloc. The last round of NATO enlargement to include countries of the former Warsaw Pact was in 2004.[90] With the invasions of Georgia in 2008 and Ukraine in 2014, the Kremlin wrecked the two countries' prospects of joining NATO because of the alliance's aversion to accepting members with unresolved territorial disputes. As long as Russia occupied Crimea and kept its Donbas proxies armed, Ukraine's NATO ambitions were crippled. It was true that increasing numbers of Ukrainians supported membership in the alliance, but it was Putin who had caused this trend by hacking off pieces of their country. The idea that the United States was secretly planning to deploy "military infrastructure," including nuclear weapons, to Ukraine was either hyperbole or paranoia. Kyiv was struggling to secure even basic defensive weapons from the United States such as Javelin antitank missiles and Stinger antiaircraft missiles.

Putin accused NATO of violating the principle of "equal and indivisible security" in Europe by enlarging. Although it was certainly unpleasant for the Kremlin to see former vassal states clamoring to join NATO, Russia's security was guaranteed not by a ring of buffer states but by the world's largest nuclear arsenal. Putin often mentioned that U.S. intermediate-range missiles deployed to eastern Europe could reduce the time Kremlin leaders would have to determine whether they were under nuclear attack. But there was no indication the United States was planning such a destabilizing step, and Putin himself had helped bring about the end of the Intermediate-Range Nuclear Forces (INF) Treaty by secretly testing missiles banned under the agreement.

After the collapse of the Soviet Union, Ukraine made much larger sacrifices in terms of security than Russia did, giving up its nuclear weapons voluntarily in the belief that it was surrounded by friendly nations. Zelensky openly expressed regret that Ukraine had forfeited its nuclear weapons for a piece of paper—the Budapest Memorandum—that failed to deter Russia in 2014. But Putin's assertion that Ukraine was seeking to acquire a nuclear bomb was a complete fabrication.

Putin's casus belli was built more on rage than on facts. Putin was driven by a desire to seek revenge for perceived slights and insults going back to the fall of the Soviet Union. By reconquering Ukraine, Russia would start to readjust Europe's balance of power in favor of Moscow. The Soviet Union had been too weak to keep its European satellite states. But Putin was not weak, and he would do everything in his power to bring Ukraine back under Russia's control.

Putin had last attended a victory parade on Kyiv's Maidan square in 2004, just weeks before the Orange Revolution. If his special military operation went to plan, he would soon be able to hold another victory parade in the Ukrainian capital.

Notes

1. Putin in Kyiv

1. Nick Paton Walsh, "Putin's Kiev Visit 'Timed to Influence Ukraine Poll,'" *The Guardian*, October 27, 2004.
2. Ilya Zhegulev, "Putin udruzhil Yanukovichu" [Putin befriended Yanukovych], Gazeta.ru, October 27, 2004, https://www.gazeta.ru/2004/10/26/oa_137752.shtml.
3. Zhegulev, "Putin udruzhil Yanukovichu."
4. Francesca Mereu, "Putin's Campaign Has Kiev on Edge," *Moscow Times*, October 28, 2004.
5. Vladimir Putin, "Interview on Ukrainian Television Channels UT-1, Inter and 1+1," The Kremlin, October 27, 2004, http://en.kremlin.ru/events/president/transcripts/22661.
6. "President Vladimir Putin Met with Ukrainian President Leonid Kuchma," The Kremlin, October 27, 2004, http://en.kremlin.ru/events/president/news/32025.
7. Anders Åslund, *How Ukraine Became a Market Economy and Democracy* (Washington, DC: Peterson Institute for International Economics, 2009), 180.
8. Åslund, *How Ukraine Became a Market Economy and Democracy*, 179.
9. Nikolai Petrov and Andrei Ryabov, "Russia's Role in the Orange Revolution," in *Revolution in Orange: The Origins of Ukraine's Democratic Breakthrough*, ed. Anders Åslund and Michael McFaul (Washington, DC: Carnegie Endowment for International Peace, 2006), 147.
10. Taras Kuzio, "The Orange Revolution," *Elections Today* 12, no. 4 (2005): 8.
11. Åslund, *How Ukraine Became a Market Economy and Democracy*, 176.
12. Åslund, *How Ukraine Became a Market Economy and Democracy*, 181.

13. Petrov and Ryabov, "Russia's Role in the Orange Revolution," 161.
14. Petrov and Ryabov, "Russia's Role in the Orange Revolution," 148.
15. Petrov and Ryabov, "Russia's Role in the Orange Revolution," 150, 161.
16. Åslund, *How Ukraine Became a Market Economy and Democracy*, 187.
17. Estimates of Russian assistance to the Yanukovych campaign ran as high as $300 million. Nikolai Petrov and Andrei Ryabov wrote that $50 million was a more probable amount. See Petrov, "Russia's Role in the Orange Revolution," 153.
18. Organization for Security and Cooperation in Europe (OSCE), *Ukraine, Presidential Election, 31 October, 21 November and 26 December 2004: Final Report* (Warsaw: Organization for Security and Cooperation in Europe, 2005), 18n41.
19. Konstantin Skorkin, "25 let donbasskogo separatizma. Chast vtoraya" [25 years of Donbas separatism. Part 2], *Realna Gazeta*, March 24, 2016, https://realgazeta.com.ua/25-let-donbasskogo-separatizma_-chast-vtoraya/.
20. Steven Lee Myers, *The New Tsar: The Rise and Reign of Vladimir Putin* (New York: Knopf, 2015), 263.
21. Myers, *The New Tsar*, 269. When I asked Yushchenko in April 2023 who had poisoned him, he said that the truth would come out once Putin lost power. Yushchenko told me that he did not hold domestic forces responsible for the poisoning.
22. Åslund, *How Ukraine Became a Market Economy and Democracy*, 176.
23. Kuzio, "The Orange Revolution," 9.
24. Petrov and Ryabov, "Russia's Role in the Orange Revolution," 157.
25. European Parliament, *Presidential Elections Ukraine, Ad Hoc Delegation: Election Observation of Second Round*, November 25, 2004, 4.
26. Myers, *The New Tsar*, 273.
27. OSCE, *Ukraine, Presidential Election*, 3.
28. Serhii Plokhy, *The Gates of Europe: A History of Ukraine* (London: Penguin, 2016), 333.
29. Mikhail Zygar, *All the Kremlin's Men: Inside the Court of Vladimir Putin* (New York: Public Affairs, 2016), 92.
30. Oleksandr Sushko and Olena Prystayko, "Western Influence," in *Revolution in Orange: The Origins of Ukraine's Democratic Breakthrough*, ed. Anders Åslund and Michael McFaul (Washington, DC: Carnegie Endowment for International Peace, 2006), 133.
31. Anatoly Medetsky, "Outrage as Yanukovych Takes the Lead," *Moscow Times*, November 23, 2004.
32. Alexei Kolesnikov, "Vladimir Putin nauchil Yevropu ukrainskoi demokratii" [Vladimir Putin taught Ukrainian democracy to Europe], *Kommersant*, November 24, 2004.
33. "Deputaty Gosdumy vyrazili obespokoyennost situatsiyei na Ukraine" [State Duma deputies expressed concern over the situation in Ukraine], RIA Novosti, November 24, 2004, https://ria.ru/20041124/742177.html.
34. For the Kremlin's translation of Putin's remarks, see "Press Statement and Answers to Questions by President of the Russian Federation Vladimir Putin at a News Conference at the End of the Russia-EU Summit," The Kremlin, November 25, 2004.
35. Former senior Bush administration official, author interview, February 2023.

36. Colin Powell, "Briefing by Secretary of State Colin L. Powell," U.S. Department of State, November 24, 2004, https://2001-2009.state.gov/secretary/former/powell/remarks/38738.htm.

37. Åslund, *How Ukraine Became a Market Economy and Democracy*, 194.

38. Åslund, *How Ukraine Became a Market Economy and Democracy*, 195.

39. Zygar, *All the Kremlin's Men*, 94.

40. Steven Lee Myers, "Putin Backs Ukrainian Leader, Dismissing Call for New Runoff," *New York Times*, December 3, 2004.

41. Åslund, *How Ukraine Became a Market Economy and Democracy*, 195–96.

42. OSCE, *Ukraine, Presidential Election*, 36.

43. Within the first months of his presidency, Yushchenko abolished visa requirements for visitors from the European Union, the United States, and other Western countries.

44. Soros, who left Hungary in 1947, took a special interest in central and eastern Europe after the fall of Communism. He spent a good part of his fortune on grants to build civil society and support scholars in the region.

45. Kirill Razumovsky and Afanasy Sborov, "Na Ukrainu sbroshena atomnaya shutka" [Atomic joke is dropped on Ukraine], *Kommersant*, October 22, 2003.

46. Razumovsky and Sborov, "Na Ukrainu sbroshena atomnaya shutka."

47. Kim Murphy. "Russia-Ukraine Ties Founder on the Shore of Tiny Isle," *Los Angeles Times*, November 3, 2003.

48. Peter Byrne, "Tussle Over Tuzla Islet Continues," *Kyiv Post*, October 30, 2003.

49. Victor Yasmann, "The Kremlin's Battle for Ukraine," Radio Free Europe/Radio Liberty, May 3, 2004, https://www.rferl.org/a/1052592.html.

50. Valeria Korchagina, "Putin Tells West Not to Meddle in Ukraine," *Moscow Times*, July 27, 2004.

51. Petrov and Ryabov, "Russia's Role in the Orange Revolution," 146.

52. Zygar, *All the Kremlin's Men*, 87.

53. "Medvedchuk rasskazal o tom, kak Putin stal krestnym yego docheri" [Medvedchuk recounted how Putin became his daughter's godfather], *Vedomosti*, July 7, 2019.

54. Zygar, *All the Kremlin's Men*, 87.

55. Condoleezza Rice, *No Higher Honor: A Memoir of My Years in Washington* (New York: Crown, 2011), 358.

56. Sergei Pugachyov, interview by Dmitry Gordon, Gordonua.com, September 29, 2021, https://gordonua.com/publications/byvshij-blizhajshij-drug-putina-milliarder-pugachev-ja-skazal-putinu-vyberi-mesto-gde-tebja-pohoronit-on-otvetil-ja-zhit-tolko-sobralsja-zachem-mne-eto-otstan-1573874.html.

57. "Yanukovich i Luzhkov priekhali v Severodonetsk" [Yanukovych and Luzhkov arrived in Sievierodonetsk], Grani.ru, November 28, 2004, https://graniru.org/Politics/World/Europe/Ukraine/m.80421.html.

58. Skorkin, "25 let donbasskogo separatizma. Chast vtoraya."

59. Jan Maksymiuk, "Analysis: Will Ukraine Split in Wake of Divisive Ballot?," Radio Free Europe/Radio Liberty, November 30, 2004, https://www.rferl.org/a/1056133.html.

60. Maksymiuk, "Will Ukraine Split in Wake of Divisive Ballot?"

61. Citing two people close to him, Catherine Belton wrote that Putin tried to resign after Yushchenko's win but could not find anyone in his inner circle to replace him. See Catherine Belton, *Putin's People: How the KGB Took Back Russia and Then Took On the West* (New York: Farrar, Straus and Giroux, 2020), 271.

62. "'Ukraina—ne Rossiya': O chyom pisal Leonid Kuchma" ["Ukraine is not Russia": What Leonid Kuchma wrote about], Korrespondent.net, September 4, 2003, https:// korrespondent.net/ukraine/politics/78346-ukraina-ne-rossiya-o-chem-pisal-leonid -kuchma.

63. "Vystupleniye Prezidenta Ukrainy Leonida Kuchmy na prezentatsii knigi 'Ukraina— ne Rossiya' v Moskve" [Speech by Ukrainian President Leonid Kuchma at the presentation of the book 'Ukraine is not Russia' in Moscow], SU.POL, September 3, 2003, http://supol.narod.ru/archive/books/cuchma.htm.

64. Mikhail Shevchuk and Dmitry Kamyshev, "Obyknovenny 'Nashizm.' Kreml sozdayot novoye molodyozhnoye dvizheniye" [Ordinary "Nashism": The Kremlin founds a new youth movement], *Kommersant*, February 21, 2005.

2. Warning Shots

1. The American Presidency Project, "The President's News Conference with President Viktor Yushchenko of Ukraine in Kiev, Ukraine," April 1, 2008, https://www .presidency.ucsb.edu/documents/the-presidents-news-conference-with-president -viktor-yushchenko-ukraine-kiev-ukraine.

2. Matt Spetalnick, "Bush Vows to Press for Ukraine, Georgia in NATO," Reuters, April 1, 2008, https://www.reuters.com/article/us-nato-*ukraine*-bush/bush-vows-to-press -for-ukraine-georgia-in-nato-idUSL0141706220080401.

3. "Public Support for Ukraine's Euro-Atlantic Course: Assessments and Recommendations," Razumkov Centre (Kyiv, Razumkov Centre, 2021), 9.

4. "Leftists Stage Protest in Kyiv," *Ukrainian Weekly*, April 6, 2008, 2.

5. George H. W. Bush, "Remarks to the Supreme Soviet of the Republic of the Ukraine in Kiev, Soviet Union," August 1, 1991, George H. W. Bush Presidential Library & Museum, https://bush41library.tamu.edu/archives/public-papers/3267.

6. Mikhail Zygar, *All the Kremlin's Men: Inside the Court of Vladimir Putin* (New York: PublicAffairs, 2016), 108.

7. George W. Bush, *Decision Points* (New York: Crown, 2010), 195–96.

8. Condoleezza Rice, *No Higher Honor: A Memoir of My Years in Washington* (New York: Crown, 2011), 62.

9. Angela Stent, *The Limits of Partnership: U.S.-Russian Relations in the Twenty-First Century* (Princeton: Princeton University Press, 2014), 62–63.

10. Bush, *Decision Points*, 196.

11. "Russia Outlines How It Will Cooperate with U.S.," CNN, September 24, 2001, https://edition.cnn.com/2001/WORLD/europe/09/24/ret.russia/index.html.

12. Bush, *Decision Points*, 196.

13. Kevin O'Flynn, "Russia Pulls Out of Its Big Spy Base in Cuba," *The Guardian*, October 17, 2001.

14. Peter Baker, " 'I'm Thrilled He's Here,' Bush Says as Putin Visits His Texas Ranch," *Washington Post*, November 15, 2001.

15. Vladimir Putin, "Vladimir Putin: The NPR Interview," by Robert Siegel, NPR, November 15, 2001, https://legacy.npr.org/news/specials/putin/nprinterview.html.

16. "Meeting the Russia Challenge: Lessons from the Foreign Policy Transition from Bush to Obama," posted by the Brookings Institution, February 24, 2023, YouTube video, 54:06 to 54:21, https://www.youtube.com/watch?v=edpdPPGAAy0.

17. Former senior Bush administration official, author interview, February 2023.

18. "President Bush Meets with Russian President Putin at Camp David," September 27, 2003, George W. Bush White House Archives, https://georgewbush-whitehouse.archives.gov/news/releases/2003/09/20030927-2.html.

19. Former senior Bush administration official, February 2023.

20. Zygar, *All the Kremlin's Men*, 108.

21. Peter Baker, *Days of Fire: Bush and Cheney in the White House* (New York: Anchor, 2014), 383.

22. Baker, *Days of Fire*, 384.

23. Bush, *Decision Points*, 433.

24. Peter Baker and Susan Glasser, *Kremlin Rising: Vladimir Putin's Russia and the End of Revolution* (New York: Scribner, 2005), 224–25.

25. Bush, *Decision Points*, 233.

26. Gleb Pavlovsky, "Interview with Gleb Pavlovsky," by Vitaly Dymarsky, *Redkollegiya*, Ekho Moskvy, March 26, 2021, https://web.archive.org/web/20220303211154/https:/echo.msk.ru/programs/beseda/2811368-echo/.

27. Vladimir Putin, "Speech and the Following Discussion at the Munich Conference on Security Policy," The Kremlin, February 10, 2007, http://en.kremlin.ru/events/president/transcripts/24034.

28. Rice, *No Higher Honor*, 670–71.

29. Mikhail Zygar and Vladimir Solovyov, "Severoatlanticheskaya blokada" [North Atlantic blockade], *Kommersant*, April 2, 2008.

30. Michael R. Gordon et al., "Vladimir Putin's 20-Year March to War in Ukraine—and How the West Mishandled It," *Wall Street Journal*, April 1, 2022.

31. Ronald D. Asmus, *A Little War That Shook the World: Georgia, Russia, and the Future of the West* (New York: Palgrave Macmillan, 2010), 120–21.

32. Asmus, *A Little War*, 123–24.

33. Rice, *No Higher Honor*, 671–72.

34. Bush, *Decision Points*, 431

35. Asmus, *A Little War*, 128.

36. Gordon et al., "Vladimir Putin's 20-Year March to War."

37. Steven Erlanger and Steven Lee Myers, "NATO Allies Oppose Bush on Georgia and Ukraine," *New York Times*, April 3, 2008.

38. Rice, *No Higher Honor*, 673–74.

39. Rice, *No Higher Honor*, 675.

40. Asmus, *A Little War*, 133.

41. Bush, *Decision Points*, 431.

42. Vladimir Putin, "Vystupleniye Vladimira Putin na sammite NATO" [Vladimir Putin's speech at the NATO summit], UNIAN, April 18, 2008, https://www.unian.net/politics /110868-vyistuplenie-vladimira-putina-na-sammite-nato-buharest-4-aprelya -2008-goda.html.

43. John F. Tefft, "Reflections on Russia, Ukraine and the U.S. in the Post-Soviet World," *Foreign Service Journal*, March 2020.

44. Andrei Kolesnikov, "Vladimir Putin skazal kak otrezal Rossiyu ot NATO" [Vladimir Putin said how he cut off Russia from NATO], *Kommersant*, April 5, 2008.

45. Olga Allenova, Yelena Geda, and Vladimir Novikov, "Blok NATO razoshyolsya na blokpakety" [The NATO bloc dispersed into blocking stakes], *Kommersant*, April 7, 2008.

46. Kolesnikov, "Vladimir Putin skazal kak otrezal."

47. Allenova, Geda, and Novikov, "Blok NATO."

48. Bush, *Decision Points*, 431.

49. Rice, *No Higher Honor*, 679.

50. In her memoirs, Condoleezza Rice wrote that she suspected the main reason for Moscow's intransigence on the issue was that U.S. missile defense components were to be stationed in Poland and the Czech Republic, two former Warsaw Pact countries that joined NATO in 1999. See Rice, *No Higher Honor*, 678.

51. Independent International Fact-Finding Mission on the Conflict in Georgia, *Report*, Council of the European Union, September 2009.

52. Bush, *Decision Points*, 434–35.

53. Russian investigators would later say that 162 South Ossetian civilians had been killed in the fighting. See Vladislav Trifonov, Zaur Farniyev, and Georgy Dvali, "Obvinitelny razgovor" [Accusatory talk], *Kommersant*, July 4, 2009.

54. Later I learned that inside the U.S. embassy American diplomats were nervously recalling the bombing of the Chinese embassy in Belgrade during the U.S.-led air campaign against Serbia in 1999.

55. Lucian Kim, "Empty Towns, Destruction in Georgia Show 'Everyone Is to Blame,'" Bloomberg, August 17, 2008.

56. Asmus, *A Little War*, 106–7.

57. The conversation was related to the French magazine *Le Nouvel Observateur* by Sarkozy's main diplomatic adviser, Jean-David Levitte. When asked directly, Putin did not deny making the remarks, and his official website republished the article in the original French with a Russian translation.

58. Zygar, *All the Kremlin's Men*, 105-6.

59. Rice, *No Higher Honor*, 684–86.

60. Rice, *No Higher Honor*, 689.

61. Asmus, *A Little War*, 187.

62. "Meeting the Russia Challenge," 19:58 to 20:13.

63. "Meeting the Russia Challenge," 24:29 to 24:35.

64. Senior State Department official, author interview, September 2008.

65. Bush, *Decision Points*, 435.

66. Michael Kofman, "Russian Performance in the Russo-Georgian War Revisited," *War on the Rocks*, September 4, 2018, https://warontherocks.com/2018/09/russian -performance-in-the-russo-georgian-war-revisited/.

67. Vladimir Putin, "Russian Prime Minister Vladimir Putin Interviewed by the German ARD TV Channel," The Russian Government, August 29, 2008, http://archive .premier.gov.ru/eng/events/news/1758/.

3. Moscow Uprising

1. Lucian Kim, *lucian in moscow*, https://www.luciankim.com/blogs/lucian-in-moscow /page/5/.

2. "'Pora sobirat dan': Nationalisty ne khotyat kormit Kavkaz i 'Yedinuyu Rossiyu'" [Time to collect tribute: Nationalists do not want to feed the Caucasus and 'United Russia'], Lenta.ru, October 24, 2011, https://lenta.ru/articles/2011/10/24 /meeting/.

3. In its final report on the Duma elections, the Organization for Security and Cooperation in Europe found that the vote was "slanted in favor of the ruling party" and "did not provide the necessary conditions for fair electoral competition." The report went on to say that "the quality of the process deteriorated considerably during the count, which was characterized by frequent procedural violations and instances of apparent manipulation, including several serious indications of ballot box stuffing." See *Russian Federation, Elections to the State Duma, 4 December 2011: Final Report* (Warsaw: Organization for Security and Cooperation in Europe, 2012).

4. Natalya Raibman, "Peskov obyasnil padeniye reitinga Putina poslevybornymi emotsiyami" [Peskov explained the drop in Putin's ratings with postelection emotions], *Vedomosti*, December 16, 2011.

5. A group of neurologists studied videos of Putin's gait to understand why his right arm swung less than his left arm when he walked. They coined the term "gunslinger's gait" and posited that it may have resulted from Putin's KGB training, when he was taught to be able to draw a gun quickly. See Rui Araújo et al., "'Gunslinger's gait': A New Cause of Unilaterally Reduced Arm Swing," *British Medical Journal*, December 14, 2015.

6. Peter Spiegel, "Biden Says Weakened Russia Will Bend to U.S.," *Wall Street Journal*, July 25, 2009.

7. Joe Biden, "Vice President Biden's Remarks at Moscow State University," Obama White House Archives, March 10, 2011, https://obamawhitehouse.archives.gov/the -press-office/2011/03/10/vice-president-bidens-remarks-moscow-state-university.

8. Russia finally joined the WTO in 2012. That same year, Obama signed the Magnitsky Act, which targeted individual Russian human rights violators and allowed for the normalization of trade relations with Russia. The law replaced the Cold War–era Jackson-Vanik Amendment in regard to Russia.

9. Nikolaus von Twickel, "Biden 'Opposes' 3rd Putin Term," *Moscow Times*, March 10, 2011.

10. Biden recounted this anecdote in even greater detail in a 2014 interview with the *New Yorker* magazine. According to Biden, he told Putin in his office: "Mr. Prime Minister, I'm looking into your eyes, and I don't think you have a soul," to which Putin responded by smiling and saying: "We understand one another."

11. Steven Lee Myers, *The New Tsar: The Rise and Reign of Vladimir Putin* (New York: Knopf, 2015), 383.

12. "News Conference by President of Russia," The Kremlin, May 18, 2011, http://www.en.kremlin.ru/events/president/transcripts/statements/11259.

13. Mikhail Zygar, *All the Kremlin's Men: Inside the Court of Vladimir Putin* (New York: PublicAffairs, 2016), 205.

14. Mikhail Khodorkovsky, "Dlya modernizatsii nuzhno mobilizovat 3 percent naseleniya" [For modernization, 3 percent of population needs to be mobilized], *Vedomosti*, October 21, 2009.

15. Mikhail Khodorkovsky, "Modernizatsii ne budet" [There will be no modernization], *Vedomosti*, October 12, 2011.

16. USAID was expelled from Russia the following year after spending almost $3 billion on aid and democracy programs in the country; Golos became the first nongovernmental organization to be designated a "foreign agent" under a 2012 law.

17. In its final report on the election, the Organization for Security and Cooperation in Europe said that the election process "deteriorated" once votes were cast because of procedural irregularities. The OSCE also found that the independence of election officials at all levels was in doubt and noted the use of administrative resources, including unfair media coverage and the "onerous" registration of candidates. See *Russian Federation, Presidential Election, 4 March 2012: Final Report* (Warsaw: Organization for Security and Cooperation in Europe, 2012).

18. Zygar, *All the Kremlin's Men*, 220.

4. Massacre on the Maidan

1. Igor Girkin, interview by Dmitry Gordon, posted by Dmitry Gordon, March 18, 2020, YouTube video, 14:23 to 14:59, https://www.youtube.com/watch?v=hf6K6pjK_Yw.

2. In a 2015 newspaper interview, Rustam Temirgaliyev, Crimea's former first deputy prime minister and a leading pro-Russian politician on the peninsula, said he was informed about the arrival of the relics in Crimea on January 13, 2014. See "Rustam Temirgaliyev: 'Yesli eto imelo opredelyonnuyu rezhissuru, rezhissyoru nuzhno postavit pyat s plyusom'" [Rustam Temirgaliyev: 'If this had stage directions, the director gets an A+'], by Pyotr Kozlov, *Vedomosti*, March 16, 2015.

3. Catherine Belton, *Putin's People: How the KGB Took Back Russia and Then Took On the West* (New York: Farrar, Straus and Giroux, 2020), 420–21.

4. Konstantin Malofeyev, "Intervyu—Konstantin Malofeyev, osnovatel 'Marshal Kapitala'" [Interview with Konstantin Malofeyev, founder of Marshall Capital], by Yelizaveta Sergina and Pyotr Kozlov, *Vedomosti*, November 13, 2014.

5. Belton, *Putin's People*, 427.

6. Girkin, Gordon interview, 17:26 to 17:39.

7. Nataliya Telegina, "Put Malofeyeva: ot detskogo pitaniya k sponsorstvu Donbassa i proshchennym $500 млн" [Malofeyev's path: from baby food to sponsorship of the Donbas and a forgiven $500 million], *Slon*, May 12, 2015, https://republic.ru/posts/50662.

8. Girkin, Gordon interview, 42:26 to 42:34.

9. Girkin, Gordon interview, 29:19 to 29:33.

10. Temirgaliyev, "'Yesli eto imelo opredelyonnuyu rezhissuru.'"

11. Temirgaliyev, "'Yesli eto imelo opredelyonnuyu rezhissuru.'"

12. Sonya Koshkina, *Maidan: Nerasskazannaya istoriya* [Maidan: The untold story] (Kyiv: Bright Star, 2015), 228–29.

13. As part of the compromise that concluded the Orange Revolution, Viktor Yushchenko agreed to constitutional amendments diluting presidential power. But after Yanukovych took office in 2010, the Constitutional Court voided the amendments, returning to him the strong presidency laid out in the 1996 constitution.

14. Koshkina, *Maidan*, 233–35.

15. Koshkina, *Maidan*, 239.

16. Koshkina, *Maidan*, 241.

17. Koshkina, *Maidan*, 249.

18. Koshkina, *Maidan*, 258.

19. "Readout of Vice President Biden's Call with Ukrainian President Viktor Yanukovych," Obama White House Archives, February 18, 2014, https://obamawhitehouse.archives.gov/the-press-office/2014/02/18/readout-vice-president-bidens-call-ukrainian-president-viktor-yanukovych.

20. Koshkina, *Maidan*, 256–57.

21. Koshkina, *Maidan*, 266–67.

22. Koshkina, *Maidan*, 269.

23. In its final report, the Organization for Security and Cooperation in Europe said the process had improved since the 2004 election, praising the campaign's "free and calm atmosphere" and a "pluralistic media environment." See Organization for Security and Cooperation in Europe, *Ukraine, Presidential Election, 17 January and 7 February 2010: Final Report* (Warsaw: Organization for Security and Cooperation in Europe, 2010).

24. Alexandra Vagner, "Ot lyubvi do nenavisti—odin shag. Ukraina i Putin" [One step from love to hate: Ukraine and Putin], *Radio Svoboda*, August 20, 2019, https://www.svoboda.org/a/30117767.html.

25. Christiane Hoffmann et al., "How the EU Lost Russia over Ukraine," *Der Spiegel*, November 24, 2014, https://www.spiegel.de/international/europe/war-in-ukraine-a-result-of-misunderstandings-between-europe-and-russia-a-1004706.html.

26. Fiona Hill and Clifford G. Gaddy, *Mr. Putin: Operative in the Kremlin*, rev. ed. (Washington, DC: Brookings Institution, 2015), 101.

27. Vladimir Putin, "Statya v gazete 'Izvestiya': Novy integratsionny proyekt dlya Yevrazii" [Article in 'Izvestia' newspaper: New integration project for Eurasia], October 4, 2011, The Russian Government, http://archive.government.ru/docs/16622/.

28. Zbigniew Brzezinski, "The Premature Partnership," *Foreign Affairs*, March/April 1994.

29. "Celebrations of Russian Navy Day and Ukrainian Navy Day," The Kremlin, July 28, 2013, http://en.kremlin.ru/events/president/news/18963.

30. Hoffmann et al., "How the EU Lost Russia over Ukraine."

31. "Orthodox-Slavic Values: The Foundation of Ukraine's Civilisational Choice Conference," The Kremlin, July 27, 2013, http://en.kremlin.ru/events/president/news/18961.

32. Yalta European Strategy, "Former US Secretary of State Hillary Clinton Provides Clear Message of Support to Ukraine at 10th Annual Meeting of YES," September 21, 2013, https://yes-ukraine.org/en/news/klyuchovi-mesedzhi-derzhavnogo-sekretarya-ssha-2009-2013-hillari-klinton-shcho-prozvuchali-na-10-iy-yaltinskiy-shchorichniy-zustrichi.

33. Shaun Walker, "Ukraine's EU Trade Deal Will Be Catastrophic, Says Russia," *The Guardian*, September 22, 2013.

34. Koshkina, *Maidan*, 28.

35. Elizabeth Piper, "Special Report: Why Ukraine Spurned the EU and Embraced Russia," Reuters, December 19, 2013, https://www.reuters.com/article/us-ukraine-russia-deal-special-report/special-report-why-ukraine-spurned-the-eu-and-embraced-russia-idUSBRE9BI0DZ20131219.

36. Koshkina, *Maidan*, 27.

37. Hoffmann et al., "How the EU Lost Russia over Ukraine."

38. Hoffmann et al., "How the EU Lost Russia over Ukraine."

39. Piper, ""Special Report: Why Ukraine Spurned the EU and Embraced Russia."

40. Hoffmann et al., "How the EU Lost Russia over Ukraine."

41. Michael R. Gordon et al., "Vladimir Putin's 20-Year March to War in Ukraine—and How the West Mishandled It," *Wall Street Journal*, April 1, 2022.

42. Viktor Yushchenko, author interview, April 2023.

43. Koshkina, *Maidan*, 31–32.

44. Olga Onuch, "The Maidan and Beyond: Who Were the Protesters?" *Journal of Democracy* 25, no. 3 (July 2014): 46–48.

45. Victoria Nuland, "Remarks at the U.S.-Ukraine Foundation Conference," U.S. Department of State, December 13, 2013, https://2009-2017.state.gov/p/eur/rls/rm/2013/dec/218804.htm.

46. "Ashton: Yanukovych Promised Solution within 24 Hours," Radio Free Europe/Radio Liberty, December 11, 2013, https://www.rferl.org/a/ukraine-protests-nuland-yanukovych/25197108.html.

47. Sergei Sidorenko, "Sergei Glazyev: Federalizatsiya—uzhe ne ideya, a ochevidnaya neobkhodimost" [Sergei Glazyev: Federalization is no longer an idea but an obvious necessity], *Kommersant Ukraina*, February 6, 2014.

48. Natalya Galimova, "Tainy poslannik: Vladislav Surkov vedyot aktivnye peregovory s ukrainskimi politikami" [Secret envoy: Vladislav Surkov is actively negotiating with Ukrainian politicians], Gazeta.ru, February 21, 2014, https://www.gazeta.ru/politics/2014/02/20_a_5919041.shtml.
49. Sonya Koshkina, "Vladislav Surkov. Ukrainsky sled" [Vladislav Surkov. Ukrainian trail], LB.ua, April 22, 2015, https://rus.lb.ua/news/2015/04/22/302707_vladislav_surkov_ukrainskiy_sled.html.
50. "V GPU obyasnili, chto FSB i Surkov delali na Maidane" [Ukrainian General Prosecutor's Office explained what FSB and Surkov did on the Maidan], *Ukrainska Pravda*, October 20, 2015, https://www.pravda.com.ua/rus/news/2015/10/20/7085511/.
51. Koshkina, "Vladislav Surkov. Ukrainsky sled."
52. Koshkina, *Maidan*, 273–76.
53. Koshkina, *Maidan*, 279.
54. Koshkina, *Maidan*, 282–83.
55. Koshkina, *Maidan*, 294.
56. "Readout of Vice President Biden's Call with Ukrainian President Viktor Yanukovych," Obama White House Archives, February 20, 2014, https://obamawhitehouse.archives.gov/the-press-office/2014/02/20/readout-vice-president-bidens-call-ukrainian-president-viktor-yanukovych.
57. "Telephone Conversation with President of Ukraine Viktor Yanukovych," The Kremlin, February 20, 2014, http://en.kremlin.ru/events/president/news/20295.
58. Koshkina, "Vladislav Surkov. Ukrainsky sled."
59. Koshkina, *Maidan*, 295.
60. Vladimir Putin, "Gala Event Marking Defender of the Fatherland Day," The Kremlin, February 20, 2014, http://en.kremlin.ru/events/president/news/20293.
61. Hill and Gaddy, *Mr. Putin: Operative in the Kremlin*, 496n63.
62. Koshkina, "Vladislav Surkov. Ukrainsky sled."
63. Gordon et al., "Vladimir Putin's 20-Year March to War."
64. Koshkina, *Maidan*, 301, 303–4.
65. Andriy Parubiy, author interview, April 2015.
66. Koshkina, *Maidan*, 304, 310.
67. Koshkina, *Maidan*, 302–3, 308, 311.
68. Roman Olearchyk and Neil Buckley, "Uncertainty in Ukraine as President Goes Missing," *Financial Times*, February 22, 2014.
69. Koshkina, *Maidan*, 315.
70. Koshkina, *Maidan*, 315, 317–319.
71. Glenn Thrush and Kenneth P. Vogel, "What Joe Biden Actually Did in Ukraine," *New York Times*, November 10, 2019.
72. Koshkina, *Maidan*, 333.
73. "Rybak: Vernus v Verkhovnuyu Radu cherez neskolko dnei" [Rybak: I'll return to the Verkhovna Rada in a few days], *Ukrainska Pravda*, February 23, 2014, https://www.pravda.com.ua/rus/news/2014/02/23/7015967/.
74. Maria Popova, "Was Yanukovych's Removal Constitutional?," PONARS Eurasia, March 20, 2014, https://www.ponarseurasia.org/was-yanukovych-s-removal-constitutional/.

5. The Gifts of the Magi

1. Mykhailo Dobkin, interview by Dmitry Gordon, Gordonua.com, October 8, 2020, https://gordonua.com/publications/dobkin-yanukovich-pzdun-eshche-tot-1521354.html.
2. Dobkin, Gordon interview.
3. Sonya Koshkina, *Maidan: Nerasskazannaya istoriya* [Maidan: The untold story] (Kyiv: Bright Star, 2015), 320–21, 323.
4. "Kolomoisky: 'Separatizm na Vostoke i Yuge Ukrainy ne proidyot'" [Kolomoiskyi: 'Separatism in the east and south of Ukraine will not pass], Censor.net, February 22, 2014, https://censor.net/ru/news/272122/kolomoyiskiyi_separatizm_na_vostoke_i_yuge_ukrainy_ne_proyidet_my_ne_dadim_raskolot_stranu.
5. Ihor Kolomoiskyi, interview by Dmitry Gordon, posted by Dmitry Gordon, March 9, 2019, YouTube video, 0:40 to 1:11, https://www.youtube.com/watch?v=7cJ_j1P6TYM.
6. Koshkina, *Maidan*, 316.
7. It was unclear exactly where Yanukovych wanted to fly, although he was likely already being lured to Russia. Putin later said the two had agreed on the phone that day to meet in the closest Russian city, Rostov-on-Don. See "Meeting of the Valdai International Discussion Club," The Kremlin, October 24, 2014, http://en.kremlin.ru/events/president/news/46860.
8. Koshkina, *Maidan*, 324–27.
9. Kobzar said that he spoke with a counterpart at the FSO whom he knew from Yanukovych's frequent meetings with Putin. Kobzar did not mention the officer's name, but it is likely that he spoke with Alexei Dyumin, one of Putin's most trusted bodyguards. Dyumin reportedly masterminded the operation to extract Yanukovych from Ukraine, and he was later promoted several times, becoming a deputy defense minister and the governor of Tula region. See "Sud nad Yanukovichem: Dopros nachalnika SB prezidenta Kobzarya. Stenogramma zasedaniya" [Yanukovych trial: Questioning of the head of the presidential security service Kobzar. Transcript of the hearing], Censor.net, July 16, 2018, https://censor.net/ru/news/3076722/sud_nad_yanukovichem_dopros_nachalnika_sb_prezidenta_kobzarya_stenogramma_zasedaniya.
10. "Kak bezhal Yanukovich. Podrobnosti rasskazali v sude" [How Yanukovych fled. Details told in court], Korrespondent.net, January 25, 2018, https://korrespondent.net/ukraine/3933172-kak-bezhal-yanukovych-podrobnosty-rasskazaly-v-sude.
11. "Podozrevayemy v otravlenii Skripalei agent GRU Chepiga-'Boshirov' vyvozil iz Ukrainy Yanukovicha—Zhurnalist" [The GRU agent suspected of poisoning the Skripals, Chepiga-'Boshirov,' took Yanukovych out of Ukraine: Journalist], Hromadske, October 1, 2018, https://hromadske.ua/ru/posts/podozrevaemyi-v-otravlenyy-skrypalei-ahent-hru-chepyha-boshyrov-vyvozyl-yz-ukrayny-yanukovycha-zhurnalyst.
12. Censor.net, "Sud nad Yanukovichem."
13. A Kyiv court would later try Yanukovych in absentia and convict him of treason. The bodyguards who testified about Yanukovych's last trip through eastern Ukraine did so during the course of the trial.
14. "Eks-okhrannik Yanukovicha: Dlya prinuditelnoi posadki vertolyota s eks-prezidentom mogli primenit boyevuyu aviatsiyu [Ex-Yanukovych guard: Military aircraft

could have been used to force down ex-president's helicopter]," Censor.net, January 25, 2018, https://censor.net/ru/news/3046599/eksohrannik_yanukovicha_dlya _prinuditelnoyi_posadki_vertoleta_s_eksprezidentom_mogli_primenit_boevuyu.

15. Korrespondent.net, "Kak bezhal Yanukovich."

16. Andriy Parubiy, author interview, April 2015.

17. *Krym. Put na Rodinu* [Crimea: The Way Home], Andrei Kondrashov (Rossiya, 2015), 1:05:40 to 1:05:46, https://smotrim.ru/video/1188898.

18. *Krym, Put na Rodinu*, 2:08 to 2:15.

19. *Krym. Put na Rodinu*, 9:42 to 9:58.

20. Gabriel Gatehouse, "Ukraine Crisis: Yanukovych Regrets Bloodshed in Kiev," BBC News, June 22, 2015, https://www.bbc.com/news/world-europe-33224138.

21. A day-by-day account of my 2014 trip to Crimea first appeared in the *Berlin Quarterly*. See Lucian Kim, "One Week in Crimea," *Berlin Quarterly* 1, no. 2 (2014): 32–39.

22. Lucian Kim, "Is Crimea Ukraine's Next Ticking Time Bomb?" *BuzzFeed News*, February 24, 2014, https://www.buzzfeednews.com/article/luciankim/is-crimea-ukraines-next -ticking-time-bomb.

23. "Krym podnimet vopros ob otdelenii pri smene legitimnoi vlasti Ukrainy" [Crimea will raise the issue of secession if Ukraine's legitimate government is replaced], RIA Novosti, February 20, 2014, https://ria.ru/20140220/996014223.html.

24. Refat Chubarov, author interview, April 2015.

25. Rustam Temirgaliyev, "Rustam Temirgaliyev: 'Yesli eto imelo opredelyonnuyu rezhissuru, rezhissyoru nuzhno postavit pyat s plyusom' " [Rustam Temirgaliyev: 'If this had stage directions, the director gets an A+'], by Pyotr Kozlov, *Vedomosti*, March 16, 2015.

26. Chubarov, April 2015.

27. Temirgaliyev, " 'Yesli eto imelo opredelyonnuyu rezhissuru.' "

28. A year after Crimea's annexation Grach told the German publication *Zeit Online* that he was first vetted as Crimean prime minister by three Russian admirals who visited Simferopol on February 20, the day of the Maidan massacre. According to Grach, the admirals connected him by satellite phone with a top-ranking Kremlin official. Grach repeated the story in an interview with the Russian-language site *Meduza* in 2017, although he claimed that his first meeting with the admirals took place on February 23, Yanukovych's last day on Ukrainian soil. Grach also named the Kremlin official he spoke to by phone: Sergei Shoigu, the Russian defense minister. Grach's *Meduza* interview revealed how the Russian military and FSB laid the groundwork for the annexation, including the organization of fake political rallies. See " 'Yesli by nas ne podderzhal Patrushev, v Krymu stoyal by amerikansky flot' " ['If Patrushev had not supported us, the American Navy would be in Crimea'], by Ilya Zhegulev, *Meduza*, March 21, 2017, https://meduza.io/feature/2017/03/21/esli -by-nas-ne-podderzhal-patrushev-v-krymu-stoyal-by-amerikanskiy-flot.

29. According to Rustam Temirgaliyev, one of Konstantinov's accomplices, fifty-three deputies were physically present during the session, suggesting that the remaining votes were cast using eleven lawmakers' electronic voting cards. The journalist Sonya Koshkina also confirmed that fifty-three deputies had been present at the

session. However, only forty-two of them voted for Aksyonov, Koshkina wrote, citing four Crimean lawmakers who were there. See Koshkina, *Maidan*, 346.

30. "I. Strelkov vs N. Starikov," posted by Neyromir-TV, January 22, 2015, YouTube video, 46:58 to 47:10, https://www.youtube.com/watch?v=G04tXnvKx8Y.

31. Temirgaliyev, " 'Yesli eto imelo opredelyonnuyu rezhissuru.' "

32. Andriy Senchenko, author interview, April 2015.

33. Oleksandr Turchynov, "Kak sorvalsya plan Rossii po zakhvatu Ukrainy?" [How was Russia's plan to seize Ukraine foiled?], posted by Krym.Realii, March 9, 2020, YouTube video, 24:07 to 24:58, https://www.youtube.com/watch?v=bT97rbyJZYw.

34. Turchynov, "Kak sorvalsya plan Rossii," 20:04 to 20:09.

35. Temirgaliyev, " 'Yesli eto imelo opredelyonnuyu rezhissuru.' "

36. Mikhail Zygar, *All the Kremlin's Men: Inside the Court of Vladimir Putin* (New York: PublicAffairs, 2016), 279.

37. A transcript of the meeting was published in February 2016 and is a matter of public record.

38. Turchynov, "Kak sorvalsya plan Rossii," 30:53 to 33:39.

39. Turchynov, "Kak sorvalsya plan Rossii," 36:43 to 41:09.

40. Turchynov, "Kak sorvalsya plan Rossii," 43:00 to 48:01.

41. For the Kremlin's translation of Putin's appeal, see "Vladimir Putin Submitted Appeal to the Federation Council," The Kremlin, March 1, 2014, http://en.kremlin.ru/events/president/news/20353.

42. According to the journalist Steven Lee Myers, on March 2—the day after the Federation Council vote—Putin finally summoned Yanukovych to his residence outside Moscow, where the Russian leader forced his Ukrainian guest to draft and sign a backdated letter asking for Russian military assistance. See Steven Lee Myers, *The New Tsar: The Rise and Reign of Vladimir Putin* (New York: Knopf, 2015), 462. On March 3, Russia's ambassador to the United Nations, Vitaly Churkin, held up a copy of the letter during a UN Security Council debate on Ukraine. The letter would later serve as a key piece of evidence in Yanukovych's in absentia treason trial. Yanukovych did not deny being the letter's author, but he claimed that it was an informal request for a "police peacekeeping mission" without any legal weight.

43. Serhii Plokhy, *The Last Empire: The Final Days of the Soviet Union* (New York: Basic Books, 2014), 176, 258.

44. Months earlier, in March 1991, a solid majority of Ukrainians had supported Ukraine joining a "union of sovereign states" in a referendum initiated by Gorbachev in an effort to save the Soviet Union. According to Vladislav Zubok, there was no contradiction here because most Ukrainians evidently believed they could pursue full independence and still join some sort of commonwealth without a central government in the future. See Vladislav Zubok, *Collapse: The Fall of the Soviet Union* (New Haven, CT: Yale University Press, 2021), 200–201.

45. Yury Meshkov returned to Crimea in March 2014 with hopes of resurrecting his political career. He ended up becoming a critic of the puppet government and was

briefly detained after he tried to meet with Putin when the Russian leader visited Simferopol. Meshkov died in 2019 at the age of seventy-three.

46. The poll, commissioned by the Washington-based International Republican Institute, also found that 40 percent of Crimeans self-identified as Russian, 24 percent as Crimean, 15 percent as Ukrainian, 15 percent as Crimean Tatar, and 5 percent as "other." See "Public Opinion Survey Residents of the Autonomous Republic of Crimea May 16–30, 2013," International Republican Institute, May 2013, https://www.iri.org/wp-content/uploads/legacy/iri.org/2013%20October%20 7%20Survey%20of%20Crimean%20Public%20Opinion,%20May%2016-30,%202013 .pdf.

47. "How Relations Between Ukraine and Russia Should Look Like? Public Opinion Polls' Results," Kyiv International Institute of Sociology, March 4, 2014, https:// www.kiis.com.ua/?cat=reports&id=236&lang=eng.

48. Konstantin Malofeyev, "Intervyu—Konstantin Malofeyev, osnovatel 'Marshal Kapitala'" [Interview with Konstantin Malofeyev, founder of Marshall Capital], by Yelizaveta Sergina and Pyotr Kozlov, *Vedomosti*, November 13, 2014.

49. See "Novaya Gazeta's 'Kremlin Papers' Article: Full text in English," UNIAN, February 25, 2015, https://www.unian.info/politics/1048525-novaya-gazetas-kremlin -papers-article-full-text-in-english.html.

50. Igor Girkin, interview by Dmitry Gordon, posted by Dmitry Gordon, March 18, 2020, YouTube video, 30:27 to 30:30, https://www.youtube.com/watch?v=hf6K6pjK_Yw.

51. Construction of the bridge began after Crimea's annexation. Putin personally opened the bridge in May 2018.

52. Temirgaliyev, "'Yesli eto imelo opredelyonnuyu rezhissuru.'"

53. Mohylov, a career law enforcement officer, had briefly served as Yanukovych's interior minister before being dispatched to Crimea. He did not collaborate with the Russian occupation.

54. Zygar, *All the Kremlin's Men*, 275.

55. Vladimir Vetrov, "Vladimir Konstantinov schitayet sebya predatelem No 1" [Vladimir Konstantinov considers himself traitor No. 1], Krym.Realii, March 4, 2016, https://ru.krymr.com/a/27589839.html. In an interview, the Crimean politician Andriy Senchenko told me that after visiting Moscow in late 2013 Konstantinov ordered documentation on the 1954 transfer of Ukraine to Russia from the head of the Supreme Council's legal service.

56. Sonya Koshkina, "Vladislav Surkov. Ukrainsky sled" [Vladislav Surkov. Ukrainian trail], LB.ua, April 22, 2015, https://rus.lb.ua/news/2015/04/22/302707_vladislav _surkov_ukrainskiy_sled.html.

57. "Spiker parlamenta Kryma sobralsya prosit Rossiyu o zashchite" [The speaker of the Crimean parliament is going to ask Russia for protection], *Vzglyad*, February 4, 2014, https://vz.ru/news/2014/2/4/671020.html.

58. "Krymsky deputat prizval vernut poluostrov Rossii" [Crimean deputy called for returning peninsula to Russia], 24 Kanal, February 19, 2014, https://24tv.ua/ru /krimskiy_deputat_prizval_vernut_poluostrov_rossii_video_n410726.

59. "Idyot voina za yedinstvo gosudarstva Ukraina, zayavil spiker Rady Kryma" [There is a war for the unity of Ukraine, speaker of Crimean parliament said], RIA Novosti, February 20, 2014, https://ria.ru/20140220/996049622.html.

60. "Attitude of the Population of Ukraine to Russia and the Population of Russia to Ukraine, November 2021," Kyiv International Institute of Sociology, December 17, 2021, https://www.kiis.com.ua/?lang=eng&cat=reports&id=1078.

61. Girkin, Gordon interview, 48:46 to 49:13.

62. Turchynov, "Kak sorvalsya plan Rossii," 17:38 to 18:44.

63. Peter Baker, "Pressure Rising as Obama Works to Rein In Russia," *New York Times*, March 2, 2014.

64. Zygar, *All the Kremlin's Men*, 281.

65. Temirgaliyev, " 'Yesli eto imelo opredelyonnuyu rezhissuru.' "

66. Temirgaliyev, " 'Yesli eto imelo opredelyonnuyu rezhissuru.' "

67. One hundred countries supported the resolution; eleven voted against it; fifty-eight abstained. Only a handful of countries went as far as to recognize Crimea as a Russian territory, among them Cuba, Nicaragua, Syria, and North Korea.

68. "How Relations Between Ukraine and Russia Should Look Like?," Kyiv International Institute of Sociology.

69. Yevgeny Bobrov, "Problemy zhitelei Kryma" [The problems of Crimea's residents], Russian Presidential Council on Human Rights, April 21, 2014, http://www.president-sovet.ru/members/blogs/post/problemy_zhiteley_kryma/.

70. For the Kremlin's translation of Putin's speech, see "Address by President of the Russian Federation," The Kremlin, March 18, 2014, http://en.kremlin.ru/events/president/news/20603.

71. Parubiy, April 2015.

72. Liliya Yapparova, "Vezhlivye batyushki. Kak svyashchenniki RPTs uchastvovali v prisoyedinenii Kryma" [Polite fathers: How Russian Orthodox priests participated in the annexation of Crimea], *Meduza*, March 16, 2020, https://meduza.io/feature/2020/03/16/vezhlivye-batyushki.

73. Koshkina, *Maidan*, 352.

74. *Krym. Put na Rodinu*, 1:29:58 to 1:30:40.

6. Zombie Revolution

1. Glazyev reacted to the publication of the recordings by saying that he would not comment on the "ravings of Nazi criminals." See "Glazyev i Zatulin otvetili na publikatsiyu proslushki ikh razgovorov o Kryme" [Glazyev and Zatulin responded to the publication of the wiretap of their conversations about Crimea], RBK, August 23, 2016, https://www.rbc.ru/rbcfreenews/57bc262b9a7947855ab36bf2.

2. Serhiy Taruta, author interview, March 2014.

3. In a leaked March 2014 letter published by the Russian newspaper *Novaya Gazeta*, Girkin complained to a colleague that he was being sidelined by local Crimean

officials, who viewed him as a "dangerous madman." See Valery Shiryayev, "Krym. God spustya. Chto my znayem teper" [Crimea one year later: What we know now], *Novaya Gazeta*, February 19, 2015.

4. Igor Girkin, interview by Dmitry Gordon, posted by Dmitry Gordon, March 18, 2020, YouTube video, 58:14 to 59:20, https://www.youtube.com/watch?v=hf6K6pjK_Yw.

5. Yuliya Polukhina, "Besslavnye gibridy" [Inglorious hybrids], *Novaya Gazeta*, July 17, 2020.

6. Girkin, Gordon interview, 1:00:03 to 1:02:04.

7. Igor Strelkov [Igor Girkin] " 'Semnadtsat kilometrov my shli marshem cherez gran-itsu' " ['We marched 17 kilometers across the border'], by Sergei Shargunov, *Svobodnaya Pressa*, November 11, 2014, https://svpressa.ru/war21/article/103643/.

8. Strelkov, " 'Semnadtsat kilometrov.' "

9. Igor Strelkov [Igor Girkin], "Kto ty, 'Strelok'?" [Who are you, 'Strelok'?], by Alexander Prokhanov, *Zavtra*, November 20, 2014, https://zavtra.ru/blogs/kto-tyi-strelok.

10. Vladimir Gladkov, "Strelkov: Malofeyev otkazalsya pomogat Donbassu, vyruchil Aksyonov" [Strelkov: Malofeyev refused to help the Donbas, Aksyonov came to the rescue], *PolitNavigator*, July 5, 2020, https://m.politnavigator.net/strelkov-malofeev-otkazalsya-pomogat-donbassu-vyruchil-aksjonov.html.

11. "Kak Rossiya otryvala Donbass. Top-5 priznanii" [How Russia tore off the Donbas: Top 5 confessions], Krym.Realii, January 26, 2021, https://www.radiosvoboda.org/a/31069837.html.

12. Girkin, Gordon interview, 1:59:19 to 1:59:39.

13. Mikhail Zygar, *All the Kremlin's Men: Inside the Court of Vladimir Putin* (New York: PublicAffairs, 2016), 284.

14. "Direct Line with Vladimir Putin," The Kremlin, April 17, 2014, http://en.kremlin.ru/events/president/news/20796.

15. Gladkov, "Strelkov: Malofeyev otkazalsya pomogat Donbassu."

16. Paweł Pieniążek, *Greetings from Novorossiya: Eyewitness to the War in Ukraine* (Pittsburgh, PA: University of Pittsburgh Press, 2017), 80–81.

17. Girkin, Gordon interview, 1:29:50 to 1:30:11.

18. Ilmari Käihkö, "A Conventional War: Escalation in the War in Donbas, Ukraine," *The Journal of Slavic Military Studies* 34, no. 1 (2021): 40.

19. Andriy Parubiy, author interview, April 2015.

20. Oleksandr Lytvynenko, author interview, April 2015.

21. European diplomat, author interview, April 2015.

22. The UN High Commissioner for Human Rights later found that both sides in the clashes were violent, exchanging gunfire and volleys of Molotov cocktails. The UN High Commissioner also blamed the police for being "passive, even negligent," in securing the rival demonstrators and criticized a "lack of political will" to bring any of the perpetrators to justice. See "7 Years with No Answers. What Is Lacking in the Investigations of the Events in Odesa on 2 May 2014?," Office of the United Nations High Commissioner for Human Rights, April 30, 2021, https://ukraine.un.org/en/126054-7-years-no-answers-what-lacking-investigations-events-odesa-2-may-2014.

23. "The Views and Opinions of South-Eastern Regions Residents of Ukraine: April 2014," Kyiv International Institute of Sociology, April 20, 2014, https://www.kiis .com.ua/?lang=eng&cat=reports&id=302&page=7.

24. "Despite Concerns about Governance, Ukrainians Want to Remain One Country," Pew Research Center, May 8, 2014, https://www.pewresearch.org/global/2014/05/08 /despite-concerns-about-governance-ukrainians-want-to-remain-one-country/.

25. In 2015, a poll conducted in Ukraine and Russia found that 47 percent of Ukrainians said the dissolution of the Soviet Union was a good thing while 34 percent said it was bad. In Russia, opinion on the Soviet collapse was split 17 percent (good) to 69 percent (bad). Furthermore, 61 percent of Russians agreed with the statement that parts of neighboring countries really belonged to Russia. See Katie Simmons, Bruce Stokes, and Jacob Poushter, "NATO Publics Blame Russia for Ukrainian Crisis, but Reluctant to Provide Military Aid," Pew Research Center, June 10, 2015, 32, 41.

26. Within months of my stay the Liverpool Hotel would be taken over by pro-Russian separatists and turned into a base for their "ministry of state security."

27. Michael Birnbaum, Fredrick Kunkle, and Simon Denyer, "Putin Calls for Postponement of Separatists' Referendum in Eastern Ukraine," Washington Post, May 7, 2014.

28. Lucian Kim, "Ukraine's Zombie Revolution," Slate, May 22, 2014, https://slate.com /news-and-politics/2014/05/donetsk-peoples-republic-vladimir-putin-has-created -a-zombie-state-within-ukraine.html.

29. Alexander Borodai, "Alexander Borodai: 'Zaklyuchat mir na usloviyakh kapitulyat-sii my nikak ne gotovy' " [Alexander Borodai: 'We are in no way ready to make peace on the terms of capitulation'], by Pavel Kanygin, Novaya Gazeta, August 12, 2014.

30. Alexander Borodai, "Alexander Borodai: 'Eta voina proyavila narodnuyu energiyu' " [Alexander Borodai: 'This war has demonstrated the people's energy'], by Pavel Kanygin, Novaya Gazeta, April 11, 2015.

31. Yelizaveta Sergina and Sergei Smirnov, "Premyerom Donestskoi respubliki izbran Alexander Borodai, byvshy konsultant 'Marshal Kapitala' " [Alexander Borodai, former Marshall Capital consultant, is elected prime minister of Donetsk republic], Vedomosti, May 16, 2014.

32. Crimeans called Borodai "the minister of propaganda," but Borodai himself said the title was a joke. See Oleg Kashin, "Iz Kryma v Donbass: Priklyucheniya Igorya Strel-kova i Alexandra Borodaya" [From Crimea to Donbas: The adventures of Igor Strel-kov and Alexander Borodai], Slon, May 18, 2014, https://republic.ru/posts/41009.

33. Alexander Borodai, " 'Strelkov pytalsya stat politicheskim liderom, no eta rol yemu podkhodit, kak pachka baleriny' " ['Strelkov tried to become a political leader, but that role fits him like a ballerina's tutu'], by Ksenia Sobchak, TV Rain, November 12, 2014, https://tvrain.tv/teleshow/sobchak_zhivem/aleksandr_borodaj_strelkov_pytalsja _stat_politiche-378007/.

34. Julia Smirnova, "Die stille Hoffnung von Putins listigen Kriegern" [The silent hope of Putin's cunning warriors], Die Welt, June 23, 2016.

35. In an interview with the official Russian government newspaper, Donetsk separatist leader Pavel Gubarev said that two-thirds of the pro-Russian separatists were living

off Akhmetov's money. See "Gubarev: Nam nuzhna byudzhetnaya avtonomiya i svoya gumanitarnaya politika" [Gubarev: We need budget autonomy and our own humanities policy], by Yury Snegiryov, *Rossiiskaya Gazeta*, May 11, 2014.

36. Sonya Koshkina, *Maidan: Nerasskazannaya istoriya* [Maidan: The untold story] (Kyiv: Bright Star, 2015), 398–400.

37. Konstantin Skorkin, "Kto pridumal, chto Donbass—eto 'russky mir'? I kak v regione raskruchivali separatistskiye idei, kotorymi Putin vospolzovalsya dlya napadeniya na Ukrainu" [Who thought up that the Donbas is the 'Russian World'? And how were separatist ideas promoted in the region that Putin used to attack Ukraine?], *Meduza*, January 22, 2023, https://meduza.io/feature/2023/01/22/kto-pridumal-chto-donbass -eto-russkiy-mir-i-kak-v-regione-raskruchivali-separatistskie-idei-kotorymi-putin -vospolzovalsya-dlya-napadeniya-na-ukrainu.

38. Kim, "Ukraine's Zombie Revolution."

39. Konstantin Skorkin, "25 let donbasskogo separatizma. Chast pervaya" [25 years of Donbas separatism. Part 1], *Realna Gazeta*, March 15, 2016, https://realgazeta.com.ua /25-let-donbasskogo-separatizma-1/.

40. Skorkin, "25 let donbasskogo separatizma. Chast pervaya."

41. Konstantin Skorkin, "25 let donbasskogo separatizma. Chast vtoraya" [25 years of Donbas separatism. Part 2], *Realna Gazeta*, March 24, 2016, https://realgazeta.com.ua /25-let-donbasskogo-separatizma_-chast-vtoraya/.

42. Skorkin, "Kto pridumal, chto Donbass—eto 'russky mir.'"

43. Prime Minister Yatsenyuk signed the political part of the agreement in March 2014.

44. Anna Arutunyan. *Hybrid Warriors: Proxies, Freelancers and Moscow's Struggle for Ukraine* (London: Hurst, 2022), 145–46.

45. Zygar, *All the Kremlin's Men*, 287.

46. Arutunyan, *Hybrid Warriors*, 156–57.

47. Girkin, Gordon interview, 1:24:37 to 1:24:46.

48. Arutunyan, *Hybrid Warriors*, 160.

49. Parubiy, author interview.

50. In his March 2020 interview with the journalist Dmitry Gordon, Girkin described Zakharchenko, a former coal mine electrician, as "dimwitted" and "uncontrollable when drunk"—which he said was an everyday occurrence. According to Girkin, Zakharchenko robbed every arms collector in Donetsk and later boasted about it.

51. Anton Zverev, "Ex-Rebel Leaders Detail Role Played by Putin Aide in East Ukraine," Reuters, May 11, 2017, https://www.reuters.com/article/us-ukraine-crisis-russia -surkov-insight/ex-rebel-leaders-detail-role-played-by-putin-aide-in-east-ukraine -idUSKBN1870TJ.

52. Zverev, "Ex-Rebel Leaders Detail Role Played by Putin Aide."

53. Lucian Kim, "The Battle of Ilovaisk: Details of a Massacre Inside Rebel-Held Eastern Ukraine," *Newsweek*, November 4, 2014.

54. Andrew E. Kramer and Michael R. Gordon, "Ukraine Reports Russian Invasion on a New Front," *New York Times*, August 27, 2014.

55. Zygar, *All the Kremlin's Men*, 290.

56. "Premyer DNR: na storone opolcheniya voyuyut dobrovoltsy iz Rossii" [DNR premier: volunteers from Russia are fighting on the side of the militia], Vesti, August 28, 2014, https://www.vesti.ru/article/1860975.

57. In his November 2014 interview with *Zavtra*, Girkin said that the Russian "vacationers" led the drive toward Mariupol and could have easily taken the city. Instead, he said, they were ordered to stop their advance and not to enter Mariupol under any circumstances.

58. Senior German official, author interview, November 2015.

59. Lucian Kim, "Putin Wins Again," *Slate*, February 12, 2015, https://slate.com/news-and-politics/2015/02/ukrainian-cease-fire-agreement-was-another-victory-for-vladimir-putin-the-deal-grants-the-russian-president-flexibility-at-little-cost.html.

60. The investigation into Nemtsov's assassination was swift, and a group of suspects from Chechnya were implicated and convicted. Although the trail led straight to the inner circle of Ramzan Kadyrov, the Kremlin-backed strongman running Chechnya, nobody was prosecuted for the organization of Nemtsov's murder.

7. Yankee, Come Back!

1. John M. Broder, "2 Soviet Vessels Bump U.S. Navy Warships in Black Sea," *Los Angeles Times*, February 13, 1988.

2. Anton Valagin and Igor Filonov, "Kak rossiiskaya REB napugala amerikansky esminets" [How Russian electromagnetic warfare frightened an American destroyer], *Rossiiskaya Gazeta*, April 30, 2014.

3. *Krym. Put na Rodinu* [Crimea: The way home], Andrei Kondrashov (Rossiya, 2015), 1:25:59 to 1:26:19, https://smotrim.ru/video/1188898.

4. *Krym. Put na Rodinu*, 1:32:45 to 1:32:55.

5. Michael R. Gordon, "U.S. Says Russia Tested Missile, Despite Treaty," *New York Times*, January 29, 2014.

6. Vladimir Putin, "Interview to American TV channel CBS and PBS," The Kremlin, September 29, 2015, http://en.kremlin.ru/events/president/news/50380.

7. Vladimir Putin, "Address by President of the Russian Federation," The Kremlin, March 18, 2014, http://en.kremlin.ru/events/president/news/20603.

8. A Gallup poll in 2013, for example, found that only 17 percent of Ukrainians saw NATO as protection, while 29 percent considered it a threat. A plurality, 44 percent, viewed the alliance as neither. See Julie Ray and Neli Esipova, "Before Crisis, Ukrainians More Likely to See NATO as a Threat," Gallup, March 14, 2014, https://news.gallup.com/poll/167927/crisis-ukrainians-likely-nato-threat.aspx.

9. Zbigniew Brzezinski, "Russia Needs to Be Offered a 'Finland Option' for Ukraine," *Financial Times*, February 22, 2014.

10. "Vladimir Putin Answered Journalists' Questions on the Situation in Ukraine," The Kremlin, March 4, 2014, http://www.en.kremlin.ru/events/president/news/20366.

11. The security analyst Mark Galeotti originally coined the term in a post for his blog, "In Moscow's Shadows." He soon disavowed the term as the ideas in question were neither Gerasimov's alone nor, strictly speaking, a doctrine.

12. A translation of Gerasimov's article was published on Mark Galeotti's blog: https://inmoscowsshadows.wordpress.com/2014/07/06/the-gerasimov-doctrine -and-russian-non-linear-war/.

13. Mark Hosenball, "Ukraine Crisis: CIA, Not Pentagon, Forecast Russian Move—Sources," Reuters, March 5, 2014, https://www.reuters.com/article/ukraine-crisis-intelligence /ukraine-crisis-cia-not-pentagon-forecast-russian-move-sources-idINDEEA2500J 20140306.

14. Eli Lake, "Exclusive: U.S. Won't Share Invasion Intel with Ukraine," Daily Beast, April 8, 2014, https://www.thedailybeast.com/exclusive-us-wont-share-invasion-intel -with-ukraine.

15. Former senior Ukrainian diplomat, author interview, October 2014.

16. Senior State Department official, off-record briefing, May 2016.

17. Joe Biden, "Remarks by Vice President Joe Biden at a Meeting with Ukrainian Leg-islators," Obama White House Archives, April 22, 2014, https://obamawhitehouse .archives.gov/the-press-office/2014/04/22/remarks-vice-president-joe-biden -meeting-ukrainian-legislators.

18. Burisma, "Hunter Biden Joins the Team of Burisma Holdings," Burisma press release, May 12, 2014.

19. Hosenball, "Ukraine Crisis: CIA, Not Pentagon, Forecast Russian Move."

20. Gary Sheftick, "Era Ends in Heidelberg as U.S. Army Europe Transforms," Army News Service, September 13, 2013, https://www.army.mil/article/111356/era_ends_in _heidelberg_as_u_s_army_europe_transforms.

21. In January 2014, twenty-nine modernized Abrams tanks were brought back to Ger-many to fill a gap in training capabilities. See Michael S. Darnell, "American Tanks Return to Europe after Brief Leave," Stars and Stripes, January 31, 2014.

22. Thom Shanker, "U.S. and Russia Discuss Olympic Security," New York Times, January 21, 2014.

23. Marcin Goettig, "With Eye on Crimea, U.S. Starts Military Drills on Russia's Door-step," Reuters, March 10, 2014, https://www.reuters.com/article/ukraine-crisis -exercises/with-eye-on-crimea-u-s-starts-military-drills-on-russias-doorstep -idINDEEA290J320140310.

24. Steven Beardsley, "Destroyer USS Truxtun Heads for Black Sea amid Heightened Tensions over Crimea," Stars and Stripes, March 6, 2014.

25. Mike Schuler, "USS Taylor Heads for Repairs Following Grounding," gCaptain, March 7, 2014, https://gcaptain.com/uss-taylor-heads-for-repairs-following-grounding/.

26. "Amerikansky esminets 'Donald Kuk' primut v Chyornom more po standartam Kholodnoi voiny" [The American destroyer 'Donald Cook' will be received in the Black Sea according to Cold War standards], Moskovsky Komsomolets, April 10, 2014.

27. "Fact Sheet: European Reassurance Initiative and Other U.S. Efforts in Support of NATO Allies and Partners," Obama White House Archives, June 3, 2014, https://

obamawhitehouse.archives.gov/the-press-office/2014/06/03/fact-sheet-european
-reassurance-initiative-and-other-us-efforts-support-.

28. Maïa de la Baume and Rick Gladstone, "France Postpones Delivery of Warship to Russia," *New York Times*, September 3, 2014.

29. Barack Obama, "Remarks by President Obama to the People of Estonia," Obama White House Archives, September 3, 2014, https://obamawhitehouse.archives.gov /the-press-office/2014/09/03/remarks-president-obama-people-estonia.

30. After being sentenced to fifteen years in prison by a Russian court, Kohver was returned to Estonia in September 2015 in exchange for a convicted FSB spy.

31. Lucian Kim, "NATO Is Holding the Biggest Exercise in Poland in a Decade, and Russia Is Not Happy," VICE News, June 11, 2016, https://www.vice.com/en/article/d39qem /nato-is-holding-the-biggest-exercise-in-poland-in-a-decade-and-russia-is-not-happy.

32. Burkhard Uhlenbroich, "Steinmeier kritisiert Nato-Manöver in Osteuropa" [Steinmeier criticizes NATO maneuvers in Eastern Europe], *Bild*, June 18, 2016.

33. Lucian Kim, "Playing to the Gallery," *Berlin Policy Journal*, July 6, 2016, https://berlin policyjournal.com/playing-to-the-gallery/.

34. For Rühe's own account, see Volker Rühe, "Opening NATO's Door," in *Open Door: NATO and Euro-Atlantic Security after the Cold War*, ed. Daniel S. Hamilton and Kristina Spohr (Philadelphia: Foreign Policy Institute, 2019), 217–33.

35. Lucian Kim, "NATO Is Having an Existential Crisis," VICE News, July 11, 2016, https:// www.vice.com/en/article/7xaj4y/nato-is-having-an-existential-crisis.

36. Giedrimas Jeglinskas, author interview, August 2018.

37. Vytautas Landsbergis, panel discussion at Nordic Embassies on the twenty-fifth anniversary of the restoration of independence of the Baltic states, Berlin, May 23, 2016.

38. Catherine Belton, *Putin's People: How the KGB Took Back Russia and Then Took On the West* (New York: Farrar, Straus and Giroux, 2020), 427–29.

39. Senior German lawmaker, author interview, December 2016.

40. For the story on how Russian state television provoked protests in Germany, see Lucian Kim, "Russia Having Success in Hybrid War Against Germany," Reuters, February 11, 2016, https://www.reuters.com/article/idUS267968876820160207.

41. Katie Simmons, Bruce Stokes, and Jacob Poushter, "NATO Publics Blame Russia for Ukrainian Crisis, but Reluctant to Provide Military Aid," Pew Research Center, June 10, 2015, 5, 9, 20.

42. Senior Merkel adviser, author interview, October 2016.

43. "Darf man jetzt mit Putin feiern?" [Is it okay to party with Putin now?], *Bild*, April 29, 2014.

44. Former senior U.S. diplomat, author interview, June 2016.

45. Carol Williams, "U.S.-Ukraine Military Exercises Rub Russians the Wrong Way," *Los Angeles Times*, August 29, 1997.

46. Katya Gorchinskaya, "Parliament Counters Sea Breeze with Hot Air," *Kyiv Post*, October 27, 1998.

47. One of the most detailed descriptions of the fiasco of Sea Breeze 2006 is in a diplomatic cable from the U.S. embassy in Kyiv. See Embassy Kyiv, Wikileaks Cable: 06KIEV2190_a, https://wikileaks.org/plusd/cables/06KIEV2190_a.html.

48. Vladimir Socor, "Bush Visit, Military Exercises Canceled in Ukraine," *Eurasia Daily Monitor*, June 13, 2006, https://jamestown.org/program/bush-visit-military-exercises-canceled-in-ukraine/.

49. "Deputat Kuryanovich pridumal, kak vernut Krym Rossii" [Deputy Kuryanovich thought up how to return Crimea to Russia], Tayga.info, May 28, 2006, https://tayga.info/92278?ysclid=lmzk1asbin582463842.

50. Russian state media helped stoke outrage with its coverage from anti-NATO protests in Crimea. But when a U.S. frigate, the USS *Robert G. Bradley*, called on St. Petersburg a few weeks later, Russia's Channel One proudly announced the visit with a fluff report from aboard the American warship.

51. Leonid Grach, " 'Yesli by nas ne podderzhal Patrushev, v Krymu stoyal by amerikansky flot' " ['If Patrushev had not supported us, the American navy would be in Crimea'], by Ilya Zhegulev, *Meduza*, March 21, 2017, https://meduza.io/feature/2017/03/21/esli-by-nas-ne-podderzhal-patrushev-v-krymu-stoyal-by-amerikanskiy-flot.

52. Vladimir Socor, "U.S.-Led 'Sea Breeze' Combined Exercise Canceled in Ukraine," *Eurasia Daily Monitor*, June 23, 2009, https://jamestown.org/program/u-s-led-sea-breeze-combined-exercise-canceled-in-ukraine/.

53. "Voyenny flot Ukrainy: skolko korablei i v kakom sostoyanii" [Ukrainian navy: how many ships and in what condition], BBC News Ukrainian Service, November 26, 2018, https://www.bbc.com/ukrainian/features-russian-46348611?fbclid=IwAR22DHf_vVzfJyaVkt7TBs-DPELQb3n9-Sfs-LqzSFxh02FzJ4G4wGu-JRI.

54. Lara Jakes, Edward Wong, and Michael Crowley, "America's Road to the Ukraine War," *New York Times*, April 24, 2022.

55. Peter Baker, "Obama Said to Resist Growing Pressure from All Sides to Arm Ukraine," *New York Times*, March 10, 2015.

56. Jack Detsch, "How Ukraine Learned to Fight," *Foreign Policy*, March 1, 2023, https://foreignpolicy.com/2023/03/01/how-ukraine-learned-to-fight/.

57. Ben Hodges, author interview, July 2023.

58. In March 2014, the Levada Center found that 88 percent of Russians approved of Crimea's annexation whereas only 7 percent disapproved. With small fluctuations, those proportions remained stable over the next seven years. See "Krym" [Crimea], Levada Center, April 26, 2021, https://www.levada.ru/2021/04/26/krym/.

59. Lucian Kim, "Putin the Pariah," *Slate*, November 18, 2014, https://slate.com/news-and-politics/2014/11/vladimir-putin-is-isolated-and-shunned-that-makes-the-russian-president-even-more-dangerous.html.

60. "Ataka na Putina na sammite G20: Obama, Ebbott i drugiye zapadnye lidery veli sebya demonstrativno" [Attack on Putin at the G20 summit: Obama, Abbott, and other Western leaders behaved defiantly], *Moskovsky Komsomolets*, November 15, 2014.

61. Mikhail Zygar, *All the Kremlin's Men: Inside the Court of Vladimir Putin* (New York: PublicAffairs, 2016), 336.

62. Vladimir Putin, "70th Session of the UN General Assembly," The Kremlin, September 28, 2015, http://en.kremlin.ru/events/president/news/50385.

63. Angela Stent, *The Limits of Partnership: U.S.-Russian Relations in the Twenty-First Century* (Princeton, NJ: Princeton University Press, 2014), 69.

64. "Strategiya natsionalnoi bezopasnosti Rossiiskoi Federatsii" [National security strategy of the Russian Federation], *Rossiiskaya Gazeta*, December 31, 2015.

65. In a 2000 interview with the British television host David Frost, Putin said that "it is hard for me to visualize NATO as an enemy." When Frost asked him if it was possible that Russia could join NATO, Putin said: "I don't see why not. I would not rule out such a possibility, but I repeat—if and when Russia's views are taken into account as those of an equal partner." See "Interview to 'BBC Breakfast with Frost,'" The Kremlin, March 5, 2000, http://en.kremlin.ru/events/president/transcripts/24194.

8. Make Russia Great Again

1. "Debaty Live. Navalny vs. Strelkov" [Live Debate: Navalny vs. Strelkov], YouTube video, posted by Navalny LIVE, July 20, 2017, https://www.youtube.com/watch?v=cjbQdbJUibc.

2. "Debaty Live. Navalny vs. Strelkov," 30:07 to 30:17.

3. Girkin acknowledged that the closest he had ever been to the dastardly West was the former Yugoslavia, where he fought as a volunteer on the side of the Bosnian Serbs in the 1990s, and Romania, where the FSB briefly sent him on an assignment in 1999.

4. "Debaty Live. Navalny vs. Strelkov," 56:59 to 57:05.

5. "Debaty Live. Navalny vs. Strelkov," 1:10:02 to 1:10:09.

6. "Debaty Live. Navalny vs. Strelkov," 1:21:15 to 1:21:45.

7. Masha Gessen, "The Evolution of Alexey Navalny's Nationalism," *New Yorker*, February 15, 2021, https://www.newyorker.com/news/our-columnists/the-evolution-of-alexey-navalnys-nationalism.

8. "Manifest Nationalnogo russkogo osvobitelnogo dvizheniya 'NAROD'" [Manifesto of the National Russian Liberation Movement 'NAROD'], APN, June 27, 2007, https://www.apn.ru/publications/article17321.htm.

9. Alexei Navalny, "'Ya dumayu, vlast v Rossii smenitsya ne v rezultate vyborov'" ['I think the government in Russia will change not as a result of elections'], by Yevgenia Albats, *New Times*, July 19, 2011.

10. For the Kremlin's translation of Putin's speech, see "Annual Address to the Federal Assembly of the Russian Federation," The Kremlin, April 25, 2005, http://www.en.kremlin.ru/events/president/transcripts/22931.

11. Alexei Navalny, "Razvyornutaya pozitsiya po Ukraine i Krymu" [Detailed position on Ukraine and Crimea], LiveJournal, March 12, 2014, https://navalny.livejournal.com/914090.html.

12. For an English translation of the interview, see "Ekho Moskvy Interview with Navalny: 'We Have to Stop Sponsoring the War'," *The Interpreter*, October 16, 2014, http://www.interpretermag.com/russia-this-week-hundreds-of-russians-poisoned-25-dead-in-spice-drug-epidemic/#4625.

13. "Navalny o svoei pozitsii po Krymu" [Navalny on his position regarding Crimea], posted by TV Rain, June 8, 2017, YouTube video, https://www.youtube.com/watch?v =zj4qZdxAons.
14. Navalny said that his family began discussing politics after the Soviet authorities attempted to downplay the Chernobyl catastrophe. When he first saw Putin on TV he had the same feeling as back then, Navalny recalled, namely, that he was watching a "political lizard looking into my eyes and lying to me." See *Navalny*, directed by Daniel Roher (Warner Bros. Pictures, 2022), 43:47 to 44:56.
15. "Iyunskiye reitingi odobreniya i doveriya" [June approval and confidence ratings], Levada Center, June 26, 2014, https://www.levada.ru/2014/06/26/iyunskie -rejtingi-odobreniya-i-doveriya-3/.
16. Navalny, "Razvyornutaya pozitsiya."
17. "Aktsii protesta 26 marta i Navalny" [The March 26 protests and Navalny], Levada Center, April 6, 2017, https://www.levada.ru/2017/04/06/aktsii-protesta-26-marta -i-navalnyj/.
18. "Navalny, 'Bolotnoye delo,' Strelkov: Znaniye i otnosheniye" [Navalny, the 'Bolotnoye' case, Strelkov: Awareness and attitude], Levada Center, November 7, 2014, https://www .levada.ru/2014/11/07/navalnyj-bolotnoe-delo-strelkov-znanie-i-otnoshenie/.
19. "Congratulations to Donald Trump on Winning the US Presidential Election," The Kremlin, November 9, 2016, http://en.kremlin.ru/events/president/news /53221.
20. "Zhirinovsky ustroil v Gosdume banket po sluchayu pobedy Trampa na vyborakh" [Zhirinovsky hosted a banquet in the Duma for Trump's election victory], RBK, November 9, 2016, https://www.rbc.ru/rbcfreenews/58230a939a7947f0d933a04f.
21. "Vladimir Putin's Annual News Conference," The Kremlin, December 23, 2016, http://en.kremlin.ru/events/president/news/53573.
22. David E. Sanger and Eric Schmitt, "Spy Agency Consensus Grows That Russia Hacked D.N.C.," *New York Times*, July 26, 2016.
23. "Assessing Russian Activities and Intentions in Recent US Elections," Office of the Director of National Intelligence, January 6, 2017, https://www.dni.gov/files /documents/ICA_2017_01.pdf.
24. Lucian Kim, "What Was Russia's Role in 2016 U.S. Election? 2 Former KGB Officials Weigh In," NPR, November 11, 2017, https://www.npr.org/sections/parallels/2017 /11/11/563287218/what-was-russias-role-in-2016-u-s-election-2-former-kgb-officials -weigh-in.
25. Lucian Kim, "In Putin's Russia, an 'Adhocracy' Marked by Ambiguity and Plausible Deniability," NPR, July 21, 2017, https://www.npr.org/sections/parallels/2017/07/21 /538535186/in-putins-russia-an-adhocracy-marked-by-ambiguity-and-plausible -deniability.
26. Vladimir Putin, "Meeting with Heads of International News Agencies," The Kremlin, June 1, 2017, http://en.kremlin.ru/events/president/news/54650.
27. "Prezidentskiye vybory v SShA" [U.S. presidential elections], Levada Center, November 24, 2016, https://www.levada.ru/2016/11/24/prezidentskie-vybory-v-ssha/.

28. Alexei Navalny, "Don't Call him 'Dimon,' " posted by Alexei Navalny, March 2, 2017, YouTube video, https://www.youtube.com/watch?v=qrwlk7_GF9g.

29. Lucian Kim, "Banned from Election, Putin Foe Navalny Pursues Politics by Other Means," NPR, February 8, 2018, https://www.npr.org/sections/parallels/2018/02 /08/584369719/banned-from-election-putin-foe-navalny-pursues-politics-by -other-means.

30. In a recurring poll by the Levada Center, respondents were asked to name the politician they would vote for. In August 2017, 48 percent named Putin and only 1 percent Navalny. Two months before the presidential vote, the Levada Center said that it would stop publishing polling information on the upcoming election because it could face penalties or be closed down for doing so as a government-labeled "foreign agent."

31. For the Kremlin's translation of Putin's speech, see "Presidential Address to the Federal Assembly," The Kremlin, March 1, 2018, http://en.kremlin.ru/events /president/news/56957.

32. Lucian Kim, "Russians, with No Real Alternatives, Give Putin 6 More Years in Power," NPR, March 19, 2018, https://www.npr.org/sections/parallels/2018/03/19/594858230 /russians-with-no-real-alternatives-give-putin-6-more-years-in-power.

33. Carol D. Leonnig, David Nakamura, and Josh Dawsey, "Trump's National Security Advisers Warned Him Not to Congratulate Putin. He Did It Anyway," *Washington Post*, March 20, 2018.

34. Mark Landler, "Trump Congratulates Putin, but Doesn't Mention Meddling in U.S.," *New York Times*, March 20, 2018.

35. Putin's only two visits to the White House, in 2001 and 2005, occurred during the presidency of George W. Bush.

36. Shane Harris, "Russian Spy Chiefs Met in Washington with CIA Director to Discuss Counterterrorism," *Washington Post*, January 31, 2018.

37. Lucian Kim, "GOP Lawmakers Hope Russia Visit Sets Stage for 'New Day' Ahead of Trump-Putin Summit," NPR, July 5, 2018, https://www.npr.org/2018/07/05/626079169 /gop-lawmakers-hope-russia-visit-sets-stage-for-new-day-ahead-of-trump -putin-summ.

9. The Education of Volodymyr Zelensky

1. Volodymyr Zelensky, "Volodymyr Zelenskyi zaklykav Yanukovycha vrozumitys" [Volodymyr Zelensky called on Yanukovych to come to his senses], posted by TSN, March 1, 2014, YouTube video, https://www.youtube.com/watch?v=OCvGLF4ePdI.

2. Serhii Rudenko, *Zelensky: A Biography* (Cambridge: Polity, 2022), 84.

3. Volodymyr Zelensky, interview by Dmitry Gordon, Gordonua.com, December 26, 2018, https://gordonua.com/publications/zelenskiy-esli-menya-vyberut-prezidentom -snachala-budut-oblivat-gryazyu-zatem-uvazhat-a-potom-plakat-kogda-uydu -609294.html.

4. Responding to a request from four lawmakers, the Ukrainian Defense Ministry stated that Zelensky had not completed his military service and ignored four call-up notices between April 2014 and May 2015. See "Zelensky proignoriroval 4 povestki v 2014–2015 godakh—Minoborony" [Zelensky ignored 4 draft notices in 2014–2015: Defense Ministry], *Ukrainska Pravda*, April 13, 2019, https://www.pravda.com.ua/rus/news/2019/04/13/7212159/.

5. Ariane Chemin, "Volodymyr Zelensky's Soviet Childhood," *Le Monde*, February 19, 2023, https://www.lemonde.fr/en/international/article/2023/02/19/volodymyr-zelensky-s-soviet-childhood_6016468_4.html.

6. Iuliia Mendel, *The Fight of Our Lives: My Time with Zelenskyy, Ukraine's Battle for Democracy, and What It Means for the World* (New York: Atria/One Signal, 2022), 17.

7. Simon Shuster, "How Volodymyr Zelensky Defended Ukraine and United the World," *Time*, March 2, 2022.

8. Zelensky, Gordon interview.

9. Rudenko, *Zelensky*, 167.

10. Zelensky, Gordon interview.

11. Zelensky, Gordon interview.

12. Zelensky, Gordon interview.

13. Rudenko, *Zelensky*, 58.

14. Rudenko, *Zelensky*, 100.

15. Ariane Chemin and Benoît Vitkine, "Volodymyr Zelensky's Russian Years," *Le Monde*, February 20, 2023, https://www.lemonde.fr/en/international/article/2023/02/20/volodymyr-zelensky-s-russian-years_6016603_4.html.

16. Zelensky, Gordon interview.

17. Mendel, *The Fight of Our Lives*, 21.

18. Rudenko, *Zelensky*, 160.

19. Zelensky, Gordon interview.

20. Zelensky, Gordon interview.

21. Mendel, *The Fight of Our Lives*, 24.

22. Michael Idov, "Behind the Scenes of Volodymyr Zelensky's Rise from Rom-Com Star to Ukraine President," *GQ*, March 4, 2022, https://www.gq.com/story/zelensky-movies-director-david-dodson-interview.

23. Mendel, *The Fight of Our Lives*, 23.

24. Rudenko, *Zelensky*, 71–72.

25. Zelensky, Gordon interview.

26. "Report on the Human Rights situation in Ukraine, 16 November 2018 to 15 February 2019," Office of the United Nations High Commissioner for Human Rights, February 2019, https://www.ohchr.org/sites/default/files/Documents/Countries/UA/ReportUkraine16Nov2018-15Feb2019.pdf.

27. Ukrainian and U.S. officials later confirmed that an elite Ukrainian paramilitary unit with CIA training was responsible for killing separatist commanders. See Adam Entous and Michael Schwirtz, "The Spy War: How the C.I.A. Secretly Helps Ukraine Fight Putin," *New York Times*, February 25, 2024.

28. Lucian Kim, "Putin's Man in Crimea: We've 'Returned to Russia Forever,' " NPR, January 27, 2018, https://www.npr.org/sections/parallels/2018/01/27/581114772/putins-man -in-crimea-we-ve-returned-to-russia-forever.

29. Lucian Kim, "Exiles in Their Country, Crimean Dissidents Resist Russian Rule," NPR, February 23, 2018, https://www.npr.org/sections/parallels/2018/02/23/587565686 /exiles-in-their-country-crimean-dissidents-resist-russian-rule.

30. In 2022, Dzhelyal was convicted of sabotaging a pipeline and sentenced to seventeen years in prison after attending an international forum in Kyiv calling for Crimea's peaceful return to Ukraine. He was released in a prisoner exchange in June 2024.

31. Lucian Kim, "Why the Crisis Between Ukraine and Russia Has Taken to the Sea," NPR, November 28, 2018, https://www.npr.org/2018/11/28/671615172/why-the-crisis -between-ukraine-and-russia-has-taken-to-the-sea.

32. Daria Shulzhenko, "Pre-election Poll Gives Poroshenko Highest 'Anti-Rating' of All Presidential Candidates," *Kyiv Post*, November 18, 2018.

33. "Public Opinion Survey of Residents of Ukraine, September 29–October 14, 2018," International Republican Institute, November 2018, https://www.iri.org/wp -content/uploads/2018/11/2018.12.4_ukraine_poll.pdf.

34. Zelensky, Gordon interview.

35. Ariane Chemin, "For Volodymyr Zelensky, Politics Was a Fiction That Became His Reality," *Le Monde*, February 21, 2023, https://www.lemonde.fr/en/international /article/2023/02/21/for-volodymyr-zelensky-politics-was-a-fiction-that-became -his-reality_6016731_4.html.

36. "Patrushev predrek raspad Ukrainy v sluchaye pobedy Poroshenko na vyborakh" [Patrushev predicted the collapse of Ukraine if Poroshenko wins the elections], *Izvestia*, March 24, 2019.

37. Rudenko, *Zelensky*, 139.

38. Lucian Kim, "A Comedian Plays Ukraine's President on TV. Will He Become One in Real Life?," NPR, March 30, 2019, https://www.npr.org/2019/03/30/707118761/a -comedian-plays-ukraines-president-on-tv-will-he-become-one-in-real-life.

39. Zelensky, Gordon interview.

40. Volodymyr Zelensky, "Pro Donbas, Krym, MVF i 'Slugu narodu.' Velike intervyu Volodymyra Zelenskogo dlya TSN" [On Donbas, Crimea, IMF and 'Servant of the People.' Volodymyr Zelensky's big interview with TSN], posted by TSN, March 24, 2019, YouTube video, https://www.youtube.com/watch?v=z7aJTzevBQ8.

41. Kim, "A Comedian Plays Ukraine's President on TV."

42. Volodymyr Zelensky, "Volodymyr Zelenskyy's Inaugural Address," President of Ukraine, May 20, 2019, https://www.president.gov.ua/en/news/inavguracijna-promova -prezidenta-ukrayini-volodimira-zelensk-55489.

43. Amid the furor over Russian election interference to help Trump, the Kremlin began talking about alleged Ukrainian interference to help Clinton. During a press conference two weeks after Trump's inauguration, Putin accused the Poroshenko administration and "certain oligarchs" of having supported the Clinton campaign.

See "Joint News Conference with Hungarian Prime Minister Viktor Orban," The Kremlin, February 2, 2017, http://en.kremlin.ru/events/president/news/53806.

44. Manafort was later convicted on charges of financial wrongdoing and served time in federal prison. A month before leaving office Trump pardoned Manafort.

45. Kenneth P. Vogel, "Rudy Giuliani Plans Ukraine Trip to Push for Inquiries That Could Help Trump," *New York Times*, May 9, 2019.

46. Aaron Blake, "After Backlash, Giuliani Cancels Ukraine Trip Meant to 'Meddle' in Investigations to Help Trump," *Washington Post*, May 11, 2019.

47. "Telephone Conversation with President-elect Volodymyr Zelenskyy of Ukraine," The White House, April 21, 2019.

48. "Plenary Session of St Petersburg International Economic Forum," The Kremlin, June 7, 2019, http://en.kremlin.ru/events/president/news/60707.

49. Alexei Navalny, "Navalny chestno o Zelenskom" [Navalny honestly about Zelensky], YouTube video, posted by Navalny LIVE, May 27, 2019, https://www.youtube.com/watch?v=luB2-vL4gJ8.

50. Rudenko, *Zelensky*, 31.

51. Mendel, *The Fight of Our Lives*, 101.

52. Mendel, *The Fight of Our Lives*, 64.

53. Mendel, *The Fight of Our Lives*, 26.

54. Rudenko, *Zelensky*, 22.

55. Zelensky, Gordon interview.

56. Simon Shuster, "'I'm Not Afraid of the Impeachment Questions': How Ukrainian President Volodymyr Zelensky Is Navigating His Role in the World's Biggest Political Drama," *Time*, December 5, 2019.

57. Victoria Nuland, the State Department's top official for Europe, had played the role of Ukraine envoy in the Obama administration. Vilified by Russian state media as one of the architects of the Euromaidan protest, Nuland met repeatedly with Vladislav Surkov, the Putin aide with his own reputation as a master of Kremlin intrigue.

58. After Zelensky's election, Lutsenko told U.S. news organizations that the Bidens had not broken any Ukrainian laws. See Paul Sonne et al., "In Gambit for Trump, Giuliani Engaged Parade of Ukrainian Prosecutors," *Washington Post*, September 26, 2019.

59. Peter Baker and Nicholas Fandos, "Bolton Objected to Ukraine Pressure Campaign, Calling Giuliani 'a Hand Grenade'," *New York Times*, October 14, 2019.

60. "Memorandum of Telephone Conversation," The White House, July 25, 2019.

61. Mendel, *The Fight of Our Lives*, 109.

62. Peter Baker, "Volker Gives New Details on Giuliani's Role in Ukraine Policy," *New York Times*, October 4, 2019.

63. Andrew E. Kramer, "Ukraine's Zelensky Bowed to Trump's Demands, Until Luck Spared Him," *New York Times*, November 7, 2019.

64. For the Kremlin's translation of the meeting, see "Russia Calling! Investment Forum," The Kremlin, November 20, 2019, http://en.kremlin.ru/events/president/news/62073.

65. "Russian Energy Week Forum," The Kremlin, October 2, 2019, http://en.kremlin.ru/catalog/regions/MOW/events/61704.

66. "Vladimir Putin Answered Russian Journalists' Questions," The Kremlin, November 14, 2019, http://en.kremlin.ru/events/president/news/62047.

67. Volodymyr Zelenksy, " 'I Don't Trust Anyone at All.' Ukrainian President Volodymyr Zelensky Speaks Out on Trump, Putin and a Divided Europe," by Simon Shuster, *Time*, December 2, 2019, https://time.com/5742108/ukraine-zelensky-interview-trump-putin-europe/.

10. Grandpa in the Bunker

1. Vladimir Putin, "New Year Address to the Nation," The Kremlin, December 31, 2019, http://www.en.kremlin.ru/events/president/transcripts/62523.

2. Volodymyr Zelensky, who lost three grandfathers in the Holocaust, was invited to the ceremony but not asked to give a speech. Zelensky forfeited his spot in protest and gave his tickets to Holocaust survivors. See Iuliia Mendel, *The Fight of Our Lives: My Time with Zelenskyy, Ukraine's Battle for Democracy, and What It Means for the World* (New York: Atria/One Signal, 2022), 28.

3. Vladimir Putin, "Remembering the Holocaust: Fighting Antisemitism Forum," The Kremlin, January 23, 2020, http://en.kremlin.ru/events/president/news/62646.

4. Anna Pushkarskaya, Pavel Aksyonov, and Pyotr Kozlov, "Kremlyovsky karantin klassa 'lyuks' " [The Kremlin's luxury-class quarantine], BBC News Russian Service, March 31, 2021, https://www.bbc.com/russian/features-56581095.

5. Anton Troianovski, "Russians Were Urged to Return to Normal Life. Except for Putin," *New York Times*, September 30, 2020.

6. Lucian Kim, "Protesters in Russia's Far East Challenge Putin's Authority, Demand His Resignation," NPR, July 24, 2020, https://www.npr.org/2020/07/24/894571311/protesters-in-russias-far-east-challenge-putins-authority-demand-his-resignation.

7. "Royal Marines Complete Training in Belarus," Royal Navy, March 23, 2020, https://www.royalnavy.mod.uk/news-and-latest-activity/news/2020/march/23/200319-royal-marines-belarus.

8. Yuras Karmanau, "President's Virus Swagger Fuels Anger ahead of Belarus Vote," Associated Press, August 7, 2020, https://apnews.com/article/virus-outbreak-alexander-lukashenko-belarus-international-news-health-f69598a2b0892925fe6217d9f00152da.

9. Sviatlana Tsikhanouskaya, author interview, December 2023.

10. Tsikhanouskaya, December 2023.

11. Vladimir Putin, "Interview with Rossiya TV Channel," The Kremlin, August 27, 2020, http://en.kremlin.ru/events/president/news/63951.

12. Sviatlana Tsikhanouskaya, "#Belarus Has Woken Up! Highlights of a Speech by Svetlana Tikhanovskaya," YouTube video, 1:37 to 2:10, posted by EPP Group, August 25, 2020, https://www.youtube.com/watch?v=Bn5CIGAz_Fc.

13. The ruling party had become so unpopular that both Putin and Moscow's mayor, Sergei Sobyanin, ran as independents in 2018. All of United Russia's candidates

for Moscow city council in 2019 registered as independents to conceal their party affiliation.

14. Alexei Navalny, "Bolshoi efir o Belarusi. Tikhanovskaya. Zabastovki. Spetsnazovtsy" [Big broadcast on Belarus. Tsikhanouskaya. Strikes. Special forces], YouTube video, posted by Navalny LIVE, August 13, 2020, https://www.youtube.com/watch?v =HMXv2zvVkEU.

15. See Lucian Kim, "Women Lead the Way Against Belarus' Patriarch, Says Svetlana Tikhanovskaya," NPR, September 4, 2020, https://www.npr.org/2020/09/04/909609074 /women-lead-the-way-against-belarus-patriarch-says-svetlana-tikhanovskaya.

16. Navalny, "Bolshoi efir o Belarusi," 2:48:49 to 2:48:59.

17. As always, Putin refused to call Navalny by his name, instead referring to him as "this patient of a Berlin clinic."

18. As Navalny rose to prominence, prosecutors saddled him with criminal cases. In 2014 a Moscow court found Navalny and his brother, Oleg, guilty of embezzlement; Alexei was given a suspended sentence and Oleg was imprisoned for three and a half years. The European Court of Human Rights later ruled that the Navalny brothers had been denied the right to a fair trial and that the Russian courts' decisions had been "arbitrary and manifestly unreasonable."

19. "'Svobodu Navalnomu'! Itogi vserossiiskoi aktsii protesta 23 yanvarya" ['Freedom for Navalny!' Results of the Russia-wide protests on January 23], OVD-Info, January 23, 2021, https://ovd.info/articles/2021/01/23/svobodu-navalnomu-itogi -vserossiyskoy-akcii-protesta-23-yanvarya.

20. "Vtoraya vserossiiskaya aktsiya protesta 'Svobodu Navalnomu'" [Second Russia-wide protest 'Freedom for Navalny.' Results of January 31], OVD-Info, January 31, 2021, https://ovd.info/articles/2021/01/31/vtoraya-vserossiyskaya-akciya-protesta -svobodu-navalnomu-itogi-31-yanvarya.

21. For the Kremlin's translation of the videoconference, see "Meeting with Public Representatives of Crimea and Sevastopol," The Kremlin, March 18, 2021, http://en .kremlin.ru/events/president/news/65172.

22. Andrew E. Kramer, "Fighting Escalates in Eastern Ukraine, Signaling the End to Another Cease-Fire," New York Times, March 30, 2021.

23. Although he issued threats against Ukraine during his April press conference, Kozak also downplayed the likelihood of an escalation by Kyiv and said that U.S. influence over the Ukrainian government should not be exaggerated. See "Kozak: nachalo boyevykh deistvii v Donbasse so storony Kiyeva stanet nachalom kontsa Ukrainy" [Kozak: the start of hostilities by Kyiv in the Donbas would be the beginning of the end of Ukraine], TASS, April 8, 2021, https://tass.ru/politika/11098963.

24. "Readout of President Joseph R. Biden Jr. Call with President Vladimir Putin of Russia," The White House, April 13, 2021, https://www.whitehouse.gov/briefing-room /statements-releases/2021/04/13/readout-of-president-joseph-r-biden-jr-call -with-president-vladimir-putin-of-russia-4-13/.

25. Volodymyr Zelensky, "Address by the President of Ukraine on the Security Situation in the Country," President of Ukraine, April 20, 2021, https://www.president.gov.ua /en/news/zvernennya-prezidenta-ukrayini-shodo-bezpekovoyi-situaciyi-v-68073.

26. In an April 15 interview, Zelensky told the French newspaper *Le Figaro* that the Kremlin had still not answered his request for a phone call with Putin after four Ukrainian soldiers were killed in shelling in the Donbas on March 26.

27. Vladimir Putin, "Presidential Address to the Federal Assembly," The Kremlin, April 21, 2021, http://en.kremlin.ru/events/president/news/65418.

28. Helene Cooper and Julian E. Barnes, "80,000 Russian Troops Remain at Ukraine Border as U.S. and NATO Hold Exercises," *New York Times*, May 5, 2021.

29. For poll results from March 2014 to January 2023, see "Zagalnonatsionalne opytuvannia #20, Zovnishnopolitichni nastroi" [National survey #20, foreign policy sentiment], Rating Group, January 14–16, 2023, https://ratinggroup.ua/files/ratinggroup/reg_files/rg_ua_international_1000_012023.pdf.

30. Volodymyr Zelensky, "Intervyu Vladimira Zelenskogo—pro voinu na Donbasse, oligarkhov i Slugu Naroda" [Volodymyr Zelensky interview: On the war in the Donbas, oligarchs and Servant of the People], YouTube video, 20:59 to 21:03, posted by Zelensky President, March 21, 2019, https://www.youtube.com/watch?v=Ls0tv5M6fMs&t.

31. Alyona Getmanchuk, "Russia as Aggressor, NATO as Objective: Ukraine's New National Security Strategy," Atlantic Council, September 30, 2020, https://www.atlanticcouncil.org/blogs/ukrainealert/russia-as-aggressor-nato-as-objective-ukraines-new-national-security-strategy/.

32. Jonathan Swan and Dave Lawler, "Exclusive: Zelensky 'Surprised' and 'Disappointed' by Biden Pipeline Move," *Axios*, June 6, 2021, https://www.axios.com/2021/06/06/zelensky-biden-ukraine-russia-nord-stream-pipeline.

33. Volodymyr Zelensky, interview by Dmitry Gordon, Gordonua.com, December 26, 2018, https://gordonua.com/publications/zelenskiy-esli-menya-vyberut-prezidentom-snachala-budut-oblivat-gryazyu-zatem-uvazhat-a-potom-plakat-kogda-uydu-609294.html.

34. Pavel Polityuk, "Zelenskiy to Biden: Give Us Clear 'Yes' or 'No' on Ukraine NATO Path," Reuters, June 14, 2021, https://www.reuters.com/world/zelenskiy-asks-us-clarity-nato-membership-plan-ukraine-2021-06-14/.

35. "Brussels Summit Communiqué," NATO, June 14, 2021, https://www.nato.int/cps/en/natohq/news_185000.htm.

36. In an interview published two days before the Geneva summit, Putin said he was concerned about NATO's cyber capabilities and obliquely suggested that cyberattacks on the United States might end if Washington would reach a cybersecurity agreement with Russia. See "Full Transcript of Exclusive Putin Interview with NBC News' Keir Simmons," NBC News, June 14, 2021, https://www.nbcnews.com/news/world/transcript-nbc-news-exclusive-interview-russia-s-vladimir-putin-n1270649.

37. "Remarks by President Biden in Press Conference," The White House, June 16, 2021, https://www.whitehouse.gov/briefing-room/speeches-remarks/2021/06/16/remarks-by-president-biden-in-press-conference-4/.

38. "News Conference Following Russia-US Talks," The Kremlin, June 16, 2021, http://en.kremlin.ru/events/president/news/65870.

39. "UK Signs Agreement to Support Enhancement of Ukrainian Naval Capabilities," U.K. Government, June 23, 2021, https://www.gov.uk/government/news/uk-signs -agreement-to-support-enhancement-of-ukrainian-naval-capabilities.

40. Lucian Kim, "Russia Says It Fired Warning Shots at a British Warship Which Approached Crimea," NPR, June 23, 2021, https://www.npr.org/2021/06/23/1009483766 /russia-says-it-fired-warning-shots-at-a-british-warship-which-approached -crimea.

41. "Patrushev zayavil, chto Kiyev mozhet popytatsya vernut Krym silovym putyom" [Patrushev said that Kyiv may try to retake Crimea by force], Interfax, April 14, 2021, https://www.interfax.ru/russia/761214.

42. "Direct Line with Vladimir Putin," The Kremlin, June 30, 2021, http://en.kremlin .ru/events/president/news/65973.

43. Vladimir Solovyov, "Dmitry Kozak sobirayetsya v novy podkhod na Ukrainu" [Dmitry Kozak is planning a new approach to Ukraine], *Kommersant*, January 25, 2020.

44. Andrew Roth and Shaun Walker, "Ukraine President: Putin Has One Year to Strike Deal to End War," *The Guardian*, March 6, 2020.

45. Ben Hall, "Ukrainian Leader Calls for Revamp of Peace Process to End Donbas War," *Financial Times*, April 26, 2021.

46. Rating Group found Servant of the People had 18.6 percent support, dipping behind the Opposition Platform with 18.9 percent; polling by the Kyiv International Institute of Sociology showed a far bigger gap, with Servant of the People garnering just 11.2 percent support against the Opposition Platform's 20.7 percent. See Oleksiy Sorokin, "Zelensky's Party Loses Support, Trails in Polls," *Kyiv Post*, February 12, 2021.

47. Simon Shuster, "The Untold Story of the Ukraine Crisis," *Time*, February 2, 2022.

48. Shuster, "The Untold Story."

49. For the Kremlin's translation of Putin's remarks, see "Meeting with Permanent Members of the Security Council," The Kremlin, May 14, 2021, http://en.kremlin .ru/events/president/news/65572.

50. The journalist Ilya Zhegulev spoke to three people in Putin's entourage who described the crackdown on Medvedchuk as "the last straw" before Putin decided on a full-scale invasion. One longtime Putin acquaintance said the Russian leader took the crackdown as a "personal attack." See "Kak Putin voznenavidel Ukrainu" [How Putin came to hate Ukraine], April 25, 2023, *Vyorstka*, https://verstka.media /kak-putin-pridumal-voynu.

51. Shuster, "The Untold Story."

52. According to *Axios*, the Biden administration initially considered inviting Zelensky to the White House before the Putin summit. The administration reversed course after Zelensky fired the head of the Ukrainian state energy company Naftogaz in April, raising concerns about his commitment to fighting corruption. See Swan and Lawler, "Zelensky 'Surprised' and 'Disappointed.'"

53. Biden met with Tsikhanouskaya informally during her visit to the United States in July 2021.

54. Dmitry Peskov, "'Ya ne dumayu, chto ona sostoitsya'" ['I don't think it will take place'], by Yelena Loriya, Pyotr Marchenko, and Tatyana Baikova, *Izvestia*, September 2, 2021.

11. Killer in the Kremlin

1. Peter Baker, "Pressure Rising as Obama Works to Rein In Russia," *New York Times*, March 2, 2014.
2. Evan Gershkovich et al., "Putin, Isolated and Distrustful, Leans on Handful of Hard-Line Advisers," *Wall Street Journal*, December 23, 2022.
3. Ilya Zhegulev, "Kak Putin voznenavidel Ukrainu" [How Putin came to hate Ukraine], April 25, 2023, *Vyorstka*, https://verstka.media/kak-putin-pridumal-voynu.
4. Zhegulev, "Kak Putin voznenavidel Ukrainu."
5. Victoria Petryk, "Survey: Most Ukrainians Disapprove of Zelensky's Actions," *Kyiv Post*, November 2, 2021.
6. Zhegulev, "Kak Putin voznenavidel Ukrainu."
7. Mikhail Zygar, "How Vladimir Putin Lost Interest in the Present," *New York Times*, March 10, 2022. For another detailed account of Kovalchuk's influence over Putin, see Betsy McKay, Thomas Grove, and Rob Barry, "The Russian Billionaire Selling Putin's War to the Public," *Wall Street Journal*, December 2, 2022.
8. Zhegulev, "Kak Putin voznenavidel Ukrainu."
9. For a discussion of the thinkers who informed Putin's worldview, see Marlène Laruelle, "The Intellectual Origins of Putin's Invasion," *UnHerd*, March 16, 2022, https://unherd.com/2022/03/the-brains-behind-the-russian-invasion/.
10. "Putin sovetvtuyet chitat dnevniki Denikina" [Putin recommends reading Denikin's diaries], RIA Novosti, May 24, 2009, https://ria.ru/20090524/172146777.html.
11. Alexander Zvyagintsev, "V 1938 godu filosof, ideolog Belogo dvizheniya Ivan Ilyin dal tochny prognoz sobytii na Ukraine" [In 1938, the philosopher and White Movement ideologue Ivan Ilyin accurately predicted events in Ukraine], *Rossiiskaya Gazeta*, May 25, 2022.
12. For the Kremlin's translation of the treatise, see "Article by Vladimir Putin 'On the Historical Unity of Russians and Ukrainians,'" The Kremlin, July 12, 2021, http://en.kremlin.ru/events/president/news/66181.
13. Michael R. Gordon et al., "Vladimir Putin's 20-Year March to War in Ukraine—and How the West Mishandled It," *Wall Street Journal*, April 1, 2022.
14. Erin Banco et al., "'Something Was Badly Wrong': When Washington Realized Russia Was Actually Invading Ukraine," *Politico*, February 24, 2023.
15. Gordon et al., "Vladimir Putin's 20-Year March to War."
16. Shane Harris et al., "Road to War: U.S. Struggled to Convince Allies, and Zelensky, of Risk of Invasion," *Washington Post*, August 16, 2022.
17. Gordon et al., "Vladimir Putin's 20-Year March to War."
18. Banco et al., "'Something Was Badly Wrong.'"

19. John Hudson, "The Ukraine War Is Antony Blinken's Defining Moment," *Washington Post*, March 16, 2023.

20. Harris et al., "Road to War."

21. See "U.S.-Ukraine Charter on Strategic Partnership," U.S. Department of State, November 10, 2021, https://www.state.gov/u-s-ukraine-charter-on-strategic-partnership/. The document replaced an earlier charter on strategic partnership signed in the waning days of the George W. Bush administration.

22. Gordon et al., "Vladimir Putin's 20-Year March to War."

23. Banco et al., " 'Something Was Badly Wrong.' "

24. Harris et al., "Road to War."

25. Banco et al., " 'Something Was Badly Wrong.' "

26. Petryk, "Survey: Most Ukrainians Disapprove of Zelensky's Actions."

27. See Elena Loginova, "Pandora Papers Reveal Offshore Holdings of Ukrainian President and His Inner Circle," Organized Crime and Corruption Reporting Project, October 3, 2021, https://www.occrp.org/en/the-pandora-papers/pandora-papers-reveal-offshore-holdings-of-ukrainian-president-and-his-inner-circle.

28. In January 2023, Putin's spokesman confirmed that Putin had not spoken with Zelensky in several years. The last Kremlin readout of a conversation between the two leaders was in July 2020. See "Peskov rasskazal o poslednem razgovore Putina s Zelenskim" [Peskov spoke about Putin's last conversation with Zelensky], RIA Novosti, January 25, 2023, https://ria.ru/20230125/peskov-1847223526.html.

29. Dmitry Medvedev, "Pochemu bessmyslenny kontakty s nyneshnim ukrainskim rukovodstvom" [Why contacts with the current Ukrainian leadership are pointless], *Kommersant*, October 11, 2021.

30. For the Kremlin's translation of the discussion, see "Valdai Discussion Club Meeting," The Kremlin, October 21, 2021, http://en.kremlin.ru/events/president/news/66975.

31. NATO did not base weapons systems in prospective member states. The U.S. missile defense installations that so angered Putin were based in Poland and Romania only after the two countries had joined the alliance. The installations did not appear overnight and became operational after years of planning.

32. In advance of the December 7 call, the Kremlin had repeatedly mentioned the possibility of a follow-up summit between Biden and Putin. The Kremlin billed the videoconference as a "meeting" with the U.S. president, while the White House simply referred to it as a "video call."

33. "Meeting with US President Joseph Biden," The Kremlin, December 7, 2021, http://en.kremlin.ru/events/president/news/67315.

34. Paul Sonne, Ashley Parker, and Isabelle Khurshudyan, "Biden Threatens Putin with Economic Sanctions if He Further Invades Ukraine," *Washington Post*, December 7, 2021.

35. John Sullivan, author interview, November 2022.

36. Two months after NATO promised eventual membership to Ukraine and Georgia in 2008, Dmitry Medvedev, as Russia's new president, proposed a treaty on European

security that would have frozen NATO enlargement and diluted the U.S. role in Europe's defense. The initiative went nowhere, especially after Russia invaded Georgia two months later, but elements of the Medvedev proposal were echoed in Russia's draft treaties given to Donfried. See "Agreement on Measures to Ensure the Security of the Russian Federation and Member States of the North Atlantic Treaty Organization," Russian Foreign Ministry, December 17, 2021, https://mid.ru/ru/foreign_policy/rso/nato/1790803/?lang=en; and "Treaty between the United States of America and the Russian Federation on Security Guarantees," Russian Foreign Ministry, December 17, 2021, https://mid.ru/ru/foreign_policy/rso/nato/1790818/?lang=en.

37. "Telephone Conversation with US President Joseph Biden," The Kremlin, December 31, 2021, http://en.kremlin.ru/events/president/news/67487.

38. According to Oleksiy Danilov, the head of Ukraine's National Security and Defense Council at the time, only about ninety Javelins were delivered before the full-scale invasion. See Yaroslav Trofimov, "How the Best Chance to Win the Ukraine War Was Lost," *Washington Post*, January 9, 2024.

39. Banco et al., " 'Something Was Badly Wrong.' "

40. "Briefing with Deputy Secretary Wendy R. Sherman on the U.S.-Russia Strategic Stability Dialogue," U.S. Department of State, January 10, 2022, https://www.state.gov/briefing-with-deputy-secretary-wendy-r-sherman-on-the-u-s-russia-strategic-stability-dialogue/.

41. Emma Farge, "U.S. and Russia Still Far Apart on Ukraine after Geneva Talks," Reuters, January 10, 2022, https://www.reuters.com/world/europe/prospects-dim-us-russia-start-tense-talks-over-ukraine-crisis-2022-01-10/.

42. Banco et al., " 'Something Was Badly Wrong.' "

43. Harris et al., "Road to War."

44. "Online Press Briefing with Ambassador John J. Sullivan, U.S. Ambassador to the Russian Federation," U.S. Department of State, January 28, 2022, https://www.state.gov/online-press-briefing-with-ambassador-john-j.-sullivan-u.s.-ambassador-to-the-russian-federation.

45. "Press Release on Submitting a Written Reaction to the US Response concerning Security Guarantees," Russian Foreign Ministry, February 17, 2022, https://mid.ru/en/foreign_policy/news/1799157.

46. Banco et al., " 'Something Was Badly Wrong.' "

47. Volodymyr Zelensky, "An Interview with Ukrainian President Volodymyr Zelensky," by Isabelle Khurshudyan, *Washington Post*, August 16, 2022.

48. Greg Miller and Catherine Belton, "Russia's Spies Misread Ukraine and Misled Kremlin as War Loomed," *Washington Post*, August 19, 2022.

49. Zelensky, Khurshudyan interview.

50. "Briefing by Aide to the President Yury Ushakov following a Telephone Conversation between Vladimir Putin and Joseph Biden," The Kremlin, February 12, 2022, http://en.kremlin.ru/events/president/news/67761.

51. It soon emerged that Macron had refused to let Kremlin doctors administer a COVID test on him for fear the Russians would store his DNA. See Michel Rose,

"Macron Refused Russian COVID Test in Putin Trip over DNA Theft Fears," Reuters, February 11, 2022, https://www.reuters.com/world/europe/putin-kept-macron -distance-snubbing-covid-demands-sources-2022-02-10/.

52. Gordon et al., "Vladimir Putin's 20-Year March to War."

53. Harris et al., "Road to War."

54. Nico Fried and Andreas Hoidn-Borchers, "Das erste Jahr als Kanzler: Olaf Scholz über bedrückende Momente, Fehler und ein wichtiges Treffen mit Putin" [The first year as chancellor: Olaf Scholz on depressing moments, mistakes, and an important meeting with Putin], *Stern*, January 1, 2023.

55. Jack Watling and Nick Reynolds, "The Plot to Destroy Ukraine," Royal United Ser-vices Institute, February 15, 2022, https://static.rusi.org/special-report-202202 -ukraine-web.pdf.

56. Watling and Reynolds, "The Plot to Destroy Ukraine." After the full-scale Russian invasion, Ukrainian investigators would accuse two top SBU officials, Oleh Kulinich and Andriy Naumov, of working for Russian intelligence. As a result of the scandals, Ivan Bakanov, the head of the SBU and Zelensky's childhood friend, lost his job in July 2022.

57. In April 2021, a poll by the Kyiv firm Research & Branding found that 84 percent of Ukrainians would view a further Russian military intervention as an occupation, while just 2 percent saw it as a liberation. Forty-eight percent of respondents said they were ready to defend their country. See Miller and Belton, "Russia's Spies Mis-read Ukraine."

58. Nick Reynolds and Jack Watling, "Ukraine through Russia's Eyes," Royal United Ser-vices Institute, February 25, 2022, https://rusi.org/explore-our-research/publications /commentary/ukraine-through-russias-eyes.

59. Roman Kravets and Roman Romaniuk, "Kremlin's Two Plans. Who Would Govern Ukraine if Kyiv Fell," *Ukrainska Pravda*, March 5, 2023, https://www.pravda.com.ua /eng/articles/2023/03/5/7391273/.

60. Miller and Belton, "Russia's Spies Misread Ukraine." Also see James Politi, Max Seddon, and Roman Olearchyk, "US Shares Fresh Claims of Moscow Coup Plot for Ukraine," *Financial Times*, February 15, 2022.

61. In November 2021, Zelensky warned of an imminent coup plot against him. In Janu-ary 2022, the British government announced that it had uncovered Russian plans to install an obscure Ukrainian politician, Yevhen Murayev, as the puppet leader in Kyiv.

62. Kravets and Romaniuk, "Kremlin's Two Plans."

63. Gershkovich et al., "Putin, Isolated and Distrustful, Leans on Hard-Line Advisers."

64. Mikhail Khodaryonok, "Prognozy krovozhadnykh politologov" [The forecasts of bloodthirsty pundits], *Nezavisimaya Gazeta*, February 3, 2022.

65. The letter was originally published on the website of the Russian Officers Assem-bly but was later taken down. It later appeared here: https://www.km.ru/v-rossii /2022/02/06/otnosheniya-rossii-i-ukrainy/895037-obrashchenie-obshcherossiiskogo -ofitserskogo.

66. According to Western intelligence officials, the Chinese government asked the Kremlin to hold off on any military action in Ukraine until after the Winter

Olympics, which closed on February 20. See Edward Wong and Julian E. Barnes, "China Asked Russia to Delay Ukraine War Until After Olympics, U.S. Officials Say," *New York Times*, March 2, 2022.

67. "News Conference Following Russian-Belarusian Talks," The Kremlin, February 18, 2022, http://en.kremlin.ru/events/president/news/67809.

68. A year and a half after the start of the Russian invasion, Lukashenko maintained that he had not received any advance notice of Putin's plan. However, Lukashenko said that at their meeting before the invasion Putin had asked Lukashenko to give him "cover" should he need it. See Alexander Lukashenko, interview by Diana Panchenko, posted by ATN, August 17, 2023, YouTube video, 19:32 to 20:35, https://www.youtube.com/watch?v=eWdDqndjN8Q.

69. Volodymyr Zelensky, "Speech by the President of Ukraine at the 58th Munich Security Conference," President of Ukraine, February 19, 2022, https://www.president.gov.ua/en/news/vistup-prezidenta-ukrayini-na-58-j-myunhenskij-konferenciyi-72997.

70. Gordon et al., "Vladimir Putin's 20-Year March to War."

71. Harris et al., "Road to War."

72. Security Council Meeting," The Kremlin, February 21, 2022, http://en.kremlin.ru/events/president/news/67825.

73. The charge of "genocide" was ludicrous. The United Nations estimated that between April 2014 and December 2021 a total of 14,200 to 14,400 people had been killed in the conflict, of which at least 3,404 were civilians on both sides of the front line, 4,400 Ukrainian troops, and 6,500 pro-Russian fighters. In 2021, the UN recorded twenty-five civilians killed, the lowest annual number for the entire conflict period. See Office of the United Nations High Commissioner for Human Rights, "Conflict-Related Civilian Casualties in Ukraine," January 27, 2022.

74. Three days after Zelensky's election in 2019, Putin signed a decree simplifying the naturalization process for residents of the Donbas. During the Security Council meeting, Dmitry Medvedev said that there were eight hundred thousand Russian citizens living in the DNR and LNR who deserved the protection of the Russian government. The Kremlin had used a similar policy of granting Russian citizenship to people living in Georgia's breakaway regions—and then justified its 2008 invasion by claiming to "protect" Russian nationals.

75. Less than two weeks earlier, on February 10, Kozak had held a fruitless round of negotiations with Zelensky's adviser Andriy Yermak in Berlin. Standing before Putin Kozak accused the Ukrainians of lying and "legal cretinism," saying they would never fulfill the Minsk agreement.

76. Banco et al., " 'Something Was Badly Wrong.' " Citing a source close to Dmitry Peskov, Putin's spokesman, Owen Matthews wrote that only three of the advisers at the Security Council meeting knew the full extent of Putin's invasion plan: Defense Minister Sergei Shoigu, Security Council Secretary Nikolai Patrushev, and FSB Director Alexander Bortnikov. See Owen Matthews, *Overreach: The Inside Story of Putin's War against Ukraine* (London: Mudlark, 2022), 12.

77. Gershkovich et al., "Putin, Isolated and Distrustful, Leans on Hard-Line Advisers."

78. For the Kremlin's translation of the speech, see Vladimir Putin, "Address by the President of the Russian Federation," The Kremlin, February 21, 2022, http://en.kremlin.ru/events/president/news/67828.
79. Lenin's readiness to grant Ukraine far-reaching autonomy was a deliberate effort to give independence-minded Ukrainians an incentive to join the nascent Soviet Union, according to historian Serhii Plokhy. See Serhii Plokhy, "Casus Belli: Did Lenin Create Modern Ukraine?," Harvard Ukrainian Research Institute, February 27, 2022, https://huri.harvard.edu/news/serhii-plokhii-casus-belli-did-lenin-create-modern-ukraine.
80. The mention of weapons of mass destruction was a direct echo of America's casus belli for its invasion of Iraq—and just as groundless.
81. Putin was referencing repairs of the dilapidated Ochakiv naval outpost hundreds of miles from Russia's internationally recognized borders and the Yavoriv joint training center in western Ukraine. This assistance was the direct result of Russia's invasion in 2014. Ukraine, as a sovereign state, was in its right under international law to seek foreign assistance in defending its territory against further aggression.
82. Donald Trump, "Full Interview: President Trump with C&B from Mar-a-Lago," Clay Travis & Buck Sexton Show, February 22, 2022, https://www.clayandbuck.com/president-trump-with-cb-from-mar-a-lago/.
83. Michael Schwirtz et al., "Putin's War," New York Times, December 16, 2022.
84. Harris et al., "Road to War."
85. Schwirtz et al., "Putin's War."
86. Roman Kravets and Roman Romaniuk, "The Three Longest Days of February. The Beginning of the Great War Which No One Thought Would Come," Ukrainska Pravda, September 5, 2022, https://www.pravda.com.ua/eng/articles/2022/09/5/7366059/.
87. "Vladimir Putin Answered Media Questions," The Kremlin, February 22, 2022, http://en.kremlin.ru/events/president/news/67838.
88. Matthews, Overreach, 18.
89. Vladimir Putin, "Address by the President of the Russian Federation," The Kremlin, February 24, 2022, http://en.kremlin.ru/events/president/news/67843.
90. NATO accepted four Balkan countries—Albania, Croatia, Montenegro, Macedonia—after 2004, but none of them had been satellites of the Soviet Union, i.e., members of the Warsaw Pact under Moscow's direct influence.

Index

deal mediated by EU, 90–91; profile of "median protester," 84; Russian interest in use of force against, 87; Russian narrative of U.S.-led coup d'état, 87, 95, 160; Russian role in negotiated settlement, 89–90; spread of demonstrations outside Kyiv, 75, 84; Yanukovych employing violence in quelling, 72, 74, 83; Yanukovych refusing to take advice from Western leaders, 74; Yanukovych's entourage evacuating in reaction to massacre, 90; Yanukovych's resignation sought by, 72, 91–92

Europe: Obama's lack of interest in, 85, 120, 159–60; U.S. troop levels in, 6, 159, 164, 250. *See also* European Union; NATO

European Court of Human Rights, 192–93, 293n18

European Deterrence Initiative/European Reassurance Initiative, 166

European Union (EU): Baltic states becoming members of, 13, 77; on enlargement as logical process, 166; Kuchma and, 25; mediating peace deal after Maidan massacre, 90–91; Nobel Peace Prize awarded to (2012), 77; observers of Ukraine election (2004), 16; Putin and, 17, 78; Putin attending his last bilateral summit (Brussels 2014), 88; Russian invasion of Georgia and, 45; Russian opposition to Ukraine joining, 80; as Russia's largest trading partner, 78, 172; sanctions against Russia, 88, 124, 150, 171, 256; Tymoshenko's imprisonment as obstacle to Ukrainian membership, 77–82; Ukraine's decision to postpone pursuit of membership, 72, 82, 85–87, 129–30; Ukraine signing association agreement, 148; Ukraine's pursuit of membership, 5–6, 77–82, 146, 159;

U.S. supporting Ukraine's pursuit of membership, 80, 85–87

Evans, Donald, 172

Fair Russia party, 67

fascism and Nazism: Azov Battalion's use of Nazi symbols, 151; Soviet enemies labeled as Nazis, 143; Ukrainian "Banderites" and, 22, 122, 129, 144; Ukrainian regime called "neo-Nazi" by Russian officials, 255; Yushchenko depicted as Nazi, 15, 146; Zelensky called fascist and Banderite, 205, 249

federalization, 87, 98, 146–47

Federation Council (Russia), 128–29, 149, 201, 257–58

Finland as model for Ukraine, 159

"foreign agent" label, 65, 70, 232, 243, 270n16, 288n30

France: doubtful of likely Russian invasion of Ukraine, 248; Islamic extremists' attacks in, 177; opposition to Iraq war, 35; opposition to NATO membership of Ukraine and Georgia, 31, 37; Russian relations with, 166, 209; on UN Security Council's resolution against Gaddafi, 62. *See also* Hollande, François; Macron, Emmanuel; Sarkozy, Nicolas

Frolov, Vladimir, 188–89

FSB, 135, 174, 233, 252–53, 275n28

FSO (Russian Federal Guard Service), 100–101

Füle, Štefan, 77, 81

Furgal, Sergei, 228

G8 suspending Russia's membership, 88, 124

G20 summit (2014), 176

G20 summit (2017), 200, 219

Gabriel, Sigmar, 171

Gaddafi, Muammar, 62, 65–66, 177

Galeotti, Mark, 189, 283n11

Gates, Robert, 36

Orange Revolution (*continued*)
east Ukraine's reaction to, 26–27; global media attention and, 21–22; Putin's reaction to, 7, 17, 29, 54, 65, 117; Russian-speaking lawmakers threatening to secede, 99, 142; support from businesses, 21; as surprise to U.S., 17
Organization for the Prohibition of Chemical Weapons, 233
OSCE (Organization for Security and Cooperation in Europe), 16–18, 137, 269n3, 270n17, 271n23
Ostpolitik, 171
Our Ukraine political bloc, 13

Page, Carter, 188
Pakistan, 33
Pandora Papers, 248
Parasyuk, Volodymyr, 92
Party of Regions (Ukraine), 13, 23, 74, 81, 90–91, 93, 143, 147, 173. *See also* Yanukovych, Viktor
Parubiy, Andriy, 91, 102, 123, 135, 151
Pasechnik, Leonid, 256
Patrushev, Nikolai, 118, 174, 212, 233
Pavlovsky, Gleb, 32, 36
Perry, Rick, 215
Peskov, Dmitry, 243, 255
Peter the Great (czar), 26
Plokhy, Serhii, 301n79
Plotnitsky, Igor, 151, 154
Poland: as model for economic transformation and renewal, 132; U.S. air exercises in, 165, 167–68; U.S. battalion stationed in, 169; U.S. missile defense installations in, 31, 164, 297n31
Polyezhai, Lyubov, 93
Pompeo, Mike, 200, 224, 229–30, 243
Pora (Ukrainian student organization), 16, 29
Poroshenko, Petro: 2018 presidential election, 213; 2019 presidential

election and runoff, 211–14; debate with Zelensky, 213; on Maidan massacre, 89; peace in Donbas and, 152–54; presidential election of (2014), 147–48; Putin and, 148; Sea of Azov challenge to Russia, 211; in Yushchenko campaign, 10; Zelensky's impersonation of, 208
Powell, Colin, 18
Pravyi Sektor (Ukrainian political group), 84, 147
Prilepin, Zakhar, 182
Prodi, Romano, 172
Prokhorov, Mikhail, 69
pro-Russian activists: Aksyonov and, 106–7; Crimea and, 110–17; Donetsk (eastern Ukraine) and, 7, 128–50; goals of, 144–45; MH17 downing and, 127–28, 149–50; Poroshenko and, 148; rejecting label of separatists, 144; Russia encouraging uprising against Kyiv, 129, 147, 162; secession threats of, 146; self-labeling as "militiamen," 144; Yanukovych and, 81
protests in Russia. *See* Moscow; Navalny, Alexei
protests in Ukraine. *See* Euromaidan protests; Orange Revolution
Pshonka, Viktor, 101
Pugachyov, Sergei, 26
Purgin, Andrei, 146
Pushilin, Denis, 256
Pussy Riot, 70
Putin, Vladimir: 2004 Russian presidential election, 69; 2004 Ukraine election and, 9–14, 18, 27; 2011 Russian Duma elections and, 67; 2012 Russian presidential election, 67–68, 270n17; 2018 Russian presidential election, 197–99, 292n13; 2018 Russian presidential inauguration, 211; American admiration for, 172; anti-Putin protesters (2011), 55, 64–65;